SNA

Theory and Practice

SNA

Theory and Practice

A comprehensive guide to
IBM's
Systems Network Architecture

Anura Guruge

PERGAMON PRESS
OXFORD · NEW YORK · BEIJING · FRANKFURT
SÃO PAULO · SYDNEY · TOKYO · TORONTO

U.K.	Pergamon Press plc, Headington Hill Hall, Oxford OX3 0BW, England
U.S.A.	Pergamon Press, Inc., Maxwell House, Fairview Park, Elmsford, New York 10523, U.S.A.
PEOPLE'S REPUBLIC OF CHINA	Pergamon Press, Room 4037, Qianmen Hotel, Beijing, People's Republic of China
FEDERAL REPUBLIC OF GERMANY	Pergamon Press GmbH, Hammerweg 6, D-6242 Kronberg, Federal Republic of Germany
BRAZIL	Pergamon Editora Ltda, Rua Eça de Queiros, 346, CEP 04011, Paraiso, São Paulo, Brazil
AUSTRALIA	Pergamon Press Australia Pty Ltd., P.O. Box 544, Potts Point, N.S.W. 2011, Australia
JAPAN	Pergamon Press, 5th Floor, Matsuoka Central Building, 1-7-1 Nishishinjuku, Shinjuku-ku, Tokyo 160, Japan
CANADA	Pergamon Press Canada Ltd., Suite No. 271, 253 College Street, Toronto, Ontario, Canada M5T 1R5

First edition 1984
Reprinted 1985, 1987, 1989

ISBN 0-08-028583-X

SNA—Systems Network Architecture is a proprietary design specification of International Business Machines Corp.

Printed in Great Britain by BPCC Wheatons Ltd, Exeter

To Kathy

Contents

Chapter 5: Half-sessions 129

Chapter 6: LU–LU sessions 189

Preface

The use of computers is burgeoning inexorably; continually and consistently surpassing all predictions and expectations, influencing and making impact on more and more facets of everyday life – whether it be at home, at work or even at play. But the way in which computers are being used is changing. While fast, powerful, extensive, centralised host computer systems still abound – and all indications are that they will continue to do so for at least another decade – the advent of extremely cost-effective but competent microcomputers, and the emergence of increasingly sophisticated, powerful and compact minicomputers are diversifying the actual and potential application spread and physical dispersement of computer systems.

Computer systems for single applications, personal computing or automating the accounting of a small business or an individual department of a company are now cost justifiably, practically and physically available to users requiring computing resources, rather than being restricted to concentrated, centralised computer facilities. These computer systems require very little space, are capable of functioning in normal office or home environments without the need for air-conditioning or special power supplies and are designed for operation by users as opposed to dedicated system operators. This increase in the number of, and the spread in the physical distribution of computer systems, with the inevitable need for accessing, monitoring, interchanging or updating data located in one system from another system or from a terminal, makes *teleprocessing* (the access to a computer system from a remote location via a telecommunication link) and *distrib-*

uted data processing (multiple computer systems interconnected by telecommunication links and capable of interacting with each other) strategies and technology key issues fundamental to planning, designing, implementing and managing current and future computer systems. This book deals with the strategy and technology of a proprietary scheme for realising the prerequisite data communications environment for a practical distributed data processing system.

SNA (Systems Network Architecture), put forward by IBM in 1974, is a design specification for the data communications-oriented facilities and functions that must be provided and performed to achieve a viable, efficient, reliable and cost-effective basis for distributed data processing and advanced teleprocessing applications. SNA is not a product. It is a design specification – an architectural blueprint – comprehensively and unambiguously stating the data communication facilities and functions that need to be provided and performed by hardware or software products such as teleprocessing access methods, control programs for communication control units and terminal control units, intended for either operating within, or for supporting, a distributed data processing system.

SNA, or, to be precise, the distributed data processing products containing data communication components conforming to it, has finally come of age. After years of languishing, during which time it was oft viewed with suspicion and cynicism as an IBM scheme to coerce its users towards IBM-dictated and –controlled data communication systems, but also lovingly nurtured, refined, protected and promoted by IBM and a few independent data communication cognosenti, it is finally gaining acceptability and respectability in the current urgency for a viable data communications strategy and for implementable products for harnessing, controlling and managing distributed data processing systems and complex teleprocessing applications.

For IBM users, SNA (the installation of SNA-based products) is no longer a question of 'whether', but of 'when?'. The current version of SNA – the fourth major revision to the original, embryonic scheme introduced in 1974 – and the products based on it represent a comprehensive, coherent, powerful, flexible and easily enhanced data communications strategy for distributed data processing or complex teleprocessing applications. The number of large and demonstrably successful, data communication environments realised through SNA-based products, the volume of documentation available from IBM and the incessant publicity it has received – favourable or otherwise – now make SNA not only the best known, but, in effect, the *de facto* standard for data communication strategies. All discussions on other data communication architectures, eg the International Standards Organisation's seven-layer Reference Model of Open Systems Interconnection, inevitably use SNA as the basis for comparison. Rumours are rife that European PTTs are to provide SNA-based public data communication environments. The question of what will unseat SNA is no longer debated: the fundamental question now posed when other data communication strategies are proffered is 'how does it interact with SNA?'

This book is a tutorial cum reference manual on SNA. It is a systematic, thorough, topic-by-topic explanation of the SNA specification (the theory of SNA) and a conceptual guide to implementing SNA-based data communications environments using products conforming to SNA (the practice of SNA). The fundamental aim is to explain SNA in terms of the specification – why the facilities and functions prescribed in the specification are needed, how the specification visualises these facilities and functions and what the specification intends to achieve; then to illustrate how these facilities and functions are realised in current, common IBM proprietary products available for implementing SNA-based data communication environments, for distributed data processing systems. It is not a step-by-step instruction manual for implementing an SNA-based system. The configurational and product permutations that are possible, and the continual introduction of new products, makes it impossible to even contemplate such a specific and definitive instruction manual. What this book attempts is a description of generalised, implementational concepts by explaining them in terms of the functions the specification is aiming to achieve. By appreciating what the specification is trying to achieve, implementors can ascertain how best to customise product-specific implementational criteria by relating and extrapolating them to the relevant functions in the specification. For example, once the concept and objective of *session-level pacing* is perceived from a specification viewpoint, supplying the relevant pacing parameters for an ACF/

VTAM or ACF/NCP generation becomes a meaningful and scientific – and even enjoyable and satisfying – exercise, rather than a vague, *ad hoc* and potentially costly experiment.

This book, though not based on them, has its origins in the public and in-house seminars on SNA I have been conducting for Pergamon Infotech since the beginning of 1982. As such, rather than being just a reiteration of SNA prose from IBM manuals, it is a genuine attempt to comprehensively and clearly *explain* SNA – the theory and application – using the techniques and methodology employed in the seminars.

The book primarily addresses, and will be of considerable benefit to, systems analysts, system programmers, system designers, DP managers, operations managers, operations staff, communications analysts and engineers and application programmers involved in developing on-line applications in IBM or IBM-compatible installations, and technical managers and staff of computer or communications equipment manufacturers developing or supporting SNA-based products. No in-depth knowledge of data communications or IBM systems is assumed in this book; thus it is suitable for non-IBM-oriented DP personnel or even students who wish to gain an appreciation of SNA in particular or who just want to discover the composition of a data communications strategy.

Trying to glean an insight into the possible background, rationale and justification that prompted a decision always helps when trying to fathom the validity of what, at face-value, appears to be an arbitrary decision. This is also true with SNA. Understanding the problems and limitations that beset data communications in the pre-SNA era, and realising what IBM was trying to overcome and cater for with SNA, is enormously helpful when studying SNA as it shows the reasons behind what initially appear to be idiosyncrasies or preoccupations of SNA. To this end, this book, after a formal definition of SNA, devotes most of the first chapter to answering the question 'Why SNA?', and to the intentions and motives of SNA. Chapter 2 continues the theme of Chapter 1 by describing the evolution of SNA in terms of the types of data communication environments that were possible with each of the five versions of SNA. Chapters 3 to 10 then concentrate on the facilities and functions available with the current version of the SNA specification, and the products that conform to this specification. In Chapter 11, SNA is viewed in terms of functional layers so that it can be compared with the International Standards Organisation's seven-layer Reference Model of Open Systems Interconnection. Chapter 12 concludes the main text of the book by describing some of the main IBM proprietary products available for realising an SNA-based distributed data processing system. Each chapter is preceded by a list of topics that will be introduced and discussed in that chapter. Each chapter finishes with a *Checkpoint*, which schematically summarises the salient topics covered in the chapter. The last section of all the chapters – other than Chapter 12, which is wholly devoted to implementational details – is entitled *Implementational notes* and describes how the facilities and functions discussed in that chapter are implemented in current and common IBM products. The data streams used by SNA – 3270 Data Stream and SCS – are described in *Appendix B*, while the *Glossary* and the *Table of acronyms and abbreviations* serve as reference aids. Though self-contained and self-sufficient, this book is not meant as a replacement of any of the manuals on SNA supplied by IBM. It supplements the SNA reference manuals – qv *Bibliography* – and complements the terse, but precise, descriptions of SNA in these manuals, by more informal, though equally accurate, explanations of the concepts and principles.

Maximum benefit can be gained from this book if it is read with occasional reference to the reference manuals, for example to study the exact format of an SNA command whose format is not reproduced in the book. However, this is in no way essential: a detailed understanding of SNA can be gained by reading this book on its own.

At this stage it is appropriate to state my affiliation to SNA. This is best done by saying that SNA is one of my hobbies: a spare-time pursuit that continually fascinates me, gives me a lot of pleasure to study and discuss, and acts as a source of relaxation! As such this book was written in my so called 'spare time' – evenings and weekends. However, my initial contact with SNA was far from promising. I had been with IBM a few weeks – joining as a junior programmer in the Systems Support Group at the Research Laboratory in Hursley, in the summer of 1974 – when I received a cryptic and curt memo to the effect that, 'Henceforth SNA will be known as Systems Network Architecture rather than Single

Network Architecture'. As I had never heard of SNA, and as both titles were equally baffling, I sought clarification from my manager – the head of System Support – who told me not to worry about it as it would never catch on! A subject so easily and callously dismissed was always worth pursuing. Eighteen months later I had my first hands-on experience of SNA when working on a prototype 3274 control unit. Since then, SNA has always been around.

Anura Gurugé
Harpenden, 1984

Acknowledgements

Some words of sincere gratitude are due to: the Management, and the members of the Customer Support Group, of ITT Business Systems – especially Steve Kane, the then Technical Manager – who gave me the opportunities, the encouragement, the scope and the resources to pursue the implementational aspects of SNA; Professor John Florentin of Birkbeck College, University of London, for widening my understanding and appreciation of data communications; Dr Tom Westerdale, also of Birkbeck, who voluntarily – and well beyond the call of duty – and with immense patience tried to teach me the art of precise writing; Phil Rowland – my ex-colleague, now with Mohawk Data Sciences – who waded through the handwritten drafts to determine their validity and readability and was always at hand with encouragement; Pete Francis and Doreen Dowding of Pergamon Infotech for their patience and dedication in producing this book; my parents for unfailing encouragement, motivation and firm insistence that I write and finish the book; and to Kathy for inspiration and understanding.

Chapter 1:
SNA – a preamble

☐ Definition ☐ 'Pre-SNA' Systems ☐ Why SNA? ☐ Application Switching ☐ 'Trunks' ☐ SNA – The Intentions ☐ SNA – What Does It Specify?

Chapter 1:
SNA – a preamble

SNA – a definition

It is becoming the vogue to put forward multiple, essentially germane, but nevertheless somewhat divergent definitions of exactly what Systems Network Architecture (SNA) is. For instance, the following descriptions have been given:

- 'SNA is a direction-setting concept'
- 'SNA is a set of products'
- 'SNA is a specification'
- 'SNA is a plan for structuring a network'
- 'SNA defines the behaviour of networks of heterogeneous, loosely-coupled processors'.

SNA *per se*, as introduced to the computing fraternity by the International Business Machines (IBM) Corporation in 1974, and as the word 'architecture' in its name unequivocally proclaims, was, and still is, fundamentally and intrinsically *a design specification*.

SNA specifies comprehensively the various *data communications-oriented* facilities and functions that need to be provided and performed by products intended for either operating within, or supporting, a distributed data processing system: the total data communications facilities and functions within the system result in an efficient, reliable, cost-effective and resource-sharable data communications environment, that not only enables the relevant products to be freely interconnected but also enables data transfer operations to be performed between these products in a homogeneous manner irrespective of the nature of the products. SNA only addresses the data communications-related aspects of these products, and even that in terms of generalised functions and facilities, rather than implementational- or product-specific detail. In other words, SNA does not specify how the various functions and facilities it describes should be implemented by a product, eg whether a function should be performed by hardware or software, the processing or storage requirements needed to realise a particular set of functions, the physical characteristics of facilities, the optimum buffer sizes for a given function, or any performance criteria such as data transfer rates. Figure 1.1 illustrates the scope and intentions of SNA relative to a distributed data processing system.

Why SNA?

Before examining SNA in detail to determine the type of data communications environment it proposes for distributed data processing systems, the question 'Why did IBM have to introduce a specification such as SNA?', should be considered. Understanding the types of data communications-related problem that existed in the 'pre-SNA' era – the problems SNA was intended to alleviate – helps in appreciating the true objectives of, the underlying rationale for, and the spirit of SNA.

An early 1970s IBM data processing system that provided an interactive service and a batch processing facility for remote locations would consist typically of a System/370 host computer with one or more I/O channels, an IBM 270X transmission control unit supporting the telecommunication links to the remote locations, remote batch terminals such as the IBM 2780s or 3780s and clustered or stand-alone interactive terminals, which were channel attached (ie locally) or remotely attached such as IBM 2741s, 2260s and 3270s. The Binary Synchronous Communications (BSC) or asynchronous (ie start/stop) data link control protocol was used to interact with the remote terminals, while the IBM Channel protocol was used to interact with locally-attached terminals. Figure 1.2 depicts a typical, early 1970s, IBM data processing system.

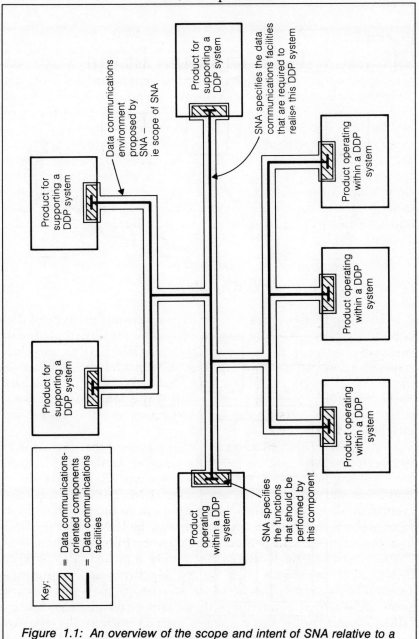

Figure 1.1: *An overview of the scope and intent of SNA relative to a distributed data processing (DDP) System*

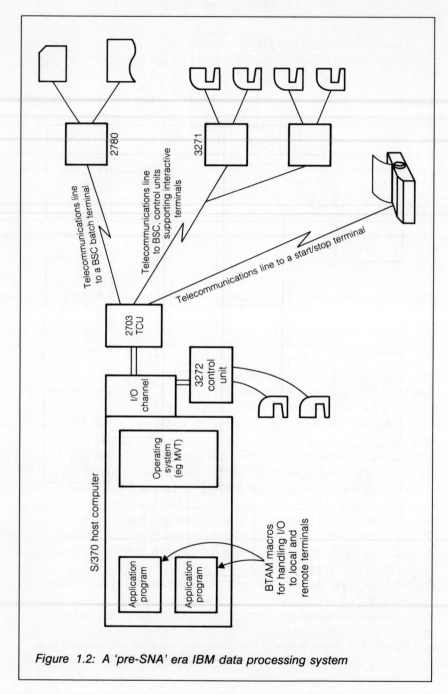

Figure 1.2: A 'pre-SNA' era IBM data processing system

6

The data communications aspects of these types of data processing system had many drawbacks. These are discussed in the following.

Inability of a terminal or a device to be dynamically switched between application programs

In 'pre-SNA' systems, every locally-attached terminal or device and every telecommunications line was assigned a unique 'Device Address' relative to the channel it was attached to or, in the case of telecommunications lines, the channel to which the 270X supporting the line was attached. (This 'Device Address' consists of the address of the channel followed by the address within this channel corresponding to the 'port' or 'slot' within the channel to which the device or telecommunication line is 'attached'. It is usually referred to as the 'Subchannel Address'.)

All I/O operations to a terminal or device, whether local or remote, had to explicitly specify a Device Address – the actual Device Address for channel-attached terminals or devices and the Device Address of the telecommunications line to which the subject terminal or device was attached, in the case of remote terminals or devices. (If a telecommunications line had multiple devices or terminals attached to it, a subaddressing scheme based on polling and selection would be used on interactions performed on the line. However, this subaddressing would still be done in the form of write operations performed on the line by output instructions that specified the Device Address of the line.) This method of operation alone, where each terminal, device and telecommunication line was assigned a unique Device Address and all I/O operations were based on it, need not have caused any restrictions to devices or terminals dynamically switching between multiple application programs executing in the host, if all the terminals and devices, whether local or remote, were 'owned' by a single 'message-switching' program. This program would route messages between a terminal or device and the relevant application program the terminal or device was communicating with at a given time, based on monitoring and intercepting 'logon' and 'logoff' messages. However, this was not the case. A terminal or device that wished to communicate with a given application program would be assigned to that application program when that program was loaded for execution. This assignment was done by specifying the actual Device Address of the terminal or device for locally-attached terminals or devices, or in the case of a remote terminal or device, the Device Address of the telecommunications line to which the terminal or device was attached, in the job control statements pertaining to the application program. The terminal or device would then stay allocated to that application program until it ceased executing. A terminal or device, whether local or remote, once assigned to an application program would only be able to communicate with that program while that program remained active. It could not 'logoff' from that application program and 'logon' to another application program: it could only 'logoff' and then 'logon' to the same application program. So, if a system had multiple, concurrently active application programs all offering interactive access, each application program required its own dedicated set of terminals and devices, even if each terminal or device only required sporadic access to the applications program it was attached to. A user who required access to two or more concurrently active application programs needed duplicate sets of equipment to achieve this. Figures 1.3 and 1.4 illustrate the kind of configuration that resulted due to the dilemma faced by a user who could not dynamically switch a terminal or device between concurrently active application programs.

This requirement for a unique device address had a secondary drawback. An I/O channel could only cater for, at most, 256 device addresses per channel. Thus, the need for a unique device address for every locally-attached device and terminal and every telecommunication line meant that in a large data communications environment the address capacity of a single channel could soon be exceeded and additional channels would need to be configured. However, this did not necessarily permit unrestricted growth; there were also restrictions on the number of channels per system. So if a very large environment were required, multiple systems had to be used, with the terminal, device and telecommunication link population spread across the systems.

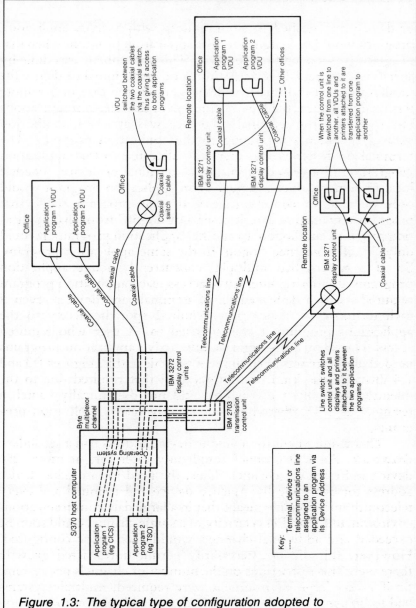

Figure 1.3: The typical type of configuration adopted to
enable users to be able to access two concurrently active
application programs in a 'pre-SNA' data processing
system

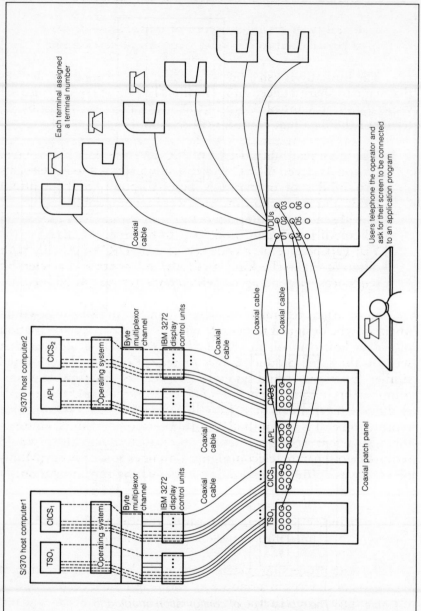

Figure 1.4: Another type of configuration used to overcome the lack of dynamic application program switching by a terminal, in a 'pre-SNA' data processing system

Inability of dissimilar types of terminal or device to be attached to the same telecommunication line

The limitations listed below dictated that terminals or devices that were to share a telecommunications line must not only use the same data link control protocol but must also be compatible in terms of the data link control features supported:

1 The incompatibility between BSC and S/S data link control protocols. Even if BSC was the only protocol to be used, its two modes of operation – point-to-point (or contention) mode and multipoint mode – were incompatible.
2 The absence of a common device and component addressing scheme if multipoint mode was to be used.
3 The dependence on a code set, ie EBCDIC or ASCII, with different error-checking methods and control character bit sequences, depending on which code set was to be used.

Since each terminal or device family in this era would invariably be designed to operate with its own particular variation of a data link control, in practice only terminals or devices that were in the same product family or related ones, and performed similar functions, could co-exist attached to the same telecommunications line. As such, a remote location requiring functionally dissimilar terminals or devices – eg a remote batch terminal for remote job entry and output, and an interactive terminal cluster – for concurrent access to services provided by a host, would require two separate telecommunication lines to that host. (Multiplexing was an option and did not resolve the root limitation.)

Inability to concentrate multiple short-haul local lines into a single long-haul 'trunk'

If a data processing system contained a large concentration of terminals or devices in a remote location, and the level of usage or the response time criteria for these terminals or devices did not warrant dedicated telecommunications lines to the host computer, significant cost benefits could be achieved by being able to use a remote communications processor (a remotely-attached Transmission Control unit). This would act as a 'concentrator' between multiple short-haul local lines and a single 'trunk' (which, if required, could consist of multiple telecommunications lines) to the host computer. Figure 1.5 depicts the concept of using 'trunks' to serve concentrations of terminals and devices in a remote location.

'Pre-SNA' systems did not cater for remote communication processors. (In addition to providing this line 'concentration' capability, a remote communication process – given sufficient processing capability – could have also increased overall data transmission efficiency in the system by handling functions such as 'device polling', ie ascertaining if a device or terminal has data that needs to be conveyed to the host, or in the event of data corruption, by the retransmission of data blocks locally, rather than having these functions provided by the host computer by transmission over the long-haul trunk.) Multipoint lines, in theory, offer a comparable facility, but the inability to mix dissimilar terminals or devices on the same line, restrictions – performance- or telecommunication-line-supplier-dictated – on the number of 'drops' permitted per line and the reliance on one line as opposed to multiple lines or a 'backup' switched line available with a trunk, limit their usefulness in practice.

Lack of a standard protocol for data transfer between application programs

The absence of a standard or appropriate protocol for communication between two application programs in the same machine – or in two separate host computers interconnected via a channel connection or a telecommunication line – resulted in the relevant applications programs taking it in turn to emulate a remote batch terminal, such as an IBM 2780 or 3780 (and in some instances even an interactive terminal such as an IBM 3270). This enabled the data transfer operations to be performed using the macros available from the existing access methods, such as BTAM, and the hardware options available on the Transmission Control units (ie neither the macros available nor the Transmission Control unit hardware option settings recognised data transfer operations between application programs and only catered for

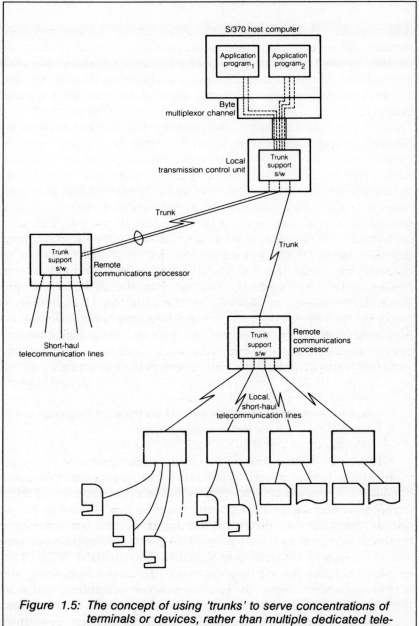

Figure 1.5: The concept of using 'trunks' to serve concentrations of terminals or devices, rather than multiple dedicated tele-communication lines (a feature not available on 'pre-SNA' systems)

data transfer between an application program and a terminal or device). While this mode of data transfer did not restrict the type or the volume of data that could be exchanged, it was not particularly efficient since the full data buffering (ie storage) and the processing capabilities offered by a host computer were not being used (eg larger block sizes and more sophisticated data compression and compaction techniques than those that could be used when emulating a remote batch terminal).

All data communications control functions being performed in the host computer

In 'pre-SNA' systems all data communications control functions, ie data link control protocol support and device control support, were performed in the host computer by the application programs that interacted with local or remote terminals or devices. For example, if an application program was to interact with a remote terminal – say a 3270 – that used multipoint BSC as its data link control protocol, it would have to do the following:

- Explicitly execute the polling and selection (or addressing) operations using the terminal-specific polling and addressing schemes
- Issue acknowledgments for data or control messages received
- Frame data blocks with the appropriate block-delimiting characters – *viz* SOH, STX, ETX, ETB etc
- Cater for retransmission or abort requests
- Handle time-outs and temporary 'wait' conditions – such as a WACK response – etc.

In these systems Transmission Control units only provided minimal data link control protocol support: insertion of pad and synchronisation characters and the calculating and checking block check characters (BCC) in the case of BSC, and supplying and checking parity for start/stop. This centralised, application program-based mode of operation not only depleted host computer processing resources but also made the development and maintenance of application programs cumbersome and long-winded as intricate data communications control functions had to be dealt with in addition to the actual functions that needed to be performed by the program.

SNA – the intentions

In view of the data communications-related drawbacks inherent in 'pre-SNA' systems, the overall intentions of SNA are easy to surmise: the specification of the data communications-oriented facilities and functions that need to be provided in order to achieve a data communications environment, for data processing systems consisting of one or more host computers that would do the following:

1 Facilitate resource sharing:
   - Enable any terminal or device to access and be able to switch between any of the application programs executing within the environment. (This facility is commonly referred to as 'application switching')
   - Enable dissimilar terminal or device types to coexist on the same telecommunications link. (However, this requirement was addressed by the introduction of a universally applicable, teleprocessing, data link control protocol, with one common mode of operation – Synchronous data link control protocol (SDLC) – which, even though announced by IBM at the same time as SNA, was not a part of SNA. SDLC is a teleprocessing protocol that SNA specifies for controlling data interchange over telecommunication links, just as the IBM S/370 channel protocol is specified by SNA for controlling data interchange across IBM S/370 channels. In other words, SDLC is just another data link control protocol referred to by SNA, rather than an integral component of SNA)
   - Enable multiple lines to be concentrated into one or more trunks.
2 Cater for efficient, effortless and unrestricted interactions between application programs, thus enabling data processing functions to be performed at multiple locations served by the environment, with the application programs at each location

being able to communicate with any other application program within the total data processing system.

3 Enable data communication functions to be distributed throughout the environment, not restricted to only the host computers in the system, and for these functions to be provided by dedicated and specialised 'system control programs' that are responsible for providing, sustaining and controlling the data communications environment, as opposed to these functions having to be performed by the individual application programs. This not only frees computing resources previously being utilised for the provision of data communication control functions to be used for true problem solving, it shifts the control function closer to the entities that need to be controlled, thus increasing overall efficiency, and also enables application programs to be developed without the distraction of having to cater for the majority of the data communication control functions. Application programs could now interact with terminals, devices or other application programs on a logical basis – concentrating only on the transfer of data – without concern for data link control or device control.

SNA – what it specifies

The SNA specification achieves the following:
- It identifies the various entities in a data processing system that need to be able to convey data via the data communications environment
- It identifies the essential characteristics of the data transfer operations between one entity type and another
- It specifies the the way in which the various entities to be served will gain access to the data communications environment
- It specifies the functions needed in the data communications environment to support the various entities it serves and also the control functions needed to provide and sustain the environment, how these functions should be provided, the grouping of them into components and how these components can be physically interconnected

- It specifies the procedure that should be followed to establish temporary relationships between two entities that are being served by the environment, if they wish to communicate with each other, and the procedure for terminating this relationship
- It specifies the data control procedures to be used to ensure that the data transfer operations are orderly and error free
- It specifies the commands and the command sequences pertaining to the various designated procedures
- It specifies the message unit formats to be used for all data transfer operations within the environment.

Implementational notes

SNA is not a product. It cannot be ordered for implementation as a single entity.

SNA is a specification: it specifies the data communication-oriented functions that need to be provided and performed by products intended for either operating within, or supporting, a distributed data processing system. SNA does not specify or recommend how the functions and facilities it postulates should be implemented by a product, whether all of them should be implemented or whether a subset would suffice, nor does it address any non-communication-related aspect of a product. This lack of implementational mandates, or even guidelines, and particularly the absence of a concept of various permissible levels (or standards) of implementation – as with the current specifications for computer languages, eg the ANSI specification for COBOL – can prove to be a severe drawback as it is sometimes difficult to ascertain what functions and features of SNA have been implemented by a given product and whether the implementation faithfully echoes the spirit of the specification, or whether the implementation is based on a technology-dictated perception of the specification.

While SNA *per se* is in essence a design specification, the term 'SNA' on its own is often used as a generic term to succinctly describe the data communication component of a distributed data processing product that conforms to the SNA specification. For example, '3274 SNA' refers to an IBM 3274 Information Display System Control Unit which, when loaded with the appropriate 'microcode', will present a data communication capability that conforms to the SNA specification. But this same 3274 with no change in the hardware but with a different set of 'microcode', which is supplied in addition to the SNA-based 'microcode', would only operate on a link using BSC as its data link control protocol and therefore not conforming to the SNA specification. Thus the post-fix SNA when applied to a distributed data processing product only refers to the fact that the product can be configured with an I/O capability that conforms to the SNA specification and does not apply to any other characteristic of the product.

Some current IBM distributed data processing products that can be configured to contain I/O components that conform to the SNA specification are as follows:

- Teleprocessing access methods:
  - ACF/VTAM
  - ACF/TCAM
  - ACF/VTAME
- Application subsystems:
  - CICS/VS
  - IMS/VS
  - DPPX
  - DPCX
- Communications controller, control programs:
  - ACF/NCP
- Terminals or devices:
  - 3270 Information Display System
  - 3730 Distributed Office Communication System
  - 3600 Finance Communication System
  - 8100 Information System
  - 6670 Information Distributor
  - SERIES/1 minicomputer etc.

Note that the current IBM communication controllers 3705 and 3725 can only be thought of as providing I/O capabilities that conform to the SNA specification when executing the relevant control program, ie ACF/NCP. A 3705 executing an Emulation Program (EP) appears and acts as a 270X Transmission Control unit which, being a 'pre-SNA'-designed device, does not contain any I/O components that conform to the SNA specification.

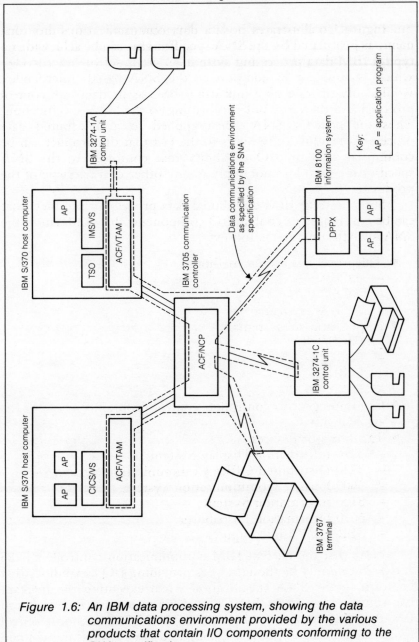

Figure 1.6: An IBM data processing system, showing the data communications environment provided by the various products that contain I/O components conforming to the SNA specification

Figure 1.6 illustrates how a data communications environment, as postulated by the SNA specification, can be achieved in a typical IBM data processing system.

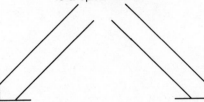

Systems Network Architecture (SNA)
is a specification

to achieve an efficient, reliable, cost-effective environment with interconnection freedom and a uniform means of communication, providing:
- 'Application switching'
- Dissimilar terminal/device coexistence on a line (⟺SDLC)
- 'Trunking'
- Application program ⇌ application program protocol
- Identification⟹ distribution of data control functions
- Data interactions based on logical entities, divorced from device or physical configuration specifics

that specifies, for a data communication environment:
- Entities that need to be served
- How the entities interact with the environment
- Control functions
- Function grouping and interconnection procedures
- Commands and command sequences
- Message formats

Checkpoint 1

Chapter 2:
The evolution of SNA

□ SNA 0 □ SNA 1 □ SNA 2 □ SNA 3 □ SNA 4

Chapter 2:
The evolution of SNA

Overview

The ease and flexibility with which complex distributed data processing environments can be postulated and implemented using distributed data processing products based on the current SNA specification belies the rather humble and inauspicious origins of SNA. Current SNA-based data processing environments can consist of multiple host computers serving a variety of locally or remotely located I/O devices and terminals via a data transmission system. These systems are capable of cost-effectively catering for most interconnection requirements and offer data link concentration, alternate paths and multiple links between communications controllers to maximise transmission efficiency and system availability. The current SNA specification, referred to as SNA 4, is the fourth revision to the original SNA specification, SNA 0, that was put forward in 1974. Each revision enhanced the control functions, the interconnection and data interchange capabilities and the configuration possibilities of SNA-based data communication environments.

This book concentrates on the SNA 4 specification and the unqualified term 'SNA' in the remainder of this book implies SNA 4. However, before discussing SNA 4 in detail it is salutory and illuminating to review, in terms of physical interconnection and topology, the kind of data communications environment that could be implemented using the products that conformed to each of the five versions of SNA. Viewing the evolution of SNA in terms of the type of physical configurations that each version catered for – notwithstanding a few restrictions imposed by the product implementations rather than by limitations in the relevant specifications – is a more tangible, succinct and indicative guide to the intentions and strategy of SNA than the analysis of the individual, intrinsic functions provided by each version.

SNA 0

SNA 0 fulfilled the crucial objective of SNA, which is application switching, but only catered for the most basic of data communications environments: a tree structure consisting of a single host computer with a locally- (ie, channel-) attached communications controller supporting a star network of cluster controllers attached to it via leased telecommunication links. Figure 2.1 illustrates the only type of SNA data communications environment that was possible with SNA 0. Although its existence is well documented now, SNA 0 was effectively a prototype and was referred to in some quarters of IBM as 'Single Network Architecture', more in deference to its limitations than in referring to its possible uniqueness as an architecture for data communications environments.

SNA 1

SNA 1, announced in 1975, was IBM's first public acknowledgment of its commitment to SNA as its data communications design strategy for future distributed data processing-related products. SNA 1 enhanced the configuration options provided by SNA 0 by permitting a second communications controller – supporting a star network of cluster controllers and stand-alone terminals on leased telecommunication links – to be attached via a leased telecommunications link to the locally-attached communications controller, ie allowing the possibility of a remote communications controller. Ironically though, the remote communications controller could only support non-SNA devices. (By 'non-SNA device' is meant a device, whether a cluster controller or a stand-alone terminal, whose data communications components are not based on SNA and instead use one of the pre-SNA

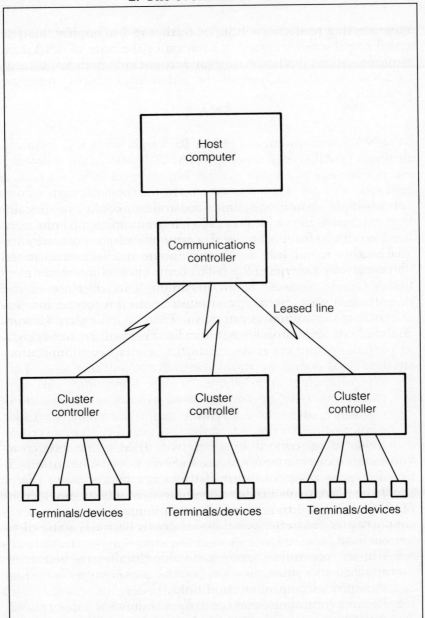

Figure 2.1: *The only kind of data communications environment possible with SNA 0 (c. 1974)*

teleprocessing protocols – BSC or start/stop – to control the data transfer operations.) Figure 2.2 illustrates the type of SNA data communications environment that was possible with SNA 1.

SNA 2

SNA 2 was announced in late 1975 and, while still retaining the fundamental system topology of SNA 1, offered the following enhancements:

1 Multiple communication controllers could be locally attached to the single host. No telecommunication links were permitted from one local communications controller to another to provide an alternate route if a communications controller experienced a fault on the channel interface.
2 A single remote communications controller could be attached via a leased telecommunications link to each locally-attached communications controller. No links were permitted between remote communications controllers, nor could a remote communications controller be attached to more than one local communications controller at any one time. This type of configuration where a remote communications controller can only be connected to a local communications controller, and where a remote communications controller cannot support the attachment of another remote communications controller is referred to as a 'remote communications controller, cascade level of one'. The analogy is drawn to a series of waterfalls to graphically stress that a remote communications controller can only be one 'drop' away from a local communications controller.
3 A cluster controller could be locally (ie channel) attached to the host.
4 Cluster controllers and stand-alone terminals could be attached to communication controllers via either leased or switched telecommunication links.
5 Remote communication controllers could now support SNA devices and not only non-SNA devices as in SNA 1.

Figure 2.3 depicts a typical SNA 2 environment.

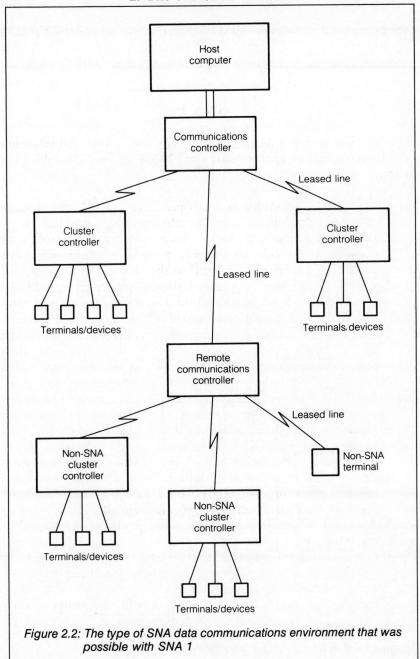

Figure 2.2: The type of SNA data communications environment that was possible with SNA 1

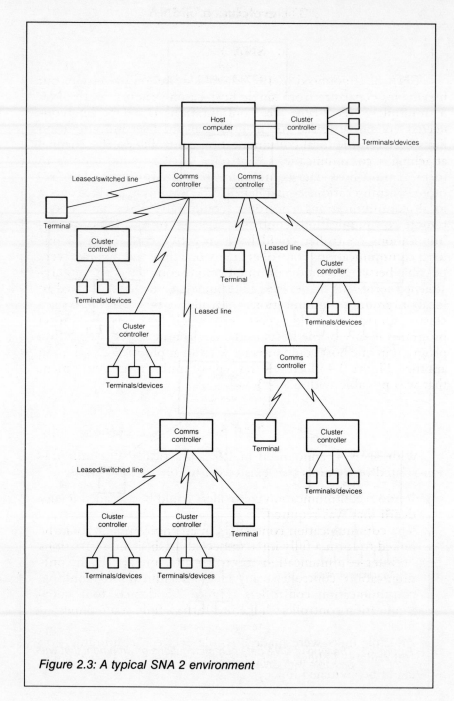

Figure 2.3: A typical SNA 2 environment

30

SNA 3

SNA 3, announced in 1977, heralded the long overdue, but inevitable, departure from single host-based systems. With SNA 3, multiple SNA 2-type tree configurations could be interconnected via single leased (or manual dial-up) telecommunication links between the local communication controllers or by channel attaching a communications controller to two or more hosts to form a multi-host data communications environment. The 'remote communications controller cascade level' remained at one, a local communications controller could only have an 'active' remote communications controller attached to it, a remote communications controller could have an active connection to one local communications controller at any one time and no links were possible between remote communications controllers. Remotely-attached terminals or devices, ie terminals or devices attached to local or remote communications controllers either directly or via a cluster controller, could access and switch between application programs in any of the hosts in the environment. An application program in one host could interact with an application program in another. Figure 2.4 illustrates the type of multi-host environment that was possible with SNA 3.

SNA 4

With SNA 4, announced in 1978, practically all configuration-related restrictions that existed with SNA 3 were lifted:

1 Remote communication controllers could be cascaded to any depth that was required.
2 The communication controllers in an environment could be linked to form a fully interconnected mesh, ie no restrictions on inter-communication-controller attachments. Each communication controller can have attachments to multiple communication controllers. Figure 2.5 depicts four communication controllers linked to form a fully interconnected mesh.
3 Multiple links were made possible between communication controllers. (These links, though operated as leased links, could be switched links.)

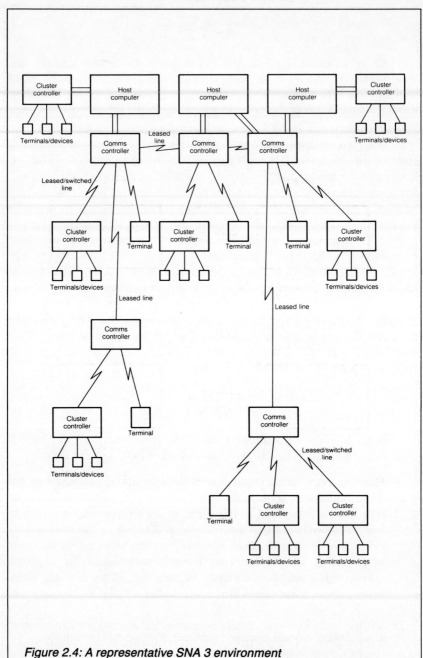

Figure 2.4: A representative SNA 3 environment

32

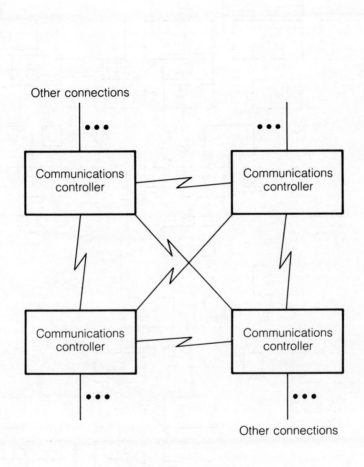

Figure 2.5: Four communications controllers linked to form a fully interconnected mesh

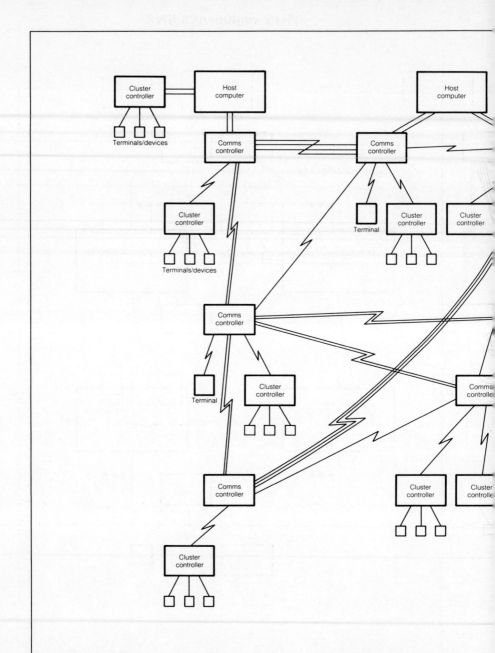

Figure 2.6: The type of data communications environment possible with SNA 4

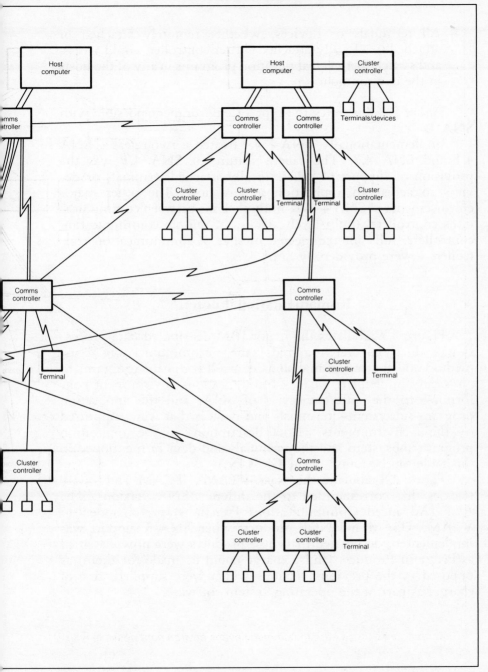

4 All terminals or devices, whether remotely attached or
attached to a locally-attached cluster controller, could access,
and switch, between application programs in any of the hosts
in the environment.

Figure 2.6 illustrates the type of environment possible with
SNA 4.

Implementationally, SNA 4 was treated as two releases: SNA
4.1 and SNA 4.2. The salient feature of SNA 4.1 was the
provision of support to enable locally-attached terminals or devices to access an application in any host. The other major
enhancements of SNA 4 – *viz* multiple links between communications controllers, multi-level cascades of remote communication
controllers, fully interconnected meshes of communication controllers – were provided by SNA 4.2.

Implementational notes

Figure 2.7 tabulates the major IBM distributed data processing products that were required, ie the telecommunications access
method and the communications controller control program, to
physically implement a data communications environment conforming to the different levels of SNA, and the application
program subsystems, terminals and devices that were supported
by these environments. (Brief descriptions of the application
program subsystem and the terminals and devices mentioned in
this table can be found in the Glossary.)

Figure 2.8 tabulates the exact 'VTAM', 'TCAM' and 'NCP'
releases that corresponded to the different SNA versions. The
ACF (Advanced Communications Functions) prefix added to
VTAM, TCAM and NCP products when SNA 3 support was
implemented, designated that these products were now classified
as Program Products (and a charge could be made for them) as
opposed to the previous versions which were supplied, free of
charge, as part of the operating system software.

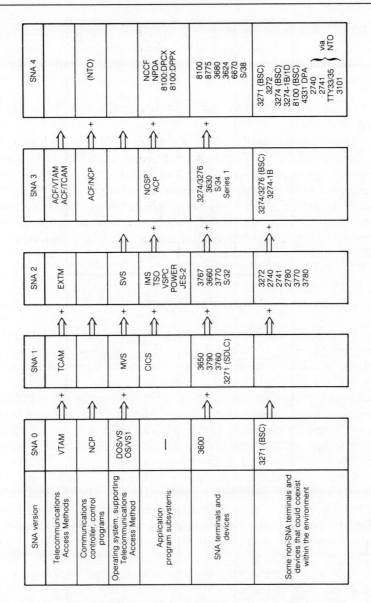

SNA version	SNA 0	SNA 1	SNA 2	SNA 3	SNA 4
Telecommunications Access Methods	VTAM	TCAM	EXTM	ACF/VTAM ACF/TCAM	(NTO)
Communications controller, control programs	NCP			ACF/NCP	
Operating system, supporting Telecommunications Access Method	DOS/VS OS/VS1	MVS	SVS		
Application program subsystems	—	CICS	IMS TSO VSPC POWER JES-2	NOSP ACP	NCCF NPDA 8100:DPCX 8100:DPPX
SNA terminals and devices	3600	3650 3790 3760 3271 (SDLC)	3767 3660 3770 S/32	3274/3276 3630 S/34 Series 1	8100 8775 3680 3624 6670 S/38
Some non-SNA terminals and devices that could coexist within the environment	3271 (BSC)		3272 2740 2741 2780 3770 3780	3274/3276 (BSC) 3274-1B	3271 (BSC) 3272 3274 (BSC) 3274-1B/1D 8100 (BSC) 4331 DPA 2740 2741 TTY33/35 3101 } via NTO

Figure 2.7: Summary of the various IBM DDP products that were required to implement SNA environments corresponding to the five versions of SNA and the terminals and devices supported within these environments

SNA version	SNA 0	SNA 1	SNA 2	SNA 3	SNA 4.1	SNA 4.2
'VTAM'	VTAM 1.1		VTAM 2	ACF/VTAM Release 1	ACF/VTAM Release 2	ACF/VTAM Release 3
'TCAM'	—	TCAM 8	TCAM 9 / TCAM 10	ACF/TCAM Version 1	ACF/TCAM Version 2 Releases 1 and 2	ACF/TCAM Version 2 Release 3
'NCP'	NCP 3		NCP 4 / NCP 5	ACF/NCP Release 1	ACF/NCP Releases 2 and 2.1	ACF/NCP Release 3

Figure 2.8: The 'VTAM', 'TCAM' and 'NCP' releases corresponding to the five SNA versions

SNA version	0	1	2	3	4
Number of hosts	1	1	1	n^*	n
Number of locally-attached communications controllers	1	1	n	n	n
Number of remote communications controllers that can be attached to a local communications controller	0	1	1	1	n
Remote communications controller, cascade level	0	1	1	1	n
Number of attachments a remote communications controller can have to other communications controllers	—	1	1	1	n
Multiple links between communications controllers	No	No	No	No	Yes
Links between locally-attached communications controllers	—	—	No	Yes	Yes
Fully interconnected meshes between communications controllers	—	—	No	No	Yes
Locally-attached cluster controllers	No	No	Yes	Yes	Yes
Switched-line support to cluster controllers and terminals	No	No	Yes	Yes	Yes
Locally-attached devices/terminals accessing application programs in other hosts	—	—	—	No	Yes

*n is an implementational-dependent value greater than 1

Checkpoint 2

Chapter 3:
Basic components

☐ End Users ☐ Network Addressable Units ☐ System Series Control Point ☐ Logical Units ☐ Path Control Network ☐ Nodes ☐ Subareas

Chapter 3:
Basic components

End users

In addition to providing data manipulation facilities, a modern DP system must cater for data communication between various types of information source and destination. Since SNA addresses the total data communications requirements of a DP system, it is necessary to look at the data transfer configurations that might be needed.

All DP systems need to be capable of transferring data between application programs and I/O devices such as card readers, line printers, tape units and disk drives. These devices can either be directly attached to the computer by multi-wire cables or, if data is required from or at a location remote from the computer, by telecommunication links. Interactive DP systems also need to provide for data communication between terminal users and application programs and, in some instances, for direct communication between two terminal users. As with I/O devices, the terminals can either be directly attached to the computer or, when the terminal is located at a location remote from the computer, by telecommunication links.

A modern DP system can consist of not just one computer but a series of computers interconnected by cables or telecommunication links. In such a system there will be a need to provide for, and control, data communication between application programs resident in, or terminals attached to, one computer, and I/O devices or terminals attached to another computer.

In distributed data processing environments particularly,

direct data transfer between application programs is required. The application programs could be resident in the same computer or in different computers.

The term 'application program', especially in the context of an interactive system, could mean not just a single 'problem-solving' program, but a programming subsystem supporting the execution of multiple 'problem-solving' programs. These programming subsystems appear to the operating system as a single application program, and the operating system is not aware of the 'subprograms' running under the control of the subsystem.

So, SNA must cater for data communication:

- Between application programs and I/O devices
- Between application programs and terminal users
- Between terminal users
- Between application programs

in single or multiple computer environments, with locally and remotely attached I/O devices and terminals. However, in spite of these various possible configurations the information sources and destinations that participate in data communication are either application programs, terminal users or I/O devices.

SNA refers to these possible sources or destinations of information – application programs, terminal users or I/O devices – as *end users*.

Network Addressable Units

The objective of SNA is to specify a data communications environment that provides for the efficient and reliable transfer of data between end users, irrespective of their physical configuration.

SNA specifies this data communication environment in terms of a collection of uniquely addressable, functional entities, called *Network Addressable Units*, interconnected by a *Path Control Network*.

Three types of Network Addressable Unit (NAU) are defined:

- *System Services Control Points* (SSCPs)
- *Logical Units* (LUs)
- *Physical Units* (PUs).

SSCP

Every SNA environment must contain at least one SSCP. SSCPs control and manage the resources that make up an SNA environment. Thus, while in an environment with only one SSCP, all the resources will be controlled by it; in an environment with multiple SSCPs, each SSCP will control the resources of a particular portion of the environment.

The set of resources controlled by an SSCP is referred to as the *domain* of that SSCP. An environment with only one SSCP will consist of one domain, while a multi-SSCP environment will consist of multiple domains.

Where SSCPs occur within a communications environment and what determines the number of SSCPs in a given environment will be dealt with in the discussion of *nodes* later in this chapter.

An SSCP will control the following:

- The physical configuration of all the resources (individually and in respect to each other) within its domain
- The addition or removal of resources to or from its domain
- The activation and deactivation of resources within its domain
- The establishment of communication paths – between resources, for data transfer (and the disconnection of these paths when data transfer is complete)
- The testing of resources within its domain
- The recovery of faulty resources
- The system operators' interactions with the resources of its domain.

LU

Though SNA acknowledges that there can only be three types of end user, each of these types encompasses a wide spectrum of continually changing capabilities, characteristics and requirements. For example, a terminal user could be using a teleprinter (consisting of a keyboard and printer) which communicates character by character in asynchronous mode, or a visual display unit equipped with a light pen, capable of multi-colour data display which communicates by means of blocks of data imbedded in a synchronous protocol. To attempt to classify all the properties of each of the end user types, and then to specify how two end users with a given set of properties would communicate with each other would be futile, even if it were possible. Therefore SNA does not attempt to specify the actual properties of the end users. As such, end users are outside the boundaries of the data communications environment described by SNA.

End users interact with the SNA-defined communications environment via LUs. LUs can be thought of as communications ports that enable end users to access and use the resources of the SNA environment for data transfer.

Before end–user–to–end–user communication can occur each end user must access the communications environment via an LU. End-user-to-end-user communication is then achieved by means of SNA-defined transactions between the LUs.

An LU performs the necessary data transformation and data-flow management functions that are needed to support end–user–to–end–user communications. So, an LU should be viewed as a set of functions that are invoked by an end user to enable it to communicate with another end user, rather than as a rigid interface to the environment.

While it is usual to have an LU per end user – ie a one-to-one relationship between end users and LUs – this is not mandatory. An LU could support multiple end users. SNA does not specify any criteria for end user-to-LU association. This is left as an implementation option.

PU

Several control functions need to be performed by a data communications environment, to establish and maintain its physical configuration. The activation, deactivation and operation of communication-specific entities, such as data links, need to be

controlled. Certain resources within the environment might need
to be loaded with software from another resource before they can
participate in data transfer operations. Diagnostic information,
such as dumps, might be needed from a failed resource to facilitate
its recovery. Such physical configuration-related control functions
– managing communications-specific physical entities and, where
necessary, loading and dumping resources – are performed by
PUs.

PUs are invariably implemented by software. Thus, a Physical
Unit – in SNA terms – is a piece of software that controls physical
entities and physical operations (not, contrary to expectations, a
physically-tangible component such as a communications control
unit or a terminal control unit). PUs will be studied in more detail
later in this chapter in the discussion on SNA nodes.

Figure 3.1 illustrates the basic relationship between end users,
Network Addressable Units and the Path Control Network.

Path Control Network

NAUs communicate with each other by means of SNA-
specified message units, transmitted via the Path Control Network. The format of these message units are:

message unit::= <nau:d,nau:o,SNA parameters,data>

where 'nau:d' denotes the address of the NAU the message is
destined for, and 'nau:o' is the address of the NAU which
originated the message. If 'nau:o' wishes to communicate with
'nau:d', it constructs a message unit and passes it to the Path
Control Network. The Path Control Network will ensure that it
is delivered to 'nau:d'. If 'nau:o' passes a series of message units, all
destined to 'nau:d', the Path Control Network will deliver these
message units to 'nau:d' in the same order that it received them
from 'nau:o'.

The Path Control Network consists of *path control* and *data
link control* components. Path Control components are responsible
for selecting and managing the overall route that a message unit
from one NAU to another NAU must traverse. The route chosen
by the Path Control components might include data links across

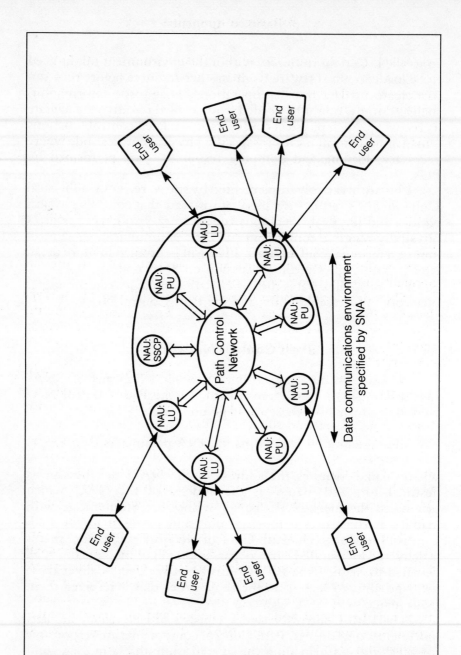

Figure 3.1: Basic relationship between end users, NAUs and the Path
Control Network

which the message unit has to be transmitted. Data link control components will control the transmission of the message unit across each data link. The Path Control Network will be dealt with in detail in Chapter 7.

Nodes

NAUs can only reside in SNA *nodes*. An SNA node consists of one or more NAUs and a set of Path Control Network components (see Figure 3.2). Nodes are interconnected by the Path Control Network. (In an SNA context the terms 'node' and 'SNA node' are synonymous, and it is customary to use the unqualified term 'node' rather than 'SNA node'.)

SNA defines four types of node. They are referred to as *Type 1 nodes*, *Type 2 nodes*, *Type 4 nodes* and *Type 5 nodes*. (Note the absence of Type 3 nodes.) The node types are distinguished by their functional capabilities and by the presence or absence of certain NAU types.

Type 1 and Type 2 nodes are called *peripheral nodes*, while Type 4 and Type 5 nodes are called *subarea nodes*. Interconnection and message unit routing capabilities are the differentiating factors between peripheral and subarea nodes.

Each peripheral node must be attached to a subarea node via Path Control Network components. Peripheral nodes cannot be attached directly to other peripheral nodes; neither can a peripheral node be concurrently attached to more than one subarea node. Multiple peripheral nodes can be attached to one subarea node (see Figure 3.3).

NAUs resident in peripheral nodes are sources of, and destinations for, message units within an SNA environment. However, the Path Control Network components of peripheral nodes have little or no message-routing capabilities. They can only transmit or receive message units to or from the subarea node that their peripheral node is attached to and, in some instances, 'route' message units between NAUs that are resident within the peripheral node.

Since NAUs resident in a peripheral node can only communicate with other NAUs in other nodes via the subarea node (that

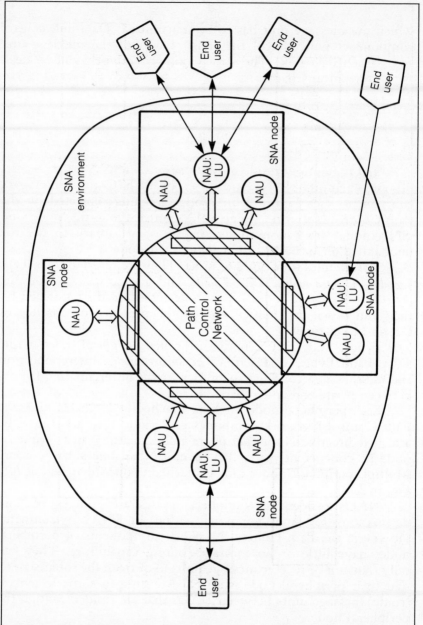

Figure 3.2: NAUs and Path Control Network components within SNA nodes

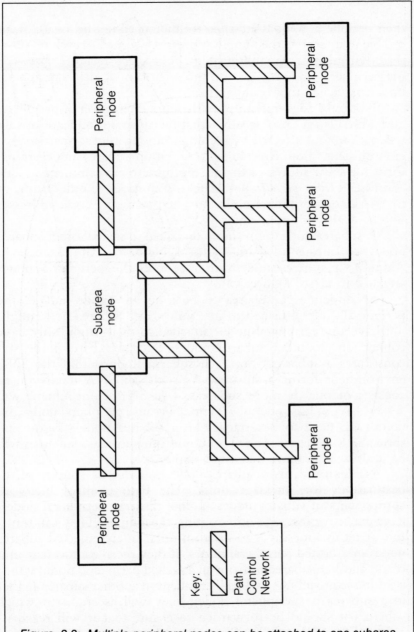

Figure 3.3: Multiple peripheral nodes can be attached to one subarea node

their peripheral node is attached to) they need not be aware of, or be able to interpret, the unique addresses assigned to each NAU in the environment. An abbreviated *local address* structure, between the peripheral node NAUs and the subarea node that a peripheral node is attached to, would suffice.

Not only does this simplify the implementation of peripheral node NAUs, it also ensures that peripheral node addressing schemes are not affected by reconfigurations in other parts of the environment. Boundary Functions within subarea nodes transform the local addresses to the appropriate environment-unique addresses or *vice versa* when dealing with message units from, or to, NAUs in peripheral nodes attached to them. Local addresses will be dealt with in Chapter 8, *SNA addressing*.

A subarea node can be interconnected to several other subarea nodes by means of Path Control Network components. In addition, a subarea node can have multiple peripheral nodes attached to it (see Figure 3.4).

SNA defines a subarea to be a subarea node and all the peripheral nodes attached to it. (Note that a subarea node might not have any peripheral nodes attached to it. It might only have connections to other subarea nodes. Such a subarea node still constitutes a subarea.) So, each subarea node within the SNA environment forms a subarea. As such, an SNA environment consists of one or more subareas. (An SNA environment will always have at least one subarea node because peripheral nodes, by definition, have to be attached to a subarea node!) Figure 3.4 shows an SNA environment with multiple subareas. Subareas will be dealt with in more detail in Chapter 8.

NAUs resident in subarea nodes can also be sources of, or destinations for, message units. The Path Control Network components of subarea nodes, unlike those in peripheral nodes, have extensive message-unit-routing capabilities. They can transmit or receive messages to or from other interconnected subarea nodes or attached peripheral nodes. If they receive a message unit (from another subarea or from an attached peripheral node) which is addressed to a NAU which is resident in another subarea (either in a subarea or peripheral node), they will ascertain to which subareas it should be forwarded to ensure that it will reach its eventual destination.

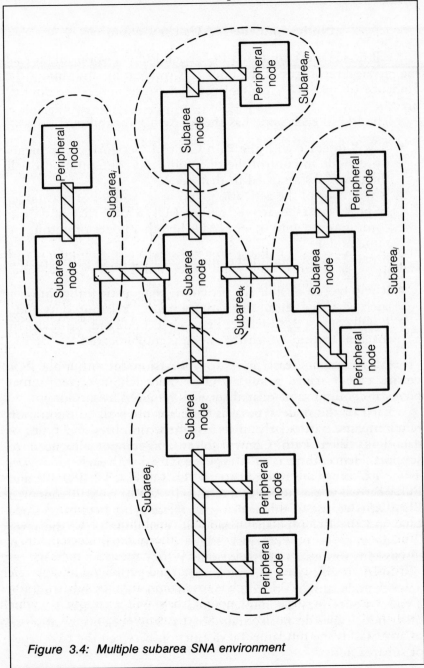

Figure 3.4: Multiple subarea SNA environment

Nodes and the NAUs they contain

All nodes must contain a PU. Each PU is responsible for all the physical resources of the node it is resident in, and (under the guidance of an SSCP) controls how these resources are configured.

The PU in each node has the following capabilities:

- It will interact with the Path Control Network components of its node to control the operation and configuration of all the data links attached to that node
- It will control the activation (and deactivation) of that node. A node must be active, before LUs within that node can communicate with other NAUs (in other nodes or within the same node)
- It may request, and then control, the loading of software into its node
- It will be responsible for providing diagnostic information – such as storage dumps or activity traces – relating to its node
- It will control the interface between its node and the device or machine within which that node is implemented.

(SNA has no concept of, or provision for, multiple PUs within a node, since a single PU embraces the complete set of physical configuration-related services required by a node.)

Each of the node types has different physical configuration requirements, particularly in terms of the numbers and types of data links their Path Control Network components need to support. Hence, there is a PU type associated with each node type. These PU types are referred to as PU_T1, PU_T2, PU_T4 and PU_T5. A Type x node (where x is 1, 2, 4 or 5) will contain a PU_Tx. (Because of this one-to-one relationship between a node type and the PU type that resides in that node type, the term 'PU_Tx node' – or even just 'PU_Tx' – is often used in SNA discussions to mean a 'Type x node'.)

SNA specifies that a Type 5 node must contain an SSCP. (A Type 5 node cannot contain more than one SSCP, but multiple Type 5 nodes may be implemented within one machine!) The other node types do not contain SSCPs. The presence or absence of an SSCP is the fundamental distinction between the two types of subarea node.

All nodes may contain LUs. (Some subarea nodes, Type 4 nodes in particular, might not contain any LUs.) Peripheral nodes must always contain at least one LU.

The two types of peripheral node differ in the maximum number of LUs that each may contain and in the number of concurrent data transfer operations that their LUs can support.

Due to the different local address structures used by the two types of peripheral node, Type 1 nodes can have a maximum of 64 LUs, while Type 2 nodes can have a maximum of 255 LUs.

An LU in a Type 1 node can only support one LU-to-LU data transfer operation at a time. An LU in a Type 2 node can support multiple concurrent data transfer operations with other LUs.

There is no specified limit to the maximum number of LUs a subarea node may contain: the number will only be restricted by the NAU addressing scheme which imposes an upper limit on the total number of NAUs that may occur within an SNA environment. This will be covered in Chapter 8.

Figure 3.5 summarises the types and numbers of NAUs that each node type can (and in some cases should) contain.

Informal names for the nodes

Based on the nature of the physical devices or machines within which each node type is usually implemented, the following informal relationships are often drawn:

- Type 5 node – 'host' node
- Type 4 node – 'communications controller' node
- Type 2 node ⎱ 'cluster controller' or
- Type 1 node ⎰ 'terminal' node.

(Note that the terms 'cluster controller' and 'terminal' can both be applied to either a Type 2 or a Type 1 node.)

When using these informal node names, it is important to bear in mind that the device or machine described by that node name will always contain other non-SNA specified components, which are not a part of the SNA node.

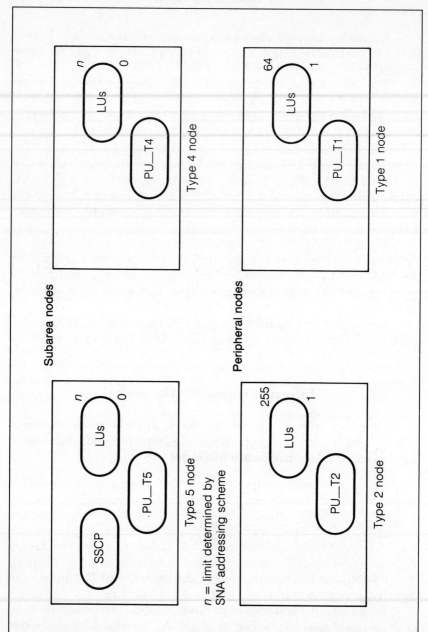

Figure 3.5: Summary of the types, and numbers of, NAUs that each node type can contain

Node interconnection

A Type 1 or Type 2 peripheral node can be attached to either a Type 4 or Type 5 subarea node. A peripheral node cannot be attached to another peripheral node, nor can it be attached to more than one subarea node at a given time. SNA does not impose any specific restrictions on the number of peripheral nodes that can be simultaneously attached to a subarea node. (The SNA resource addressing scheme and physical connection limits dictated by the way the node is implemented will, in practice, govern how many peripheral nodes a given subarea node can support.) Figure 3.6 illustrates the interconnection possibilities between peripheral and subarea nodes. Note that each subarea node forms the hub of a typical 'star' network and that the data links – provided by the Path Control Network components – can be either point-to-point or multipoint. (Loops, where the subarea node acts as the Loop Control Station, are also feasible, though not explicitly stated in SNA.)

It is theoretically possible to connect subarea nodes to each other – with multiple data links between the nodes, if necessary – to form a generalised, fully interconnected 'mesh' network. Figure 3.7 illustrates some of the interconnection possibilities that exist between subarea nodes. Note that peripheral nodes, though not shown in Figure 3.7, can be attached to any of the subarea nodes depicted in the figure.

Implementational notes

So far the basic components of SNA have been discussed in terms of their formal specifications. The discussion has not included how, or where, these components are implemented within a typical data processing system to create an SNA-based data communications environment. This was to avoid the danger of implementational features being misconstrued as SNA specification-imposed criteria. When dealing with SNA, it is very important that a clear distinction is drawn between how a certain entity (or concept) is specified by SNA, and how it may have been implemented within a given product. An implementation might not fully reflect the spirit of the specification: even if it did, the manner in which an entity is implemented need not be unique.

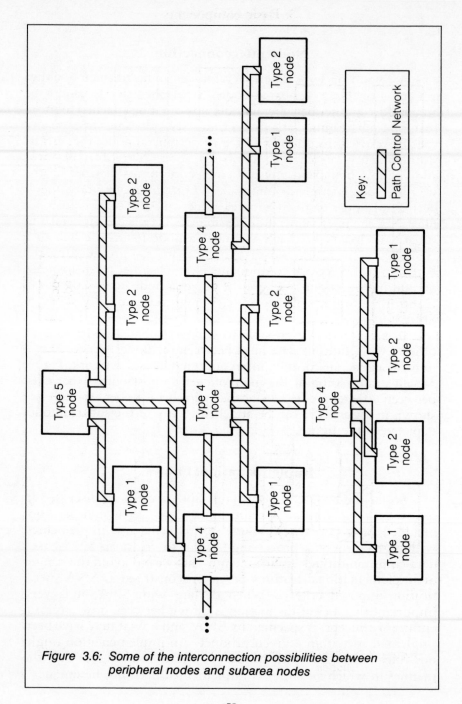

Figure 3.6: Some of the interconnection possibilities between peripheral nodes and subarea nodes

Key:

Path Control Network

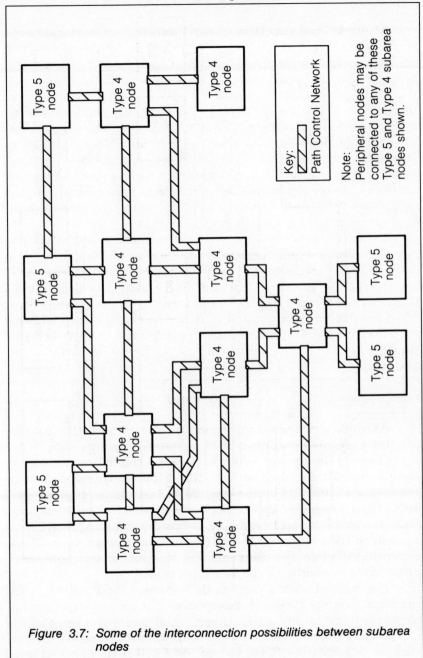

Key:
Path Control Network

Note:
Peripheral nodes may be connected to any of these Type 5 and Type 4 subarea nodes shown.

Figure 3.7: *Some of the interconnection possibilities between subarea nodes*

Multiple implementational variations that all conform to the specification could be possible. For example, SNA specifies that an SNA environment must contain at least one SSCP, and that SSCPs reside in Type 5 nodes. It does not specify the characteristics of the physical devices within which Type 5 nodes should be implemented. Currently, Type 5 nodes are only implemented on general-purpose computers. But this only indicates an implementational interpretation rather than an SNA specification-imposed restriction. The SNA specification *per se* does not preclude the postulation of an environment where Type 5 nodes may occur within communications controllers, and general-purpose computers will only contain Type 2 nodes to support their application program (or I/O device) end users.

However, now the unrestrictive and generalised manner in which the basic components are specified has been shown, it is instructive to examine the way in which they are normally implemented – to create practical SNA-based data communications environments – in real data processing products. Since most SNA environments are found in data processing systems hosted by IBM System/370 (or compatible) computers, the products that implement the SNA components on such systems will be examined.

Type 5 nodes

As implied by their informal name – 'host node' – these nodes are always located within an IBM System/370 computer.

(Type 5 nodes are sometimes implemented within minicomputers, for example in the IBM 8100 Information System running a DPPX Operating System. These minicomputers run application programs and act as hosts to attached terminals and I/O devices. However, if they need to communicate with a Type 5 node in an IBM System/370 host they do so by employing a Type 2 peripheral node also implemented within the minicomputer, rather than as another Type 5 subarea node.)

The bulk of each Type 5 node – viz the SSCP, the PU_T5, the Path Control Network components, the boundary function to support any locally attached peripheral nodes and most of the LU services – is provided by a telecommunications access method such as VTAM, ACF/TCAM or ACF/VTAM. (The relevant access methods are listed in Chapters 2 and 12.) Figure 3.8 depicts the interrelationships between a Type 5 node, the access method and the application program end users within a host computer. (Note that the access method contains non-SNA specified components. These components support locally attached devices which do not contain SNA nodes, eg IBM 3274-1B or 1D cluster controllers.)

Type 5 nodes will directly support Type 2 peripheral nodes in channel-attached, ie local cluster controllers, eg IBM 3274-1As or programmable controllers, eg IBM 3791s. (Type 1 nodes are not normally implemented on channel-attached devices.)

The LUs in these Type 5 nodes only support application program end users. Terminal operator end users on a channel-attached device (or I/O device end users attached to one) will be supported by LUs in a peripheral node implemented within that device, rather than by LUs in a Type 5 node.

It is important to note at this stage that the data link control components of Type 5 nodes only support data transfer on IBM System/370 channels. Telecommunications links are handled by Type 4 nodes. (The exception is Type 5 nodes provided by ACF/VTAME, which support telecommunications links attached to an IBM 4331 host via a communications adaptor.)

Two Type 5 nodes could be implemented on the same host by installing two different access methods – eg ACF/VTAM and ACF/TCAM. One access method, on its own, will only provide for one Type 5 node.

Type 4 nodes

These nodes are provided by network control programs, such as IBM's NCP or ACF/NCP, resident in IBM 3704, 3705 or 3725 communications controllers. See Chapters 2 and 12 for details.

The communications controllers that contain Type 4 nodes can be interconnected with hosts containing Type 5 nodes, or other communications controllers containing Type 4 nodes, in a variety of configurations as summarised in Figure 3.7. The connections to host computers will be via channel attachments while the interconnections to other communications controllers will be via telecommunications links.

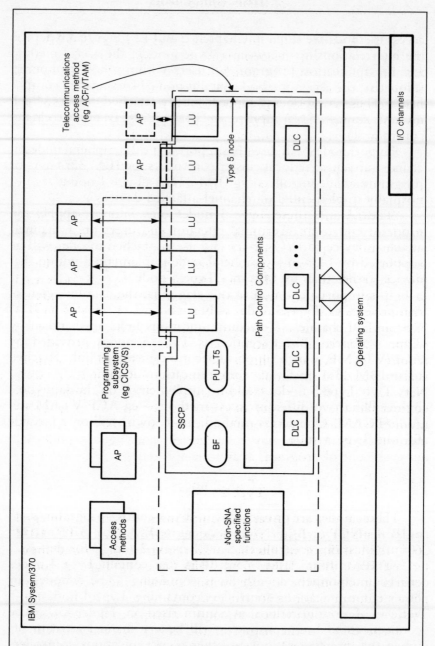

Figure 3.8: A Type 5 node within an IBM System/370 host computer

Type 4 nodes will only support peripheral nodes that are attached to it by telecommunications links. Devices with peripheral nodes could be attached to the same IBM System/370 channel as a communications controller with a Type 4 node, but these peripheral nodes will be supported by a Type 5 node in the host. Any communication between these peripheral nodes and the Type 4 node has to be conducted via the Type 5 node.

Since the IBM communications controllers do not contain facilities to support end users, Type 4 nodes do not contain any LUs: they only contain a PU_T4 and Path Control Network components to support attached data links.

A communications controller with a Type 4 node is not a mandatory prerequisite for all SNA data communications environments. Type 4 nodes are only required if telecommunications links need to be supported (and Type 5 nodes are not being provided by ACF/VTAME), or if two or more Type 5 nodes need to be interconnected. An SNA environment consisting only of 'channel-attached' peripheral nodes communicating with a Type 5 'host node' (or consisting only of application program end users within a host communicating only among themselves) will not require a Type 4 node. (This is why the term 'SNA Environment' is always used in this book, rather than the more common 'SNA Network', as the term 'Network' in a data communications context has the propensity of conjuring up visions of telecommunications links and communications controllers!) A communication controller may only contain one Type 4 node, ie, network control program, at any given time.

Type 2 nodes

These nodes are invariably implemented either as integral components of a cluster controller, eg IBM 3274-1A/1C, IBM 3601, IBM 8775, or within the control program of a minicomputer, eg IBM 8100, IBM 3790, IBM Series/1. Type 2 nodes, depending upon the device within which the node is implemented, can either be attached via IBM System/370 channels to Type 5 nodes, or via telecommunications links to Type 4 nodes.

Depending on the nature of the device within which it is implemented, a Type 2 node may contain LUs to cater for any of the end user types.

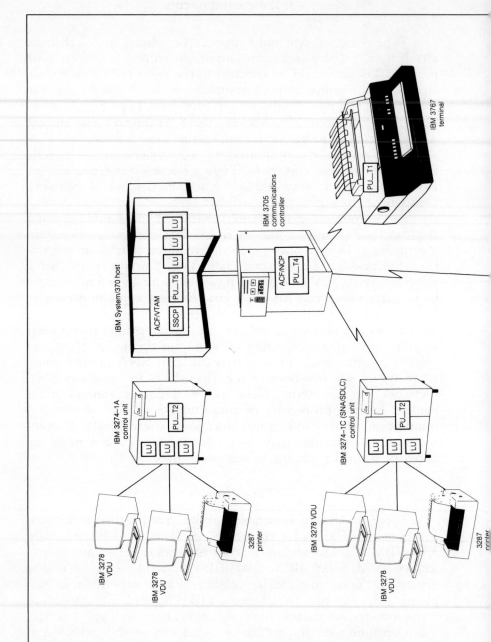

Figure 3.9: A typical IBM System/370-based SNA environment

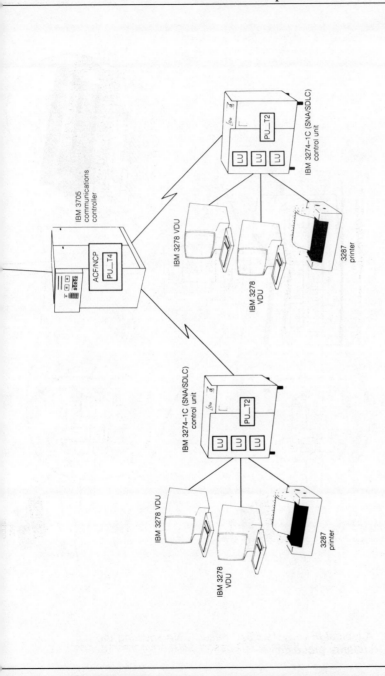

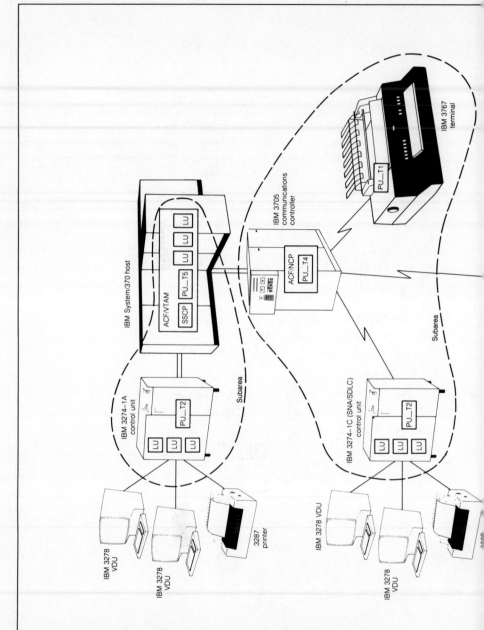

Figure 3.10: A typical IBM System/370-based SNA showing the subarea grouping

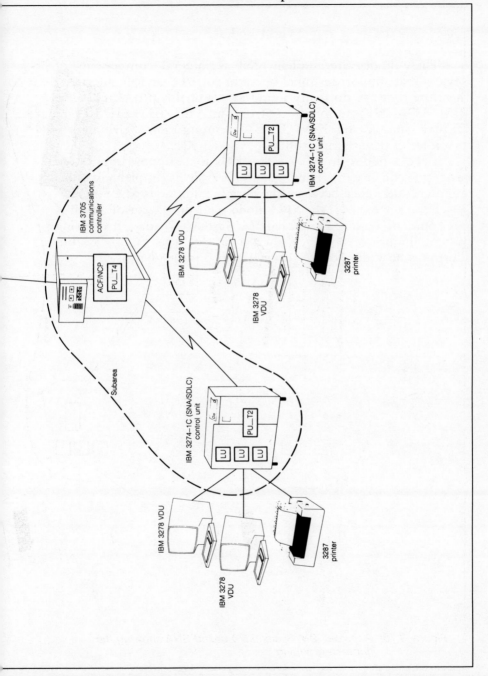

Type 1 nodes

These nodes are implemented as integral components of devices that support terminal operator (or I/O device) end users: therefore they are normally found in terminal control units. The IBM 3271-11/12 terminal control unit, the IBM 3275-11/12 Display Station and IBM 3767 Communication Terminal are examples of devices that contain Type 1 nodes.

Type 1 nodes do not contain LUs that support application program end users. This is another, albeit implementation-imposed, difference between the peripheral node types.

Figure 3.9 shows the SNA nodes and the extent of an SNA environment within a typical IBM System/370 data processing system. Figure 3.10 depicts the same system as Figure 3.9 but illustrates how the nodes will be grouped into subareas.

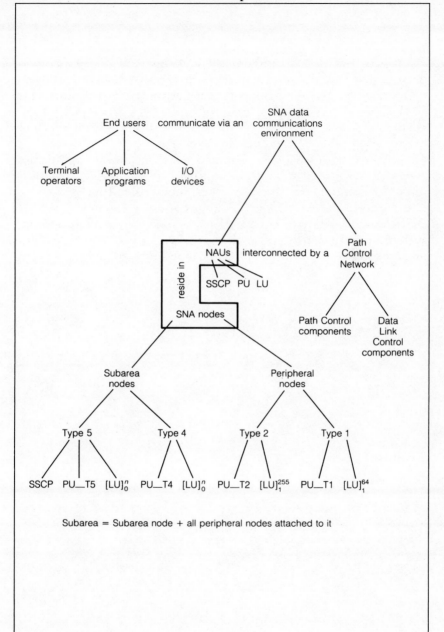

End users communicate via an SNA data communications environment

Terminal operators   Application programs   I/O devices

NAUs interconnected by a Path Control Network

reside in

SSCP PU LU

SNA nodes

Path Control components   Data Link Control components

Subarea nodes   Peripheral nodes

Type 5   Type 4   Type 2   Type 1

SSCP PU__T5 $[LU]_0^n$ PU__T4 $[LU]_0^n$ PU__T2 $[LU]_1^{255}$ PU__T1 $[LU]_1^{64}$

Subarea = Subarea node + all peripheral nodes attached to it

Checkpoint 3

69

Chapter 4:
Sessions

☐ Primary NAU ☐ Secondary NAU ☐ Half-sessions ☐ Domain ☐ Shared Control ☐ LU-LU Sessions ☐ SSCP-LU Sessions ☐ SSCP-PU Sessions ☐ SSCP-SSCP Sessions ☐ ACTPU/DACTPU ☐ ACTLU/DACTLU ☐ ACTCDRM/DACTCDRM ☐ BIND/UNBIND ☐ REQDISCONT ☐ INIT-SELF ☐ CINIT ☐ SESSST/BINDF ☐ NSPE/NOTIFY ☐ CDINIT/CDCINIT ☐ CDSESSST/CDSESSSF ☐ INIT-OTHER/INIT-OTHER-CD TERM-SELF ☐ CTERM ☐ SESSEND/UNBINDF ☐ CDTERM ☐ CDSESSEND/CDSESSTF ☐ TERM-OTHER/TERM-OTHER-CD

Chapter 4:
Sessions

Overview

A formal, bilateral and temporary relationship must be established between two NAUs before they can participate in any form of dialogue. This relationship is referred to, in SNA, as a *session*. The session is a fundamental and intrinsic concept of SNA: all communications within an SNA environment are based on sessions, and a hierarchy of sessions between the various types of NAU exists to control the environment and the data communication operations between end users.

When a session is established between two NAUs the characteristics of the communications that will occur in that session, and the protocols that will be used to control the communications, are agreed upon, explicitly or implicitly, by both NAUs. The characteristics that are agreed upon are those such as the mode of communication (full or half duplex), the error recovery responsibilities, the maximum data block sizes for each direction, the acknowledgment scheme and data block sequence numbering scheme. (The full set of characteristics that can be agreed upon at session establishment, will be discussed in Chapter 5.)

The NAU which requests a session to be established is known as the *primary NAU* of the session. The NAU which accepts a session establishment request is known as the *secondary NAU* of the session.

The primary NAU will specify (as a part of the session establishment request) the communications characteristics of the session and the protocols that will be used by it, and the secondary

NAU, to control these communications. If the NAU that receives a request for a session establishment (ie the potential secondary NAU) cannot support the communications characteristics or the protocols specified by the primary NAU, it will normally reject the session establishment request and a session will not be established between those two NAUs. During the establishment of certain types of session the primary NAU can specify that the potential secondary NAU can indicate agreement to a session being established only if certain characteristics or protocols specified by the primary NAU are modified. Such a session establishment request is known as a negotiable request.

Half-sessions

A session consists of two *half-sessions*; one in the primary and one in the secondary NAU. A half-session is the set of functions used by a NAU to provide the protocols needed to support the communications within a particular session. Two half-sessions that form a session are interconnected by the Path Control Network. This is illustrated in Figure 4.1. Chapter 5 concentrates on half-sessions.

Provided it has sufficient resources a NAU can support multiple, concurrent half-sessions: thus it can participate in multiple, concurrent sessions with other NAUs. Figure 4.2 illustrates NAUs supporting multiple sessions. Note the possibility of having *parallel sessions*, ie multiple, concurrent sessions between two NAUs.

Domain

An SNA *domain* consists of an SSCP and all the PUs, LUs and Path Control Network components that the SSCP can activate via SNA-specified 'activation' requests. These activation requests (which have names of the form 'type of resource being activated', prefixed by '*Activate*', eg *Activate Physical Unit, Activate Logical Unit, Activate Link*) will be discussed later in this chapter and in Chapter 7. Thus, each SSCP in an SNA data communications environment will have a domain associated with it.

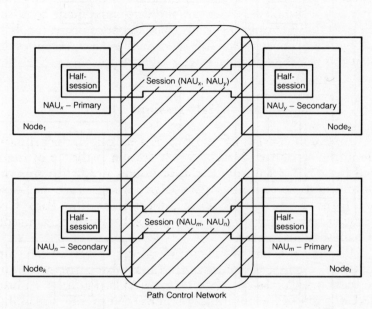

Note:
A session is usually identified by the ordered pair
<primary NAU address, secondary NAU address>

*Figure 4.1: A session consists of two half-sessions,
interconnected by the Path Control Network*

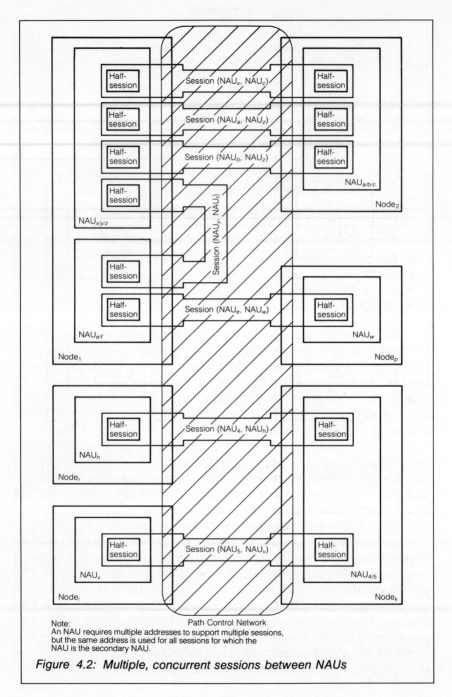

Half-session

Session (NAU$_x$, NAU$_c$)

Half-session

Half-session

Session (NAU$_a$, NAU$_z$)

Half-session

Half-session

Session (NAU$_b$, NAU$_z$)

Half-session

NAU$_{a/b/c}$

Half-session

Node$_2$

NAU$_{x/y/z}$

Session (NAU$_y$, NAU$_i$)

Half-session

Half-session

Session (NAU$_e$, NAU$_w$)

Half-session

NAU$_{e/f}$

NAU$_w$

Node$_1$

Node$_p$

Half-session

Session (NAU$_4$, NAU$_h$)

Half-session

NAU$_h$

Node$_r$

Half-session

Session (NAU$_5$, NAU$_v$)

Half-session

NAU$_v$

NAU$_{4/5}$

Node$_l$

Node$_k$

Path Control Network

Note:
An NAU requires multiple addresses to support multiple sessions,
but the same address is used for all sessions for which the
NAU is the secondary NAU.

Figure 4.2: Multiple, concurrent sessions between NAUs

Each PU, LU and Path Control Network component in an SNA environment must belong to at least one domain. It is possible for PUs and Path Control Network components to belong to more than one domain. Such resources are referred to as being under *shared control*.

Figure 4.3 depicts a single–domain SNA environment, while a multi–domain environment is shown in Figure 4.4.

Sessions between NAUs

SNA specifies four types of session that can be established between NAUs:

- *LU-LU sessions*
- *SSCP-LU sessions*
- *SSCP-PU sessions*
- *SSCP-SSCP sessions.*

End–user–to–end–user communication is achieved via LU-LU sessions. Thus, before two end users can communicate with each other the LUs associated with them must establish an LU-LU session. Before an LU-LU session can be established each LU must establish an SSCP-LU session with the SSCP that controls the domain that the LU belongs to. An LU that wishes to establish a session with another LU needs to inform the other LU of its wish and also indicate to it certain basic attributes of the proposed session, such as which LU will be the primary LU which will issue the session activation request. These session initiation messages can only be conveyed from one LU to another via the SSCP(s) that control(s) the respective LUs.

The SSCP-LU sessions are used to transmit the LU-LU session initiation messages. (However, the session activation request that is transmitted by the designated primary LU, as a result of the initiation messages, is not conveyed via the SSCP-LU sessions.) SSCPs are therefore involved in, and control, monitor and arbitrate in, all LU-LU session establishments. The SSCP-LU sessions remain in force even after the LUs have established the necessary LU-LU sessions. Session termination messages, status and test information and subsequent session initiation messages for LUs that can support multiple LU-LU sessions are all

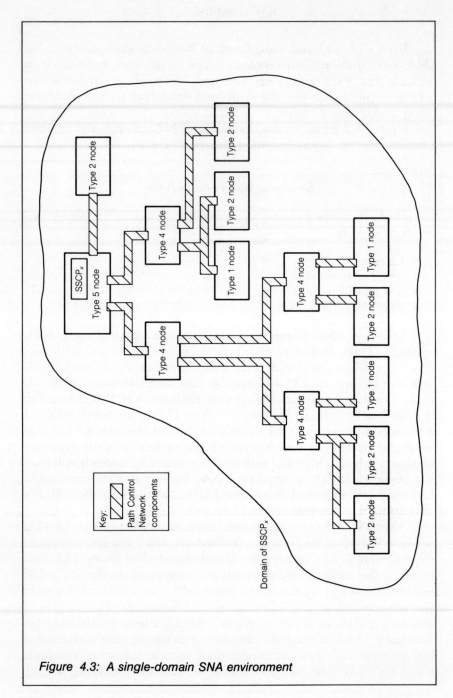

Figure 4.3: A single-domain SNA environment

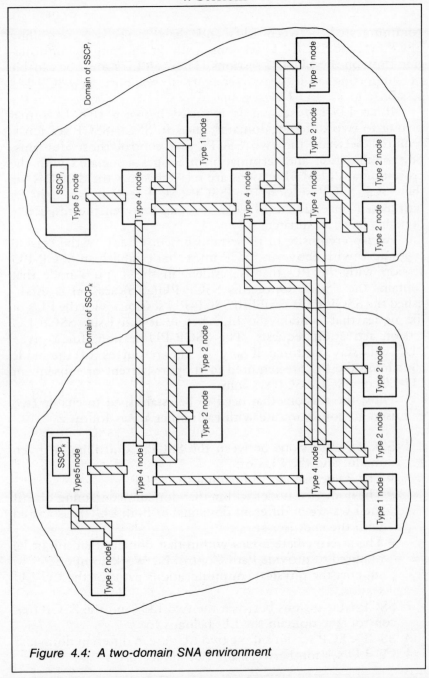

Figure 4.4: A two-domain SNA environment

communicated between LUs and their respective controlling SSCPs via the SSCP-LU sessions, without affecting the information flow on the LU-LU sessions. Thus, all LUs must be capable of supporting at least two concurrent sessions: an SSCP-LU session and an LU-LU session.

If an LU-LU session is required between two LUs that belong to two different domains, then an SSCP-SSCP session is required between the two SSCPs that control those domains. Session initiation and termination messages associated with the cross-domain LU-LU sessions are relayed across the domains via the SSCP-SSCP session. An SSCP-SSCP session can only be terminated once all the LU-LU sessions between the respective domains have terminated.

As a prerequisite to the establishment of any of the session types dealt with above an SSCP must first establish an SSCP-PU session with the PU that is resident in the Type 5 node that contains the SSCP. Once this SSCP-PU(_T5) session is established the SSCP must establish SSCP-PU sessions with the PUs of the nodes that contain the LUs before it can issue SSCP-LU session activation requests. The SSCP-PU session, for a given PU, will stay in force if any of the resources of the node containing the PU are required to support current or subsequent LU-LU or SSCP-SSCP sessions.

Thus, the sessions that need to be established to enable two end users to communicate with each other are as follows:

1 SSCP-PU sessions between the SSCP, controlling a given domain, and the PUs of:
   • The Type 5 node, containing the SSCP
   • The nodes (or node) within that domain, containing one (if the LUs are in different domains) or both LU(s) associated with the end user(s)
   • The intermediate nodes within that domain that might be required to provide Path Control Network components to support the physical communications path for the LU-LU session.
2 SSCP-LU sessions between the two LUs and the SSCP that controls the domain the LU belongs to.
3 SSCP-SSCP sessions if the two LUs are in different domains.
4 LU-LU session between the two subject LUs.

Figure 4.5 depicts a cross-domain LU-LU session, three intra-domain LU-LU sessions and the SSCP-PU, SSCP-LU and SSCP-SSCP sessions that are required to initiate and sustain these LU-LU sessions.

SNA does not define the possibility of sessions between PUs, ie no session activation requests exist for a PU to request the establishment of a session with another PU. However, PUs in adjacent nodes sometimes do communicate with each other – using the Path Control Network, but outside the scope of the other sessions – to exchange control information on certain Path Control Network components or to cooperate in the loading of software into peripheral nodes.

SNA also does not define sessions between PUs and LUs. Any LU-PU interactions that might be required – such as the, notification of status or statistical information – are relayed via the relevant SSCP-LU and SSCP-PU sessions or via implementation-specific control paths within the node itself.

SSCP-PU sessions

Before it can proceed with the establishment of SSCP-LU or SSCP-SSCP sessions each SSCP must establish SSCP-PU sessions with the following PUs:

- The PU in the Type 5 node it resides in
- The PUs of the nodes that contain LUs that intend to establish LU-LU sessions
- The PUs of the nodes that are required to provide Path Control Network components to implement communications paths for subsequent SSCP-LU, SSCP-SSCP and LU-LU sessions.

An SSCP initiates the establishment of an SSCP-PU session by dispatching a session activation request, called an *Activate Physical Unit* (ACTPU), to the relevant PU via the Path Control Network. The SSCP-PU session is established when the PU agrees to the establishment of the session by sending an acceptance message – referred to as a positive response – to the SSCP. (Since

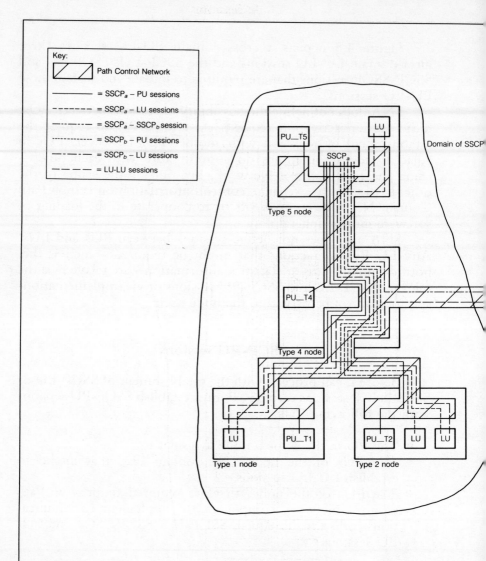

Key:

▨ Path Control Network

——— = SSCP$_a$ – PU sessions

– – – – – = SSCP$_a$ – LU sessions

–·–·– = SSCP$_a$ – SSCP$_b$ session

·········· = SSCP$_b$ – PU sessions

–··–··– = SSCP$_b$ – LU sessions

— — — = LU-LU sessions

PU__T5

SSCP$_a$

LU

Domain of SSCP

Type 5 node

PU__T4

Type 4 node

LU   PU__T1

PU__T2   LU   LU

Type 1 node

Type 2 node

Figure 4.5: Four LU-LU sessions and the SSCP-PU, SSCP-LU and SSCP-SSCP sessions that are required to initiate and sustain these four LU-LU sessions

82

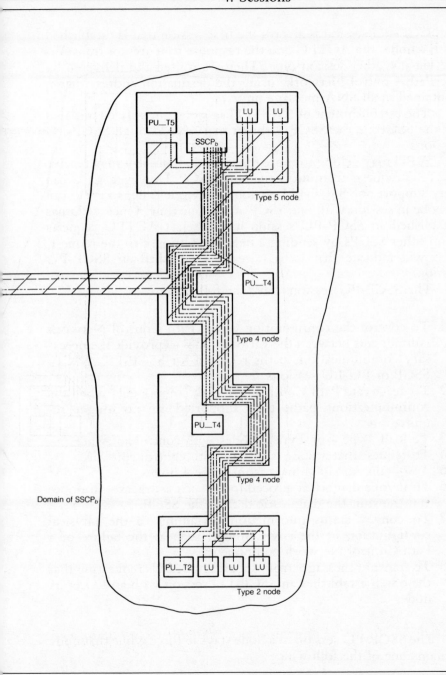

the SSCP-PU session is always the first session that is established with a node, the ACTPU and the response to it are not transmitted via any other session type. They are routed and delivered by the Path Control Network, using the destination address that is contained in all SNA message units.)

The establishment of SSCP-PU sessions can only be initiated by the SSCP, ie the SSCP is the primary NAU of all SSCP-PU sessions.

A PU may belong to more than one domain, ie it may receive ACTPU requests from more than one SSCP. However, a PU can only support one SSCP-PU session at any one time, so a PU can only be in session with one SSCP at any one time. Once a PU has established an SSCP-PU session it will reject ACTPU requests from other SSCPs by sending a negative response to the request, ie it will indicate that it has already established an SSCP-PU session.

The SSCP-PU sessions have the following uses:

1 To control the configuration of the Path Control Network components between the various nodes to provide the necessary communications paths required for SSCP-LU, SSCP-SSCP or LU-LU sessions.
2 To deactivate Path Control Network components when the communications paths they supported are no longer required.
3 To load Type 4 or Type 2 nodes with control software.
4 To request that a node is loaded with control software.
5 To obtain storage dumps from Type 4 nodes.
6 To invoke diagnostic procedures – such as traces – in nodes and transmit the diagnostic data to the SSCP.
7 To convey status information pertaining to the physical configuration of the environment, such as the failure of a Path Control Network component.
8 To transmit messages from subarea node PUs requesting that the SSCP establishes an SSCP-LU session with an LU in its node.

The SSCP-PU session of a node stays in force while that node contains one of the following:

- LUs that are participating in, or intending to establish, LU-LU sessions
- Path Control Network components providing communications paths for other sessions.

An SSCP-PU session can only be terminated by the SSCP. (A PU in a peripheral node can ask the SSCP to terminate the SSCP-PU session – and thereby deactivate the node – by sending a *Request discontact* (REQDISCONT) message to the SSCP, via the SSCP-PU session.) The SSCP initiates the termination of an SSCP-PU session by dispatching a *Deactivate Physical Unit* (DACTPU) request to the PU. The session is terminated when the PU sends the SSCP a positive response to the DACTPU request.

SSCP-LU sessions

An LU must have an SSCP-LU session established with the SSCP that controls the domain it belongs to before it can participate in the establishment of any LU-LU sessions. This is because the LU-LU session initiation messages that must be exchanged between two prospective session partners, before the designated primary LU issues the session activation request, can only be conveyed via the respective SSCP-LU sessions. The LU-LU session initiation process is described later in this chapter.

The establishment of SSCP-LU sessions can only be initiated by the SSCP ie, the SSCP is the primary NAU of all SSCP-LU sessions.

An SSCP initiates the establishment of an SSCP-LU session by dispatching a session activation request, called an *Activate Logical Unit* (ACTLU) to the subject LU via the Path Control Network. The SSCP-LU session is established when the LU agrees to the establishment of the session by sending a positive response to the SSCP.

Before an SSCP can issue an ACTLU request to an LU it must have an operational SSCP-PU session with the PU of the node the subject LU resides in. But the ACTLU request is not transmitted to an LU via the SSCP-PU session corresponding to its node. (In common with ACTPU requests, ACTLU requests and the responses to them are routed and delivered by the Path Control Network, using the destination address contained in the message unit.) As such, PUs are not directly involved in the establishment of SSCP-LU sessions.

An LU can only support one SSCP-LU session, and that session must be with the SSCP that controls the domain it belongs to. If an LU intends to establish an LU-LU session with an LU that is in another domain, it still transmits the session initiation messages to its controlling SSCP, via their SSCP-LU session. The SSCP will convey these messages to the SSCP that controls the domain the other LU belongs to via an SSCP-SSCP session. That SSCP will relay the session initiation messages to the relevant LU via their SSCP-LU session.

The SSCP-LU sessions have the following uses:

1 To convey LU-LU session initiation messages from one LU to another (but note that the LU-LU session activation request issued by the primary LU, as a result of these session initiation messages, or the response to this request, is not transmitted on the SSCP-LU sessions).

2 To convey LU-LU session termination messages from one LU to another. (As with the session activation request, the session deactivation request, which is issued by the primary LU as a result of the termination message or the response to it, is not transmitted on the SSCP-LU sessions.)

3 To convey status information pertaining to LU-LU session initiation or termination, between the SSCP and an LU.

4 To convey LU or end-user status information to the SSCP.

5 To request and conduct test procedures between the SSCP and an LU.

The SSCP-LU session of an LU must stay in force while the LU is participating in, or intends to participate in, LU-LU sessions. An SSCP-LU session can only be terminated by the SSCP. There is no explicit way of an LU requesting the SSCP to terminate their SSCP-LU session. (However, if a peripheral node PU transmits a REQDISCONT to request the termination of the SSCP-PU session, the SSCP-LU sessions of the LU in that node will be terminated prior to the SSCP-PU session being terminated.) An SSCP initiates the termination of an SSCP-LU session by dispatching a *Deactivate Logical Unit* (DACTLU) request to the LU. The session is terminated when the LU sends the SSCP a positive response to the DACTLU request.

SSCP-SSCP sessions

An SSCP that has an LU in its domain that wishes to establish an LU-LU session with an LU in another domain must establish an SSCP-SSCP session with the SSCP that controls the other domain as a prerequisite to the LU-LU session initiation process. The LU-LU session initiation messages that are conveyed within a domain via SSCP-LU sessions are relayed between the two domains via the SSCP-SSCP session.

An LU wishing to initiate an LU-LU session does not need to know whether or not its prospective session partner belongs to the same domain as it. An LU sends the same session initiation message to its controlling SSCP – via their SSCP-LU session – irrespective of whether the other LU is in the same domain as it, or in another domain. The SSCP is responsible for ascertaining which domain the prospective session partner belongs to. If it is in another domain the SSCP establishes an SSCP-SSCP session with the SSCP that controls the other domain. The communications path for the SSCP-SSCP session establishment request – which may also be used for subsequent cross-domain LU-LU sessions – is established by activating the necessary Path Control Network components via the relevant SSCP-PU sessions. The information that was contained in the session initiation messages that the first SSCP received from its LU is then conveyed by the first SSCP to the other via a set of SSCP-SSCP messages. The other SSCP will pass this information to the target LU – in the same manner as for an intra-domain session initiation – via their SSCP-LU session. The initiation process proceeds with both LUs only communicating with their controlling SSCPs and using the same messages as for an intra-domain session initiation. The two SSCPs relay the relevant information between themselves using the SSCP-SSCP session. However, the LU-LU session activation request, issued by the designated primary LU as a result of the session initiation process, or the response to it, is not conveyed across the domains via the SSCP-SSCP session nor within each domain via the SSCP-LU session. The transportation of the cross-domain LU-LU session activation request and the response to the request are handled entirely by the Path Control Network in the same way that an intra-domain request is conveyed within the domain. The cross-domain LU-LU session initiation process is described later in this chapter.

An SSCP initiates the establishment of an SSCP-SSCP session by despatching a session activation request called an *activate cross-domain resource manager* (ACTCDRM). This is sent to the other SSCP via the Path Control Network. The SSCP-SSCP session is established when the other SSCP agrees to the establishment of the session by sending a positive response.

Unlike SSCP-PU or SSCP-LU sessions, where the SSCP is always the primary, or LU-LU sessions where the primary is designated during the initiation process, SSCP-SSCP sessions do not have a predesigned primary or a procedure to designate a primary. Any SSCP can initiate an SSCP-SSCP session, and thus be the primary, by sending an ACTCDRM request to another SSCP. Thus, it is conceivable that two SSCPs might issue ACTCDRM to each other simultaneously. In this situation, the SSCP which has the higher SSCPID – an installation-assigned SSCP identification number – is treated by the other SSCP as the primary.

An SSCP can support multiple SSCP-SSCP sessions, but only one SSCP-SSCP session can be established between any two SSCPs.

A cross-domain LU-LU session may span several intermediate domains. The two SSCPs controlling the subject LUs do not need SSCP-SSCP sessions with the SSCPs controlling the intermediate domains to establish their SSCP-SSCP session. An SSCP-SSCP session is only needed if LU-LU sessions are required between LUs belonging to the domains controlled by the SSCPs. Figure 4.6 illustrates the SSCP-SSCP session requirement for a cross-domain LU-LU session traversing across one intermediate domain.

The SSCP-SSCP sessions are used in the following ways:

1 By the SSCPs to relay LU-LU session initiation messages between LUs that are in different domains.

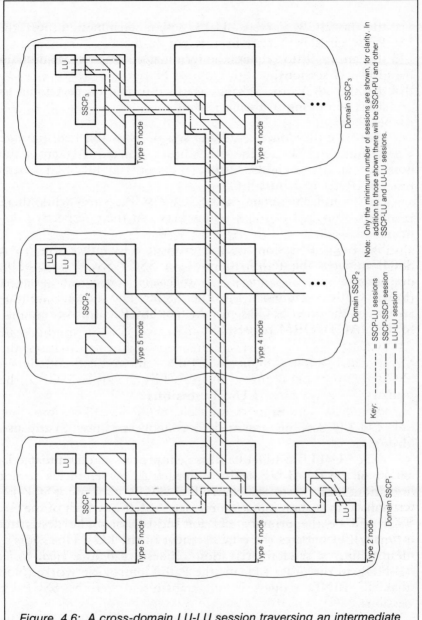

Figure 4.6: A cross-domain LU-LU session traversing an intermediate domain, and the SSCP-SSCP session needed to initiate and sustain this session

2 By the SSCPs to relay LU–LU session termination messages between LUs that are in different domains.
3 By an SSCP to request the termination of all cross–domain LU–LU sessions.
4 By the SSCPs to exchange status information pertaining to LUs belonging to their domains.

Once a cross–domain LU–LU session is established message units from one LU to the other are a transported across the domains via the LU–LU session and not via the SSCP–SSCP session. (Refer to Figure 4.6.)

SSCPs must maintain their SSCP–SSCP session while there are cross–domain LU–LU sessions between their respective domains.

SSCP–SSCP sessions can be terminated by either SSCP. An SSCP initiates the termination of an SSCP–SSCP session by despatching a *deactivate cross-domain resource manager* (DACTCDRM) request to the other SSCP. The session is terminated when the other SSCP sends the first SSCP a positive response to the DACTCDRM request.

LU–LU sessions

LU–LU sessions are used to conduct end–user–to–end–user dialogues.

The LU–LU session establishment process can be initiated by either of the two LUs, or by a third LU, by sending a session initiation message to its controlling SSCP via their SSCP–LU session. This session initiation message specifies which of the two LUs will be the primary LU for the session. The designated primary LU initiates the establishment of the LU–LU session by despatching a session activation request, called a *bind session* (BIND), to the other LU, via the Path Control Network. (Note that the BIND request is not transmitted via the SSCP–LU sessions.)

Two types of BIND request are possible: negotiable or non–negotiable. With a negotiable BIND, the primary LU proposes a set of characteristics and protocols for the LU-LU session, to the secondary LU. The secondary LU can either: agree to the establishment of the session with the characteristics and protocols that were specified by the primary by sending a positive response; agree to the session provided that certain characteristics or protocols are modified by sending a positive response that indicates the modifications; or reject the establishment of the session by sending a negative response. (If the primary finds the modifications indicated by the secondary unacceptable it will proceed to terminate the session.)

With a non-negotiable BIND, the primary LU specifies the characteristics and the protocols for the session. The secondary LU cannot request any modifications to them. It can either agree to the establishment of the session by sending a positive response or reject the establishment of the session by sending a negative response.

An LU can support multiple LU-LU sessions provided it has sufficient resources.

The LU-LU sessions are used to:

1 Conduct end-user-to-end-user dialogues.
2 Control the message flow of end-user-to-end-user dialogues.
3 Request invocation of, and control, recovery procedures if any errors are detected in the message flow.

An LU-LU session can only be terminated by the primary LU. The secondary LU could invoke the termination of the session by sending its controlling SSCP – via their SSCP-LU session – a session termination request. The SSCP will then convey this to the primary LU via their SSCP-LU session if the primary is in its domain, or relay it to the primary LU's controlling SSCP via an SSCP-SSCP session if the primary LU is in another domain. The primary LU initiates the termination of an LU-LU session by despatching an *unbind session* (UNBIND) request to the secondary LU. The session is terminated when the secondary LU sends the primary LU a positive response to the UNBIND. The LU-LU session termination process is described later in this chapter.

LU-LU sessions are discussed in more detail in Chapter 6.

LU-LU session initiation: intra-domain

An end user who wishes to communicate with another end user informs the LU through which it accesses the SNA environment of its intention, using an implementation-dependent protocol. It identifies the other end user in terms of the LU through which that end user accesses the environment. This LU is referred to by a name assigned to it by the system implementor, rather than by an address. This enables SNA environments to be implemented and modified without the end users and their LUs having to be customised each time to the addresses of the other LUs. In addition, the end user, or its LU, does not know, or care, whether the proposed session is an intra- or cross-domain session. The same procedure is used by the end user and its LU to establish the session, irrespective of whether it is intra- or cross-domain. The difference between intra- and cross-domain LU-LU session establishment processes is only apparent to SSCPs and is restricted to SSCP-SSCP interactions via SSCP-SSCP sessions.

An LU, on being instructed by an end user to provide a means of communication with another end user, will initiate the establishment of an LU-LU session with the LU that serves the other end user. The LU that initiates the LU-LU session establishment process is known as the *Initiating LU* (ILU). The LU that serves the other end user is called the *Destination LU* (DLU).

The LU-LU session initiation process begins when the ILU issues an *initiate-self* (INIT-SELF) request to its controlling SSCP via their SSCP-LU session. The INIT-SELF request specifies the following:

- The name of the DLU
- Which of the LUs will be the primary LU for the session (the ILU does not necessarily have to be the primary LU; it could specify that the DLU should be the primary)
- A set of session characteristics and protocols for the proposed session.

On receipt of the INIT-SELF, the SSCP first ascertains whether the DLU is in the domain it controls. If the DLU *is* in its domain, it resolves the DLU name to an address assigned to the DLU. (If the DLU can support multiple LU-LU sessions it will have more than one address.) The SSCP will then determine whether it has an SSCP-LU session established – and as such a communications path via the Path Control Network exists – with the DLU. (If the SSCP-LU session does not exist it will attempt to establish it.) The SSCP next ascertains whether the DLU is able to support the session – the DLU could already be in session with other LUs and as such have insufficient resources for another half-session for the proposed session. The SSCP also converts the session characteristics and protocols specified in the INIT-SELF to a set of parameters that will be included in the BIND request.

If the DLU is active (ie, it has an SSCP-LU session established with the SSCP) and is capable of supporting the proposed session, the SSCP will send a positive response to the ILU to indicate that it has successfully processed the INIT-SELF request. (Note that at this stage the DLU is unaware of the proposed session.) If the DLU is not active (ie, the SSCP cannot establish an SSCP-LU session with it), or if it is unable to support another LU-LU session (ie, it is already participating in one or more LU-LU sessions), or if there was a conflict in the session characteristics and protocols specified by the ILU, the SSCP would send a negative response to indicate that it cannot progress any further with the initiation process.

Once the SSCP has determined that the DLU should be able to participate in the proposed session it proceeds to construct a request, called a *control initiate* (CINIT), that will be sent to the primary LU(PLU). The CINIT request advises the PLU to attempt to establish an LU-LU session. The CINIT request contains the following:

- An address for the PLU and an address for the potential secondary LU(SLU)
- Parameters that should be incorporated in the BIND request, that will be issued by the PLU.

Once it constructs the CINIT, the SSCP transmits it to the PLU that was designated in the INIT-SELF request, via their SSCP-LU session.

If the PLU is able to support the proposed LU-LU session, with the characteristics and protocols indicated in the CINIT, it will send a positive response to the SSCP. If it cannot, it will send a negative response. (Note that if the PLU was not the ILU, the CINIT would be its first intimation of the proposed LU–LU session.)

If the PLU can support the proposed session it will proceed to construct a BIND request based on the session parameters indicated in the CINIT. The PLU may modify some of the session parameters indicated in the CINIT – within SNA defined limits – when constructing the BIND. Once the PLU has constructed the BIND, and appended to it the address of the SLU and its own address as contained in the CINIT, it passes it to the Path Control Network, which ensures that it is delivered to the potential SLU.

The SLU, on receipt of the BIND request, will determine whether it can support the proposed session according to the session parameters specified in the BIND. If it is able to support the session, it will agree to the establishment of the LU–LU session by sending a positive response to the PLU. If it is unable to support the session according to the session parameters specified in the BIND, and the BIND request was non–negotiable, it will reject the establishment of the session by sending a negative response to the PLU. If the BIND request was negotiable, and the SLU could support the session if certain session parameters were modified, it would indicate this to the PLU by sending a positive response that included a list of the modified parameters. If the SLU cannot support the proposed session because it has not got the relevant resources, it will reject the establishment of the session by sending a negative response to the PLU, irrespective of whether or not the BIND request was non–negotiable.

When the PLU receives from the SLU a positive response to either type of BIND request, or a positive response to a negotiable BIND request that contained a set of modified session parameters that it finds acceptable, the establishment of the subject LU–LU session is complete. This session can now be used for end–user–to–end–user communication. The PLU informs its controlling SSCP that the LU–LU session it was instructed to establish by the CINIT request has been successfully established by sending it a *session started* (SESSST) message via their SSCP–LU session. Since an SESSST is essentially a courtesy message, with no functional implications, the PLU indicates to the SSCP by means of a flag within the SESSST message unit that it does not expect a response to the SESSST from the SSCP.

If the PLU receives from the SLU a negative response to the BIND request, or a positive response to a negotiable BIND request that contains a set of modified session parameters that is unacceptable to it, the subject LU-LU session is not established. (In the case where the PLU receives a positive response to a negotiable BIND, it initiates the termination of the session by immediately sending an UNBIND request to the SLU.) The PLU informs the SSCP that it was unable to establish the proposed session by sending the SSCP a *bind failure* (BINDF) message via their SSCP-LU session. The PLU will specify within the BINDF message why the session could not be established. As with the SESSST, the PLU indicates to the SSCP that it does not require a response to the BINDF message.

On receipt of a BINDF message, the SSCP must inform the ILU that the PLU was unable to establish the proposed LU-LU session. It does so by sending the ILU either a *network services procedure error* (NSPE) or a *NOTIFY* message, via their SSCP-LU session. Whether NSPE or NOTIFY is sent depends on which message was requested by the ILU in its INIT-SELF request. The ILU acknowledges the receipt of either the NSPE or the NOTIFY by sending a positive response to the SSCP.

Figure 4.7 illustrates an intra-domain, LU -LU session initiation process where the ILU is the potential SLU of the session. Figure 4.8 illustrates the initiation process when the ILU is the PLU of the session. An unsuccessful session initiation process is illustrated in Figure 4.9.

LU- LU session initiation: cross–domain

The initial stages of a cross-domain or an intra-domain LU-LU session initiation process are the same.

An LU, on being instructed by an end user to provide it with a means of communication with another end user, will issue an INIT-SELF request to its controlling SSCP. The INIT-SELF will specify the name of the DLU, the LU which will be the primary LU for the session and a set of session characteristics and protocols.

On receipt of the INIT-SELF, the SSCP will check whether the DLU is in its domain. If it is not it will determine the domain

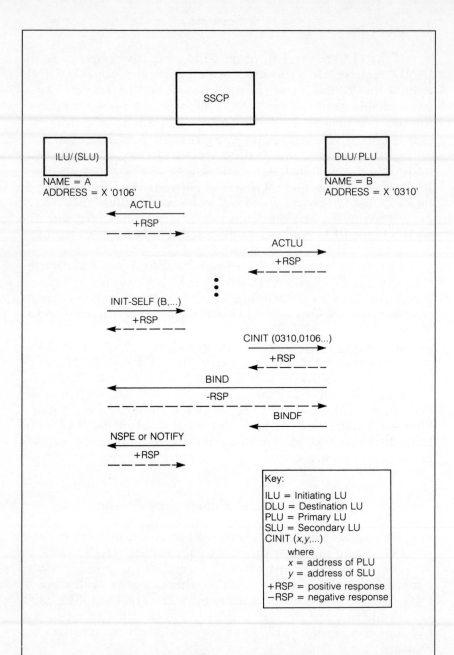

Figure 4.7: Intra-domain, LU-LU session initiation sequence, where the ILU is the potential SLU

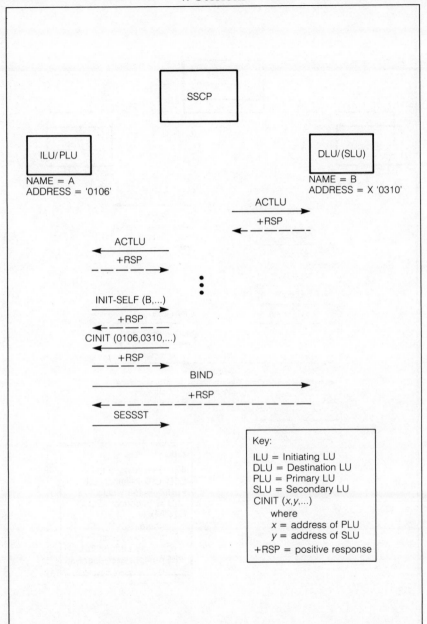

Figure 4.8: Intra-domain, LU-LU session initiation sequence, where the ILU is the PLU

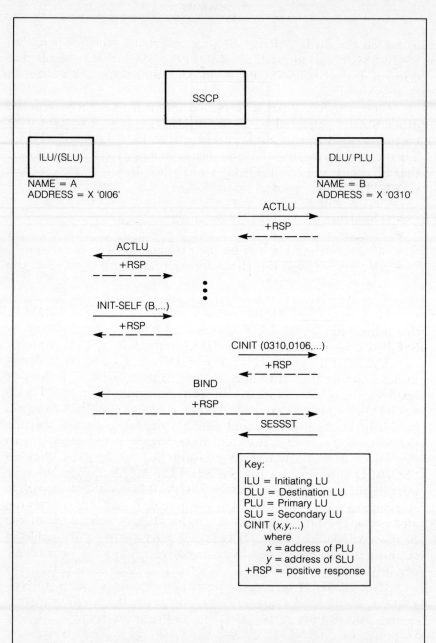

Figure 4.9: An unsuccesful, intra-domain, LU-LU session initiation sequence

to which the DLU belongs. It then ascertains whether it has an SSCP-SSCP session established with the SSCP that controls that domain. If the SSCP-SSCP session does not exist it will initiate its establishment.

Once the SSCP has determined that it is in session with the other SSCP – referred to as SSCP(DLU) – it will request it to participate in initiating the session between the ILU and the DLU. This is done by means of a *cross-domain initiate* (CDINIT) request that is sent to the SSCP(DLU) via the SSCP-SSCP session. The CDINIT request specifies the following:

- The name of the DLU
- The address of the ILU
- Which of the LUs will be the primary LU for the session
- The set of session characteristics and protocols for the session.

Note that the CDINIT request conveys to the SSCP(DLU), the information the ILU's controlling SSCP – referred to as SSCP(ILU) – received from the ILU in the INIT-SELF request.

SSCP(DLU), on receiving an CDINIT request, first determines whether the DLU does belong to its domain. If it does, it resolves the DLU name to an address assigned to the DLU. SSCP(DLU) then ascertains whether it has an SSCP-LU session established with the DLU and whether the DLU can support the proposed session. (If it does not have an SSCP-LU session with the DLU it will attempt to establish it.) If the DLU has an SSCP-LU session with the SSCP(DLU), and is capable of supporting the proposed session, the SSCP(DLU) will send a positive response to the SSCP(ILU). The positive response will contain the address of the DLU. At this stage the DLU is not aware of the proposed session. (If the DLU is not active, or if it is unable to support the proposed session, a negative response is sent to the SSCP(ILU).)

If SSCP(ILU) receives a positive response to the CDINIT request, it will send a positive response to the ILU to indicate that it has successfully processed the INIT-SELF request. (If the response to CDINIT is negative, SSCP(ILU) sends a negative response to the ILU to indicate that it cannot progress any further with the initiation process.)

Once SSCP(ILU) has received a positive response to the CDINIT request, both SSCPs have the following information:

- The address of the ILU
- The address of the DLU
- Which of the LUs is the primary LU for the session
- The set of session characteristics and protocols for the session.

At this point, the SSCP that controls the potential SLU – referred to as SSCP(SLU) – will request the SSCP that controls the designated PLU – referred to as SSCP(PLU) – to instruct the PLU to attempt to establish a session with the SLU. SSCP(SLU) does this by sending a *cross-domain control initiate* (CDCINIT) request to the SSCP(PLU), via their SSCP-SSCP session. The CDCINIT request specifies:

- An address for the PLU and an address for the SLU
- Parameters for the BIND request.

The SSCP(PLU), on receipt of the CDCINIT request, checks that the PLU is still active and capable of supporting the proposed session. If the PLU is still able to support the proposed session SSCP(PLU) constructs a CINIT request based on the data that was contained in the CDCINIT. It then sends a positive response to the SSCP(SLU) to indicate that it has successfully processed the CDCINIT request. (If the PLU is not able to support the proposed session, a negative response will be sent to the SSCP(SLU). SSCP(ILU) will convey this to the ILU via an NSPE or a NOTIFY request.)

The CINIT request constructed by the SSCP(PLU) to instruct the PLU to attempt to establish a session with the SLU is the same as that used for an intra-domain LU-LU session initiation. It contains an address for the PLU and for the SLU and parameters for the BIND. The BIND parameters included in the CINIT by the SSCP(PLU) need not be the same as those specified in the CDCINIT. SSCP(PLU) may modify certain parameters to accommodate the capabilities of the PLU or the Path Control Network components in its domain. The SSCP(PLU) transmits the CINIT request to the PLU via their SSCP-LU session.

Since there is no explicit or implicit indication in the CINIT request as to whether the proposed session is intra- or cross-domain, the PLU processes the CINIT in the same manner as described for an intra-domain session initiation.

On receipt of the CINIT, the PLU constructs a BIND request and despatches it to the potential SLU by means of the Path Control Network. If it receives from the SLU an acceptable positive response to the BIND – which could have been negotiable or non-negotiable – the PLU will send an SESSST to the SSCP(PLU) to indicate that it has successfully established the LU–LU session. SSCP(PLU) will inform SSCP(SLU) that the subject LU–LU session has been successfully established by sending it a *cross-domain session started* (CDSESSST) message via their SSCP–SSCP session. The subject LU–LU session is specified in CDSESSST either by the names of the two LUs or by their addresses.

If the PLU receives from the SLU a negative response to the BIND, or an unacceptable positive response to a negotiable BIND, it sends a BINDF to the SSCP(PLU). SSCP(PLU) will inform the SSCP(SLU) that the PLU was unsuccessful in establishing the proposed session by sending it a *cross-domain session set-up failure* (CDSESSSF) message via their SSCP–SSCP session. The session that could not be established is identified in the CDSESSSF either by the names of the two LUs or by their addresses. Once both SSCPs are aware that the proposed session cannot be established, the SSCP controlling the ILU will send it an NSPE or a NOTIFY to inform it of this.

A cross-domain LU–LU session initiation process where the ILU is the potential SLU of the session is illustrated in Figure 4.10. Figure 4.11 illustrates a cross-domain initiation process where the ILU is the PLU of the session. An unsuccessful cross-domain initiation process is illustrated in Figure 4.12. (Note that the transmitted initiation requests received by the two LUs are the same as those used for intra-domain session initiation.)

Third-party LU–LU session initiation

SNA caters for the situation where an LU may wish to initiate an LU–LU session between two other LUs. This is

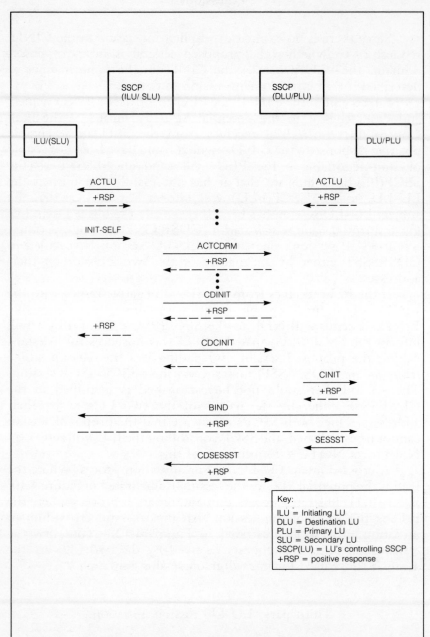

Figure 4.10: Cross-domain, LU-LU session initiation sequence, where the ILU is the potential SLU

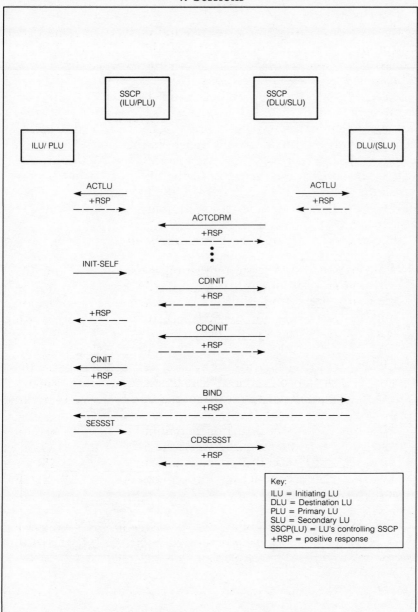

Figure 4.11: Cross-domain, LU-LU session initiation sequence, where the ILU is also the PLU for the session

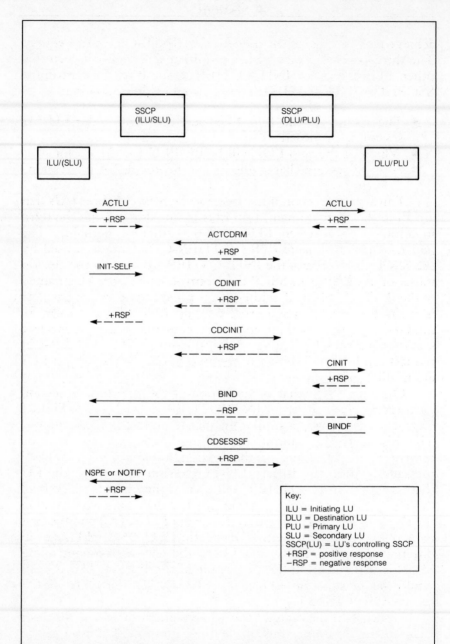

Figure 4.12: An unsuccessful, cross-domain, LU-LU session initiation sequence

achieved by means of an *initiate-other* (INIT-OTHER) request. The third-party LU that wishes to initiate a session between two other LUs issues an INIT-OTHER request to its controlling SSCP. The INIT-OTHER request specifies the following:

- The names of the two LUs between whom the LU-LU session is proposed
- Which of the two LUs will be the PLU for the session
- A set of session characteristics and protocols for the session.

Third-party session initiation may be between three LUs that are all in the same domain, two LUs in one domain and the third in another or between LUs in three different domains. The *initiate-other cross-domain* (INIT-OTHER-CD) request is used by the SSCP that receives the INIT-OTHER, to convey the session initiation request to an SSCP that controls one of the LUs named in the INIT-OTHER, if neither of the prospective session partners is in its domain. (Since a cross-domain LU-LU session can be initiated by either of the two SSCPs controlling the prospective session partners – by issuing a CDINIT – the INIT-OTHER-CD request can be sent to either of the two SSCPs, if the subject LUs are in different domains.)

Once an SSCP that controls one of the prospective session partners receives either an INIT-OTHER or an INIT-OTHER-CD, it processes it in a similar manner to an INIT-SELF request. The third-party LU, and its controlling SSCP, can request to be informed of the status of the session initiation via NOTIFY messages. (With third-party LU-LU session initiations, the LU that issues the INIT-OTHER is known as the Initiating LU. If all three LUs are in the same domain, the LU that is named second in the INIT-OTHER is known as the *Origin LU* (OLU) and the first named LU is known as the Destination LU. If the LUs are in different domains the Origin LU is the LU whose controlling SSCP issued the CDINIT as a result of the INIT-OTHER-CD, while the Destination LU is the LU whose controlling SSCP received the CDINIT.)

Figure 4.13 illustrates a third-party initiation where all three LUs are in the same domain, while Figure 4.14 illustrates the initiation process when the subject LUs are in three different domains.

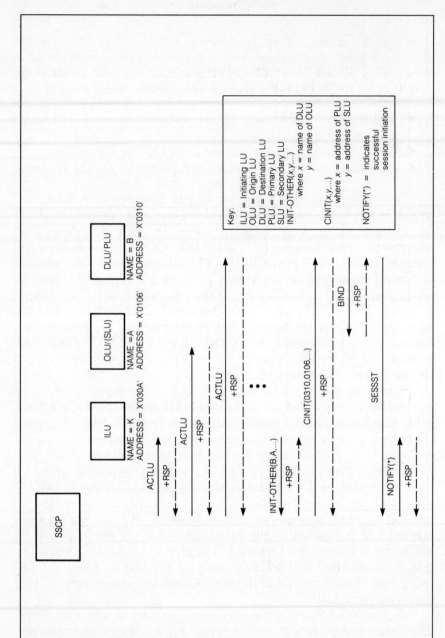

Figure 4.13: Intra-domain, third party LU-LU session initiation sequence

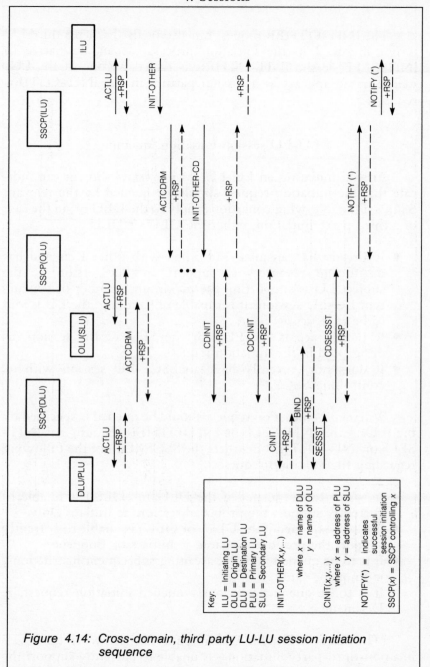

Figure 4.14: Cross-domain, third party LU-LU session initiation sequence

The INIT-OTHER request can also be used when a third LU is not involved in the initiation process, as an alternative to INIT-SELF, ie the INIT-OTHER is issued by one of the LUs whose name appears as a session partner in the INIT-OTHER request.

LU-LU session initiation: queuing

An LU initiating an LU-LU session establishment can indicate that the initiation request should be queued by the relevant SSCPs if the following conditions apply to the DLU or, in the case of a third-party initiation, either the OLU or DLU:

- It already has sessions established with other LUs and has insufficient resources to support another session, ie the subject LU is supporting the maximum number of concurrent LU-LU sessions it is capable of handling: the LU is said to be at its *session limit*
- It cannot act as the PLU or the SLU of the session, as designated in the initiation request
- It does not currently have an SSCP-LU session with its controlling SSCP.

Whether an initiation request should be queued is specified by the ILU in the INIT-SELF or INIT-OTHER request. An INIT-SELF or INIT-OTHER instructs the SSCP(ILU) of the following regarding the initiation request:

- It is not to be queued if the DLU (or OLU) is unable to currently support the proposed session, ie Initiate Only
- It is to be queued if the DLU (or OLU) is unable to currently support the proposed session, ie Initiate or Enqueue
- It is to be queued initially, awaiting subsequent instructions, ie Enqueue Only
- It is to de-queue a previously queued initiation request, ie De-queue.

(The Enqueue Only initiation request is used when the ILU – in a non-third-party initiation – is unable to currently support the session it is proposing but wishes to proceed with its initiation as soon as it is able to support it. In the case of a third-party initiation, the Enqueue Only can be used when the ILU does not want the proposed session established immediately, but at a later stage. An Enqueue Only initiation request will be released from the queue, when the SSCP receives a De-queue request for it from the ILU.)

An initiation request that indicates that it can be queued will specify a set of criteria for queuing it. The queuing criteria will be one or more of the following:

• Session limit of subject LU(s) exceeded
• Subject LU(s) cannot act as the PLU or the SLU as designated
• Subject LU(s) does not have an SSCP-LU session.

If there are multiple initiation requests between two LUs, the requests will specify whether it should be placed at the bottom or top of the queue and in what order the queue should be de-queued.

Even if the queuing criteria are satisfied an initiation request will only be queued if all the relevant SSCPs support queuing and the queuing limit for the subject LUs has not been exceeded.

An intra-domain session initiation, whose request specified Initiate or Queue, will be queued if the DLU (or OLU if it is a third-party initiation) is currently unable to support the proposed session. A positive response to the INIT-SELF or INIT-OTHER request will be sent to the ILU, by the SSCP, when the request is queued. The SSCP will de-queue the request and resume processing it when it ascertains that the status of the DLU (or OLU) has changed and that it can now support the proposed session. An LU will inform its SSCP of status changes – change of session limit, ability to act as a PLU or SLU – via NOTIFY messages. An SSCP informs the ILU that a previously queued initiation request has been de-queued and is being processed by sending it a NOTIFY message.

For a cross-domain session initiation, where the request specified that it can be queued, the queuing criteria are conveyed in the CDINIT request to the SSCP(DLU) along with the status of the DLU's potential session partner – is it as its session limit?

can it act as the PLU or SLU as designated? (For a third-party initiation, queuing criteria for the DLU and OLU are conveyed to the SSCP(OLU) from the SSCP(ILU) in the INIT-OTHER-CD request.) If SSCP(DLU) queues the initiation request, it informs the SSCP that issued the CDINIT of this in the positive response it returns. If it was an Initiate or Enqueue request, and the status of the DLU changes such that it can support the proposed session, SSCP(DLU) will send a NOTIFY to the SSCP that issued the CDINIT to inform it that the initiation process can resume. On receipt of the NOTIFY, the SSCP must issue another CDINIT – which specifies De-queue – to the SSCP(DLU). When SSCP(DLU) receives the De-queue CDINIT request it will return a positive response and proceed as for a non-queued initiation process. (For a third-party initiation, SSCP(OLU) will inform SSCP(ILU) that the initiation process has resumed by sending it a NOTIFY. SSCP(ILU) will convey this information to the ILU by sending it a NOTIFY.)

LU-LU session termination

Either LU of an LU-LU session, whether it is intra- or cross-domain, can request the termination of that session by sending a *terminate-self* (TERM-SELF) request to its controlling SSCP, via their SSCP-LU session. (The PLU of a session can directly terminate that session by instructing the SLU to cease message transmission and then issuing it an UNBIND request, rather than involving the SSCP by using a TERM-SELF request.)
The LU that issues the TERM-SELF is known as the *Terminating LU* (TLU), while its session partner is called the Destination LU (DLU). The TERM-SELF request specifies the following:

- The name of the DLU (or the addresses of the DLU and the TLU)
- Whether the DLU is the PLU or the SLU of the session
- Whether the session is active, or whether it refers to a proposed session that has been queued during session initiation
- The type of termination to be performed:

- Orderly, where the PLU can execute a predefined end-of-session procedure before terminating the session
- Forced, where the PLU must attempt to terminate the session immediately and unconditionally
- Clean-up, which is similar to Forced but the session is terminated immediately the UNBIND is issued rather than when a positive response to the UNBIND is received from the SLU

- Whether or not the SSCP-LU session of the TLU should be deactivated when this LU-LU session is terminated.

The SSCP(TLU), on receiving a TERM-SELF, first ascertains the domain to which the DLU belongs. (A positive response to the TERM-SELF will then be sent to the TLU to indicate that it is processing the request.)

If it is an intra-domain session, the SSCP will issue a *control terminate* (CTERM) request to the PLU, via their SSCP-LU session. The CTERM instructs the PLU to attempt to terminate the session identified in the request by means of the addresses of the PLU and SLU. (Note that the PLU could have multiple LU-LU sessions, some of which could be parallel sessions with the SLU.) The CTERM request specifies the following:

- The addresses of the PLU and SLU
- The type of termination to be performed – orderly, forced or clean-up.

The PLU, on receipt of the CTERM, will determine whether it is in session with the specified SLU and, if so, issue an UNBIND request to it (after executing the end-of-session procedure, if orderly termination was specified) via their LU-LU session. It will also send to the SSCP a positive response to the CTERM. The UNBIND request will indicate by means of a one-byte code the reason for the session termination.

The session is terminated when the SLU returns to the PLU a positive response to the UNBIND. The PLU informs the SSCP of the successful termination of the session by sending it a *session ended* (SESSEND) message, via their SSCP-LU session. (The PLU does not expect a response to the SESSEND.) If the PLU could not terminate the session, for example, because it cannot contact the SLU due to a fault in a Path Control Network component, it will send an *unbind failure* (UNBINDF) message to the SSCP. The SSCP will inform the TLU of this by means of a NOTIFY message.

Figure 4.15 illustrates a successful intra-domain LU–LU session termination sequence. Compare this figure with Figure 4.7, which illustrates an intra-domain LU–LU session initiation sequence and note the symmetry between the initiation and termination sequences.

If the session to be terminated is a cross-domain session, the SSCP(TLU) will despatch a *cross-domain terminate* (CDTERM) request to the SSCP(DLU), via their SSCP–SSCP session. The CDTERM conveys the information that was contained in the TERM-SELF, with the addition of the addresses or names of the PLU and SLU to uniquely identify the subject session. The CDTERM requests the SSCP(DLU) to participate in the termination of the subject session. SSCP(DLU) will check that the DLU is in its domain and then send a positive response to the SSCP(TLU). The SSCP(PLU) – which could be SSCP(DLU) or SSCP(TLU) – will then issue a CTERM to the PLU, and the termination process will proceed as for an intra-domain termination. SSCP(PLU) will inform the other SSCP of a successful termination by sending it a *cross-domain session ended* (CDSES-SEND) via their SSCP–SSCP session. A termination failure will be conveyed by means of a *cross-domain session takedown failure* (CDSESSTF).

Figure 4.16 illustrates a successful cross-domain LU–LU session termination sequence. Compare this figure with Figure 4.10 and again note the symmetry between the session initiation and termination sequences. (Since there is no need to convey information about the SLU to the PLU during termination there is no termination request corresponding to the CDCINIT.) Also note that the termination requests transmitted or received by the two LUs are the same as those used for intra-domain session termination.

The TERM-SELF can also be used by a TLU to request the termination of all the LU–LU sessions it is a partner in, or where it has parallel sessions with the DLU to selectively terminate some or all of these sessions. If the TLU wishes all – active, queued, or both – sessions that it is a partner in to be terminated, it does not

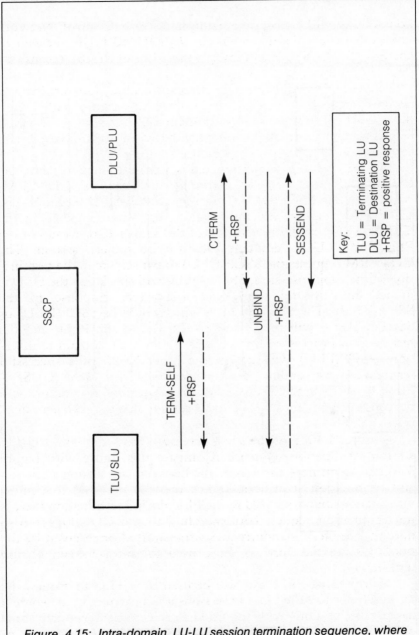

Figure 4.15: Intra-domain, LU-LU session termination sequence, where the TLU is the SLU of the session

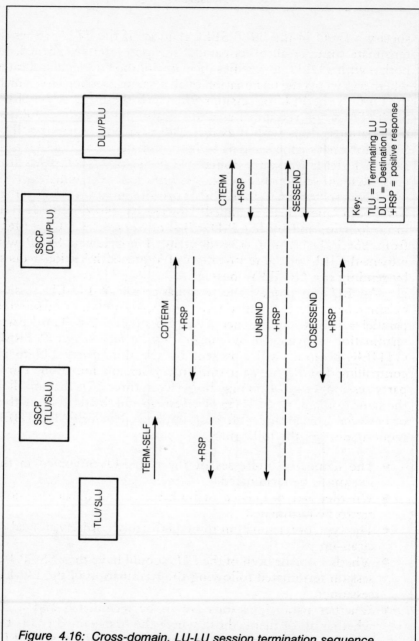

Figure 4.16: Cross-domain, LU-LU session termination sequence,
where the TLU is the SLU of the session

114

specify a DLU in the INIT-SELF request. If the TLU wishes to terminate some or all of its parallel sessions – active, queued, or both – with a DLU, it specifies the name of the DLU and indicates whether it wants the termination of all sessions, sessions for which the DLU is the PLU or sessions for which the DLU is the SLU. SSCP(TLU), on receipt of an INIT-SELF that specifies multiple terminations, deals with it as if it had received a separate INIT-SELF for each of the sessions to be terminated. SSCP(TLU) will issue CTERMs (for intra-domain sessions) and CDTERMs (for cross-domain sessions) for each session it has to terminate.

Requests for the termination of session initiation requests that have been queued are handled directly by the SSCP(TLU) if intra-domain, and by SSCP(DLU) – on receipt of a CDTERM from SSCP(TLU) – if cross-domain. The relevant SSCP will inform the ILU of the termination of a queued initiation request by sending it a NOTIFY message.

An LU can request the termination of an LU-LU session existing between two other LUs, or the termination of selected parallel sessions existing between two other LUs. Third-party termination is achieved by means of a *terminate-other* (TERM-OTHER) request, which is sent by the third-party LU to its controlling SSCP. As with third-party session initiation, third-party session termination may be between three LUs that are all in the same domain, two LUs in one domain and the third in another or between LUs in three different domains. The TERM-OTHER request specifies the following:

- The names or addresses of the two LUs involved in the session to be terminated
- Whether active, queued or both active and queued sessions are to be terminated
- The type of termination to be performed: orderly, forced or clean-up
- Whether one or both of the LUs should have their SSCP-LU session terminated following the termination of the LU-LU session(s)
- Whether parallel sessions are to be terminated and if so, whether all of them, those where the first-named LU is the PLU or those where the second-named LU is the PLU, should be terminated.

If neither of the LUs involved in the session(s) to be terminated are in the domain controlled by the SSCP that receives the TERM-OTHER, it conveys the information that was in it to an SSCP that controls one or both the subject LUs by means of a *terminate-other cross-domain* (TERM-OTHER-CD) request, transmitted via an SSCP-SSCP session. (If the two subject LUs are in two different domains the TERM-OTHER-CD can be sent to either of the two controlling SSCPs.) Once an SSCP that controls one of the subject LUs has received the INIT-OTHER information, directly or via a TERM-OTHER-CD, termination proceeds as for a TERM-SELF request received from one of the subject LUs. The only difference is that the third-party LU and its controlling SSCP are informed of the status of the termination by means of a NOTIFY message.

TERM-OTHER can also be used by an LU as an alternative to TERM-SELF, to request the termination of one or more sessions it has with another LU, ie the TERM-OTHER is issued by one of the two LUs involved in the session(s) to be terminated. When TERM-OTHER is used in this way the issuing LU cannot request the termination of all its LU-LU sessions as with a TERM-SELF, since the TERM-OTHER insists that a target DLU is always specified.

Implementational notes

Domains

A domain consists of all the PUs, LUs and Path Control Network components that have been explicitly defined to, and subsequently activated by, an SNA-oriented teleprocessing access method, such as VTAM, ACF/TCAM or ACF/VTAM. Thus, in practice, a domain will consist of one or more of the following entities that have been defined to, and have been activated by, an access method:

- The PU_T5 in the access method
- Network Control Programs – *viz* PU_T4 and Path Control Network components – for local and remote communications controllers

- PU_T2s and LUs in locally attached control units
- LUs that serve application programs resident in the host computer
- PU_T2s, PU_T1s and LUs of devices specified within active Network Control Programs
- Path Control Network components within the access method, needed to support the locally attached, and active, communications controllers and control units.

ACT/VTAM (Releases 2 and 3), which is becoming increasingly popular as the standard teleprocessing access method for realising SNA environments, will be used as the reference access method in this section, so that specific, rather than generic, examples can be used.

An ACF/VTAM domain, for a given activation, consists of all the SNA resources that have been defined to it, and activated by it, in terms of ACF/VTAM *major* and *minor nodes*. (ACF/VTAM major and minor are not related to SNA nodes, and should not be confused with, or related to, SNA nodes.) A major node is a set of resources of a given type that have been grouped together, while a minor node is an individual resource within a major node.

Each ACF/VTAM major node will define the following:

- A network control program for a locally or remotely attached communications controller and all the devices and teleprocessing links specified within the network control program
- A set of PU_T2s and LUs for locally attached control units
- A set of application programs, resident in the same host as ACF/VTAM, that will use ACF/VTAM
- A set of devices that may access the environment via switched SDLC lines (these switched lines are also defined in the appropriate network control programs).

Each major node is a separate file (a member in OS/VS, a book in DOS/VS) in the ACF/VTAM definition library, SYS1.VTAMLST. With the exception of network control program major nodes all the other major nodes are specified by means of ACF/VTAM VBUILD macros. The TYPE operand of the VBUILD macro specifies the type of major node being defined:

TYPE=LOCAL for local control unit major node, TYPE=APPL for application program major node and TYPE=SWNET for a switched device major node.

A network control program major node is defined by filing the complete network control program definition, which includes the specifications on all the PUs, LUs and links controlled by that network control program, prefixed by an ACF/VTAM PCCU (Programmed Communication Control Unit) macro, which identifies the communications controller which will execute the network control program.

An application program major node consists of a set of application programs that uses ACF/VTAM. Each application program is defined within the major node by an APPL macro. Each APPL macro is assigned a name, and it is this name that is used as the LU name during LU-LU session initiation and termination. (An alternative name for the application program (and the LU that serves it) that is only valid for intra-domain session initiations or terminations, can be specified in the APPL macro by means of the ACBNAME operand. This permits a copy of an application program to be run in multiple domains. An LU can access the copy in its domain using the alternative name specified in the ACBNAME which will be the same in all domains, or a copy in another domain, by using the name assigned for that program in the APPL macro, in the other domain.)

A local control unit major node consists of a set of locally attached node Type 2 control units. Each control unit is defined by an ACF/VTAM PU macro – which specifies the channel address of the device – and a set of ACF/VTAM LU macros for each LU available within that control unit. Each PU and LU macro is assigned a name. This will be the LU name used in LU-LU session initiations and terminations.

A switched device major node consists of a set of node Type 1 and node Type 2 devices that access the environment – via a network control program – by means of switched SDLC lines. Each device is defined by a PU macro, which specifies whether it is Type 1 or Type 2 node. A set of LU macros follows each of the PU macros and defines the LUs available within each device.

A network control program major node consists of one network control program for a locally or remotely attached communications controller. The teleprocessing lines that are supported by the network control program are specified by means of the network control program macros GROUP and LINE. (A GROUP macro specifies the characteristics that are common to a set of lines, whereas a LINE macro represents a line and specifies the characteristics unique to that line, including its name and a communications control unit relative address for that line.) Devices – node Type 1 or Type 2 – attached to each line are defined, following the LINE macro, by means of the network control program macro's PU and LU. The PU defines each device on the line, while the LU macros following a PU macro define all the LUs available within that device. Each PU and LU macro is assigned a name. It is this name that is used for LU-LU session initiations and terminations.

Figure 4.17 illustrates the use of major and minor nodes to define SNA resources to ACF/VTAM.

Major nodes can be activated either when ACF/VTAM is started, or dynamically once ACF/VTAM is operational. The major nodes to be activated are specified by the names under which they are filed in the ACF/VTAM definition library. The domain of an ACF/VTAM, at any given time will consist of all the resources that are defined within the currently active major nodes.

Multi-domain environments

In a multi-domain SNA environment each teleprocessing access method must have defined to it every other teleprocessing access method it might need to communicate with in order to support cross-domain LU-LU sessions. (Note that only the ACF versions of VTAM, TCAM and NCP support cross-domain sessions.) The relevant access methods are defined to each other in terms of *cross-domain resource managers* (CDRMs). (A CDRM is the subset of an SSCP that deals with cross-domain sessions.)

In ACF/VTAM, the CDRMs that each ACF/VTAM might have to deal with are defined by means of CDRM major and minor nodes. (ACF/VTAM and ACF/TCAM can co-exist in multi-domain environments.) Each CDRM major node defines a set of CDRMs for a particular multi-domain configuration, while

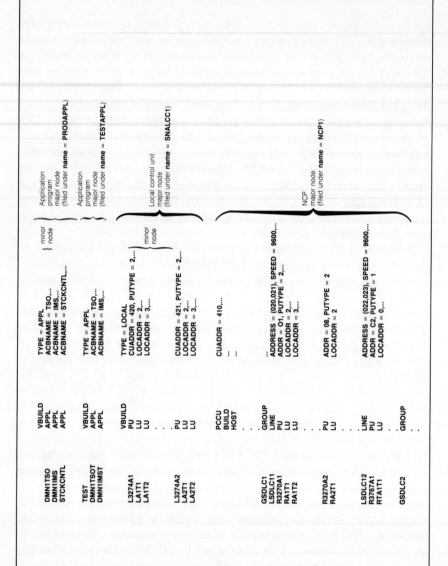

Figure 4.17: Defining SNA resources to ACF/VTAM using major and minor nodes

each CDRM in that configuration is defined by a minor node. (Since a CDRM major node defines a complete configuration, each of these nodes will contain a minor node definition for the CDRM for that domain.) A CDRM major node is defined with a VBUILD macro with a TYPE=CDRM operand. Each of the CDRMs for a given configuration is defined within the major node by means of a CDRM macro. A CDRM is identified by the subarea address of its SSCP. This is specified in the SUBAREA= operand of the CDRM macro. Each CDRM macro is also assigned a name. This name is used when defining cross-domain usable resources.

Each ACF/VTAM must also have defined to it all the LUs outside its domain, with whom it might have to initiate LU-LU sessions. These LUs are defined by means of *cross-domain resources* (CDRSC) major and minor nodes. A CDRSC major node defines a set of LUs that are in other domains for a given configuration, while each of these foreign LUs are defined by a CDRSC minor node. A CDRSC major node is defined with a VBUILD macro with a TYPE=CDRSC operand. Each of the foreign LUs for a given configuration is defined within the major node, by means of a CDRSC macro. The CDRM= operand of the CDRSC macro specifies the domain this LU belongs to by naming the CDRM for that domain. The CDRSC macro is assigned a name: it is this name that is used when initiating or terminating sessions with it. (The names assigned to foreign LUs must not conflict with names assigned to local LUs. In addition, the name by which an LU is known in other domains must correspond to the name given to it in its own domain.)

The communications paths between the various domains must also be defined. These are defined by means of PATH macros in ACF/VTAM and in ACF/NCP. The route is defined in terms of adjacent and destination subarea addresses. (In ACF/NCP the SDLC line that serves as the cross-domain link is defined in much the same way as a local line serving a device. The PU statement associated with this line will contain PUTYPE=4 and SUBAREA= operands to denote the communication controller in the other domain.)

Figure 4.18 illustrates the basic definitions required for a multi-domain environment.

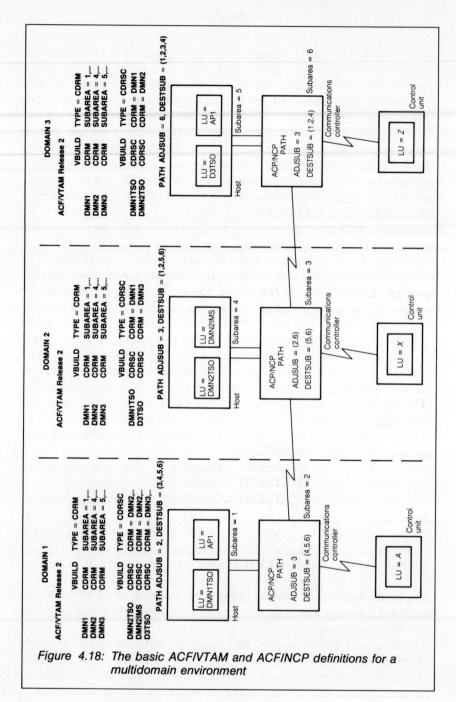

Figure 4.18: The basic ACF/VTAM and ACF/NCP definitions for a multidomain environment

122

Session characteristics and protocols

During LU–LU session initiation, the specification of the session characteristics and protocols for the proposed session are done by means of *log mode tables* and *log mode names*.

The set of session characteristics and protocols are represented by a string of bits that can be directly embedded into the BIND request by the PLU. (The PLU may modify certain values prior to using the string in the BIND.) Rather than transmitting this bit string to denote the session characteristics and protocols in INIT-SELF, INIT-OTHER, CDINIT and INIT-OTHER-CD requests, each bit string is filed – with an assigned name, ie the log mode name – in a log mode table, within the SSCP (in practice, a file in one of the access methods' libraries). The LU–LU initiation request then specifies the session characteristics and protocols by quoting the appropriate log mode name. The SSCP will retrieve the bit string corresponding to the log mode name, and convey this string to the PLU via CINIT and CDINIT requests.

A log mode table is defined to ACF/VTAM by means of a MODETAB macro. Each set of session characteristics and protocols is defined within a log mode table using an MODEENT macro. The log mode name for the entry is assigned via the LOGMODE= operand. An ACF/VTAM mode table has the following structure:

```
log mode table name MODETAB
                MODEENT LOGMODE= log mode name,...
                MODEENT LOGMODE= log mode name,...
                MODEENT LOGMODE= log mode name,...
                      .
                      .
                      .
                MODEEND
```

If multiple log mode tables are present, the table to be searched for and the log mode name quoted by an LU can be specified by means of the MODETAB= operand in ACF/VTAM APPL, LU and PU macros and ACF/NCP LU and PU macros. (If MODETAB= is specified in the PU macro, it applies to all the LUs in that device, unless explicitly overridden in the LU macro.)

Terminal/device LU initiated sessions

In an ACF/VTAM environment terminal or device LUs can only have LU-LU sessions with ACF/VTAM application program LUs. Though the terminal or device LU can initiate a session with an application program LU, the application program LU is always the PLU for these sessions.

A terminal or device LU initiates a session with an application program LU either as a result of encountering a predefined condition, eg initial activation, or as a result of a product specific instruction from the terminal (operator) or device it supports. The type of initiation request that is generated by the LU depends on the processing capabilities of the control unit or device within which it is resident. Two types of initiation request are possible: *field-formatted logon* or *character-coded logon*.

A field-formatted logon is a *bona fide* INIT-SELF request. Field-formatted logons are only produced by LUs in control units or devices that have sufficient processing capabilities to construct an INIT-SELF request. ACF/VTAM can directly process a field-formatted logon without recourse to auxiliary translations.

Character-coded logons are produced by LUs in control units or devices that are unable to construct INIT-SELF requests. When a character-coded logon is used, a 'logon message' entered by the terminal or device operator is passed directly to ACT/VTAM. ACF/VTAM will translate it to an INIT-SELF request and then process it. ACF/VTAM expects character-coded logons to be of the format:

LOGON APPLID (*LU name of application program*) **LOG-MODE** (*log mode name*) **DATA** (*some user data*)

However, if a different character-coded logon format is required, ACF/VTAM will transform the non-standard logon format to the standard format prior to translating it to an INIT-SELF. Transformations for non-standard logon formats are specified to ACF/VTAM by means of *Unformatted System Services* (USS) tables. This table is defined using a USSTAB macro.

The type of logon that will be used by an LU is defined to ACF/VTAM by means of the SSCPFM= operand of the ACF/VTAM and ACF/NCP PU and LU macros. (If coded for the PU

124

macro it applies to all the LUs within the device.) If a USS table is used its name is specified in the USSTAB= operand of ACF/VTAM and ACF/NCP PU and LU macros.

Application program LU initiated sessions

An ACF/VTAM application program LU initiates a session in which it will be the PLU by either executing an OPNDST (open destination) macro, or an SIMLOGON (simulated logon) macro.

With an OPNDST, two types of initiation are possible: Accept and Acquire.

Accept

The application program will accept session initiation requests from potential SLUs. OPNDST with Accept can be issued either when ACF/VTAM has informed the program of an initiation request by invoking the program's LOGON exit routine, or in anticipation of potential initiation requests.

Acquire

OPNDST with Acquire results in an INIT-SELF request to be sent to ACF/VTAM. If the potential SLU is available, ACF/VTAM will return a CINIT, which will be accepted for further processing by the OPNDST.

A SIMLOGON macro, as with an OPNDST with Acquire, causes an INIT-SELF request to be sent to the ACF/VTAM. However, unlike OPNDST with Acquire, there is no OPNDST ready to accept the potential CINIT. When SIMLOGON is used an OPNDST with Accept must either have been issued in anticipation of, or as a result of, the LOGON exit routine being invoked.

An ACF/VTAM application program LU can initiate sessions with other ACF/VTAM or ACF/TCAM application programs. These sessions can be intra- or cross-domain. In application-program-to-application-program sessions, either program could be the PLU for the session. In addition, parallel sessions are also permitted between two application program LUs. (When parallel sessions exist, each session is independent of the others, and it is possible for an application program LU to have some parallel sessions for which it is the PLU, and some for which it is the SLU.)

An application program that wishes to be the SLU, in an application-program-to-application-program session, does so by executing a REQSESS macro.

Third-party session initiations

There are three possibilities for an LU-LU session being initiated by a third-party LU:

1 An application program LU which is the PLU of a session can attempt to initiate a session between its session partner and another application program PLU, by terminating the session with a CLSDST (close destination) macro which specifies OPTCD=PASS and the name of the potential PLU in the AAREA= operand.

2 The ACF/VTAM operator issuing either a VARY NET,LOGON= or VARY NET,ACT,LOGON= command which specifies an LU name and an application program LU name.

3 An application program LU name is specified in the LOGAPPL= operand of an ACF/VTAM or ACF/NCP PU or LU macro. (The name specified in a PU macro will apply to all the LUs of a device, unless it is overriden in the LU macro.) ACF/VTAM will attempt to initiate the specified session when the LU is activated.

Session termination

An application program LU can terminate a session for which it is the PLU by executing a CLSDST macro and a session in which it is the SLU by executing a TERMSESS macro.

Terminal or device LUs can terminate a session by issuing a field-formatted logoff (equivalent to a TERM-SELF) or by issuing a character-coded logoff, which will be translated by ACF/VTAM to a TERM-SELF (cf character-coded logons).

The ACT/VTAM operator can terminate sessions – third-party terminations – by issuing either a VARY NET,INACT,... or VARY NET,TERM,... .

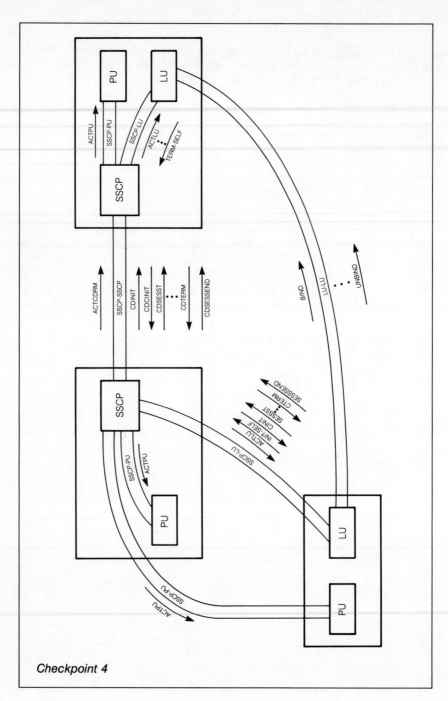

Checkpoint 4

128

Chapter 5:
Half-sessions

□ Requests/Responses □ RU □ RH □ Definite/Exception/No Response □ Exception Requests □ Immediate/Delayed Request Mode □ Immediate/Delayed Response Mode □ CHASE □ Normal/Expedited Flow □ Sequence Numbers and Identifiers □ Transmission Control □ Data Flow Control □ Function Management Data Services □ Session Network Services □ Session Presentation Services □ NAU Services Manager □ NAU Services Layer □ Session Control □ Connection Point Manager □ SDT/CLEAR □ CRV □ STSN □ Pacing □ Cryptography □ Chains □ Brackets □ CANCEL □ BID □ RTR □ SBI/BIS □ Send/Receive Modes □ SIG □ Quiescing □ QEC/QC/RELQ □ Shutdown □ SHUTC/RSHUTD □ LUSTAT □ Sync Points □ CDTAKED/CDTAKEDC □ CLEANUP □ DSRLST

Chapter 5:
Half-sessions

Requests and responses

All message units that are transmitted within an SNA environment are classified as being either *requests* or *responses*. A request, in the SNA context, is a message unit that conveys data or initiates a data transfer or control operation. A request may consist of end-user data (eg an enquiry from one end user to another, a reply to an end-user enquiry, a command to an application program end user to perform a designated operation, a command to control the operation of an end-user terminal or device) or of SNA commands for controlling the environment (eg session initiation and activation messages, configuration control messages, message unit flow control messages). A response in SNA, contrary to the expected connotation, is not the reply to a request: a response only indicates that a request reached its destination and whether the receiver of the request can process it or not. Therefore a response is, in effect, a positive or negative acknowledgement of the feasibility of a request. (A response should not be confused with a data link control protocol acknowledgement. A data link control acknowledgement only deals with whether or not a data block was received in the correct sequence and was uncorrupted during transmission.)

Each response relates to a particular request. A request may only have, at most, one response. Multiple responses to the same request, even if they are generated at different stages during the processing of the request, are not permitted. A response identifies the request it refers to by quoting both the sequence number or

identifier of the request, and, if present, the numeric code –
referred to as the *request code* – contained in most requests to
specify their function. A response can be either a positive or a
negative response.

A positive response indicates that the request that it refers to
can be, or is being, processed or that it has been successfully
processed. (At what point during the processing of a request a
positive response may be sent depends on the nature of the
request. A request may specify that if it cannot be processed
immediately it should be queued and processed at a later stage. If
such a request is queued, a positive response may be sent at that
point to indicate the successful queuing of the request rather than
the successful processing of it. But the positive response will not
specify whether it refers to the successful processing or to the
queuing of the request: the requester can only ascertain that by the
time it takes to receive the reply – not the response – to the
request. If an error is encountered when a queued request – to
which a positive response has already been sent – is eventually
processed, a reply is sent notifying the requester of the error.)

A negative response indicates that the request cannot be
processed or that an error was encountered during the processing
of the request. A negative response will contain a four-byte code –
referred to as *sense data* – specifying why the request could not be
processed or the nature of the error that was encountered during
the processing of the request.

The reply to, or the results of, a particular request that was
successfully processed will be conveyed to the requester by means
of another request. For example, an LU that intends to establish an
LU-LU session with another LU, issues an INIT-SELF request
specifying its intentions to its controlling SSCP. The SSCP,
receiving the INIT-SELF request, determines, in conjunction with
another SSCP if the other LU is in another domain, whether or
not the other LU is active and is capable of supporting the
proposed LU-LU session. It will then send the LU that issued the
INIT-SELF request either a positive response if the other LU is
active and is capable of supporting the proposed session immediately or later (if queuing was acceptable), or a negative
response if the other LU is inactive or is unable to support the
proposed session. A positive response to the INIT-SELF request
does not, in itself, establish, or provide information necessary to

establish, the proposed LU-LU session. All that the positive response indicates is that the other LU is active and is able to support the proposed session. The actual reply to the INIT-SELF request (which will be a BIND request if the issuer of the INIT-SELF was the potential SLU, or a CINIT request if the issuer of the INIT-SELF was the PLU) will follow some time after the positive response. If an unexpected error was encountered in the session initiation processes, after the positive response had been sent, a NOTIFY request will be sent to the issuer of the INIT-SELF request to inform it of the error.

The only exceptions to the convention of the reply to a request being conveyed by another request rather than by the response to the request, are 17, of the 125, SNA commands. The positive responses to ACTCDRM, ACTLU, ACTPU, ADDLINK, ADDLINSTA, BIND, CDINIT, CDSESSEND, CDTERM, CINIT, DSRLST, DUMPINIT, DUMPTEXT, INIT-OTHER-CD, RNAA, ROUTETEST and STSN requests, may contain data which relates to the request (even though this data might not be interpreted as replies in the traditional sense.)

Figure 5.1 illustrates the relationship between requests and responses.

Each SNA message unit either contains a request or a response. Requests and responses, multiple requests or multiple responses cannot be grouped into one SNA message unit. If an SNA message unit contains a request, the portion of the message unit containing the request is referred to as the *Request Unit*. Similarly, in a message unit containing a response, the portion of the message unit occupied by the response is referred to as the *Response Unit*. Request Units and Response Units share the common abbreviation RU. Request Units and Response Units are always prefixed by a three-byte header. The header prefixing a Request Unit is known as a *request header*, while the header prefixing a response unit is known as a *response header*. These headers share the common abbreviation RH. The leading bit – ie bit 0 of byte 0 – of these headers, referred to as the *request/response indicator* (RRI), specifies whether the submessage unit prefixed by the RH contains a request – ie it is a Request Unit – or whether it contains a response – ie it is a Response Unit.

Every request does not necessarily have to have a response. A request specifies one of three possible types of response it expects.

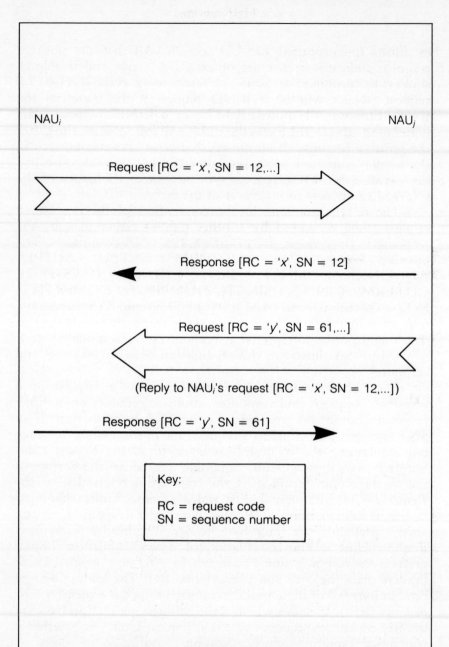

NAU$_i$ NAU$_j$

Request [RC = 'x', SN = 12,...]

Response [RC = 'x', SN = 12]

Request [RC = 'y', SN = 61,...]

(Reply to NAU$_i$'s request [RC = 'x', SN = 12,...])

Response [RC = 'y', SN = 61]

Key:

RC = request code
SN = sequence number

Figure 5.1: The relationship between requests and responses –
a response is not the reply to a request

These three types are:

1 *Definite response* – a response to the request, whether positive or negative, must be sent.
2 *No-response* – a response is not required and should not be sent (eg, an SESSST request specifies 'no-response' as it is essentially a courtesy message).
3 *Exception response* – a response is only required – and should only be sent – if the request cannot be processed or if an error was encountered during the processing of the request. Since the inability to process a request or an error during the processing of a request is indicated by a negative response, the only response sent when exception response is specified will be a negative response.

Three bits, known as *definite response 1 indicator* (DR1I), *definite response 2 indicator* (DR2I) and *exception response indicator* (ERI), are provided in a request header to specify the type of response expected by the request. No-response is specified by setting all three of these bits to 0. Exception response is specified by setting ERI to 1, and DR1I and DR2I to either <0,1>, <1,0> or <1,1>. Definite response is specified by setting ERI to 0, and DR1I and DR2I to either <0,1>, <1,0> or <1,1>. Note that it is the setting of the ERI that differentiates between the specification of an exception or a definite response, rather than the settings of DR1I or DR2I. SNA does not define any explicit use for DR1I and DR2I setting. All that SNA specifies is that the bit combination set for DR1I and DR2I in a definite or exception response specification must be returned without any change, in the response header prefixing the appropriate response.

The response header also has three bits to indicate the type of response being conveyed: DR1I and DR2I, which reflect the setting of the corresponding bits in the request header of requests specifying definite or exception response, and the *response type indicator* (RTI) which denotes whether the response is positive (set to 0) or negative (set to 1). Figure 5.2 summarises how the type of response expected for a request is specified, and how the response to it indicates whether it is a positive or negative response. (Response headers also contain a bit known as the *sense data included indicator* (SDI) which, when set to 1, denotes that sense

Response expected	Request header bits: DR1I	DR2I	ERI	Response header bits for the response: DR1I	DR2I	RTI	Type of response
No-response	0	0	0	-	-	-	None
Definite	0	1	0	0	1	0	Positive
				0	1	1	Negative
	1	0	0	1	0	0	Positive
				1	0	1	Negative
	1	1	0	1	1	0	Positive
				1	1	1	Negative
Exception	0	1	1	0	1	1	Negative
	1	0	1	1	0	1	Negative
	1	1	1	1	1	1	Negative

Figure 5.2: How the type of response expected for a request is specified in the request header and how the response header indicates the type of response being conveyed

136

data is included in the response. Since all negative responses contain sense data, this bit is set to 1 in all negative responses and to 0 in positive responses.)

SNA specifies the type of response that must be sent, and the settings of DR1I and DR2I if definite or exception response is specified, for Request Units containing SNA commands. The type of response for end-user requests – and the settings of DR1I and DR2I – within an LU–LU session is left to the discretion of the end users. The LU–LU session initiator suggests the type of response expected by the requests that will flow from the PLU to the SLU, and for those from the SLU to the PLU, when it proposes the session characteristics and protocols for the session by specifying an appropriate logmode entry name. The session initiator does not specify the settings for DR1I and DR2I. The response type that will be used, which may differ from those suggested by the session initiator, for the requests in both directions for the duration of the session are designated by the PLU in the BIND request.

The types of response that can be specified in the BIND, for the requests in each direction are no-response, exception response, definite response or a combination of definite and exception responses. The requests from the PLU to the SLU can have a different type of response from those from the SLU to the PLU, but once it has been specified in the BIND, for each direction, and agreed upon by both LUs, it cannot be changed for another response type within the duration of the session. The response type indicated in the request headers of all the request units associated with an LU–LU session must be consistent with the type of response specified in the BIND. If definite or exception response was specified, the DR1I and DR2I of the request header will be set to denote the bit setting expected on the response, on a Request-Unit-by-Request-Unit basis. The DR1I and DR2I settings, when specified, do not have to be the same for all the Request Units in a given direction.

Exception requests

An error in a request may be detected by an intermediate component before the request reaches its destination NAU. For example, an intermediate component might detect an error in the sequence number assigned to a Request Unit. When an intermediate component does detect such an error, it would be inappropriate for it to issue a negative response – even if definite or exception response was specified in the request header – to the originator of the request, as this would not only contravene the principle of a session between two NAUs, but would also preclude the NAU to whom the request was addressed from being able to process the request and issue its response or reply. Instead, errors detected by intermediate components are dealt with by means of *exception requests* (EXR).

Request headers, in common with response headers, contain a sense data included (SDI) bit. When an intermediate component discovers an error, it inserts four bytes of sense data, which describe the nature of the error, at the start of the Request Unit containing the incorrect request and sets the SDI bit in the request header to 1. The SDI bit being on denotes that the request is no longer a 'normal' request, but an exception request. Up to three bytes from the start of the original request – usually just the request code, if present – are then concatenated at the end of the sense data. The rest of the original request is then discarded. The exception request, which still contains the original destination and origin addresses and the sequence number or identifier, is then forwarded, by the intermediate component, to the NAU to whom the original request was destined. (Note that the intermediate component does not notify the originator of the request of the error that was detected, and that it does not identify itself in the exception request.)

A NAU, on receiving an EXR, will process the sense data and the portion of the original request included in the EXR, and issue an appropriate response or a reply.

It is possible that another intermediate component might detect another error, this time in the EXR, before it reaches its destination. In such an instance, the sense data inserted by the first intermediate component can be overwritten by four bytes of 'new' sense data describing the latest error. However, such updating of EXR sense data is rare, as the original error that caused the EXR to be created is usually considered as being the most significant error that needs to be brought to the attention of the NAU that receives the EXR.

Request and response control modes

In addition to specifying the types of response a request may ask for, SNA also specifies a set of rules governing when requests and responses may be issued by a given half-session. These rules, which are aimed at providing a means of regulating the flow of message units within a session, and of facilitating error recovery, are known as the *request and response control modes*.

These control modes, which are used in all the four types of SNA session (SSCP-PU, SSCP-LU, SSCP-SSCP and LU-LU), are assigned when the session is established. In each session, a request control mode and a response control mode are specified, for the requests and responses flowing in each direction, ie each half-session is assigned a request control mode and a response control mode. The modes specified for one direction need not be the same as those specified for the other direction. Once these modes have been assigned at session establishment they cannot be changed during the duration of the session. For LU-LU sessions, the control modes to be used, in each direction, are suggested by the session initiator when specifying the session characteristics and protocols, and confirmed by the PLU and the SLU when the BIND request is processed.

Two control modes are defined for regulating the issuing of requests: *immediate request mode* and *delayed request mode*.

If immediate request mode is selected for requests flowing in one direction no requests may be sent in that direction until a response is received for a previously sent request that specified that it needed a definite response. (That is, once a request that specified definite response is transmitted, no other requests can be transmitted in that direction until a response is received for that request.) With immediate request mode, multiple requests that specify exception response or no response may be transmitted without any restrictions, but only when the half-session is not waiting for a response to a request that specified definite response.

With delayed request mode there are no restrictions as to when a request – irrespective of the response a previously transmitted request specified – may be issued. Multiple requests all specifying definite response may be transmitted without waiting for the response to each request.

Two control modes are also defined for regulating the order in which responses may be issued: *immediate response mode* and *delayed response mode*.

If immediate response mode is specified for a half-session, it must issue the responses in the same order that it received the requests, ie it must process requests and issue responses to those requests that require responses on a first-in, first-out basis. This means that the other half-session, ie the one issuing the requests, on receiving a response, can be sure that all the requests that it had sent, prior to the request for which it has received the response, have been processed and that responses to these requests, if any, have been dispatched. This is particularly useful if a series of requests that specified exception response had been transmitted. By sending a subsequent request, which specifies definite response, and then waiting for a response to it from the half-session operating in immediate response mode the half-session issuing the requests can ascertain that all the previous requests – that specified exception responses – have by then been processed and that it will not receive an exception response for one of them at a later stage.

With delayed response mode, responses may be issued in any order, irrespective of the order in which the requests that the responses refer to were received. This could present processing difficulties to the other half-session, especially if it is issuing requests that specify exception response. It can never be sure when it may receive an exception response to one or more of those requests. To overcome this problem, on LU-LU sessions, SNA provides a command known as a *CHASE* request.

When an LU half-session receives a CHASE request (which will always ask for a definite response) from its session partner, it must send all the responses that may be outstanding for requests previously received on that session, before it can issue a response to the CHASE request. Thus, by issuing a CHASE request, a half-session can ensure that it receives all outstanding responses for requests that it has previously transmitted.

Normal and expedited flow

Within each session of an SNA environment, the flow of requests and responses in each direction is divided into two independent categories, referred to as the *normal flow* and the *expedited flow*.

Requests or responses transmitted on the normal flow, in one direction, are delivered to the opposite session partner in the same order in which they were transmitted. However, requests or responses transmitted on the expedited flow can overtake normal flow requests or responses flowing in the same direction at queuing points within the session. As such, a request or a response transmitted on the expedited flow could reach the opposite session partner before requests and responses that were transmitted prior to it; on the normal flow. (But within the expedited flow requests and responses are kept in the order in which they were transmitted.)

End-user requests and responses can only be transmitted on the normal flow. The expedited flow, within each session, is reserved for certain designated SNA commands and the responses to these commands. These commands are those related to session initiation and termination, session activation and deactivation, configuration control and message flow control. The other SNA commands and their responses share the normal flow with the end-user requests and responses. The flow that each SNA command and its response must use is specified by SNA and cannot be changed. (Note that a response will always use the same flow as that used by the request it refers to.) The type of flow used by each of the SNA commands is tabulated in Chapter 9, *SNA commands*.

Expedited flow uses immediate request mode and immediate response mode in both directions. Normal flow, however, can use either of the two request and response modes, in either direction. Requests transmitted in each of the two flows, in each direction, are assigned sequence numbers or identifiers, totally independent of each other, ie there is no relationship between sequence numbers or identifiers used in the two different flows, in a given direction.

Having these two distinct flows, and restricting end-user traffic to one of them, enables session control, configuration control or error recovery information to be exchanged, and acted upon, by the two half-sessions, without normally disrupting the orderly flow of end-user traffic or, if disruption is inevitable because of catastrophic errors, to minimise the disruption to the end-user traffic flow.

Sequence numbers and identifiers

Each request transmitted in an SNA session is assigned either a sequence number or an identifier, which will uniquely identify that request, relative to a given direction and a flow, during the period in which it is 'active'. The sequence number or identifier is used to ensure that requests flowing in either of the two flows, in a given direction, are kept in the order in which they were transmitted within that flow, and to correlate responses with the requests they refer to. (A response identifies the request that it refers to by using the request's sequence number or identifier as *its* sequence number or identifier, ie responses are not assigned separate sequence numbers or identifiers but echo those assigned to the requests they refer to.) Except when being transmitted between NAUs resident in a Type 1 node and the boundary function in the subarea node to which the Type 1 node is attached, each request or response is prefixed by a 16-bit field, referred to as the *sequence number field* (SNF), which contains its sequence number or identifier. Sequence numbers and identifiers are always numeric and are in the range 0 to 65 535.

Sequence numbers are assigned to a stream of contiguous requests, in a given direction, in serially ascending order, while identifiers can be assigned to requests in an arbitrary manner rather than in any specific order.

Requests (and their responses) transmitted on the expedited flow of a session are always assigned identifiers rather than sequence numbers. Requests (and their responses) transmitted on the normal flow of a session can be assigned either sequence numbers or identifiers. Whether sequence numbers or identifiers will be used on the normal flow, in both directions, is specified at session activation, for all four types of SNA session. The scheme chosen to identify normal flow requests cannot be changed once the session is established and will apply to all normal flow requests flowing in either direction.

The sequence numbers used by the two half-sessions of a given session are independent of each other. The sequence number counts used by each half-session are initialised to 0 when the session is activated. Before a request that uses sequence numbers is transmitted by a half-session, it increments its current sequence number count by one and then assigns it to the request that is to be transmitted. (So, the sequence number assigned to the first request that uses sequence numbers, transmitted by a half-session, following the activation of the session, is 1.) The sequence number count will wrap-around to 0 once it has reached, and had assigned, sequence number 65 535. (Thus, the request transmitted after the one assigned sequence number 65 535 will have a sequence number of 0.)

Since the two half-sessions use independent sequence number counts — which are both initialised to 0 at session activation — the same sequence number (or, for that matter, identifier) can be assigned to requests (and echoed by the respective responses) flowing in opposite directions. This does not cause any ambiguity since the direction in which a request or response is flowing is always unequivocally specified by the destination and origin addresses, and there is a clear distinction between requests and responses.

Half-sessions in NAUs resident within Type 1 nodes — due to the limited processing capability of these nodes — do not support sequence numbers or identifiers, ie they will not assign sequence numbers or identifiers to requests or responses they transmit, or expect to receive requests or responses with sequence numbers or identifiers. As such, requests or responses to or from these half-sessions are not pre-fixed by an SNF. But, sequence numbers or identifiers will be used, and expected, by the opposite, ie non–Type 1 node-located, half-session and by certain Path Control Network components. The boundary function, in the subarea node, to which a Type 1 node is attached will assign and check sequence numbers or identifiers of requests and responses to or from half-sessions in NAUs resident in that Type 1 node.

Half-session structure

Each half-session of an SNA environment, irrespective of the type of session it is a part of or the type of NAU it is located in, consists of three hierarchically structured components:

- *Transmission Control* (TC) component
- *Data Flow Control* (DFC) component
- *Function Management Data Services* (FMDS) component.

Within each half-session, the transmission control component is the innermost, ie lowest level, component, relative to the SNA environment and acts as the half-session's interface with the Path Control Network. The function management data services component is the outermost, ie highest level, component, while the data flow control component is functionally situated between the TC and FMDS components. Figure 5.3 depicts the structure of the half-session components within a given session, while Figure 5.4 shows the half-session components within a NAU supporting multiple half-sessions.

The functions performed by the FMDS component of a given half-session depend on the type of session the half-session is a part of. For sessions involving an SSCP – *viz* SSCP-PU, SSCP-LU or SSCP-SSCP sessions – the FMDS components of the two half-sessions forming the session are responsible for controlling and monitoring the various resources associated with the subject NAUs. As such, the FMDS components of half-sessions forming SSCP-related sessions are known as *Session Network Services* (SNSs). However, the FMDS components of half-sessions forming LU-LU sessions are responsible for the manipulation of data that has been accepted from an end user, or is to be presented to an end user. As such, the FMDS components of half-sessions forming LU-LU sessions are known as *Session Presentation Services* (SPSs).

In addition to containing one or more half-sessions, each active NAU also contains a *NAU services manager*. The NAU services managers, within the appropriate NAUs, control and monitor the configuration and operation of the SNA environment by exchanging *network services* (NS) requests and responses with one another, via the relevant SSCP-oriented sessions, viz SSCP-PU, SSCP-LU or SSCP-SSCP. (Network services requests and responses are described in Chapter 7, *The Path Control Network*.) NAU services managers interact with the relevant half-sessions within the NAU they are in via the FMDS components of the half-sessions. Therefore, any given NAU's NAU services manager and the FMDS components of the half-sessions within it are known as the *NAU services layer*. Figure 5.5 illustrates the relationship between the NAU services manager and half-sessions within an LU and a PU.

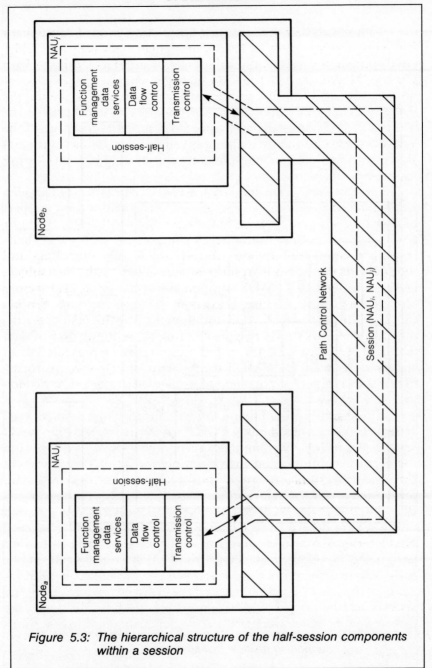

Figure 5.3: The hierarchical structure of the half-session components within a session

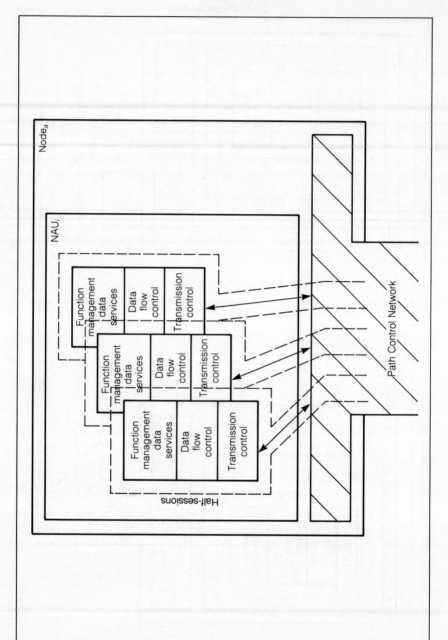

Figure 5.4: *The structure of half-session components within a NAU supporting multiple half-sessions*

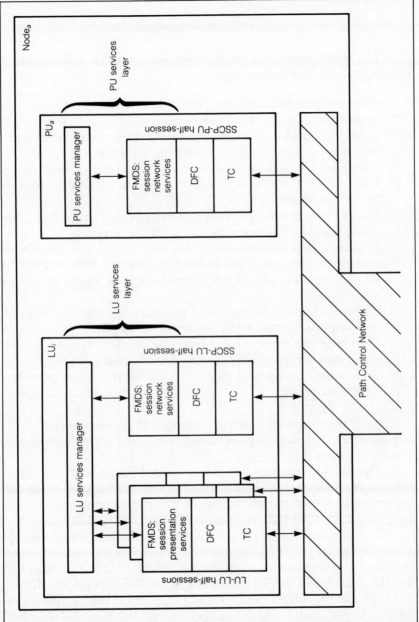

Figure 5.5: NAU services manager and half-sessions within an LU and a PU

Transmission control

The Transmission Control component of a half-session is responsible for the following:

1 Activating and deactivating the session which its half-session is to be, or already is, a partner in.
2 Activating and deactivating the data flow within a session.
3 Recovering the data flow following an error.
4 Checking the sequence numbers of normal flow requests.
5 Controlling the rate at which data flows within the session, by means of *pacing*.
6 Controlling the enciphering and deciphering of end-user data if *cryptography* has been specified for the session.
7 Ensuring that request units do not exceed the maximum request unit length stipulated for the session. (The maximum RU length for LU-LU sessions is agreed upon at session activation.)
8 Constructing the request and response headers for requests and responses emanating from its half-session.
9 Checking the requests and response headers of requests and responses it receives from the opposite half-session.
10 Separating the normal flow data traffic from the expedited flow data traffic.

Each transmission control component consists of two sub-components: a *session control* component and a *connection point manager* (CPMGR).

The session control subcomponent handles the first three items – *viz* session and data activation and deactivation, and data flow recovery – of the above list of TC component responsibilities, while the CPMGR is responsible for the remainder.

The session control subcomponent executes its duties by means of a set of SNA commands referred to as *session control requests* (and responses) – viz ACTCDRM, ACTLU, ACTPU, BIND, CLEAR, CRYPTOGRAPHY VERIFICATION (CRV), DACTCDRM, DACTLU, DACTPU, REQUEST RECOVERY (RQR), SET AND TEST SEQUENCE NUMBERS (STSN), START DATA TRAFFIC (SDT) and UNBIND. (The functions of ACTCDRM/DACTCDRM, ACTLU/DACTLU,

ACTPU/DACTPU and BIND/UNBIND were described in Chapter 4, *Sessions*.)

SDT and CLEAR requests are used by the session control subcomponents to activate or deactivate the flow of non-TC component-related requests and responses within LU-LU, SSCP-PU and SSCP-SSCP sessions. Whether both SDT and CLEAR, one of them, or neither, will be supported during a session is determined at the activation of that session as a session characteristics and protocols option. (CLEAR is only supported on LU-LU sessions.)

If the support of SDT was agreed upon at session activation, the transmission of non-TC component-originated requests or responses, by either half-session, can only take place once the session control subcomponent in the primary NAU has issued an SDT request and the session control subcomponent in the secondary NAU has sent a positive response to it. (If SDT is not supported by a session, transmission of any type of request and response can begin immediately the session is established.)

CLEAR – if supported by the session – is used by the session control subcomponent in the primary LU to halt the transmission of non-TC component-originated requests or responses, by either half-session, and to reset the data flow-related parameters of the session such as the sequence number counts. Once a CLEAR request has been issued and received by the secondary LU no non-TC-originated requests or responses can be transmitted by either half-session until either the primary LU issues SDT – if SDT is supported – or if SDT is not supported, the primary LU processes a positive response to the CLEAR and resumes transmission.

A CLEAR request – if supported by the session – can be issued by the primary LU at any time during the session. CLEAR is normally used as the first step in recovering the data flow in a session following a catastrophic, but potentially recoverable, error condition.

RQR – if supported – is used in LU-LU sessions by the session control subcomponent of the secondary LU to request the primary LU to initiate the recovery of the data flow. On receipt of an RQR request the session-control subcomponent in the primary LU will attempt to recover the data flow by either issuing a CLEAR request, providing CLEAR is supported by the session, or if CLEAR is not supported, by issuing an UNBIND request to deactivate the session. Whether or not RQR is supported by a given LU-LU session is determined at session activation as one of the session characteristics and protocol options. (The CRV and STSN requests are discussed later in this chapter.)

Pacing

The technique used in SNA to regulate the rate at which data flows between two components is referred to as pacing. The object of pacing is to ensure that, during a given data transfer operation, the receiving component is not inundated with data from the transmitting component, especially in instances where the transmitting component is capable of transmitting data faster than the receiving component is able to process or store it. When pacing is used in a data transfer operation the receiving component – rather than transmitting – dictates the rate at which data (ie requests) will be transmitted. Pacing is SNA's fundamental data flow rate regulating mechanism and is used on a session basis – *session-level pacing* – as well as on a route (ie path) basis within the Path Control Network – *virtual-route pacing*.

The technique used in session-level and virtual-route pacing is essentially the same. The concept of pacing and how it is used on a session basis are described in this chapter, while virtual-route pacing is discussed in Chapter 7, *Path Control Network*.

Pacing is based on three pacing-specific entities:

1 *A pacing window size.*
2 *Pacing requests.*
3 *Pacing responses.*

The pacing window size is the maximum number of SNA requests that the receiving component of a data transfer operation can accept at a time. (That is, once the receiver has received the number of SNA requests corresponding to the pacing window size, it would cease to have sufficient processing or storage resources to accept any more requests until it has processed some or all of the requests it has already received.) The receiver and transmitter agree on the receiver's pacing window size – N requests – prior to initiating the data transfer operation. Once the transmitter begins to transmit requests it cannot transmit more than N requests to the receiver at a time. When the receiver has received all or some of those requests and is able to accommodate N more requests it sends a pacing response to the transmitter to indicate that another N requests can be transmitted to it.

Pacing operates in the following iterative manner. The pacing window size, N, for the receiver is determined prior to initiating the data transfer operation. When the data transfer operation begins, the transmitter can initially transmit up to N requests. (It cannot transmit any further requests until it receives a pacing response from the receiver.) With the first request transmitted the transmitter includes a pacing request indicator.

Once the receiver has received the request containing the pacing request indicator it will issue a pacing response, to the transmitter, either after it has received and processed the first N requests or before it has received all N requests. (Whether the receiver waits to receive and process all N requests before issuing a pacing response, or whether it issues a pacing response after only receiving some of them is an implementation–dependent option.)

When the transmitter receives a pacing response from the receiver it can again transmit a further N requests, the first request of which will include a pacing request indicator. If the transmitter receives a pacing response before it has transmitted all N requests it resets to N its count of the number of requests it can transmit before having to wait for a pacing response.

A pacing response can be sent by the receiver either as an indicator included on a response to a request it has received or by means of a pacing-specific response known as an *isolated pacing response* (IPR). IPR can be used as the only means of signalling the pacing response, but it is normally only used if there is no response to a request available on which to include the pacing response indicator, eg if the requests received specified no response or exception response. (Note that only one pacing response will be issued for each batch of requests received, and that a pacing response will only be issued after the receiver receives a pacing request.)

Figure 5.6 illustrates the use of pacing, in both directions, within a data transfer operation.

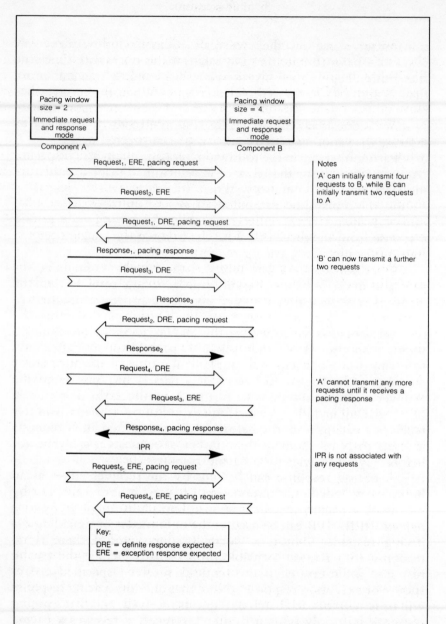

Figure 5.6: *The use of pacing to regulate the rate of flow of requests between two components*

Session-level pacing is used, in both directions, to regulate the rate of transmission of requests on the normal flow within SSCP-SSCP and LU-LU sessions. (Session-level pacing is not used within SSCP-PU or SSCP-LU sessions, or on the expedited flow of any of the session types.)

With session-level pacing, pacing requests are denoted by setting the *pacing indicator* bit provided in request headers to 1, while pacing responses are denoted by setting the pacing indicator bit in response headers to 1, or by means of IPRs. The format of an IPR is described in Chapter 10, *SNA message units*. (The pacing indicator in request headers when set to 1 is sometimes referred to as the pacing request indicator, while the pacing indicator in response headers when set to 1 is referred to as the pacing response indicator.)

Session-level pacing window sizes, which need not be the same for each direction, are established when an SSCP-SSCP or an LU-LU session is activated. The window sizes agreed upon at session activation stay in force for the duration of that session.

For SSCP-SSCP sessions, the primary SSCP's pacing window size, ie the maximum number of normal flow requests that it can receive from the secondary SSCP at a time, is specified in the ACTCDRM request. The secondary SSCP specifies its pacing window size in the positive response to the ACTCDRM. (A positive response to an ACTCDRM is one of the 17 positive responses that may convey data.) If either SSCP specifies a window size of 0 (which is referred to as 'no pacing'), that indicates that there is no need for the requests being sent to it to be paced, ie it can accept as many requests as the other SSCP is able to transmit to it over a given period of time.

With an LU-LU session the implementation of session-level pacing depends on the type of node in which the secondary LU is located. If the SLU is located in a subarea node, session-level pacing in both directions will be done on an 'end-to-end' basis by the two half-sessions. This method of end-to-end pacing is referred to as 'one-stage pacing'. However, if the SLU is located in a peripheral node, session-level pacing in both directions can be done either in one stage, in two separate stages – *viz* two-stage pacing – or in one stage in one direction and two stages in the other. With two-stage pacing, in both directions, pacing is not done on an end-to-end basis by the two half-sessions, but between each half-session and the boundary function supporting the SLU. So with two-stage pacing, in both directions, normal flow requests from the PLU to the SLU are paced as follows:

- Stage 1 – the PLU to the boundary function supporting the SLU
- Stage 2 – the boundary function supporting the SLU to the SLU.

Normal flow requests from the SLU to the PLU are paced as follows:

- Stage 1 – the SLU to the boundary function supporting it
- Stage 2 – the boundary function supporting the SLU to the PLU.

If two-stage pacing is to be used, pacing window sizes have to be established not only for the half-sessions in the PLU and SLU but also for the boundary function supporting the SLU. If two-stage pacing in both directions is used the boundary function will receive requests from both the PLU and the SLU that need to be paced. Therefore it needs two independent pacing window sizes to ensure that it is not 'flooded' by requests in one or both directions: one pacing window size for requests from the PLU and another for those from the SLU.

The initiator of an LU–LU session will indicate by means of an appropriate mode name whether one-stage pacing in both directions, two-stage pacing in both directions or one-stage pacing in one direction and two-stage pacing in the other is to be used, and also the relevant pacing window sizes for the PLU, SLU and (if two-stage pacing is being used) for the boundary function. These pacing parameters will be conveyed to the PLU as a subset of the BIND parameters in the CINIT request. The PLU, especially if it was not the session initiator, can modify its pacing window size from that specified in the CINIT BIND parameters. (But the PLU cannot change it to 0, which would indicate no pacing.) The pacing parameters will then be incorporated into the BIND request. If the BIND is negotiable, the SLU may attempt to reduce (but never increase) its pacing window size by quoting its preferred value in the response to the BIND. (If two-stage pacing is being used in a given direction and the BIND for the session is negotiable the boundary function supporting the SLU may also attempt to modify its pacing window size by inter-cepting the response to the BIND and inserting its preferred value in it.)

Cryptography

SNA supports cryptography in LU-LU sessions as a security measure for end-user data. If cryptography is to be used in a given LU-LU session, two 'levels' of cryptography are available: Ses-sion-Level Mandatory Cryptography and Session-Level Selective Cryptography. If mandatory cryptography is chosen all request units containing end-user data will be enciphered by the transmit-ting half-session's CPMGR subcomponent (and deciphered at the opposite end by the receiving half-session's CPMGR). If selective cryptography is chosen only certain request units containing end-user data are enciphered. When selective cryptography is being used the transmitting end user specifies to its LU, when it passes the LU a request, whether or not that request should be enciphered. If the request is to be enciphered, the *enciphered data indicator* (EDI) bit in the request header for that request is set to 1. The CPMGRs will then only encipher and decipher request units that have the EDI in their request headers set.

In SNA, session-level cryptography employs a cryptographic algorithm that uses a 64-bit cryptographic key to encipher and decipher the requests that need to be protected by cryptography. This cryptography scheme complies with the Data Encryption Standard (DES) algorithm specified in *Federal Information Proces-sing Standards Publication* 46, 15 January 1977. With this scheme the cryptographic algorithm does not have to be kept secret or unique for each application. Only the cryptographic key that was used to encipher the data needs to be guarded.

Whether or not cryptography is to be used within an LU-LU session, and if so the 'level' to be used, is specified by the ILU by means of an appropriate log mode entry name. The cryptographic key to be used for a given LU-LU session, to encipher and decipher the end-user RUs – referred to as the session cryptography key – is a pseudo-random number chosen by the SSCP(PLU). (For cross-domain LU-LU sessions, SSCP(SLU) may specify the session cryptography key.) This session cryptography key is needed by both the PLU and SLU so that they can encipher and decipher the end-user RUs. Since the cryptography scheme used relies on the cryptographics key being kept secret, rather than the cryptographic algorithm, the session cryptographic key needs to be protected while it is being transmitted to the PLU and the SLU (and if it is a cross-domain session, when it is being conveyed across the domains). To this end the session cryptography key is itself enciphered before being transmitted. Each LU (and SSCP, if cross-domain sessions are envisaged) that supports cryptography is assigned an LU (or SSCP) cryptographic key. Each SSCP is privy to the LU cryptographic keys that have been assigned to the LUs in its domain. The session cryptography key to be used for a given session is conveyed to the PLU of that session in the CINIT request – enciphered under the PLU's cryptographic key – and to the SLU in the BIND request – enciphered under the SLU's cryptography key. (Since the SSCP(PLU) supplies the PLU with the parameters for the BIND request, via the CINIT request, the session key enciphered under the SLU cryptography key is also embedded within the CINIT as a BIND parameter.)

The cryptography algorithm used requires, in addition to the session cryptography key, a 64-bit initial value (which must be the same at either end of the session) to initialise its internal registers prior to enciphering or deciphering the first end-user RU. This initial value is referred to as the session cryptography seed. The session cryptography seed is a non-zero, pseudo-random number chosen by the SLU. The SLU conveys to the PLU the session cryptography seed it has chosen for the session – enciphered under the session cryptography key for security – via the positive response for the BIND request. When the PLU receives the positive response to the BIND it extracts the enciphered cryptography seed and deciphers it using the session cryptography key. It then inverts (changes 0s to 1s and *vice versa*) the first 32 bits of the deciphered cryptography seed. This modified 'seed' is then enciphered, using the session cryptography key, and transmitted to the SLU via a CRV request. (A CRV request consists only of a request code and the enciphered 'seed'.) The SLU deciphers the seed conveyed in the CRV, inverts the first 32 bits and compares this value with the seed it chose. If they match, it indicates that not only did the PLU receive the seed correctly but also that the session cryptography key being used by the PLU and the SLU are the same. A successful match is signalled to the PLU by means of a positive response to the CRV. Once the PLU receives the positive response to the CRV, end-user data transfer can begin. If supported, an SDT will be issued on receipt of the positive response to the CRV. If the SLU finds that the seed it received did not match the seed it chose for the session, a negative response will be issued. On receipt of a negative response to the CRV the PLU will deactivate the session. (Once the cryptographic seed has been exchanged, using the response to the BIND, and verified, using CRV and its response, the actual seed that will be used by the algorithm as its initial value is the original seed with its first 32 bits inverted.)

In addition to session-level cryptography SNA supports two other 'levels' of cryptography referred to as *private cryptography* and *end-user cryptography*. With the former, both the session cryptographic key and the cryptographic algorithm (or protocols) are privately supplied by the end user, while in the latter the SSCP(s) specify the session cryptography key – as in session-level cryptography – but the algorithm (or protocols) are privately supplied by the end users.

Data flow control

The data flow component of a half-session is responsible for the following:

1 Chaining – the facility to enable a series of related, but separately transmitted, requests to be grouped together to form a message.
2 Brackets – a set of protocols to enable a series of requests and responses representing a specific unit of work – say an end-user transaction – to be delimited and, as such, be identifiable as a total entity.
3 Controlling the transmit and receive mode of the half-session, ie can both half-sessions transmit concurrently (full-duplex) or can only one half-session transmit at a time (half-duplex)?
4 Imposing the appropriate request and response control modes – *viz* immediate or delayed request mode and immediate or delayed response mode – specified for the half-session at session activation.

5 Assigning sequence numbers to normal-flow requests.
6 Correlating responses with the requests they refer to.
7 Providing a mechanism to temporarily interrupt the flow of normal-flow requests – in a given direction – without disrupting the other protocols being used within the session to control the flow of requests (and responses).

Chaining

Chaining provides a means whereby a transmitting half-session can indicate to its session partner that a series of requests that it is transmitting are all a part of the same message and should be treated as a group, rather than as a set of individual requests. Thus, a message that might be too long, either in terms of intermediate buffers at the receiving end or in terms of efficient error recovery, or is not available in its entirety at the start of its transmission, can still be conveyed, processed and, if an error is encountered in it, recovered, as a total entity.

The maximum request unit size that can be transmitted in each direction of an LU–LU session is agreed upon at session activation, ie the maximum RU size for each direction is specified in the BIND request. The ability to chain requests together ensures that the maximum RU size that can be transmitted in a given direction does not constrict the length of end-user messages that can be transmitted on that session.

A chain consists of one or more request units that belong to the same flow (normal or expedited flow) and are flowing in the same direction.

Two bits are provided in request headers (and for that matter, in response headers too) to support chaining: *begin chain indicator* (BCI) and *end chain indicator* (ECI). (The following notation is used when describing the composition of a chain in terms of these two indicators. If BCI and ECI are on, ie set to 1, they are referred to as BC and EC respectively. If they are off, ie set to 0, they are referred to as ¬BC and ¬EC.)

For consistency, all requests and responses that flow within any SNA session are thought of in terms of chains. However, multi-unit requests or responses are not always required, applicable or permitted. In such instances a 'chain' can consist of a single unit – a single-RU chain. Responses, expedited-flow requests and SNA commands that flow on the normal-flow can only ever be transmitted as single-RU chains. (As such multi-RU chains will only be used with end-user data.) The RUs of a multi-RU chain must be transmitted in the correct sequence, with respect to the message they are conveying.

The first request unit of a multi-RU chain has BCI and ECI set as BC, ¬EC. The last request unit of a multi-RU chain has BCI and ECI set as ¬BC, EC. The request units of a multi-RU chain that are neither the first nor the last RU, ie the request units in the middle, have BCI and ECI set as ¬BC, ¬EC. Single-RU chains have BCI and ECI set as BC, EC (referred to as 'only in chain').

A chain is the basic unit of error recovery within a session. As such, each chain can only have, at most, one response. Only three types of chain, differentiated by the type of response each requires, are permitted:

- No-response chains: each request in the chain specifies 'no-response'
- Exception-response chains: each request in the chain specifies 'exception response'
- Definite-response chains: the last (or only in the case of a single-RU chain) request in the chain specifies 'definite response'; all the other requests specify 'exception response'.

If the receiver of a chain detects an error in one of the requests of the chain it will proceed to discard all further requests of that chain until it receives either a request indicating end-of-chain, ie ¬BC, EC, a CANCEL request or a session-control request such as CLEAR or UNBIND. If the request in error was a part of an exception-response or definite-response chain, a negative response would be sent to the transmitter.

A transmitter of a chain may terminate that chain prior to transmitting the end-of-chain RU by issuing a CANCEL request. On receipt of a CANCEL request, the receiver of a chain may discard all previously received requests that were part of the chain. A CANCEL request is sent by the transmitter of a chain either because it detected an error in one of the requests of the chain, is unable to complete the chain or received a negative response to a request in the chain. (Whether the receiver of a CANCEL request discards all previously received requests in that chain, irrespective of why the CANCEL was issued, depends on how the receiver of the chain processes each individual request. Some LUs – especially those serving terminal operator or I/O device end users – tend to dispatch requests to the end user as they are received rather than when the complete chain has been received. In such instances, the 'processing' of the requests received prior to the CANCEL is left as an implementational option. The same applies if the transmitter of a chain aborts it prematurely following a negative response, by issuing an end-of-chain RU.)

Brackets

Whereas chaining enabled a series of requests to be grouped together to form a complete message, brackets provide a means of grouping together a series of messages and their responses – flowing in either or both directions – that represent a unit of work. As such a bracket delimits, or, as the name suggests, literally brackets, a series of requests and their responses, in either or both directions, that form a unit of work. Brackets prevent unrelated or unsolicited requests (or responses) interfering with the integrity of a specific unit of work.

A good example of a unit of work that could be delimited by a bracket is a database enquiry or update transaction from a terminal-operator end user. The first request from the terminal to the LU serving the application program managing the database, soliciting information from the database, will indicate that it is the start of a bracket – in much the same manner that a '(' is used when writing to delimit and isolate a group of sentences. Once the application program has received the enquiry and ascertained that it is valid and feasible, it will issue a positive response, if a definite response was requested. It will then access the database, extract the relevant information and transmit the information to the terminal-operator end user via their respective LUs, either in the form of a single request or a series of requests, ie as a chain.

These requests to the terminal operator will not contain any indication of brackets, ie these requests are within the bracket started by the initial request. (But if one of these requests indicated that it was the start of a bracket, the LU serving the terminal operator would know that this request – or if it is the start of a chain, the chain – is not related to the bracket initiated by the terminal operator.) The terminal operator, on receipt of the request(s) containing the information from the database – and following the issue of a response if one was requested – may decide to update certain records containing the information it sought. To achieve this, it will issue a series of requests, ie a chain. As these requests are still part of the original transaction they do not contain any indication of brackets, ie they are part of the original bracket. Once the terminal operator has received confirmation, in the form of a request(s), from the application program that the database update was successful, it may decide that no further related enquiries or updates are required and that it should terminate the current transaction and also the bracket. The bracket is terminated by the terminal operator issuing a request indicating 'end of bracket'. Figure 5.7 summarises the above transaction.

A bracket is defined as being a series of normal-flow chains and their responses, transmitted in either or both directions, between the two half-sessions of an LU–LU session. Therefore, a bracket may consist of the following:

- One request (ie Only in chain, specifying no response)
- One request and its response (ie Only in chain, specifying definite response)
- A series of requests (ie a no-response chain)
- A series of requests and a response (ie definite-response chain)
- A series of chains.

Whether or not brackets are to be used within a given LU–LU session is specified in the BIND request for that session. If brackets are to be used, all normal-flow transmissions within that session will be conducted in terms of brackets. When brackets are to be used, the BIND request will also specify the half-session that will have priority if a contention condition arises by both LUs trying to begin a bracket at the same time, whether only one or both half-sessions can terminate a bracket and one of two possible rules on how a bracket is terminated. The half-session that has priority in a 'begin bracket contention' condition is referred to as the *first speaker*, while the other half-session is referred to as the *bidder*, in the context of bracket usage.

The designated first speaker of a session can begin a bracket without seeking permission from the other half-session to do so.

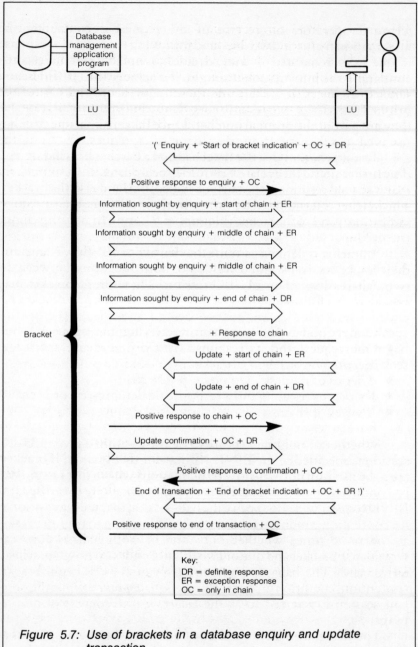

Figure 5.7: *Use of brackets in a database enquiry and update transaction*

Key:
DR = definite response
ER = exception response
OC = only in chain

However, the bidder must request and receive permission from the first speaker before it may begin a bracket.

Two bits are provided on request headers (but not on response headers) to support brackets: *begin bracket indicator* (BBI) and *end bracket indicator* (EBI). (The same notations as used with BCI and ECI are used with these two indicators to denote their setting. BB and EB denote that the indicators are on, while ¬BB and ¬EB denote that they are off.)

The first request, of the first chain, of a bracket has BBI set to 1. The first request, of the last chain, of a bracket has EBI set to 1. All the other requests within the bracket have both BBI and EBI set to 0. A bracket that consists of a single chain has both BBI and EBI set to 1, on the first request of the chain. (Note, that BBI or EBI may only be set on the first or only request of a chain, and not on subsequent requests. If the transmitter of a chain aborts the chain with a CANCEL request, EB may be sent with the CANCEL.)

A half-session can only have one bracket, ie one request that was issued with BB, outstanding at any one time. When a bracket has ended – referred to as the session being *between brackets* – the first speaker may unilaterally start another bracket; but a bidder cannot begin a bracket without the consent of the first speaker. A bidder seeks permission to begin a bracket in one of two possible ways:

1   By issuing a BID request.
2   By transmitting a chain whose first request specifies BB – known as an 'implied bid'. (If the bracket being started is to consist of a single chain the first request of that chain must specify BB and EB and the chain can be a no-response, exception-response or definite-response chain. However, if the bracket is to be a multi-chain bracket, the first chain must be a definite-response chain.)

In either case, permission is granted with a positive response, or denied with a negative response. If permission was sought with a BID request and the permission was granted, the first speaker enters receive mode and awaits the receipt of a chain whose first request will specify BB. (If a negative response is returned for an implied bid, ie permission was not granted, the bidder will need to retransmit that chain, at a later stage, as the first speaker would not have processed the original chain.)

If the first speaker prevents the bidder from starting a bracket by sending a negative response to either a BID or an implied bid, it may send a *ready to receive* (RTR) request to the bidder at a later stage to indicate that the bidder may now initiate a bracket if it so desires. Whether or not RTR will be sent at a later stage is indicated in the negative response by means of two different sense codes. A sense code of X'0813' indicates 'Bracket Bid Rejected – No RTR Forthcoming', while a sense code of X'0814' indicates 'Bracket Bid Rejected – RTR Forthcoming'. A first speaker's promise to send an RTR when it is ready to accept a bracket does not preclude – nor necessarily deter – the bidder from persevering with further bids before it receives the RTR. The first speaker may grant permission to one of these bids, even though it has not sent the promised RTR! (In the case of the RTR not being sent the bidder must carry on bidding if it still needs to begin a bracket, using explicit or implied bids.) When a bidder receives an RTR it may issue either a positive response to indicate that it will initiate the next bracket or a negative response to indicate that it will not. On receipt of a positive response to an RTR the first speaker must enter receive mode and wait for a chain whose first request specifies BB.

Whether only one half-session (and, if so, which one) or both half-sessions may terminate a bracket, irrespective of who started the bracket, is specified in the BIND request. In addition, one of the two following bracket termination rules is specified for each session using brackets:

1   Bracket Termination Rule 1 (conditional termination).
2   Bracket Termination Rule 2 (unconditional termination).

Bracket termination rule 1 (conditional termination)

When the bracket is to end, ie when the scope of that bracket is to be terminated, depends on the type of request expected by the last chain of that bracket. If the last chain is a definite-response chain, the bracket is terminated when the transmitter of the last chain receives a positive response to that chain. If, however, a negative response is issued to the last chain the bracket is not terminated. (A negative response to an intermediate chain in the bracket gives the half-session that transmitted that chain the option of terminating or continuing the bracket. It may terminate the bracket by issuing a CANCEL request with EB or by ending the chain with a request specifying exception or no-response, or it may continue the bracket by issuing a CANCEL request with EB or by ending the chain with a request specifying definite response.)

If the last chain of the bracket specifies that it is a no-response chain or an exception-response chain, the bracket is terminated, unconditionally, when the last request of the last chain of the bracket is processed.

If the bracket consists of a single chain (first request of the chain specifies BB and EB) the bracket is terminated, unconditionally, when the last request of the chain is processed, irrespective of the type of response defined for the chain.

Bracket termination rule 2 (unconditional termination)

A bracket is terminated unconditionally when the last request of the last chain of the bracket is processed, irrespective of the type of response defined for that chain.

Figure 5.8 illustrates some of the principles of bracket usage.

Two SNA commands are provided to enable the half-session of an LU-LU session to stop the initiation of new brackets within that session: *stop bracket initiation* (SBI) and *bracket initiation stopped* (BIS). The support of these two commands is not compulsory. Whether or not they are to be supported is specified in the BIND request for the session.

SBI can be sent by either half-session to request the other half-session to cease initiation of further brackets. The receiver of an SBI request does not necessarily have to stop the initialisation of further brackets immediately. However, when it does decide to cease initialising further brackets it must notify the other half-session of this by issuing a BIS request. (SBI and BIS are normally used to stop the data traffic in an LU-LU session in an orderly and controlled manner prior to the session being deactivated.)

Send/ receive modes

Even though it would be conceptually convenient, and more efficient operationally for all sessions to be capable of full-duplex data transfer, all NAUs may not have sufficient processing or

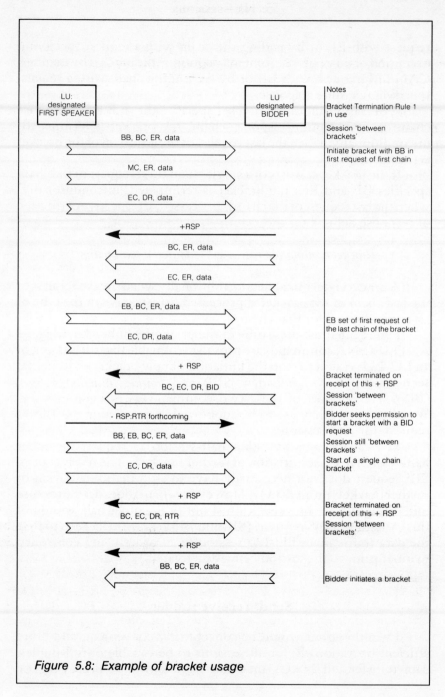

Figure 5.8: Example of bracket usage

storage resources to support full-duplex operation. Therefore SNA caters for both full- and half-duplex modes of operation at a session level (totally independent of the mode of data transfer of the physical links allocated by the Path Control Network for a session). Four modes, referred to as the *send/receive modes*, are defined by SNA to coordinate the transmission and reception of normal-flow requests within a session. Three of them are variations of half-duplex operation. The four modes are as follows:

1 *Full-duplex* (FDX)
2 *Half-duplex flip-flop* (HDX-FF): without brackets
3 *Half-duplex flip-flop* (HDX-FF): with brackets
4 *Half-duplex-contention* (HDX-CONT).

The transmission and reception of expedited-flow requests or responses – either for normal-flow or expedited-flow requests – by a half-session, are not affected by the send/receive mode in force for the normal-flow requests. The send-receive mode for a given session is specified at session activation and stays in force for the duration of that session.

Full-duplex

Both half-sessions of a full-duplex session can transmit and receive normal-flow requests simultaneously.

Half-duplex flip-flop: without brackets

In this mode the two half-sessions take turns in being the sender and receiver of normal-flow requests. The sender transmits normal-flow requests to the receiver, while the receiver issues the relevant responses. The receiver of an HDX-FF session can only become the sender if the current sender gives it explicit permission to do so. This permission is granted by means of a bit (the *change direction indicator* (CDI)) in the request header. When the sender completes the transmission of a batch of normal-flow requests (which could be one or more chains) and expects replies, not responses, to these requests from its session partner, it transfers the 'send capability' to its partner. It does this by setting the CDI to 1 in the last normal-flow request it transmits. A half-session on receipt of a normal-flow request that has CDI set to 1 in its RH, can begin transmission of normal-flow requests to the new receiver. (If a receiver, in an LU-LU session, has an urgent normal-flow request(s) to transmit, it can request its session partner to grant it permission to become the sender, ie request a CDI to be sent, by transmitting the SNA command *signal* (SIG), with a request code of 'request to send', on the expedited-flow.)

When a session is defined at session activation as using HDX-FF one of the half-sessions is designated as the first-sender. Following the activation of an HDX-FF session, or after a CLEAR command has been used to reset the data flow, the designated first-sender automatically becomes the sender.

Figure 5.9 illustrates normal-flow request transmission within an LU-LU session using HDX-FF: without brackets send/receive mode.

Half-duplex flip-flop: with brackets

When brackets are used with the HDX-FF mode of operation a first sender is not designated at session activation time as is the case when brackets are not being used. Instead, the bracket protocol's first-speaker and bidder conventions are used to determine the half-session that will initiate transmission – ie begin a bracket – whenever the session is 'between brackets'. However, once a bracket has been initiated, the same HDX-FF protocol specified for when brackets are not being used (ie the receiver can only become the sender of normal-flow requests if it receives a request with the CDI bit in the RH set to 1) applies for the duration of that bracket.

Half-duplex-contention

In this mode either half-session may unilaterally begin transmitting normal-flow requests. If both attempt to transmit simultaneously, a contention condition occurs. Such contention is resolved by designating one of the half-sessions as the 'contention winner' at session activation time.

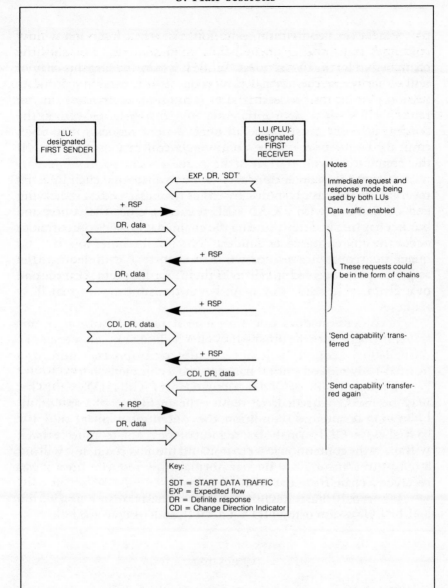

Figure 5.9: Normal-flow request transmission within an LU-LU session using HDX-FF: without brackets send/receive mode

Whenever a contention condition arises the contention winner continues transmitting normal-flow requests until it finishes the chain begun by the first request. While it is transmitting this chain it will either queue the normal-flow requests it is receiving from its session partner for processing after it has finished transmitting or reject them with an appropriate negative response. However, the contention loser must queue all normal-flow requests it receives from the contention winner, following a contention condition. (If the contention winner rejects the requests sent to it while it is transmitting, the contention loser will terminate that chain when it receives the negative response by either issuing a request specifying end-of-chain or with a CANCEL request.) Once the contention winner has finished transmitting the chain that caused contention to occur the contention loser (and the contention winner too, if it did queue the request it received while transmitting) will dequeue the requests it has received and process them. At this point, ie at the end of a chain, either side can again begin transmitting normal-flow requests.

If contention does not arise – ie if one half-session begins transmitting before the other – the other half-session, on receipt of a normal-flow request, will not attempt to begin transmitting a normal-flow request until it has received a complete chain.

Though the use of CDI is not mandatory with HDX-CONT it may be used, if needed, to reduce the incidence of contention. Following a contention condition, the contention winner could, if it so wishes, set CDI on in the last request of the chain, to indicate that it will allow the contention loser to transmit the next chain, ie it will not attempt to transmit any further normal-flow requests until it has received a chain from the contention loser.

Figure 5.10 illustrates normal-flow request transmission within an LU-LU session using HDX-CONT send/receive mode.

Quiescing

The DFC components of LU-LU sessions support a protocol, referred to as the *quiesce protocol*, which allows either half-session to temporarily stop its partner from transmitting requests on the normal-flow. (That is, as the term 'quiesce' suggests, ask its partner to become silent.) Quiescing is normally

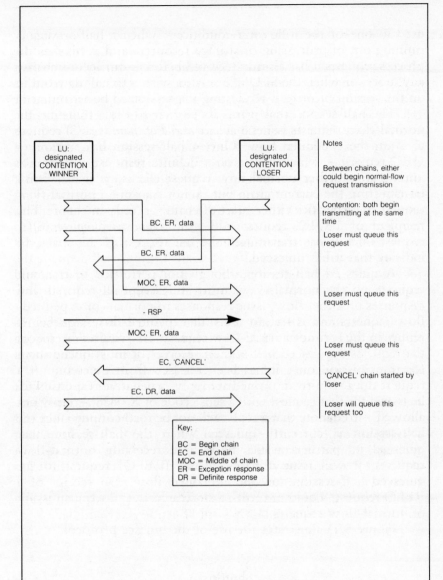

Figure 5.10: Normal-flow request transmission within an LU-LU session using HDX-CONT send/receive mode

used in one of the following conditions: when a half-session is running out of processing or storage resources and needs time to process requests it has already received before it can accommodate any more; or when the SLU of a session wishes to halt data traffic on the session prior to it requesting the session to be terminated.

The half-session that wants its partner to cease transmitting normal-flow requests issues a *quiesce at end of chain* (QEC) request to it on the expedited flow. Once a half-session has received a QEC request – which insists on a definite response – it cannot initiate any further normal-flow request chains, ie it can finish transmitting the current chain but cannot transmit a normal-flow request that specifies either 'start of chain' or 'only in chain'. The recipient of a QEC request will issue a *quiesce complete* (QC) request once it has transmitted the last request of the chain, to indicate that it has quiesced.

A quiesced half-session, though not permitted to transmit requests on the normal-flow, must still accept all requests and responses on either flow, issue responses to normal- or expedited-flow requests and is free to transmit expedited-flow requests. If replies in the form of normal-flow requests are required by any of the requests a quiesced half-session receives, it must queue them for transmission once it has been released from quiescing. If a request does require an immediate reply, a negative response will be issued for that request with a sense code of X'0828' – 'reply not allowed' – to denote that a reply will not be forthcoming since the half-session is currently quiesced. When the half-session that quiesced its partner wishes to resume receiving normal-flow requests, it will issue a *release quiesce* (RELQ) request to the quiesced half-session, on the expedited flow. On receipt of a RELQ request, a quiesced half-session can restart the transmission of normal-flow requests.

Figure 5.11 illustrates the use of the quiesce protocol.

Shutdown

In addition to the quiesce protocol, which either half-session can invoke and which permits the traffic on the normal flow to be temporarily halted, the DFC components of LU-LU sessions also provide a *shutdown protocol*. This enables the PLU of a session to

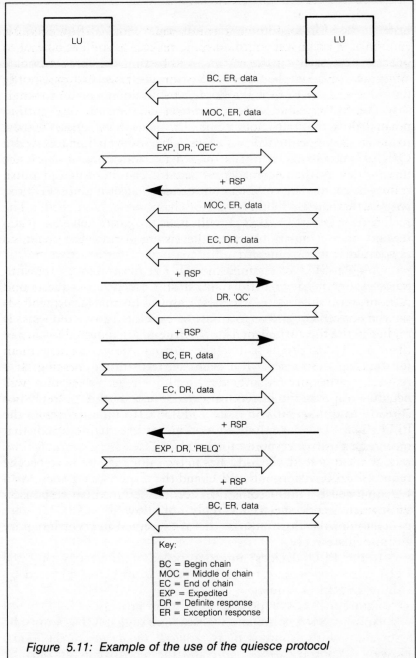

Figure 5.11: Example of the use of the quiesce protocol

instruct the SLU to stop the transmission of normal-flow requests as soon as it is convenient to do so (ie quiesce as soon as possible – but not necessarily at the end of transmitting the current chain). Whereas QEC implies that the stop in transmission is only temporary, ie a RELQ will follow, 'shutdown' normally indicates that the SLU will not be permitted to transmit any further normal-flow requests following the 'shutdown' prior to the session being deactivated. As such, 'shutdown' is invoked when the PLU intends to terminate the session and wishes to stop the flow of data traffic in an orderly manner. The shutdown protocol is implemented via two SNA commands: *shutdown* (SHUTD) and *shutdown complete* (SHUTC).

A PLU issues a SHUTD request on the expedited flow when it wants the secondary to stop transmitting normal-flow requests as soon as it is convenient (and prepare itself for deactivating the session). An SLU receiving a SHUTD request does not have to quiesce after it has finished transmitting the current chain, as it does on receiving a QEC request. The SLU can decide when it will be convenient and appropriate to quiesce, eg it could quiesce at the end of the current bracket. Before quiescing, the SLU may issue a CHASE request (on the normal flow), to solicit all outstanding responses to previously transmitted normal-flow requests so that any requests that might have been rejected with a negative response can be retransmitted if necessary. Once the SLU is ready to quiesce, it will issue a SHUTC to indicate this to the PLU. The SLU enters 'shutdown' (ie quiesced) mode when it receives a positive response to the SHUTC.

While quiesced, the SLU acts in the same manner in respect of requests it receives from the PLU and the responses it issues, as an LU quiesced by means of a QEC request. (Negative responses, with a sense code specifying 'reply not allowed' – X'0828' – are issued to normal-flow requests that are received and which require an immediate reply.)

If the PLU decides not to proceed with deactivating the LU-LU session it may release the SLU from being quiesced by issuing an RELQ request.

Figure 5.12 illustrates the 'shutdown' process.

Another SNA command whose name suggests that it must be associated with shutdown is *request shutdown* (RSHUTD). However, contrary to its name and the fact that it can only be

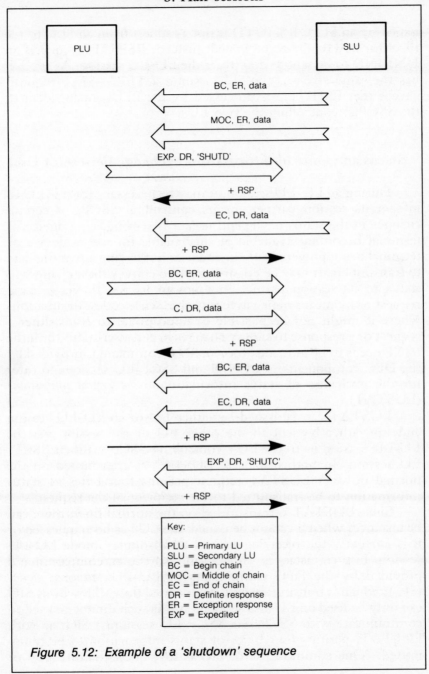

Figure 5.12: Example of a 'shutdown' sequence

issued by an SLU, RSHUTD is not a request from an SLU to the PLU for a SHUTD to be issued! Instead, RSHUTD requests an UNBIND to be sent to deactivate the LU-LU session. As such, it has the same effect as the SLU issuing a TERM-SELF request, except that RSHUTD is processed by the PLU, independent of the SSCP(s) controlling the two LUs.

Status and control information exchange between LUs

During an LU-LU session, it may be necessary for one LU to inform its session partner, or its controlling SSCP, of certain changes in the status of the end user it is serving, eg a device or terminal becoming available or unavailable for use, a device or terminal being powered-off, an end user not having any more data to transmit etc. It may be possible for it to convey these changes in status to its session partner, but not to its SSCP, via a 'data' request or by means of negative response sense codes. In situations where it might not be possible or appropriate to issue either a request or a response to signify changes in end-user status, or if the SSCP needs to be informed too, an SNA command is provided by the DFC components of LU-LU and SSCP-LU sessions to cater for the exchange of status information: it is *logical unit status* (LUSTAT).

LUSTAT can be issued by either LU of an LU-LU session and can either be sent to the other LU of the session via the LU-LU session or to the LU's controlling SSCP via their SSCP-LU session. In both instances, LUSTAT is transmitted on the normal flow. A LUSTAT request permits four bytes of status information to be transmitted to the recipient of the request.

Since LUSTAT is transmitted on the normal flow, there can be instances when it cannot be issued: the LU has been quiesced or it is currently the receiving LU in a half-duplex mode LU-LU session. In such instances, an LU can resort to another command provided by the DFC components of LU-LU sessions, *signal* (SIG), which is transmitted on the expedited flow. (However, SIG can only be used on LU-LU sessions and as such cannot be used to communicate with SSCPs via SSCP-LU sessions.) SIG, as with LUSTAT, permits four bytes of status information to be transmitted. (One common use of SIG is to request the direction of transmission to be changed in an LU-LU session using HDX-FF mode of transmission.)

Sync points

On certain LU-LU sessions the successful completion of specific units of work – such as updating or deleting a database entry – is critical to the maintenance of the integrity of the system and provisions need to be made to 'back-track' units of work if they did not complete satisfactorily. This is true particularly of those LU-LU sessions serving a transaction processing system: between a database management application program end user and terminal operator end users or between two database management application program end users. The means by which SNA caters for this requirement is referred to as *sync point* processing.

Sync points operate on the principle of allowing an end user to reserve for its exclusive use the resources it needs to complete a unit of work and ensuring that the LU serving that end user records all changes made to these resources in the form of the state prior to each change and the state following each change while each unit of work is being processed. If a unit of work completed satisfactorily the LU can discard the information it recorded on the changes made to the resources as it will not need to 'back-track' the resources to the state they were in prior to the beginning of the unit of work in question. A successful completion, which enables the LU to discard the change activity information, establishes a sync point and the unit of work processed is said to have been *committed*. If the unit of work did not complete satisfactorily, the LU can restore the resources to the state they were in prior to the unit of work beginning, by using the change activity information it recorded.

The resources that are protected by this mechanism against permanent corruption are referred to as protected resources. What constitutes a protected resource is an implementational option.

Whether or not sync points will be used by a given LU-LU session is specified in the BIND request for that session. If sync points are being used, either LU can inform the other LU that a unit of work has been successfully completed, eg successful termination of a bracket, and the change activity information being maintained for the protected resources by the LU can be discarded, ie the unit of work can be committed. An LU informs its partner that a unit of work has been committed by issuing it a '*commit*' request. A positive response to a 'commit' request establishes a new sync point, while a negative response results in both LUs restoring the relevant protected resources to the state they were in at the previous sync point.

An LU can ask its partner to issue a 'commit' request so that it can relinquish the change activity information it is maintaining for the protected resources that it is responsible for and establish a new sync point. An LU asks for a 'commit' request to be sent to it by means of a 'prepare' request. Whether or not '*prepare*' is supported is an implementational option. If it is not, the sync point process is referred to as being '*one-phase commit*' while, if 'prepare' is used, the process is referred to as being '*two-phase commit*', because a 'commit' will only be sent in reply to a 'prepare'.

There are no explicit SNA commands to represent 'commit' and 'prepare' requests. A 'commit' request is denoted by means of the response type indicator bits, *viz* DR1I, DR2I and ERI, in request headers. When sync points are being used in an LU-LU session, these three bits, in addition to specifying the type of response expected by the request, also indicate whether or not a unit of work has successfully completed and whether it can be committed or not as follows:

DR1I	DR2I	ERI	
0	0	0	} Unit of work not as yet
1	0	0	completed; it cannot be
1	0	1	committed
0	1	0	
0	1	1	} Commit unit of work
1	1	0	
1	1	1	

A 'prepare' request is conveyed either by means of a LUSTAT request (with a request mode of X'0005') or by means of a Type-10 function management header. (Function management headers are described in Chapter 6, *LU-LU sessions*.)

If sync points are being used by an LU-LU session they can still be used to ensure the integrity of the protected resources, even if the session fails and has to be reactivated. An SNA session control command *set and test sequence numbers* (STSN) and its response, which is one of the 17 responses that may contain data, is provided for this purpose. When sync points are in use, both half-sessions maintain two separate sets of sequence number counts. The first set is of the standard, normal-flow sequence number counts: the sequence numbers of the last normal-flow request transmitted and of the last valid normal-flow request received. The second set, referred to as the transaction processing program's sequence numbers, duplicate the standard set but, unlike the standard counts, cannot be reset by any SNA command (such as BIND) other than an STSN request specifying 'reset'. As such, these transaction processing program's sequence numbers can be used to determine the last normal-flow request transmitted and received by each half-session, prior to the session failing. If the counts agree at each end, ie no normal-flow requests were lost when the session failed, the processing of the interrupted unit of work could resume immediately without the need to 'back-track' to the last sync point and start the unit of work again. If the counts do not agree, they will have to be reset to the values at the last sync point, the protected resources restored to the state at that sync point and the unit of work which was interrupted restarted from the last sync point.

STSN, which can only be issued by a PLU, can be used either to reset the sequence numbers at the SLU (ie set), to ask the SLU to return (via the positive response to the STSN request) its current transaction processing program sequence numbers (ie sense), or to ask the SLU to check its current transaction processing program sequence numbers against the 'expected' sequence numbers specified in the STSN and respond if they do not agree (ie set and test). With each of these operations, it can be specified whether the operation applies to both sequence number counts at the SLU, ie transmit count and receive count, or to just one of the sequence number counts. (If STSN is to be used to resynchronise the normal-flow traffic, it must be issued immediately after the BIND has been processed and before other session control commands, such as SDT.)

Network services

FMDS components of SSCP-related sessions, viz SSCP-PU, SSCP-LU and SSCP-SSCP, in conjunction with the appropriate NAU services managers, support the network services requests and responses, which are used to control and monitor the configuration and operation of SNA environments. Five categories of network services request are defined:

1 *Network services: session services.*
2 *Network services: configuration services.*
3 *Network services: maintenance and management services.*
4 *Network services: measurement services.*
5 *Network services: network operator services.*

Network services: session services

These consist of the SNA commands used on SSCP-LU and SSCP-SSCP sessions to support the initiation and termination of LU-LU sessions – viz BINDF, CDCINIT, CDINIT, CDSES-SEND, CDSESSF, CDSESSST, CDSESSTF, CDTERM, CINIT, CTERM, INIT-OTHER, INIT-OTHER-CD, INIT-SELF, NOTIFY, NSPE, SESSEND, SESSST, TERM-OTHER, TERM-OTHER-CD, TERM-SELF and UNBINDF. These are as described in Chapter 4, *Sessions*. In addition to these commands, this category also includes four more: *cross-domain takedown* (CDTAKED), *cross-domain takedown complete* (CDTAKEDC), CLEANUP and *direct search list* (DSRLST).

CDTAKED can be issued by either SSCP of an SSCP-SSCP session to request the other SSCP to initiate the termination of all cross-domain LU-LU sessions that have been established between LUs in their respective domains, and to stop initiating any further cross-domain LU-LU sessions with LUs in the domain controlled by the SSCP issuing the CDTAKED.

CDTAKEDC is sent by each SSCP to the other – after one of them has issued CDTAKED – once each has finished terminating the relevant cross-domain LU-LU sessions in its domain.

CLEANUP is issued by an SSCP to an SLU (in a subarea node) to request that it attempts to deactivate the LU-LU session specified in the CLEANUP request.

DSRLST is issued by one SSCP to another SSCP – via their SSCP-SSCP session – to solicit status information pertaining to the LU-LU session-supporting capabilities of an LU in the other SSCP's domain.

Network services: configuration services

These are the SNA commands used on SSCP-PU sessions to execute the following activities:

- Activate and deactivate Path Control Network components
- Convey status changes in Path Control Network components
- Load Type 4 or Type 2 nodes with control software
- Request that a node is loaded with control software
- Obtain storage dumps from Type 4 nodes
- Dynamically assign network addresses
- Convey status changes in resources, within a node, associated with that node's physical configuration.

These SNA commands will be discussed in Chapter 7, *The Path Control Network*.

Network services: maintenance and management services

These are the SNA commands used on SSCP-PU and SSCP-LU sessions to:

- Activate and deactivate diagnostic procedures, such as traces and tests
- Convey data obtained from diagnostic procedures
- Record statistics on various resources.

These commands will be discussed in Chapter 7, *The Path Control Network*.

Network services: measurement services

No SNA commands have been defined as yet to provide measurement services. At present, any measurements performed on any resources within an SNA environment will be implementation dependent.

Network services: network operator services

Again no SNA commands have been defined as yet to provide an interface between SSCPs and the operator(s) controlling the SNA environment. At present the interfaces used are implementation dependent.

Implementational notes

Requests/responses

An ACF/VTAM application program uses the ACF/VTAM SEND macro to transmit end-user data and DFC-related requests, and the responses to end-user data requests and DFC-related requests. With the SEND macro, in common with most other ACF/VTAM macros, the macro operands are not supplied directly, but via a control block set up by another macro: the Request Parameter List (RPL) macro. A SEND macro refers to an RPL control block – by name – which will contain the operands it should use. The operands in an RPL control block can be specified either when the RPL is being created, via a Modify Control Block (MODCB) macro or by specifying the relevant operands in the macro which refer to the RPL control block, along with the name of the RPL.

The STYPE= operand in the RPL denotes whether the SEND macro is to transmit a request or a response. STYPE=REQ indicates a request, while STYPE=RESP indicates a response. When a request is being transmitted the CONTROL= operand – in the RPL – specifies whether the request contains end-user data, *viz* CONTROL=DATA, or a DFC-related SNA command. When a DFC-related command is to be transmitted, the CONTROL= operand will specify the command by name (or by an abbreviation of the name), *viz* BID, BIS, CANCEL, CHASE, LUS (ie LUSTAT), QC, QEC, RELQ, RSHUTD, RTR, SBI, SHUTC, SHUTD and SIGNAL. (The four bytes of status information conveyed with a LUSTAT command are specified by means of the RPL operands SSENSEO, SSENSMO and USENSEO, while the four bytes of data conveyed by a SIGNAL command are specified via the SIGDATA= operand.) When a response is being transmitted the CONTROL= operand, using the same keywords as for a request transmission, specifies the type of request being responded to. If end-user data is being transmitted, the AREA= operand specifies the start address of the data and the RECLEN= operand specifies the number of bytes of data to be transmitted.

If a response is expected to a request transmitted by a SEND macro, three different methods of obtaining it are available. If a definite response was sought, the response could be obtained directly via the SEND macro itself. POST=RESP will indicate that the SEND macro will only complete once a response has been received for the request that was transmitted and has been stored in the relevant fields within the RPL in use. If a definite response was not sought or if the program does not want to wait until it receives a response to a request transmitted, POST=SCHED can be specified and the response obtained at a later stage either via a RECEIVE macro or by means of a 'response' exit-routine, which will be activated when a response is received by ACF/VTAM.

Session Control (SC)-related requests or responses are transmitted not by means of the SEND macro, but by a SESSIONC macro. As in the case of a SEND macro, the operands for SESSIONC are specified via an RPL. STYPE=REQ or STYPE=RESP indicates whether a request or response is to be transmitted by the SESSIONC macro. If an ACF/VTAM application program is the PLU of an LU-LU session it may issue SDT, CLEAR and STSN commands via SESSIONC. The command to be issued is denoted via the CONTROL= operand by means of the keywords SDT, CLEAR or STSN. If an application program is the SLU of an LU-LU session, it can use SESSIONC to issue an RQR request (CONTROL=RQR) or the responses to BIND, SDT or STSN requests. When a response is being transmitted, the CONTROL= operand denotes the type of request it refers to. If an SDT, CLEAR or STSN command is issued by a SESSIONC, it will only complete once it has received a response to the request transmitted, ie equivalent to using SEND with POST=RESP.

ACT/VTAM application programs use the RECEIVE macro to 'read-in' end-user data requests or DFC-related requests that have been sent to it by its session partners. As with the SEND macro, the operands for a RECEIVE macro are specified via an RPL. The AREA= operand specifies the start address into which end-user data should be read, while the AREALEN= indicates the maximum length that may be read in. Only the actual data portion of an end-user data request is read into the area specified by AREA=. The information contained in the request header and, in the case of DFC-related requests, the keyword denoting the command, is placed in the relevant fields of the RPL being used. The CONTROL= operand of the RPL is updated on the completion of a RECEIVE to indicate the type of response that has been read in. The same CONTROL= keywords as those used in the SEND macro, *viz* DATA, BID, BIS, LUS etc, are used. The RECEIVE macro can also be used to obtain responses to requests issued on the normal flow. (ACF/VTAM application programs cannot receive responses to requests issued on the expedited flow. These responses are intercepted and processed by ACF/VTAM itself.)

The RTYPE= operand specifies the type of input that will satisfy a given RECEIVE operation. The keyword DFSYN indicates that the RECEIVE can read in either an end-user data request or a DFC-related request transmitted on the normal flow. The keyword DFASY indicates that the RECEIVE should only read in a DFC-related request transmitted on the expedited flow, while the keyword RESP indicates that the RECEIVE should only read in a response to a normal-flow request. An 'N' prefixed to either of these three keywords – NDFSIN, NDFASY or NRESP – indicates that the corresponding type of input will not satisfy the RECEIVE operation. Multiple keywords, including the 'negative' keywords, can be specified for the RESP= operand if more than one type of input will satisfy the RECEIVE operation.

Specifying response type

The type of response expected by a given request transmitted

by a SEND macro is specified by means of the RPL operand
RESPOND=. Three keywords, EX, FME and RRN, along with
their negative 'settings', NEX, NFME and NRRN, are used as
follows:

No-response expected:	¬ **DR1I,¬DR2I,¬ERI = NEX,NFME,NRRN**
Definite response expected:	**DR1I,¬DR2I,¬ERI = NEX,FME,NRRN**
Definite response expected:	¬ **DR1I,DR2I,¬ERI = NEX,NFME,RRN**
Definite response expected:	**DR1I,DR2I,¬ERI = NEX,FME,RRN**
Exception response expected:	**DR1I,¬DR2I,ERI = EX,FME,NRRN**
Exception response expected:	¬ **DR1I,DR2I,ERI = EX,NFME,RRN**
Exception response expected:	**DR1I,DR2I,ERI = EX,FME,RRN**

If a response is being transmitted by the SEND macro, the
RESPOND= with the same keywords as used when specifying
the type of response expected is used to specify the type of
response. NEX indicates a positive response, while EX indicates a
negative response. FME indicates DR1I being set, RRN indicates
DR2I being set while their negative settings indicate that the
respective indicators are not set. (With Session Control requests
transmitted with a SESSIONC macro, the response type expected
is not explicitly specified; a definite response with DR1I and
¬DR2I is automatically assigned.)

The RESPOND= operand, in the RPL being used, is updated when a request or response is read in by the RECEIVE
macro. In the case of a response, RESPOND= will indicate, by
means of the same keywords as used in SEND, the type of
response, while with a request it will specify the type of response
expected by the request.

Sequence numbers

ACF/VTAM will automatically assign sequence numbers to
normal-flow requests transmitted by an ACF/VTAM application

program. ACF/VTAM will also ensure that normal–flow requests destined for ACF/VTAM application programs are in sequence. If ACF/VTAM detects an out–of–sequence request it will issue an exception request to the relevant application program to notify it that an error in transmission has occurred.

An application program must specify the sequence number of the request being responded to when it issues a response. This is done via the RPL operand SEQNO=.

Chaining

The position of a given request within a chain, whether the request is being transmitted or received, is specified via the RPL operand CHAIN= and the keywords FIRST, MIDDLE, LAST or ONLY.

Brackets

The position of a given chain within a bracket is specified via the RPL operand BRACKET=, when the first or only request of each chain is being transmitted or received. The keywords BB and EB, along with their negative settings NBB and NEB, are used to specify the following:

- Beginning of a bracket = BB, NEB
- Middle of a bracket = NBB, NEB
- End of a bracket = NBB, EB
- Only in bracket = BB, EB.

Requests that specify middle of, or last in, chain must have BRACKET= set to (NBB, NEB).

Change direction indicator

If a half–duplex transmission mode is being used, the RPL operand CHNGDIR= specifies when a request is being transmitted or indicates when one has been received, and whether the CDI bit should be, or is, set. The key-word CMD corresponds to CDI being set to 1, while NCMD corresponds to CDI being set to 0.

Cryptography

The ACF/VTAM Encrypt/Decrypt Feature, the 'Programmed Cryptographic Facility' program product and the relevant encrypt/decrypt features on terminal or I/O device control units need to be installed if encryption is to be used in an ACF/VTAM environment.

The 'Programmed Cryptographic Facility' generates and stores the cryptographic keys to be used in the environment.

The ENCR= operand in ACF/VTAM minor-node definition macros APPL, PU and LU specify the 'level' of cryptography – required (REQD), selective (SEL), optional (OPT) or none (NONE) – that will be used by LUs serving application program, terminal or I/O device end users.

The RPL operand CRYPT=YES or CRYPT=NO specifies whether a request being transmitted by a SEND macro is to be enciphered or whether a request read in by a RECEIVE macro is enciphered.

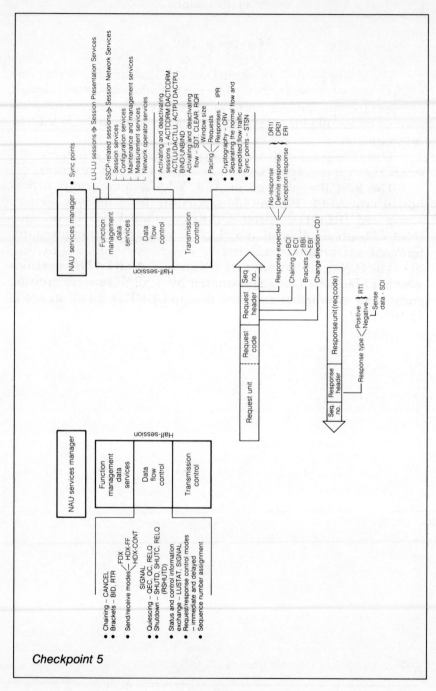

Checkpoint 5

Chapter 6:
LU–LU sessions

☐ Profiles ☐ TS Profiles ☐ FM Profiles ☐ PS Profiles ☐ LU–LU Session Types ☐ Peer-to-peer Sessions ☐ Non-SSCP Environments ☐ Function Management Headers ☐ Data Compression and Data Compaction ☐ SCB ☐ BIND Request ☐ URC ☐ BIND Response

Chapter 6:
LU–LU sessions

Overview

An end user accesses an SNA environment through an LU, so that it can communicate with other end users via LU–LU sessions. Each of the end-user types, and different end users within each type, have different functional characteristics and capabilities which in turn dictate their communications requirements and capabilities. Since LUs are the only means by which end users can access and utilise an SNA environment, LUs need to cater not only to the communications requirements *per se* of a given end user, but also to the provision of an efficient, reliable and usable 'access mechanism' whereby the end user can transmit and receive data and status information to and from the SNA environment. However, the precise end user/LU association for a given end user – while being implementation dependent anyway, as discussed in Chapter 3 – is only of generic interest. It is what an end user intends to do once access has been gained to an SNA environment which is crucial in terms of 'access mechanism' and communication requirements, that need to be catered for.

All end-user-to-end-user interactions are based on LU–LU sessions. Hence, an end user's 'access', communications requirements and capabilities can be specified in terms of the characteristics of the LU–LU sessions the end user proposes to participate in, rather than in terms of the end user/LU association (or interface). This has the added benefit of an end user, while using the same end user/LU association, being able to have different types of dialogue with other end users, either concurrently or one at a time.

The characteristics of any SNA session are totally dictated by the functions provided and performed by the two half-sessions forming that session. (The Path Control Network is effectively a 'transparent' communications path for a session and NAU services managers always work in conjunction with the FMDS components of half-sessions.) So the different types of LU-LU session that are needed to satisfy the requirements of the three end-user types, and the different end user within each type, can be defined in terms of the type of end user at either end of the session and the functions that need to be provided and performed by the two half-sessions forming that session to support the 'access' and communications requirements of the two end users.

The functional repertoire of any half-session is clearly and cleanly sub-divided into the functions provided and performed by each of the three half-session subcomponents: the FMDS component, the DFC component and the TC component.

In Chapter 5, *Half-sessions*, the functional capabilities of each of the half-session subcomponents were discussed. For a given LU-LU session only a subset of the functions provided and performed – and where there is a choice in how a function is performed, only one of these options – by each half-session subcomponent, will be required. For example, only one of the send/receive modes and one of the request and response control modes can be used by a given session. Therefore, the functional characteristics of an LU-LU session can be specified by means of the functions provided and performed by the half-session subcomponents of that session within the PLU and SLU. While these FMDS, DFC and TC functions for a given session could be explicitly stated in a structured list of keywords, the interpretation and transmission of such a list could be implementationally cumbersome and inefficient. Instead, SNA groups together related functions that can be offered by two half-session subcomponent partners into units – which are referred to as *profiles* – which can be selected and specified by means of a number relative to the subject half-session subcomponent.

Functions provided by TC components are specified by means of *transmission services* (TS) profiles, functions provided by DFC components are specified by means of *function management* (FM) profiles, while the function provided by FMDS session presentation services components in conjunction with LU services managers are specified by means of *presentation services* (PS) profiles. Thus the characteristics of an LU–LU session can be specified in terms of the two end-user session partners and the appropriate TS, FM and PS profiles.

LU–LU session types

SNA specifies six types of *LU-LU session: LU-LU session type 0,1,2,3,4* and *6* (note that there is no session type 5). The fundamental distinction between these six session types is the type of the end-user pair served by each session type. The six LU–LU session types are defined as follows:

- LU–LU session type 1 supports data communication between an application program end user and a single or multiple component I/O device end user in an interactive, batch or distributed data processing environment
- LU–LU session type 2 supports data communication between an application program end user and a single display terminal (operator) end user, in an interactive environment
- LU–LU session type 3 supports data communication between an application program end user and a single printer terminal (operator) end user, in an interactive environment
- LU–LU session type 4 supports data communication between an application program end user and a single or multiple component I/O device or terminal (operator) end user in an interactive, batch or distributed data processing environment *or* between two terminal operator end users in an interactive environment
- LU–LU session type 6 supports data communication between two application program end users in a distributed data processing environment
- LU–LU session type 0 supports data communication between two end users whose types, and therefore functional characteristics, are unknown (ie the FMDS session presentation services components of these sessions cannot perform any data manipulation function to data to or from these end users as the two LUs are not aware of the end users' characteristics or requirements. However, the end users of

these types of session still wish to use the functions provided by the DFC and TC components).

Figure 6.1 provides a schematic summary of the type of end-user pair served by each of the LU-LU session types.

In addition to the type of end-user pair served by each LU-LU session type, SNA specifies the permissible session characteristics for each session type by specifying which TS, FM and PS profiles can be used with each. The various profiles that can be used with each of the LU-LU session types are discussed in detail in the next section, *Profiles*.

The session type of an LU-LU session is nominated by the session initiator by means of an appropriate log mode entry name. The PLU will specify the session type – which may be different from that nominated by the ILU – of an LU-LU session in the BIND request. (On negotiable BINDs, the SLU may request, via a positive response to the BIND, that an LU-LU session type is used that is different from that suggested by the PLU.)

Profiles

SNA specifies seven TS profiles: TS profiles 1,2,3,4,5,7 and 17; nine FM profiles: FM profiles 0,2,3,4,5,6,7,17 and 18 and six PS profiles: PS profiles 0,1,2,3,4 and 6. The TS and FM profiles are listed in Appendix A, *TS and FM profiles*.

Some of the functional characteristics that are included in a profile will require more information, usually of a session-specific nature, than can be specified in the profile. (For example, TS profiles 2,3,4 and 17 each specify that session-level pacing will be used in both directions, but these profiles do not, and feasibly cannot, specify the pacing window sizes that should be used in each direction. Similarly, FM profile 3 indicates that HDX-FF send/receive mode will be used, but it does not specify whether the PLU or the SLU is the first sender. Such additional information that is required to augment certain of the functional characteristics included in a profile are provided via profile *usage fields*. Profiles that include functional characteristics that require supplementary information not only list a set of functional characteristics but also what supplementary information must be supplied

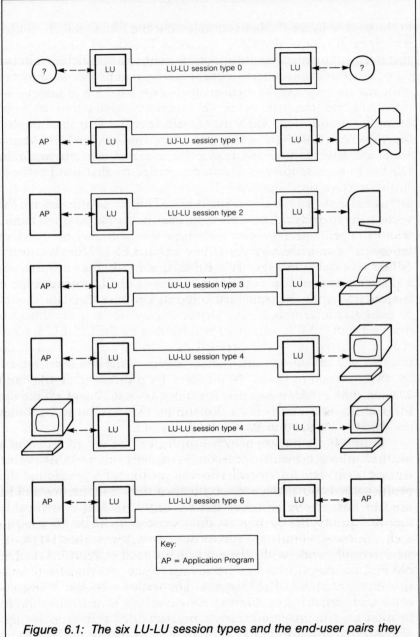

Figure 6.1: The six LU-LU session types and the end-user pairs they
support

Key:

AP = Application Program

in the profile usage fields to complement the functional characteristic specifications. (In some instances functional characteristics that need supplementary information might not be included in the set of functional characteristics supplied by that profile because the information required by that profile's usage field will unequivocally indicate the use of those functional characteristics. For example, if an FM profile's usage field specifies that 'half-duplex flip-flop reset rules' (ie which LU is the first sender following a reset or session activation) need to be specified, it is obvious that HDX-FF is the send/receive mode specified by that FM profile.)

There are six PS profiles: PS profiles 0,1,2,3,4 and 6; one for each of the six LU-LU session types. The PS profile associated with a given LU-LU session type has the same number as the session type, ie PS profile x defines the presentation services functions of an LU-LU session type x. Each PS profile, by means of its usage field, will specify the data stream – ie the end-user-to-end-user protocol that is used to convey control information, in conjunction with the actual data, specifying how the data should be used and interpreted – the character code-set and the function management (FM) headers that will be used by the LU-LU session type associated with the profile. Also specified will be certain relevant and session-specific characteristics of the end users served by such session types. (FM headers are described in the next section, while the two data streams that can be specified for LU-LU sessions (3270 Data Stream and SNA Character String (SCS)) are described in Appendix B.)

Figure 6.2 tabulates which profiles can be used with which LU-LU session types, the presentation services characteristics that are implicitly defined for each session type by its PS profile and the main characteristics that are specified via the PS usage fields. The TS and FM profile to be used with a given LU-LU session is specified in the BIND request for that session. (The PS profile, with its one-to-one correspondence with the session type, is automatically and implicitly defined for each session.) The TS, FM and PS usage fields corresponding to the profiles selected are also specified in the BIND request. The session initiator, by means of an appropriate logmode entry name, will indicate the profiles to be used for the proposed session and suitable parameters for the relevant usage fields. The PLU does not have to specify the same profiles or the usage field parameters as suggested by the ILU in

LU-LU session-type (PS profile)	Permitted TS profiles	Permitted FM profiles	PS characteristics: implied and specified via PS usage field
0	2,3,4	2,3,4	Not known. Implementation defined
1	3,4	3,4	Data stream used: SCS FM Header usage: none, FMH-1, 2 or 3 Device support: single or multiple component I/O device PS usage fields: FM Header and SCS usage rules
2	3	3	Data stream used: 3270 FM Header usage: none Device support: single display terminal PS usage fields: default and alternate screen sizes
3	3	3	Data stream used: 3270 FM Header usage: none Device support: single printer PS usage fields: default and alternate print buffer sizes
4	7	7	Data stream used: SCS FM Headers: none, FMH-1, 2 or 3 Device support: single or multiple component I/O device or word processor terminal PS usage fields: FM Header and data stream usage
6	4	18	Data stream used: SCS or specially defined data streams FM Headers: FMH-4, 5, 6, 7, or 8 Device support: none. Application program to application program PS usage fields: FM Header usage

Figure 6.2: The profile types that can be used with each of the six LU-LU session types, and a summary of the characteristics specified for each session type by its PS profile and PS usage fields

the BIND request. The same applies to the SLU in the case of a negotiable BIND: it may request the profiles or the profile usage fields to be changed.

While the characteristics specified by PS profiles due to their end-user orientation are only applicable to LU-LU sessions, TS and FM profiles specify session characteristics applicable to the other SNA session types. Figure 6.3 tabulates which TS and FM profiles can be specified for which of the SNA session types. (Note that the profile numbers, while appearing to be random at first sight, do indeed follow a pattern in terms of which profiles can be used with which session types.)

The TS and FM profile to be used by, and thereby defining the functions to be provided and performed by the TC and DFC components of, a given SSCP-PU, SSCP-LU or SSCP-SSCP session are specified in the session activation request – *viz*: ACTPU, ACTLU and ACTCDRM respectively – for that session. The formats of these session activation requests are described in Chapter 9, *SNA commands*.

Peer-to-peer sessions

So far the session partners of an LU-LU session were always viewed in terms of a primary/secondary, master/slave type relationship. The designated PLU of an LU-LU session, in addition to activating that session by issuing a BIND request – and in the case of a non-negotiable BIND, dictating all the characteristics for that session – is also the only one of the two session partners who is able to activate or deactivate the data traffic (ie issue SDT and CLEAR), or to shutdown and deactivate the session (ie issue SHUTD and UNBIND). All six LU-LU session types cater for this asymmetrical, primary/secondary type relationship and types 1, 2 and 3 insist on it. In practice, most LU-LU sessions are of this type. However, LU-LU session types 0, 4 and 6 also cater for symmetrical, peer-to-peer type sessions, ie LU-LU sessions where both LU partners are of equal standing.

With peer-to-peer sessions there is no pre-designated PLU for a proposed session: either of the two potential session partners may issue a BIND request. Befitting the intrinsically bilateral nature of peer-to-peer sessions, the BINDs for such sessions are

TS profile	FM profile	Session type			
		LU-LU	SSCP-LU	SSCP-PU	SSCP-SSCP
-	0		✓	✓	
1	1	✓	✓	✓	
2	2	✓			
3	3	✓			
4	4				
5	5	✓	✓	✓	
-	6				
7	7	✓			✓
17	17				
-	18				

Figure 6.3: The TS and FM profiles that may be used with each of the SNA session types

always negotiable. (In the interest of consistency, the LU that issues the BIND to establish a peer-to-peer session is still referred to as the PLU, and the LU that receives the BIND as the SLU, even though the other characteristics attributed to PLUs and SLUs in an asymmetrical session do not apply in a peer-to-peer session.)

In a peer-to-peer LU–LU session either LU can invoke the operational procedures that in primary/secondary type sessions could only be performed by the PLU. As such, in peer-to-peer sessions each LU is responsible for its own error recovery, since either LU is able to deactivate, reset and activate the data traffic by means of CLEAR, (STSN) and SDT requests, if it detects an error.

Type 4 LU–LU sessions also cater for the possibility of establishing and sustaining an LU–LU session between two terminal operator end users, without any SSCP involvement or intervention, provided that the two terminals are directly attached to each other via a point-to-point data link configuration, ie a two terminal-operator end-users data communications environment, without an SSCP. In such an environment the two LUs – and the PU(s) within the node(s) containing the LUs – provide the basic subset of the 'SSCP' functions that are required to establish, maintain and deactivate a type 4 LU–LU session, that will enable the two terminal-operator end users to interact with each other. A negotiable BIND is issued by either of the two LUs to establish a type 4 LU–LU session. (Note that an SNA environment that does not contain an SSCP, can only consist of two nodes at most, which must be directly interconnected by a point-to-point data link, and can only support two end users.)

Function management headers

Function management headers (FMHs) are a mechanism to enable one function management data services: session presentation services component to convey control information to its counterpart, either to instruct it on how certain data requests bound for the end user it serves should be restructured and presented, or to update operational parameters relevant to the data stream or operational procedures being used by the end users. That is, FMHs are a set of protocols used by FMDS:SPS components of LU-LU sessions to interchange control information needed to support the data streams and operational procedures being used by the end users they serve.

FMHs are used for the following:

1 To select the ultimate end-user destination for a given data request if an LU is serving either a multicomponent I/O device end user or multiple end users.
2 To specify end user-specific data management functions, eg creating or deleting a data file or record, requesting special stationery for a print file, indicating the number of copies of a print file that should be printed etc, that need to be performed by the end user or, in the case of a multicomponent end user, by a component previously selected by a preceding FMH.
3 To support data compression, ie a repetitive sequence of a character is replaced by a count specifying the number of repetitions followed by the character to be repeated.
4 To support data compaction, ie represent certain preselected characters using half the number of bits (4) normally used to represent a character (8), thereby being able to compact two contiguous, compactable characters into the number of bits normally used to represent one character.
5 To exchange parameters, eg the set of characters that can be compacted, needed to support data compression and data compaction.
6 To exchange application program end-user-specific commands between application program end users.
7 To provide additional information after a negative response has been issued.
8 To issue a sync point processing 'prepare' request.

The use of FMHs within an LU-LU session is optional and only LU-LU session types 1, 4 and 6 support their use. (Type 0 LU-LU sessions do not exploit any of the functions offered by the FMDS components, including FMHs. Session types 2 and 3, which are always between single component end users, do not require the component selection capability offered by FMHs, and as the 3270 data stream used in these sessions caters for all the relevant data management functions needed by the end users, the data management options offered by FMHs are also superfluous and, as such, not used.) Whether or not a type 1, 4 or 6 LU-LU session will use FMHs is specified in the BIND request for that session.

FMHs can only be used with end-user data requests (never with responses) and when present will either precede the end user data in the request unit or occupy a complete request unit. All FMHs begin with a byte denoting the total length of the subject FMH, followed by another byte whose first bit indicates whether another FMH follows the subject FMH and whose next seven bits specify the type or function of the subject FMH. Figure 6.4 depicts the format of the first two bytes of all FMHs while Figure 6.5 illustrates the possible request unit configuration for end-user data requests when FMHs are being used. For LU-LU sessions that support FMHs, a bit in the request header – the Format Indicator (FI) – specifies whether or not FMHs are present in the request unit. (If present, FMHs will always precede any end-user data contained within the request unit.)

SNA defines nine types of FMH: they are known as FMH-1, –2, –3, –4, –5, –6, –7, –8 and –10 (FMH-9 is not yet defined). Their functions are as follows.

FMH-1

FMH-1s are used to select a particular end-user destination and to support data compression and compaction. (Data compression and compaction are described in the next section.) The destination selected by an FMH-1 may be a component in a multicomponent I/O device end user, a medium on which the end-user data is presented, or a file residing on an I/O device. (FMH-1 may also be used to specify the type of data stream to be used with a given end-user component.)

In addition to explicitly selecting an end-user destination, FMH-1s can also be used to temporarily suspend the currently selected destination so that a new destination can be selected for the next data transfer operation, to restore a previously suspended destination to again be the current destination and to deselect a previously selected destination. The FMDS:SPS components maintain a push-down stack to cater for the suspension and reinstatement of destinations.

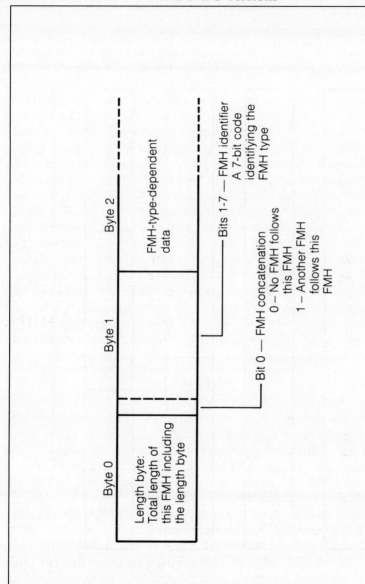

*Figure 6.4: The format of the first two bytes of any function man-
agement header*

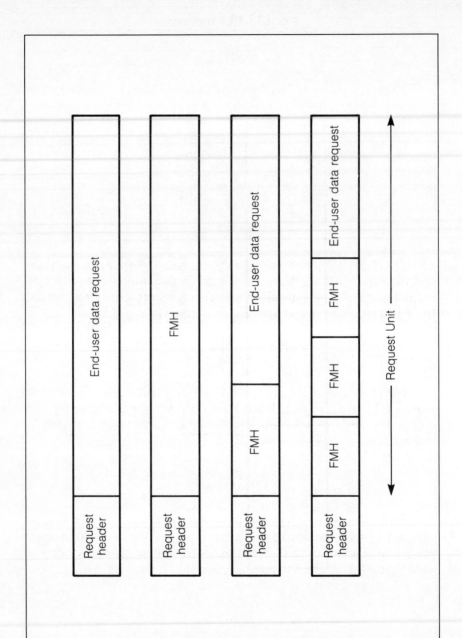

Figure 6.5: Possible Request Unit configurations when function management headers are being used in an LU-LU session

FMH-2

FMH-2s are used to specify destination-dependent data management operations that need to be performed on the end-user data by an end-user destination previously selected by an FMH-1. The typical data management functions that may be specified are the creation and deletion of files, insertion, replacement and deletion of records within a file, password validation and operator intervention requests for special media requirements.

FMH-3

FMH-3s are used to specify the same functions as those specified by FMH-2s, but are used when the subject data management functions apply to all the destinations served by the subject LU rather than just one specific destination.

FMH-4

FMH-4s are used in type 6 LU–LU sessions to prefix the data requests being exchanged between the two application program end users with the parameters required to process a particular request.

FMH-5

FMH-5s are used by an application program end user, using a type 6 LU–LU session, to select the 'process', ie a sub-application program or a subroutine, at the opposite application program end user that is to be the recipient of the next data requests.

FMH-6

FMH-6s are used by an application program end user, using a type 6 LU–LU session, to issue a command to a previously selected 'process' at the opposite application program end user.

FMH-7

FMH-7s are used to provide additional error information after certain error responses are issued.

FMH-8

FMH-8s are used by application program end users, using type 6 LU-LU sessions, to exchange a variety of control information, viz commands, parameters and status, required by the 'processes' handling the processing of the data requests.

FMH-10

FMH-10s serve as a 'prepare' request for sync point processing: this has the advantage that the FMH-10 can be included in data requests whereas LUSTAT, which can also act as a 'prepare' request, cannot contain any end-user data.

Figure 6.6 illustrates how FMH-1s can be used to select destinations during an LU-LU session.

Data compression and data compaction

Data compression and data compaction enable the length of suitable end-user data requests to be reduced while that request is being transmitted from one LU to the other LU via the Path Control Network, thereby increasing the overall efficiency of the data transmission resources. A transmitting LU compresses or compacts the data it receives from its end user before forwarding the requests to the Path Control Network. A receiving LU decompresses or decompacts the compressed or compacted requests before delivering them to the destination end user.

With data compression, a repetitive sequence of a character is replaced by a one- or two-byte code: which code is used depends on the character that appears in the repetitive sequence. For each end-user destination served by an LU a 'special' compression-specific character – referred to as the *prime compression character*

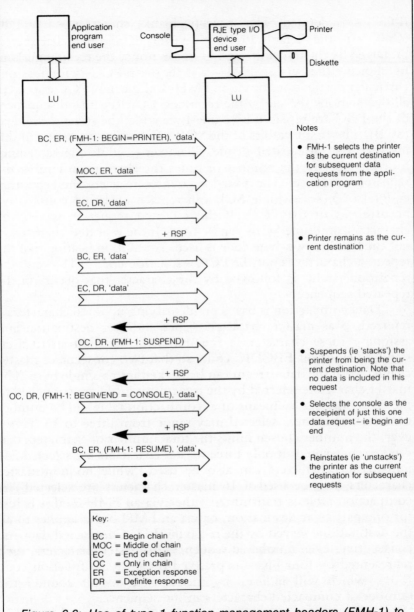

Notes

- FMH-1 selects the printer as the current destination for subsequent data requests from the application program

- Printer remains as the current destination

- Suspends (ie 'stacks') the printer from being the current destination. Note that no data is included in this request

- Selects the console as the receipient of just this one data request – ie begin and end

- Reinstates (ie 'unstacks') the printer as the current destination for subsequent requests

Key:

BC = Begin chain
MOC = Middle of chain
EC = End of chain
OC = Only in chain
ER = Exception response
DR = Definite response

Figure 6.6: Use of type 1 function management headers (FMH-1) to select the component in a multi-component I/O device end user, which is to receive a set of end-user data requests

(PCC) – is defined. The space (ie blank) character – EBCDIC X'40' – is the default PCC. However, if another character is preferred by the transmitting LU, it can notify the receiving LU of its choice either via an FMH-2, if the new PCC is for just one particular destination, or via an FMH-3, if the new PCC applies to all destinations served by the receiving LU. Repetition sequences of the PCC are replaced by a one-byte code: the *string control byte* (SCB). The first two bits of the SCB indicate its function – in this instance B'10':Repeated Prime Character – while the remaining four bits specify the number of times the character occurs in the repeated sequence. The four-bit counter restricts the repetition count to 63, so a single SCB can replace up to 63 consecutive occurrences of the PCC. If the repeated sequence exceeds 63 characters, multiple SCBs can be used. If the repeated character is not the PCC, a two-byte code is used. An SCB indicating that the repeated character is not the PCC – function code B'11' – and the repetition count, is followed by the character that occurs in the repeated sequence.

Data compaction is based on identifying up to 16 characters – referred to as master characters – per end-user destination and assigning these characters a four-bit code, in addition to their standard eight-bit EBCDIC code, so that two consecutive master characters in the data stream can be packed into a single byte. The master characters selected by the transmitting LU are conveyed to the receiving LU by means of a 'compaction table'. (The number of master characters selected may range from three to 16. However, the number chosen limits the total number of characters that can be represented. If only three master characters are selected 244 non-master characters can also be used, while no non-master characters may be used if 16 master characters are selected.) A compaction table is transmitted either via an FMH-2, if it is just for one particular destination, or via an FMH-3 if it applies to all the destinations served by the receiving LU. Compacted data – ie consecutive, even numbered sequences of master characters, each represented by four bits – is prefixed by an SCB, function code B'01', which will indicate by means of a six-bit counter the number of compacted characters in the sequence.

Data compression and data compaction can only be used in conjunction with FMH-1s. Two bits, the *Compression Indicator* (CMI) and the *Compaction Indicator* (CPI), are provided on

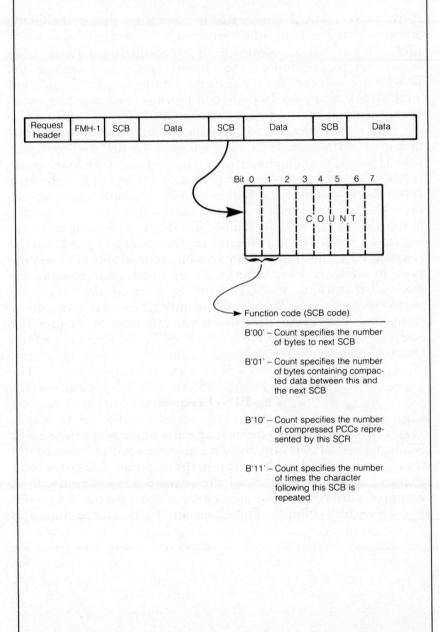

Figure 6.7: The format of an SCB and its location within a request unit

FMH-1s to specify if compressed or compacted data occurs in the end-user data following the header. (Once the presence of compressed or compacted data has been specified in a FMH-1, all request units that follow the request unit that contained the FMH-1 are also checked for compressed or compacted data until an FMH–1 that specifies no compression nor compaction is encountered at the start of a request unit.)

When data compression or data compaction has been specified in a FMH-1, an SCB must precede the first end-user data character in the request unit (see Figure 6.7). This SCB either specifies that the characters immediately following it have been compressed or compacted and the number of characters involved, or, if that is not the case, it specifies the number of bytes – range 1 to 63 – between it and the next SCB. This next SCB again could either be a compressed or compacted data count or a pointer to the next SCB. Sequences of compressed or compacted characters must be followed by another SCB (or if the sequence is longer than 63 characters, an SCB must be inserted after every 63 characters). This SCB will again either be a compressed or compacted data count or a pointer to the next SCB, ie SCBs within a request unit are always forward linked to form an SCB chain.

The BIND request

A BIND request has a generic format as shown in Figure 6.8. While the first 27 bytes are mandatory, the exact length of a BIND request will depend on the cryptography options, LU names and end-user data specified within the request. However, the total length of a BIND request cannot exceed 256 bytes.

The fields within the BIND request are defined as follows:

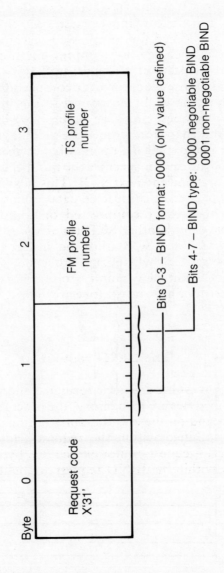

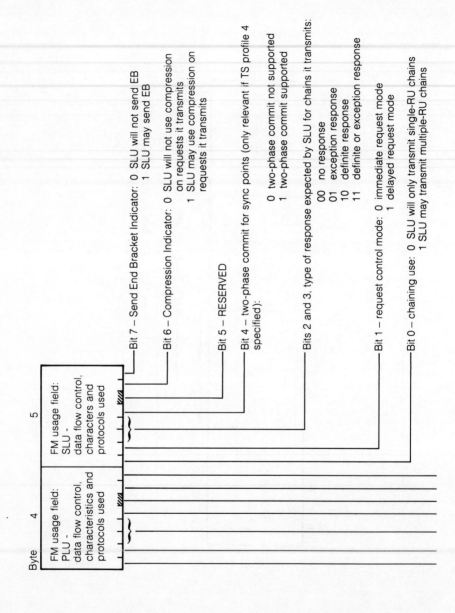

Byte

4
FM usage field:
PLU -
data flow control,
characteristics and
protocols used

5
FM usage field:
SLU -
data flow control,
characters and
protocols used

Bit 7 – Send End Bracket Indicator: 0 SLU will not send EB
                                     1 SLU may send EB

Bit 6 – Compression Indicator: 0 SLU will not use compression
                                   on requests it transmits
                                1 SLU may use compression on
                                   requests it transmits

Bit 5 – RESERVED

Bit 4 – two-phase commit for sync points (only relevant if TS profile 4
specified):

        0 two-phase commit not supported
        1 two-phase commit supported

Bits 2 and 3, type of response expected by SLU for chains it transmits:

        00 no response
        01 exception response
        10 definite response
        11 definite or exception response

Bit 1 – request control mode: 0 immediate request mode
                               1 delayed request mode

Bit 0 – chaining use: 0 SLU will only transmit single-RU chains
                       1 SLU may transmit multiple-RU chains

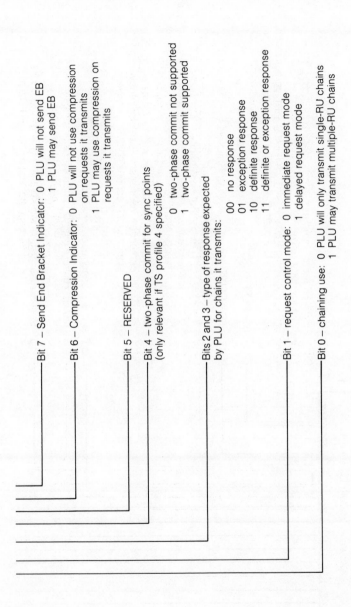

Bit 7 – Send End Bracket Indicator: 0 PLU will not send EB
1 PLU may send EB

Bit 6 – Compression Indicator: 0 PLU will not use compression on requests it transmits
1 PLU may use compression on requests it transmits

Bit 5 – RESERVED

Bit 4 – two-phase commit for sync points (only relevant if TS profile 4 specified)
0 two-phase commit not supported
1 two-phase commit supported

Bits 2 and 3 – type of response expected by PLU for chains it transmits:
00 no response
01 exception response
10 definite response
11 definite or exception response

Bit 1 – request control mode: 0 immediate request mode
1 delayed request mode

Bit 0 – chaining use: 0 PLU will only transmit single-RU chains
1 PLU may transmit multiple-RU chains

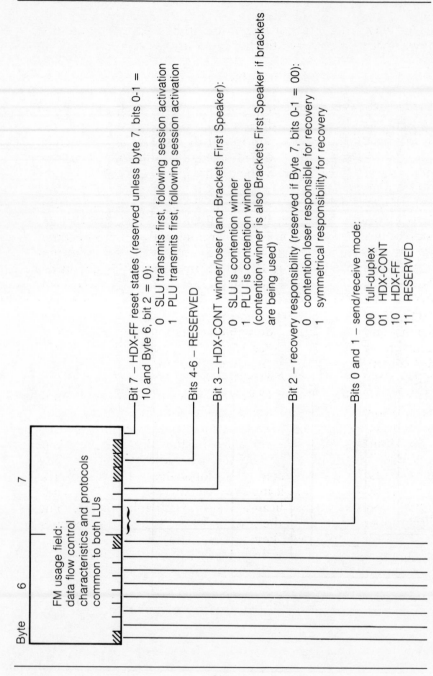

Byte 6 7

FM usage field:
data flow control
characteristics and protocols
common to both LUs

Bit 7 – HDX-FF reset states (reserved unless byte 7, bits 0-1 =
10 and Byte 6, bit 2 = 0):
  0 SLU transmits first, following session activation
  1 PLU transmits first, following session activation

Bits 4-6 – RESERVED

Bit 3 – HDX-CONT winner/loser (and Brackets First Speaker):
  0 SLU is contention winner
  1 PLU is contention winner
  (contention winner is also Brackets First Speaker if brackets
  are being used)

Bit 2 – recovery responsibility (reserved if Byte 7, bits 0-1 = 00):
  0 contention loser responsible for recovery
  1 symmetrical responsibility for recovery

Bits 0 and 1 – send/receive mode:
  00 full-duplex
  01 HDX-CONT
  10 HDX-FF
  11 RESERVED

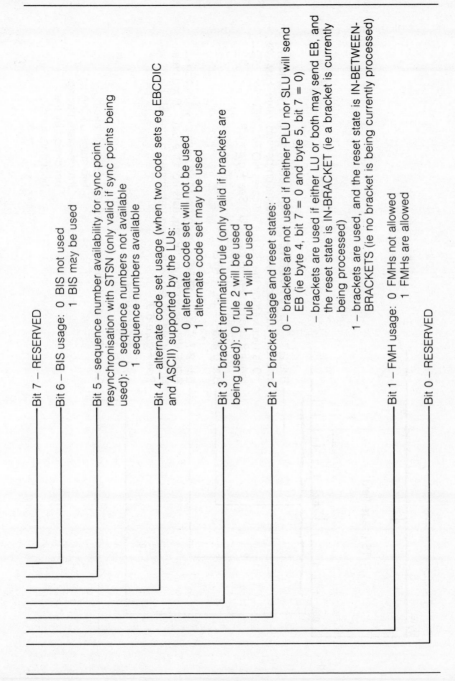

Bit 7 – RESERVED

Bit 6 – BIS usage: 0 BIS not used
1 BIS may be used

Bit 5 – sequence number availability for sync point resynchronisation with STSN (only valid if sync points being used): 0 sequence numbers not available
1 sequence numbers available

Bit 4 – alternate code set usage (when two code sets eg EBCDIC and ASCII) supported by the LUs:
0 alternate code set will not be used
1 alternate code set may be used

Bit 3 – bracket termination rule (only valid if brackets are being used): 0 rule 2 will be used
1 rule 1 will be used

Bit 2 – bracket usage and reset states:
0 – brackets are not used if neither PLU nor SLU will send EB (ie byte 4, bit 7 = 0 and byte 5, bit 7 = 0)
– brackets are used if either LU or both may send EB, and the reset state is IN-BRACKET (ie a bracket is currently being processed)
1 – brackets are used, and the reset state is IN-BETWEEN-BRACKETS (ie no bracket is being currently processed)

Bit 1 – FMH usage: 0 FMHs not allowed
1 FMHs are allowed

Bit 0 – RESERVED

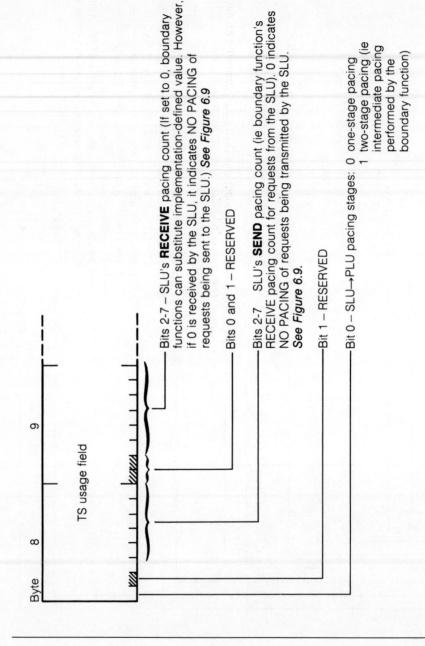

Byte 8 9

TS usage field

Bit 0 – SLU→PLU pacing stages: 0 one-stage pacing
1 two-stage pacing (ie intermediate pacing performed by the boundary function)

Bit 1 – RESERVED

Bits 2-7 SLU's **SEND** pacing count (ie boundary function's RECEIVE pacing count for requests from the SLU). 0 indicates NO PACING of requests being transmitted by the SLU. *See Figure 6.9.*

Bits 0 and 1 – RESERVED

Bits 2-7 – SLU's **RECEIVE** pacing count (If set to 0, boundary functions can substitute implementation-defined value. However, if 0 is received by the SLU, it indicates NO PACING of requests being sent to the SLU.) *See Figure 6.9*

216

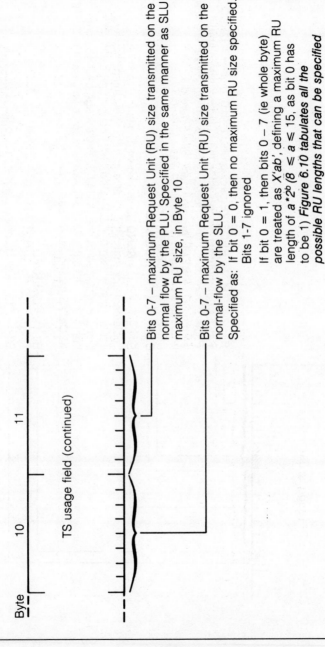

Byte

10   11

TS usage field (continued)

Bits 0-7 – maximum Request Unit (RU) size transmitted on the normal flow by the PLU. Specified in the same manner as SLU maximum RU size, in Byte 10

Bits 0-7 – maximum Request Unit (RU) size transmitted on the normal-flow by the SLU.

Specified as: If bit 0 = 0, then no maximum RU size specified. Bits 1-7 ignored

If bit 0 = 1, then bits 0 – 7 (ie whole byte) are treated as $X'ab'$, defining a maximum RU length of $a*2^b$ ($8 \leq a \leq 15$, as bit 0 has to be 1) *Figure 6.10 tabulates all the possible RU lengths that can be specified*

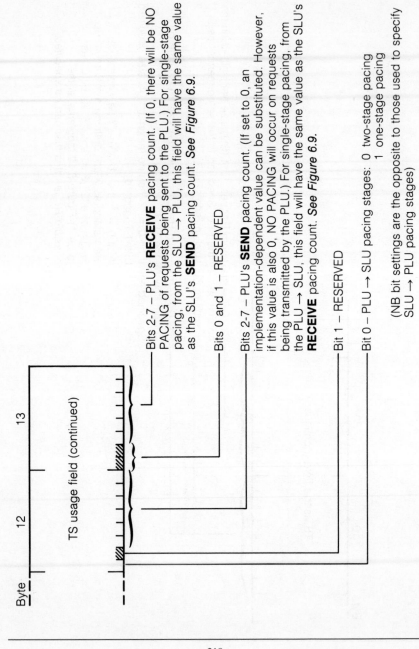

Byte 12 13

TS usage field (continued)

Bits 2-7 – PLU's **RECEIVE** pacing count. (If 0, there will be NO PACING of requests being sent to the PLU.) For single-stage pacing, from the SLU → PLU, this field will have the same value as the SLU's **SEND** pacing count. *See Figure 6.9.*

Bits 0 and 1 – RESERVED

Bits 2-7 – PLU's **SEND** pacing count. (If set to 0, an implementation-dependent value can be substituted. However, if this value is also 0, NO PACING will occur on requests being transmitted by the PLU.) For single-stage pacing, from the PLU → SLU, this field will have the same value as the SLU's **RECEIVE** pacing count. *See Figure 6.9.*

Bit 1 – RESERVED

Bit 0 – PLU → SLU pacing stages: 0 two-stage pacing
1 one-stage pacing

(NB bit settings are the opposite to those used to specify SLU → PLU pacing stages)

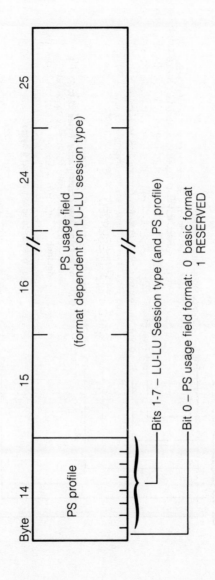

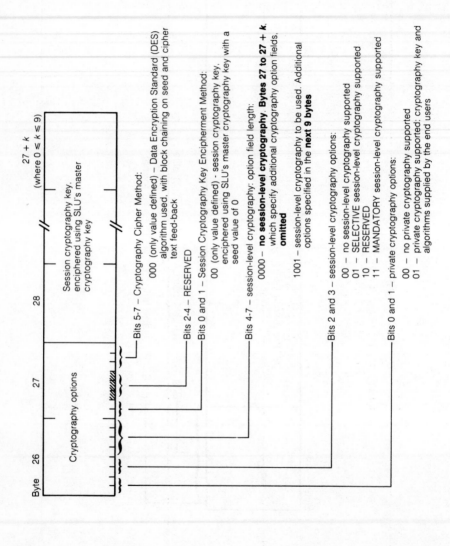

Byte 26   27   28   27 + k
(where 0 ≤ k ≤ 9)

Cryptography options

Session cryptography key, enciphered using SLU's master cryptography key

Bits 5-7 – Cryptography Cipher Method:

   000 (only value defined) – Data Encryption Standard (DES) algorithm used, with block chaining on seed and cipher text feed-back

Bits 2-4 – RESERVED

Bits 0 and 1 – Session Cryptography Key Encipherment Method:

   00 (only value defined) - session cryptography key, enciphered using SLU's master cryptography key with a seed value of 0

Bits 4-7 – session-level cryptography: option field length:

   0000 – **no session-level cryptography. Bytes 27 to 27 + k**, which specify additional cryptography option fields, **omitted**

   1001 – session-level cryptography to be used. Additional options specified in the **next 9 bytes**

Bits 2 and 3 – session-level cryptography options:

   00 – no session-level cryptography supported
   01 – SELECTIVE session-level cryptography supported
   10 – RESERVED
   11 – MANDATORY session-level cryptography supported

Bits 0 and 1 – private cryptography options:

   00 – no private cryptography supported
   01 – private cryptography supported: cryptography key and algorithms supplied by the end users

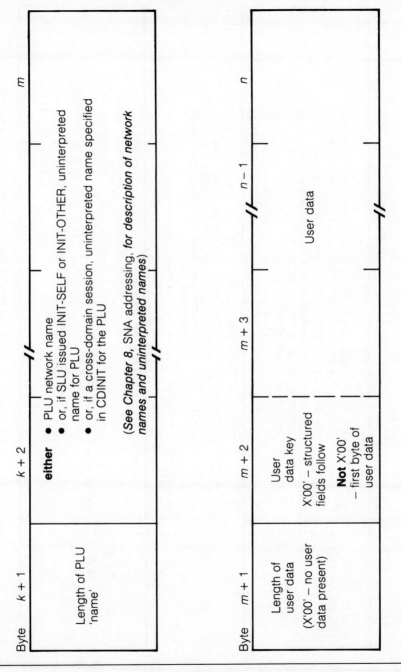

Byte $k + 1$ | $k + 2$ | m

Length of PLU 'name'

either ● PLU network name
● or, if SLU issued INIT-SELF or INIT-OTHER, uninterpreted name for PLU
● or, if a cross-domain session, uninterpreted name specified in CDINIT for the PLU

(*See Chapter 8,* SNA addressing, *for description of network names and uninterpreted names*)

Byte $m + 1$ | $m + 2$ | $m + 3$ | $n - 1$ | n

Length of user data

(X'00' – no user data present)

User data key

X'00' – structured fields follow

Not X'00' – first byte of user data

User data

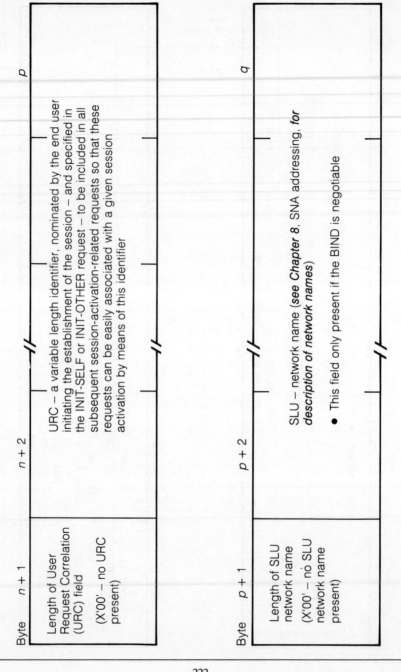

Byte $n + 1$ $n + 2$ p

Length of User Request Correlation (URC) field

(X'00' – no URC present)

URC – a variable length identifier, nominated by the end user initiating the establishment of the session – and specified in the INIT-SELF or INIT-OTHER request – to be included in all subsequent session-activation-related requests so that these requests can be easily associated with a given session activation by means of this identifier

Byte $p + 1$ $p + 2$ q

Length of SLU network name

(X'00' – no SLU network name present)

SLU – network name (*see Chapter 8*, SNA addressing, *for description of network names*)

● This field only present if the BIND is negotiable

222

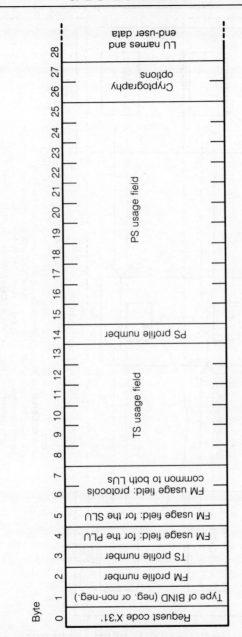

Figure 6.8: The generic format of the BIND request

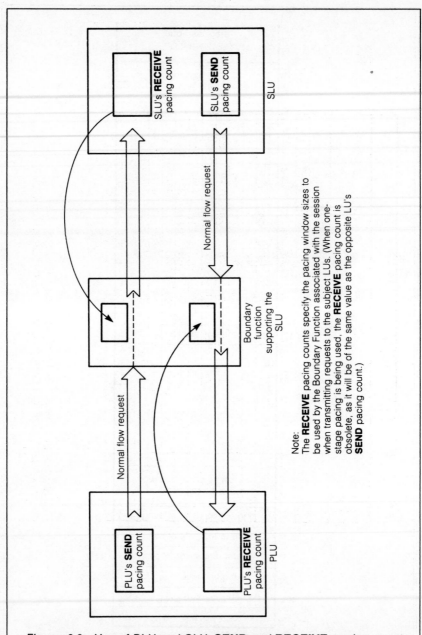

Note:
The **RECEIVE** pacing counts specify the pacing window sizes to be used by the Boundary Function associated with the session when transmitting requests to the subject LUs. (When one-stage pacing is being used, the **RECEIVE** pacing count is obsolete, as it will be of the same value as the opposite LU's **SEND** pacing count.)

*Figure 6.9: Use of PLU and SLU, **SEND** and **RECEIVE** pacing counts when two-stage pacing is being used*

Exponent (b)	Mantissa (a)							
	8	9	A	B	C	D	E	F
0	8	9	10	11	12	13	14	15
1	16	18	20	22	24	26	28	30
2	32	36	40	44	48	52	56	60
3	64	72	80	88	96	104	112	120
4	128	144	160	176	192	208	224	240
5	256	288	320	352	384	416	448	480
6	512	576	640	704	768	832	896	960
7	1024	1152	1280	1408	1536	1664	1792	1920
8	2048	2304	2560	2816	3072	3328	3584	3840
9	4096	4608	5120	5632	6144	6656	7168	7680
A	8192	9216	10240	11264	12288	13312	14336	15360
B	16384	18432	20480	22528	24576	26624	28672	30720
C	32768	36864	40960	45056	49152	53248	57344	61440
D	65536	73728	81920	90112	98304	106496	114688	122880
E	131072	147456	163840	180224	196608	212992	229376	245760
F	262144	294912	327680	360448	393216	425984	458752	491520

Note:

X'ab' corresponds to a maximum RU length of $a \cdot 2^b$ eg X'86' corresponds to $8 \cdot 2^6 = 8 \cdot 64 = 512$. X'87' corresponds to $8 \cdot 2^7 = 8 \cdot 128 = 1024$

Figure 6.10: Request Unit (RU) maximum lengths, corresponding to the X'ab' specification of BIND request bytes 10 or 11

The positive responses to a BIND request

The format of the positive response issued to a BIND request by an SLU depends on whether the BIND was negotiable or non–negotiable and whether or not session–level cryptography is being used.

If a BIND is non–negotiable and session–level cryptography is not specified, the positive response to it would consist of just one byte: the BIND request code, ie X'31':

Bytes   0   1   2

Response header	X'31' BIND request code Response Unit

If session–level cryptography is specified in either a negotiable or non–negotiable BIND request, the positive response to that BIND will consist of the total BIND request as transmitted by the PLU, with bytes 26 to 27 + k, ie the cryptography option fields, now defining:

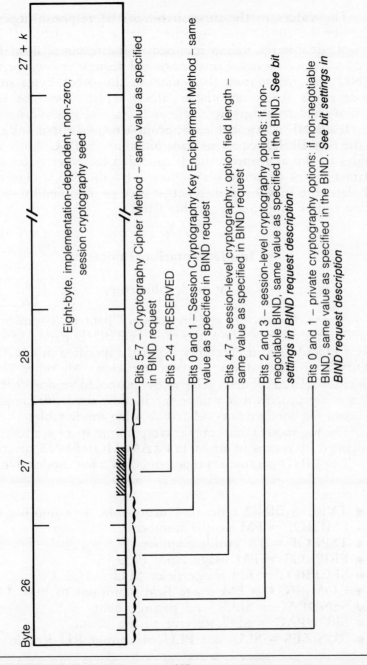

Byte 26   27   28   27 + k

Eight-byte, implementation-dependent, non-zero, session cryptography seed

Bits 5-7 – Cryptography Cipher Method – same value as specified in BIND request

Bits 2-4 – RESERVED

Bits 0 and 1 – Session Cryptography Key Encipherment Method – same value as specified in BIND request

Bits 4-7 – session-level cryptography: option field length – same value as specified in BIND request

Bits 2 and 3 – session-level cryptography options: if non-negotiable BIND, same value as specified in the BIND. *See bit settings in BIND request description*

Bits 0 and 1 – private cryptography options: if non-negotiable BIND, same value as specified in the BIND. *See bit settings in BIND request description*

The values in the other bytes of the response depend on whether the BIND was negotiable or non-negotiable. If it was non-negotiable the values returned in the response must be the same as those specified in the original request. However, if the BIND was negotiable, the values in the other bytes may be modified as for a negotiable BIND which does not specify session-level cryptography.

If a BIND is negotiable, the positive response to it will consist of the total BIND request as transmitted by the PLU, but with the values of the appropriate fields modified to indicate the session characteristics or protocols preferred by the SLU. Figure 6.11 tabulates the BIND parameters that may be modified by the SLU when responding to a negotiable BIND.

Implementational notes

Log mode table entry

Session characteristics and protocols in Chapter 4's implementational notes describes how the proposed BIND parameters for a given LU-LU session are only explicitly specified in CINIT and CDINIT requests during session initiation. All other session-initiation-related requests refer to the proposed session characteristics and protocols that will be specified by the BIND request in terms of log mode names relative to a log mode table.

The log mode table entry corresponding to a log mode name is defined by means of an ACF/VTAM MODEENT macro.

The BIND parameters represented by a log mode table entry

- TYPE = BIND type: 0 = negotiable, 1 = non-negotiable
- FMPROF = FM profile number
- TSPROF = TS profile number
- PRIPROT = FM usage field: PLU
- SECPROT = FM usage field: SLU
- COMPROT = FM usage field: common to both LUs
- SSNDPAC = SLU Send pacing count
- SRCUPAC = SLU Receive pacing count
- RUSIZES = SLU and PLU maximum RU lengths

BIND parameter	SLU may modify a positive response to a negotiable BIND
BIND format and type	Yes – but not applicable
FM profile	Yes
TS profile	Yes
FM usage fields	Yes
TS usage fields:	
SLU → PLU pacing stages	No
SLU **SEND** pacing count	No – (Boundary function may decrease if two-stage pacing used)
SLU **RECEIVE** pacing count	Yes – but can only reduce the value specified by the PLU
PLU → SLU maximum RU size	Yes – but can only reduce the value specified by the PLU
SLU → PLU maximum RU size	Yes – but can only reduce the value specified by the PLU
PLU **SEND** pacing count	Yes – if one-stage pacing, can reduce, to equal, SLU **RECEIVE** pacing count
PLU **RECEIVE** pacing count	No
PLU → SLU pacing stages	No
PS profile	Yes
PS usage field	Yes
Cryptography options	'Yes' – but only as specified when session cryptography used
PLU 'name'	No – but can omit from response by setting 'name' length = 0
User data	Yes
URC	No – but can omit from response by setting URC length = 0
SLU 'name'	No – but can omit from response by setting 'name' length = 0

Figure 6.11: The BIND parameters that may be modified by an SLU when responding to a negotiable BIND request

- PSNDPAC = PLU Send pacing count
- PSERVIC = PS profile and PS usage field
- ENCR = Cryptography option.

Pacing counts

In addition to being capable of specifying the SLU send and receive pacing counts and the PLU send pacing count in the BIND parameters represented by a log mode table entry (using the MODENT macro operands SSNDPAC=, SRCVPAC= and PSNDPAC= respectively), pacing counts can also be specified when defining an LU to ACF/VTAM or ACF/NCP.

The APPL macro used to define an application program (LU) to ACF/VTAM has a VPACING= operand. A value in the range 0 to 63 can be assigned to this operand. For LU-LU sessions where the application program LU is to be the PLU, the value assigned to the VPACING= operand is used as the PLU receive pacing count. (Refer to Figure 6.9.) For sessions where the application program LU is to be the SLU, the VPACING= value will be used as the SLU receive and the PLU send pacing counts. (Since an application program LU will only be an SLU in an application-program-LU-to-application-program-LU, (ie Type 6) session, both PLU and SLU will be in subarea nodes and, as such, one-stage pacing will be in force.) VPACING=0 indicates that pacing will not be used in that direction.

The ACF/VTAM LU macro used to define LUs within local SNA or switched major nodes, and the ACF/NCP LU macro have PACING= and VPACING= operands. The LUs defined by these macros will only participate in LU-LU sessions that employ two-stage pacing. For these sessions, the PACING= operand can be used to specify the SLU receive pacing count, while the VPACING= operand can be used to specify the PLU send pacing count. (Refer to Figure 6.9.) The ACF/NCP, PACING= and VPACING= operands will accept two numeric values. The first value specifies the pacing count, while the second specifies which of the requests in the pacing 'group' will contain the pacing request indicator. Since a pacing response cannot be issued until a pacing request is received, this parameter provides a means of further optimising buffer pool utilisation by dictating when a receiver may send a pacing response within a pacing iteration to indicate that it can receive further requests.

Issuing a BIND request

ACF/VTAM application programs that are to be the PLUs in proposed LU-LU sessions do not issue BIND requests directly. Instead, the BIND requests are issued by ACT/VTAM when an ACF/VTAM application program executes an OPNDST macro. Application programs specify the parameters to be included in the BIND request by means of operands in a session initiation and establishment related control block: the node initiation block (NIB). Two NIB operands, BNDAREA= and LOGMODE= are used to indicate the location of the parameters that the application program wants embedded in the BIND request. If the application program is happy to use the BIND parameters as specified in the CINIT request, it specifies LOGMODE=0 and BNDAREA=0. However, if the application program does not wish to use these BIND parameters it can specify its own choice of parameters either by quoting a log mode name corresponding to the set of parameters – LOGMODE=*log mode name* and BNDAREA=0 – or by constructing a BIND request image in a storage buffer – LOGMODE=0 and BNDAREA=*address of storage buffer*. (An ACF/VTAM macro, INQUIRE, is provided to enable application programs to obtain BIND parameters either from a designated log mode table entry or from a CINIT request that has been sent to it.)

In addition to being specified in the BIND parameters themselves, the BIND type and the session-level cryptography requirements are reiterated by operands in the NIB. PROC=NEGBIND indicates a negotiable BIND while PROC=NNEGBIND indicates a non-negotiable BIND. The ENCR= operand specifies the session-level cryptography requirements with one of three key-words: REQD (all requests are enciphered); SEL (selective encipherment); and NONE (cryptography not used).

Response to a BIND

In sessions between ACT/VTAM application programs and I/O-device or terminal-operator end users the response to a BIND request issued by ACF/VTAM on behalf of the application program will be generated by the LU supporting the I/O-device or terminal-operator end user. The application program is notified by ACF/VTAM whether the SLU issued a positive or negative response to the BIND via the completion code returned for the OPNDST macro that requested the BIND to be issued. If the BIND was negotiable, and the response to it is positive, the ARECLEN= operand of the RPL associated with the OPNDST will indicate the length of the BIND response received. The actual response itself will be located at the storage address specified by the RPL, AAREA= operand, when the OPNDST is executed.

In the case of sessions between ACF/VTAM application program end users, the potential SLU will receive a BIND for a proposed session from ACF/VTAM. An SCIP (session control request interrupt processing) exit routine in the SLU will be invoked on receipt of a BIND request. The BIND request received will be located at the address of the RPL associated with the exit routine specified by the AREA= operand. The SLU can either issue a positive response to the BIND by executing an OPNSEC macro, or it can reject the proposed session by issuing a negative response by executing a SESSIONC macro that specifies 'CONTROL=BIND,STYPE=RESP,RESPOND=(EX,FME)'. In the case of a negotiable BIND, the SLU constructs the BIND response image in a storage buffer pointed to by the BNDAREA= operand of an NIB, sets the PROC= operand of that NIB to NEGBIND and then issues an OPNSEC macro specifying that NIB.

Function management headers

If FMHs are being used, ACF/VTAM application programs will construct them as part of the data request. The RPL operand OPTCD= is set to FMHDR when there are FMHs present in the Request Unit, and to NFMHDR when there are not. ACF/VTAM sets the FI bit in RH based on the setting of OPTCD=.

If an application program receives an RU with FMHs, ACF/VTAM will set to FMHDR the OPTCD= operand of the RPL associated with the RECEIVE macro that is used to read in the RU.

LU-LU session type

	0		1		2		3		4		6	
	PLU	SLU	PLU	SLU	PLU	SLU	PLU	SLU	PLU	SLU	PLU	SLU
Representative IBM products	CICS/VS IMS/VS JES2 JES3 NCCF DPCX DPPX	3270 3600 3630 3650 3660 3790 Series/1 S/34	CICS/VS IMS/VS JES2 JES3 POWER/VS TSO NCCF VSPC 3630	3270 3600 3630 3640 3767 3770 3790 Series/1 S/32 S/34 S/38 DPCX DPPX	CICS/VS IMS/VS NCCF TSO VSPC	3270 3600 3790 8775 DPPX DPCX	CICS/VS	3270 3790 S/34 DPCX DPPX	CICS/VS IMS/VS	5250 6670 S/34 S/38	CICS VS IMS VS	CICS VS IMS VS

*Figure 6.12: The types of LU-LU session supported by some of the
common IBM products*

LU–LU session types

Figure 6.12 tabulates the types of LU–LU session supported by some of the common IBM products. The products shown for each session type are only a representative selection (with generic, rather than specific, product numbers given) and is not an exhaustive list of all the IBM products that can participate in that type of LU–LU session. The products itemised on the PLU column for a given session type may establish sessions with not just one of the products itemised in the SLU column, but with most or even all of them, ie the PLU-to-SLU relationship is one-to-many rather than one-to-one.

LU-LU session type	End user served	Data stream	FMHs	TS profiles	FM profiles
0		?	-	2, 3, 4	2, 3, 4
1		SCS	None, 1, 2 or 3	3, 4	3, 4
2		3270	None	3	3
3		3270	None	3	3
4		SCS	None, 1, 2 or 3	7	7
6		SCS or product specific	4, 5, 6, 7, 8	4	18

Checkpoint 6

235

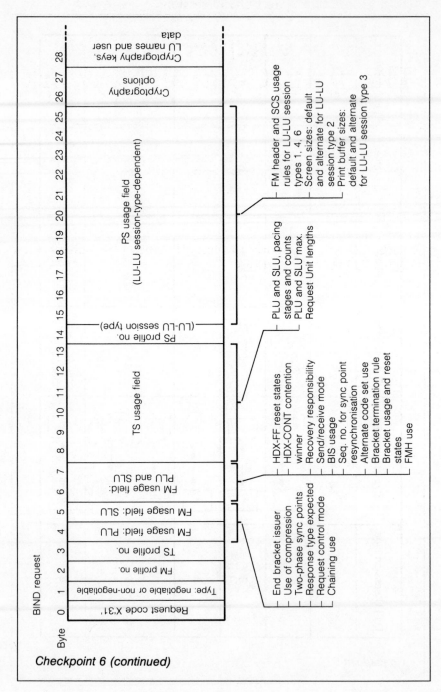

Checkpoint 6 (continued)

The diagram shows a BIND request structure:

Byte layout:

Byte	Field
0	Request code X'31'
1	Type: negotiable or non-negotiable
2	FM profile no.
3	TS profile no.
4	FM usage field: PLU
5	FM usage field: SLU
6–7	FM usage field: PLU and SLU
8–13	TS usage field
14	PS profile no. (LU-LU session type)
15–25	PS usage field (LU-LU session-type-dependent)
26–27	Cryptography options
28–	Cryptography keys, LU names and user data

FM usage field: PLU / SLU (bytes 4, 5):
- End bracket issuer
- Use of compression
- Two-phase sync points
- Response type expected
- Request control mode
- Chaining use

FM usage field: PLU and SLU (bytes 6, 7):
- HDX-FF reset states
- HDX-CONT contention winner
- Recovery responsibility
- Send/receive mode
- BIS usage
- Seq. no. for sync point resynchronisation
- Alternate code set use
- Bracket termination rule
- Bracket usage and reset states
- FMH use

TS usage field (bytes 8–13):
- PLU and SLU, pacing stages and counts
- PLU and SLU max. Request Unit lengths

PS usage field (bytes 15–25):
- FM header and SCS usage rules for LU-LU session types 1, 4, 6
- Screen sizes: default and alternate for LU-LU session type 2
- Print buffer sizes: default and alternate for LU-LU session type 3

Chapter 7:
The Path Control Network

☐ Path Control Network ☐ Link ☐ Primary/Secondary Link Stations ☐ Link Connections

Chapter 7:
The Path Control Network

Overview

The Path Control Network, which is responsible for transmitting SNA message units between the various NAUs in an SNA environment, consists of a set of Path Control components and data link control components. The Path Control components select and manage the overall route – or path – through the environment that a message unit from one NAU to another NAU must traverse. The data link control components control the transmission of the message unit across the physical data links that form the route chosen by the Path Control components.

Each SNA node contains a Path Control component and one or more data link control components.

An NAU will deliver to the Path Control component located within the node it is resident in, a message unit it wishes to transmit to another NAU. This Path Control component will determine the route that the message unit should traverse to reach the destination NAU. It will then dispatch it to the appropriate data link control component, within the node, supporting the first data link of this route, along with the relevant routing information, which will be in the form of a header. This header, which will prefix the request or response header preceding the request or response unit, is called the *transmission header* (TH). The message unit will be conveyed along the route specified by the originating node's Path Control component by intermediate Path Control and data link control components as necessary, until it reaches the Path Control component of the node containing the destination NAU. (See Figure 7.1.)

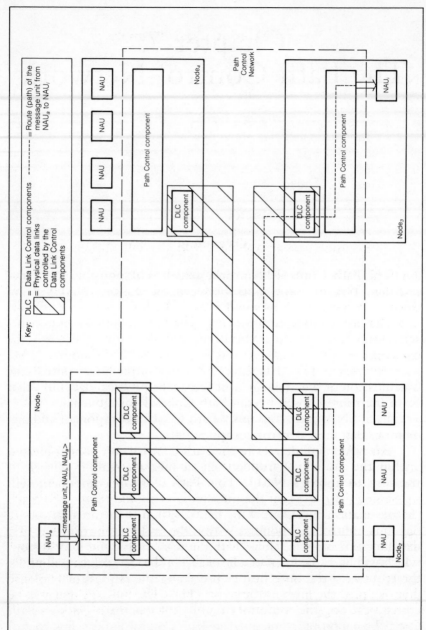

Key:
DLC = Data Link Control components
‑‑‑‑‑ = Route (path) of the message unit from NAU_a to NAU_j
= Physical data links controlled by the Data Link Control components

$Node_1$

NAU_a

<message unit, NAU_j, NAU_a>

Path Control component

DLC component

DLC component

DLC component

$Node_2$

NAU

NAU

NAU

Path Control component

DLC component

DLC component

DLC component

Path Control Network

$Node_4$

NAU

NAU

NAU

NAU

Path Control component

DLC component

$Node_3$

DLC component

Path Control component

NAU_j

Figure 7.1: Transmission of a message unit from one NAU to another via the Path Control Network

240

Data link control components

The data link control components of the Path Control Network are responsible for transferring SNA message units between nodes via SNA *links*.

An SNA link consists of the following:

- A single *primary link station*, associated with a Primary Link Station User
- A set of one or more *secondary link stations*, each associated with a Secondary Link Station User
- A single *link connection*, which physically interconnects the primary link station with each of the secondary link stations, to enable message units to be exchanged between the primary link station and any of the secondary link stations.

Figure 7.2 illustrates the composition of an SNA link. Notice that the definition of a link caters for point-to-point, multipoint and even loop data-link configurations.

A link connection is either an IBM System/370 channel or a switched or non-switched telecommunication link along with the appropriate data circuit-terminating equipment (DCE).

A link station consists of the hardware and software required to attach the link connection to the device or machine containing the SNA node, and to support the data link protocol used to establish, coordinate and sustain error-free data transfer over the link connection.

The primary link station of a link is responsible for controlling all the data transfer operations that occur over that link, using the command and procedure repertoire of the data link protocol – eg SDLC – specified for that link. All data transfer operations on a link are either from the primary link station to one or more of the secondary link stations or from a secondary link station to the primary link station. (Secondary link stations cannot communicate with each other directly.) These data transfer operations, irrespective of the direction of transmission, can only be initiated by the primary link station, ie secondary link stations cannot transmit to the primary until they are given permission to do so by the primary link station.

The number of link stations located within a given node will depend on the number of link connections supported by that

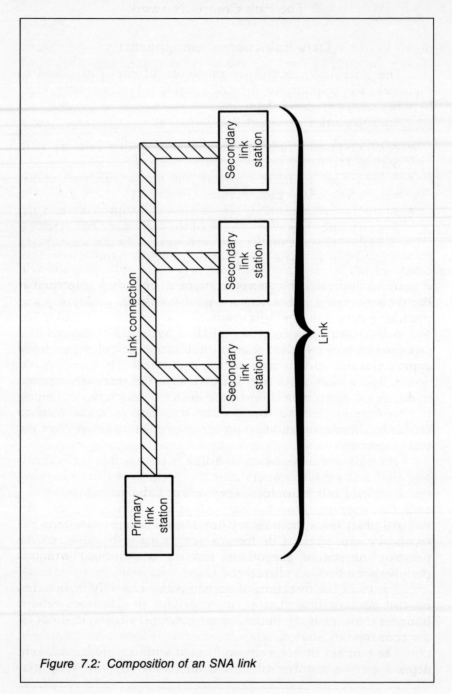

Figure 7.2: Composition of an SNA link

node. Each link connection supported will require a link station within the node to cater for the physical attachment of that link connection and to provide the data link control functions. The type of the link station terminating a link connection at a given node will depend on the node type and the manner in which that node is configured in relation to other nodes within the SNA environment. A peripheral node, because it can only be attached to one subarea node at any one time, will only contain one link station and that will be a secondary one since the subarea node it is attached to will control all the data transfer operations that take place between them. A subarea node, however, could contain multiple link stations: primary link stations to support the link connections to all the peripheral nodes it is responsible for and primary or secondary link stations if it has link connections with other subarea nodes. For example, a Type 4 subarea node will contain secondary link stations to support any link connections it has with Type 5 subarea nodes, primary link stations to support the link connections to the peripheral nodes it is responsible for and either primary or secondary link stations, depending on the topography of the environment or the order in which the nodes were activated, to support link connections with other Type 4 nodes. Figure 7.3 illustrates the link structure between various nodes in a typical SNA environment.

Irrespective of whether a link station is a primary or a secondary, its link station user will always be the Path Control component of the node that the link station is located in.

The Path Control component: subarea nodes

All SNA nodes contain a Path Control component. However, the structure of and the functions performed by a given Path Control component depend on whether it is located within a peripheral node or a subarea node.

The Path Control component of a peripheral node only has to control data traffic either between NAUs in its node and the boundary function of the subarea node the peripheral node is attached to via a single link, or between LUs within the peripheral node. But a Path Control component of a subarea node has many more functions to perform, in addition to that of controlling data

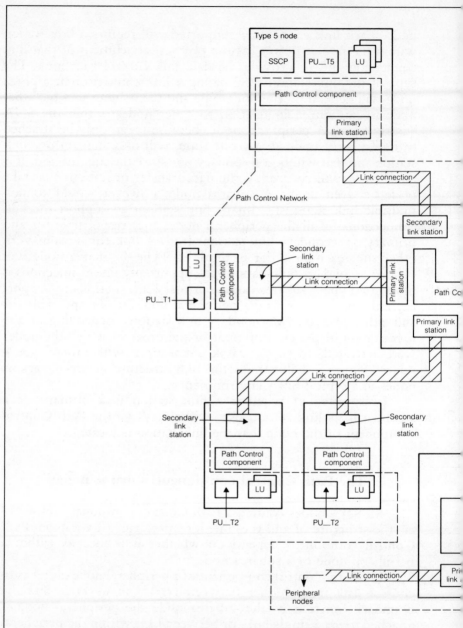

Figure 7.3: Link structure between subarea and peripheral nodes in a typical SNA environment

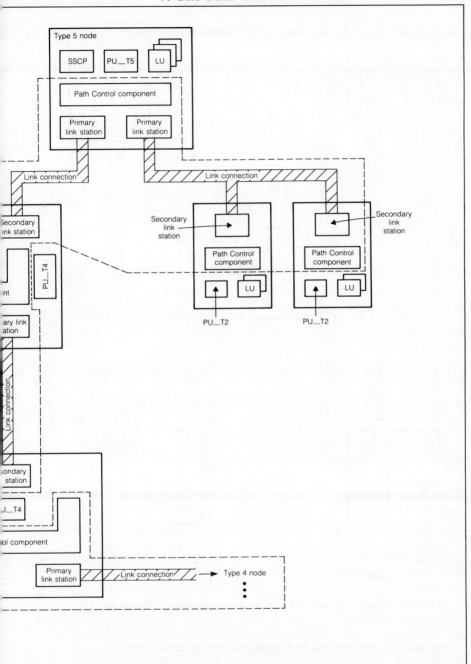

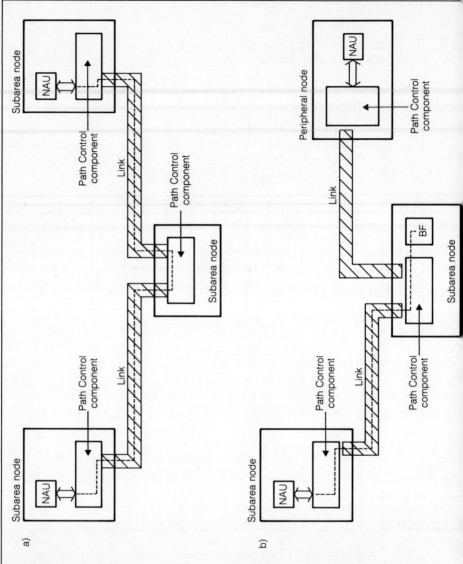

a: Route or path between two NAUs located in two different subarea nodes

b: Route or path between an NAU in a subarea node and an NAU in a peripheral node

Figure 7.4: The concept of a route between subarea nodes

246

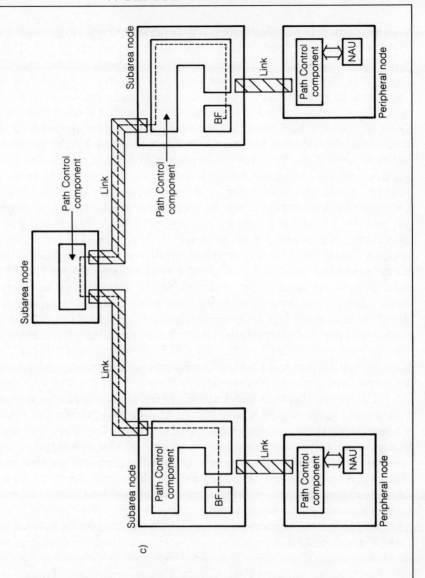

c: *Route or path between two NAUs located in two different peripheral nodes*

traffic to and from the boundary function of its node and the NAUs in the peripheral nodes attached to the subarea node. Path Control components in subarea nodes are responsible for providing and maintaining routes – or paths – through the Path Control Network to enable NAUs in a given node (subarea or peripheral) to exchange message units with NAUs in another node. If the two NAUs wishing to communicate with each other are located in two different subarea nodes, the route provided by the relevant subarea node Path Control components will be between the two subarea nodes containing the two NAUs. If one NAU is in a subarea node and the other is in a peripheral node, the route provided will be between the subarea node containing one of the subject NAUs and the subarea node to which the peripheral node containing the other NAU is attached. If the NAUs are in two different peripheral nodes, attached to different subarea nodes, the route provided will be between the two subarea nodes that the two peripheral nodes are attached to. Whether a given route between two end-to-end subarea node Path Control components involves the Path Control components of intermediate subarea nodes will depend on the link configurations available between the two end-to-end subarea nodes. Figure 7.4 illustrates the concept of a route, which is always between end-to-end subarea nodes, rather than the actual end-to-end nodes.

The route through the Path Control network between two end-to-end subarea nodes is made up of one or more transmission groups, an explicit route and a virtual route. The Path Control component of a subarea node consists of three hierarchically structured subcomponents, each of which supports one of the three entities that must be combined to form a route:

- *Transmission Group Control*
- *Explicit Route Control*
- *Virtual Route Control.*

For a given subarea Path Control component, the Transmission Group Control subcomponent is the innermost – ie lowest-level component, relative to the SNA environment, and acts as the Path Control components interface with the link stations located in that node, while the Virtual Route Control subcomponent is the outermost – ie highest-level component.

Transmission Group Control

Transmission Group Control subcomponents are responsible for providing one or more bidirectional logical connections between adjacent subarea nodes. These connections are referred to as *Transmission Groups* (TGs).

A TG is a bidirectional logical – connection between two adjacent subarea nodes and consists of one or more links between the two subarea nodes. As such, a TG consists of a set of primary and secondary link stations and a set of link connections which are either one or more telecommunications links of similar or dissimilar transmission capacity, or a single IBM System/370 channel.

Irrespective of the number of links forming a TG, the Transmission Group Control subcomponents responsible for that TG represent it to the higher levels of their Path Control components as a single link between two adjacent subarea nodes. Traffic between subarea nodes interconnected by a TG will be evenly distributed over the active links forming that TG, and the Transmission Group Control subcomponents responsible for it will ensure that the 'first in-first out' (FIFO) characteristic of a single link is preserved for the TG as a whole. That is, the receiving Transmission Group Control subcomponents will ensure that the message units that it conveys to the next higher layer of the Path Control component are in the same order that the transmitting Transmission Group Control subcomponent received them in. A TG is operative as long as at least one of its links is active, and a TG is only deemed to have failed when all its links are inoperative. This capability to combine several links to form a larger composite connection has the benefit of providing greater transmission bandwidth and 'link' availability than can be provided by a single link.

SNA does not specify an upper limit on the number of links that can be grouped together to form a TG. This is left as an implementational option and will depend on the total number of links that can be supported by a given subarea node.

A maximum of 255 TGs are possible between any two adjacent subarea nodes. A particular TG between two adjacent subarea nodes is identified by a *Transmission Group number* (TGN) – in the range 1 to 255 – and the network addresses of the two subarea nodes. (Network addresses are discussed in Chapter 8, *SNA addressing*.)

Figure 7.5 illustrates the concept of TGs between two adjacent subarea nodes.

A link can only belong to one TG at any one time. However, SNA permits a link to be dynamically reassigned from one TG to another TG.

When a Transmission Group Control subcomponent is given message units to be transmitted over a TG, it queues them on an outbound queue associated with that TG. Message units are then taken from the queue on a FIFO basis and transmitted on the first available link belonging to that TG. When a TG consists of multiple links, message units transmitted across the TG may arrive at the opposite end out of sequence to that in which they were de-queued from the outbound queue, and transmitted. This may be because of the following reasons:

- The links operating at different transmitting speeds
- The message units being of different lengths
- Transmission errors on the link.

To ensure that a receiving Transmission Group Control subcomponent can check that message units are in the correct sequence and, if they are not, for it to be able to resequence them, a TG-specific sequence number is assigned by the transmitting subcomponent to all message units when they are de-queued and prior to being transmitted across a TG. (This TG sequence number is independent of, and in addition to, the sequence number or identifier assigned to each request and response.) These TG sequence numbers are also used by the receiving Transmission Group Control subcomponent to check for duplicate message units that may be received as a result of the transmission error recovery mechanism used by Transmission Group Control subcomponents to retransmit message units following a transmission error.

If a transmission error is encountered while transmitting a message unit and the TG consists of multiple links, the transmitting subcomponent seeks to minimise the potential retransmission attempts by retransmitting that message unit over another link, in case the transmission error is data dependent and therefore liable

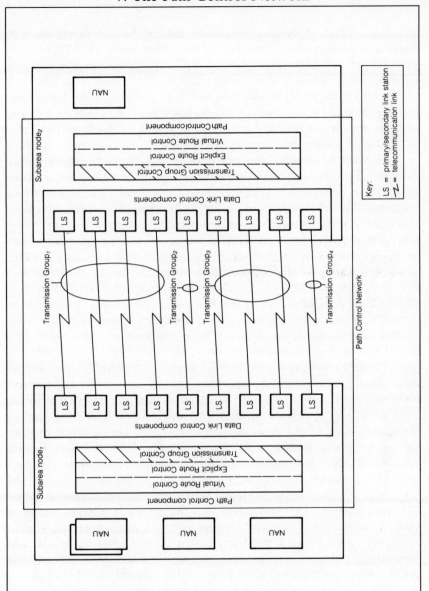

Figure 7.5: Two subarea nodes interconnected by four Transmission Groups

to recur. (This process overcomes errors due to faults on one particular link.) The transmitting subcomponent will repeat this process of retransmitting on a different link, until either the message unit is successfully transmitted over a link or it has been attempted over all the links belonging to the TG. (SNA does not specify how the transmitting subcomponent should select the next link on which the failing message unit is to be retransmitted. This is left as an implementational option.)

However, there is another process of retransmissions that is attempted in addition to this process of attempting retransmissions over different links. The link station that notifies the transmitting subcomponent of a transmission error – the first time the error occurs – will also attempt to retransmit that message unit over the original link, in parallel to the transmitting subcomponent's attempts to retransmit over another link. (Note that this process applies to all link stations and not just to the first one used.) A link station only notifies the transmitting subcomponent of the first transmission error it encounters. Subsequent errors detected when attempting retransmissions are not reported. Retransmissions continue until one is successful, the data link protocol-specified retransmission count is reached, or until the link becomes inoperative. But if it does eventually succeed in successfully transmitting the message unit, or the link becomes inoperative, it will report it to the transmitting subcomponent. This 'multi-level' retransmission process can result in duplicates of the same message unit – all bearing the same TG sequence number though – being received by the opposite Transmission Group Control subcomponent. These duplicates are discarded.

TG sequence numbers are assigned sequentially from the range 0 to 4095. The receiving Transmission Control subcomponent checks the TG sequence number of each message unit it receives against the sequence number it is expecting next. If the sequence number of a message unit is lower than expected it is discarded as it must be a duplicate, while a message unit with a higher sequence number than expected is queued on a FIFO queue until the message units that were transmitted ahead of it are received.

The 'multi-level' retransmission process does present a problem when the sequence numbers for a particular TG reach 4095. The customary sequence number wrap-around technique will not suffice if the TG consists of multiple links. If a message unit with a sequence number of 0 is received following one with a sequence number of 4095 it is still impossible for the receiving subcomponent to determine whether it is a duplicate of the last message unit that was assigned a sequence number of 0 or whether it is a new message unit. This problem is overcome by the use of a process referred to as a *Transmission Group Sweep* and a *Transmission Group sequence number field wrap acknowledgement* message.

A TG sweep is a process performed by a transmitting subcomponent, whereby it suspends the de-queuing of any new message units from the outbound queue for transmission across a given TG, until at least one copy of all previously transmitted message units has been successfully received at the opposite end and all retransmission attempts have ceased – either because a transmission was successful or because the retransmission count was reached. Thus, when a TG sweep is performed, all message units transmitted across the TG prior to the sweep would have been successfully received by the opposite end, before it receives any message units transmitted subsequent to the sweep.

Once a transmitting subcomponent has transmitted a message unit with a TG sequence number of 4095, it performs a sweep on that TG. On receipt of a message unit with a sequence number of 4095, and providing it has successfully received all previous message units, a receiving subcomponent will issue a TG sequence number field wrap acknowledgement message to its counterpart. This acknowledgement delimits a 'block' of 4096 message units. The transmitting subcomponent will not resume transmission following the sweep until it receives a wrap acknowledgement message. It will then transmit the next message unit, to which 0 will be assigned as a sequence number: it then does another sweep. This second sweep ensures that message units with sequence numbers greater than 0 will not be received at the opposite end prior to it receiving at least one copy of the message unit with a sequence number of 0. Any message units with a sequence number of 0 received after this second sweep, and before the next sweep, can immediately be discarded as they must be duplicates. Following this second sweep, all message units received are treated as part of the new 'block' of 4096 message units.

When a Transmission Group Control subcomponent is given a message unit to be transmitted across a TG, it has one of three transmission priorities assigned to it: high, medium or low. Message units are queued on the outbound queue ranked according to this priority, with message units of the same priority being queued in chronological order. Message units are de-queued for transmission in descending order of priority, on a FIFO basis within each priority. (A TG sweep is used in instances where certain environment control requests – especially those deactivating a Path Control Network component – should not overtake previous requests, even if they are of higher priority than the previous requests.)

In addition to the above functions, Transmission Group Control subcomponents are also responsible for the following:

1 Blocking and deblocking message units into and from larger units that may be used for transmission across a TG. This process is described in detail in Chapter 10, *SNA message units*.
2 Converting message units that are too long into exception requests.
3 Signalling the higher subcomponents when message unit congestion is detected within a subarea node.

Explicit Route Control

Explicit Route Control subcomponents are responsible for providing bidirectional, physical connections between end-to-end subarea nodes. These connections are referred to as *Explicit Routes* (ERs).

An ER is a physical path between two end-to-end subarea nodes, consisting of a fixed set of TGs and a set of subarea node Path Control components. Multiple ERs may be defined between two subarea nodes. Figures 7.6 and 7.7 illustrate the concept of ERs between end-to-end subarea nodes.

An ER is composed of a sequence of TGs between each pair of adjacent subarea nodes in the selected physical path between two end-to-end subarea nodes. An ER can only have defined to it, and use, one TG between any two adjacent subarea nodes, ie the total number of TGs in an ER must always be just one greater than the number of intermediate subarea nodes traversed by that ER. The same set of TGs are used by an ER for data transfer in both

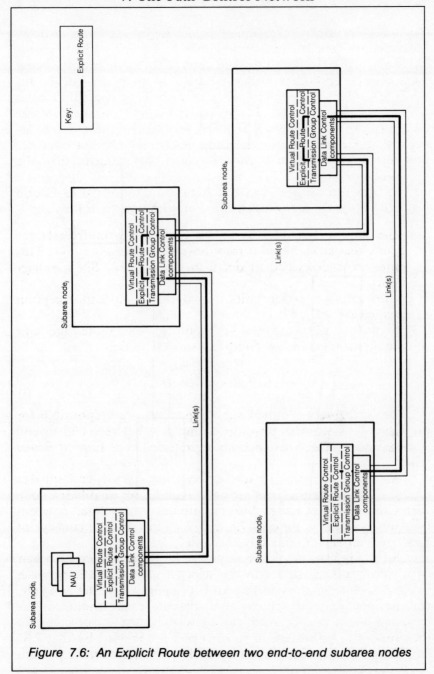

Figure 7.6: An Explicit Route between two end-to-end subarea nodes

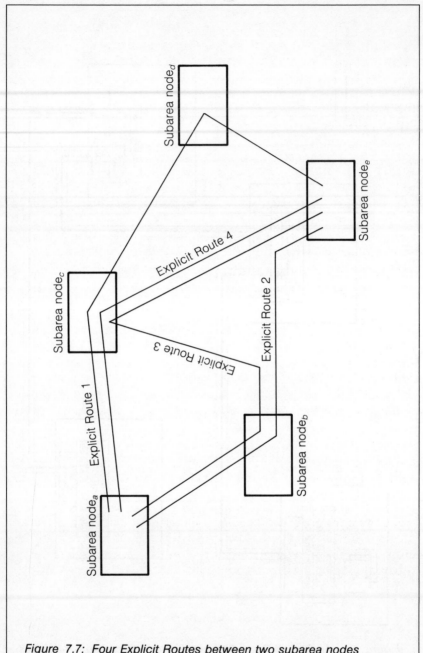

Figure 7.7: Four Explicit Routes between two subarea nodes

directions. The same TG may be shared by multiple ERs. Figure 7.8 illustrates how an ER consists of a sequence of TGs, while Figure 7.9 illustrates the sharing of a TG by multiple ERs.

An ER is identified by the ordered quadruple $<SA_1, SA_2, ERN, RERN>$, where SA_1 and SA_2 are the network addresses of the two end-to-end subarea nodes, ERN is the Explicit Route number for message units transmitted from SA_1 to SA_2 and RERN is the Explicit Route number for message units transmitted from SA_2 to SA_1. (RERN is Reverse Explicit Route Number.) ERN and RERN can each be in the range 0 to 15, and need not be the same value.

Even though the 'source' and 'destination' subarea node addresses and two Explicit Route numbers – ERN and RERN – are used to identify a given ER, the Explicit Route Control subcomponents use a route selection technique, referred to as 'source-independent routing'. This technique utilises only the destination subarea node address and the ERN to select the TG to the next adjacent subarea node, irrespective of the origin subarea node address or the RERN. That is, given the same destination subarea node address and the same ERN, an Explicit Route Control subcomponent will always select the same TG to the next adjacent subarea node, irrespective of the origin subarea node addresses or the RERNs. Therefore, if two ERs that terminate at the same destination subarea, and have the same ERNs, intersect at an intermediate subarea node along their respective physical paths, they will use the same set of TGs from that intermediate node onwards to the destination subarea node. For example, in Figure 7.10, two ERs are depicted, one between subarea node$_1$ and subarea node$_6$ and the other between subarea node$_2$ and subarea node$_6$. They have both been assigned the same ERN value of 2. Both ERs pass through subarea node$_3$. The Explicit Route Control subcomponent of this node will not differentiate between the message units assigned to the two ERs. It will transmit message units corresponding to both ERs on the same TG (to either subarea node$_4$ or subarea node$_5$).

Virtual Route Control

Virtual Route Control subcomponents are responsible for establishing and sustaining *Virtual Routes* (VRs). Virtual Routes are bidirectional, logical connections between two end-to-end

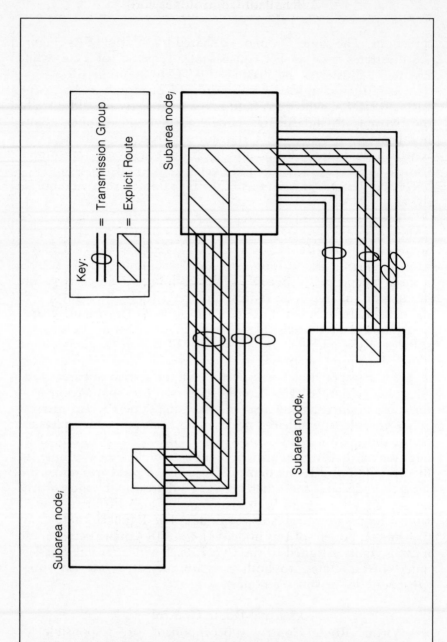

Figure 7.8: An Explicit Route is composed of a sequence of Transmission Groups between adjacent subarea nodes

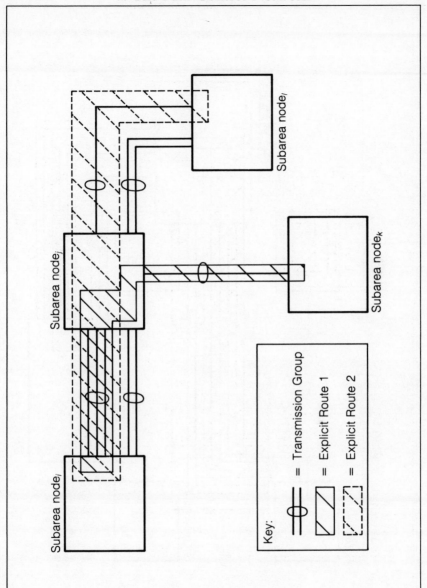

Figure 7.9: Two Explicit Routes sharing the same Transmission Group between subarea node_i and subarea node_j

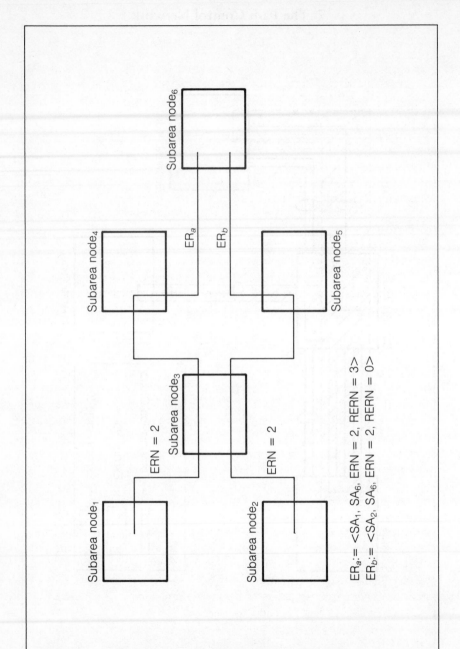

Figure 7.10: Example of intersecting Explicit Routes with the same destination subarea addresses and ERNs

ER$_a$:= <SA$_1$, SA$_6$, ERN = 2, RERN = 3>
ER$_b$:= <SA$_2$, SA$_6$, ERN = 2, RERN = 0>

Subarea node$_6$

ER$_a$
ER$_b$

Subarea node$_4$
Subarea node$_5$

Subarea node$_3$

ERN = 2
ERN = 2

Subarea node$_1$
Subarea node$_2$

subarea nodes that are supporting one or more sessions either between NAUs resident within the two end-to-end subarea nodes, NAUs in one of the subarea nodes and NAUs within a peripheral node supported by the other subarea node, or between NAUs in two peripheral nodes, each supported by one of the end-to-end subarea nodes. (VRs are also used by intra-subarea node NAU-NAU sessions. In each instance, the VR is contained within the subarea node.)

Each VR is associated with an underlying ER. An ER can be associated with multiple VRs.

Each session within an SNA environment is assigned to a VR at session activation. A session can only be assigned to one VR at any one time. However, multiple sessions can share the same VR, between two end-to-end subarea nodes.

Each VR has assigned to it one of three transmission priorities: high, medium or low. These transmission priorities are used by Transmission Group Control subcomponents to determine the order in which message units are de-queued for transmission across the TGs, forming the ER, associated with the VR. All message units belonging to sessions that are assigned to a particular VR are transmitted – along the ER – at the priority specified for the VR. When multiple VRs share the same ER, message units assigned to the VRs with the higher transmission priority are transmitted ahead of message units assigned to VRs that have lower priority.

A VR is identified by the ordered quadruple $<SA_1, SA_2$ VRN, TP>; where SA_1 and SA_2 are the network addresses of the two end-to-end subarea nodes, VRN is a Virtual Route number in the range 0 to 15 assigned to the VR and TP is the transmission priority – high, medium or low – assigned to the VR. The combination of VRN and TP permit up to 48 VRs to be defined between any two subarea nodes. A <VRN, TP> pair, identifying a VR between two subarea nodes, is referred to as a *class of service* (COS). End users can specify the COS for proposed LU-LU sessions by means of a class of service name in the INIT-SELF (or INIT-OTHER) request used to initiate the session.

VRs provide both end-to-end, data flow integrity assurance with VR sequence number assignment and checking for all message units (with the exception of VR pacing responses, which are discussed later in this chapter) transmitted across a VR, and data flow regulation by means of *VR pacing*.

Whereas session pacing, described in Chapter 5, was for regulating the rate of data flow between two session partners, VR pacing regulates the rate, in both directions, at which the combined data flows of all the sessions associated with a particular VR are transmitted.

The VR pacing process is effectively the same as that used by session pacing. However, instead of a fixed pacing window size as used by session pacing, VR pacing uses a dynamic pacing window size, which is varied between a minimum pacing window size and a maximum pacing window size.

VR pacing, in each direction, is based on the following entities:

1 Minimum pacing window size.
2 Maximum pacing window size.
3 VR pacing request.
4 VR pacing response.
5 Pacing count: a count of the number of further message units that can be transmitted before a VR pacing response is required, ie current pacing window size, less the number of message units transmitted since the last VR pacing response was received.
6 VR pacing count indicator: denotes whether the pacing count has reached 0 or not. (When the pacing count reaches 0, no further message units can be transmitted until a VR pacing response is received.)
7 VR reset window indicator: used to instruct the receiving Virtual Route Control subcomponent to reduce its transmission pacing window size and pacing count to the minimum pacing window size.
8 VR change window indicator: used by intermediate nodes to request the receiving Virtual Route Control subcomponent to instruct its counterpart to decrease (or increase) its pacing window size by 1.
9 VR change window reply indicator: used by Virtual Route Control subcomponents to instruct their counterpart to decrease (or increase) its pacing window size by 1.

VR pacing requests, VR pacing responses, VR pacing count

indicators, VR reset window indicators, VR change window indicators and VR change window reply indicators are all realised by specific bits in the FID4-type transmission headers that prefix all message units transmitted on VRs. (FID4-type transmission headers are described in Chapter 10, *SNA message units*.) The FID4-type transmission header bits that correspond to these VR pacing entities are: *VRPRQ* – VR pacing request, *VRPRS* – VR pacing response, *VR_PAC_CNT_IND* – VR pacing count indicator, *VR_RWI* – VR reset window indicator, *VR_CWI* – VR change window indicator and *VR_CWRI* – VR change window reply indicator.

The end-to-end Virtual Route Control subcomponents supporting a given VR totally control the VR pacing of the message units flowing on that VR, in both directions. However, the Path Control components of intermediate subarea nodes that are a part of the ER underlying the VR can influence the VR pacing process by notifying one of the end Virtual Route Control subcomponents of message unit congestion within their nodes.

VR pacing, which is performed independently in each direction, operates in the following manner, in a given direction.

When a VR is activated – by means of an NC_ACTVR request – the minimum and maximum pacing window sizes for it (which are the same for both directions) are specified in the NC_ACTVR request. (The minimum pacing window size is normally set to equal the number of transmission groups in the ER underlying the VR, while the maximum window size is set to be three times the minimum window size.) Upon activation, the minimum window size is used as the 'current' pacing window size. The first message unit transmitted will have the VR pacing request bit – VRPRQ – set in the TH. The transmitter can then transmit further message units until the number transmitted reaches the 'current' pacing window size. On the last message unit transmitted, before the pacing window size is exceeded (ie the pacing count has reached 0), the VR pacing count indicator – VR_PAC_CNT_IND – is set to notify the receiving subcomponent that no further message units can be transmitted to it until it issues a VR pacing response. (A VR response always consists of just a FID4 TH, with the VR pacing response bit – VRPRS – set, with no RH and RU following the TH. VR pacing responses are not assigned VR sequence numbers.)

If the transmitter receives a VR pacing response prior to the pacing count reaching 0, it will begin another pacing iteration, but will not change the pacing window size being used because the current window size is adequate for the rate at which it is transmitting. (That is, since it did not have to suspend transmission awaiting a VR pacing response, the current window size does not restrict its expected rate of transmission.) The 'current' pacing window size is added to the residual count in the pacing count to obtain the new pacing count for the new iteration. Since the pacing count has not reached 0, the new pacing count, ie the number of message units that can be transmitted before a VR pacing response is required, will be greater than the 'current' pacing window size.

However, if the VR pacing response was only received after the pacing count had reached 0 – and a message unit whose TH had VR_PAC_CNT_IND set had been transmitted – the transmitter increases its 'current' pacing size by 1, as the previous window size was inadequate for its desired rate of transmission. This process can be repeated until the 'current' pacing window size reaches the maximum window size specified for the VR. Figure 7.11 depicts the VR pacing process.

If an intermediate node along a VR begins to experience message unit congestion, it can request a gradual reduction in the rate at which message unit s are being transmitted, in a given direction, by setting the VR change window indicator – VR_CWI bit in the TH – on any message units, including VR pacing responses transmitted from that direction. (Once VR_CWI is set, no other node can reset it.) When a message unit arrives at the receiving Virtual Route Control subcomponent with VR_CWI set, it realises that at least one intermediate node along the VR is experiencing difficulty coping with the rate at which its opposite end is transmitting message units and that it must inform it to decrease its rate of transmission. The receiving subcomponent signals the transmitter to reduce its 'current' pacing window size by 1, by setting the VR change window reply indicator – VR_CWRI bit in the TH – on the next VR pacing response it issues. (VR_CWRI is only valid on VR pacing responses and it can only be set by an end Virtual Route Control subcomponent and not by intermediate node Path Control components. Once set, this bit cannot be reset by intermediate nodes.) An end Virtual

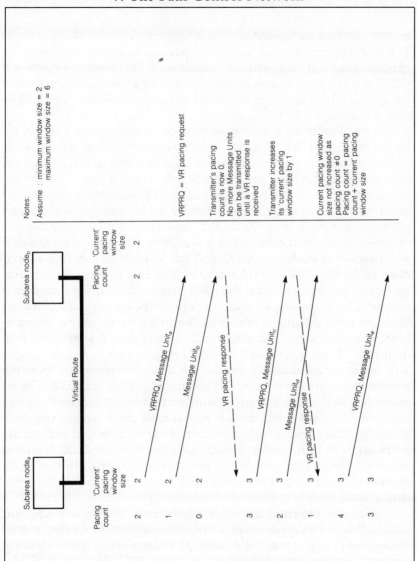

Figure 7.11: Virtual Route Pacing – dynamic adjustments to the 'current' pacing window size based on whether or not the pacing count was 0 when a VR pacing response was received

Route Control subcomponent may also set VR_CWRI to request a reduction in the transmitter's pacing window size if it is experiencing difficulty coping with its rate of transmission, even if it had not received a message unit where an intermediate node had set VR_CWI. That is, an end subcomponent may use VR_CWRI independent of VR_CWI.

A transmitting subcomponent, on receipt of a VR pacing response with VR_CWRI set, decreases its 'current' pacing window size by 1, unless the 'current' size is equal to the minimum window size specified for that VR. (A 'current' pacing window size can never be set to be less than the minimum window size nor more than the maximum window size.) This process whereby an intermediate node sets VR_CWI, and the receiving subcomponents – as a result of receiving a VR_CWI or because of congestion within its own node – sets VR_CWRI on a VR pacing response to request the transmitter to decrease its 'current' pacing window size by 1, will be repeated until the congestion clears. If the congestion was at an intermediate node it will stop setting VR_CWI on message units passing through it. When the receiving subcomponent stops receiving message units with VR_CWI set – or if its own congestion has eased – it will stop setting VR_CWRI on the VR pacing responses it issues to the transmitter. Once the transmitter ceases to receive VR pacing responses with VR_CWRI set, it can again start the process of increasing its 'current' pacing window size by 1 each time it has to wait for a pacing response after its pacing count has reached 0. That is, it will revert to the process it was using before being requested to decrease its 'current' window size. Note that since message unit congestion will be related to a ER, all VRs using that ER will be notified of the congestion.

When an intermediate node experiences severe message unit congestion it can request an immediate reduction in the overall throughput of a given VR's message units passing through it by setting the VR reset window indicator – VR_RWI bit in the TH – on any message unit it forwards along that VR. (As with VR_CWI and VR_CWRI, once VR_RWI is set it cannot be reset by any other node.) On receipt of a message unit with VR_RWI set, a receiving subcomponent will immediately reduce its pacing count to equal the minimum window size for that VR (unless the pacing count is already less than the minimum window size) and also reset its 'current' pacing window size to the minimum window size. (Note that it is the receiver's pacing window size which is reset on receipt of a VR_RWI, in contrast to the transmitter's whose pacing window size is decreased by 1 when VR_CWI is used in conjunction with VR_CWRI.) VR_RWI can also be used by an end Virtual Route Control subcomponent to instruct its counterpart to reset its 'current' pacing count and 'current' pacing window size to equal the minimum window size. Once a receiving subcomponent ceases to receive message units with VR_RWI set it can resort to the normal process for gradually increasing its 'current' pacing window size each time it has to wait for a pacing response once its pacing count has reached 0.

Figure 7.12 illustrates how VR_CWI, VRCWRI and VRRWI are used to govern the end-to-end VR pacing process. Figure 7.13 depicts the relationship between sessions and VRs.

Route extension

When a session involves a NAU in a peripheral node, the route through the Path Control Network used by that session will include a *route extension* between the peripheral node containing the NAU and the boundary function in the subarea node to which the peripheral node is attached. A route extension consists of the SNA link between the peripheral node and the subarea node to which it is attached, the Path Control component in the peripheral node and a portion of the Path Control component in the subarea node.

A session between a NAU in a subarea node and a NAU in a peripheral node will use a route consisting of a VR between the subarea node containing the subarea node NAU and the boundary function in the subarea node to which the subject peripheral node is attached, followed by a route extension between the boundary function and the subject peripheral node.

Figure 7.14 illustrates the concept of a route extension.

Network Control requests

ERs and VRs are controlled by a set of SNA commands referred to as *Network Control* (NC) requests. NC requests which are exchanged either between SSCPs or between an SSCP and a

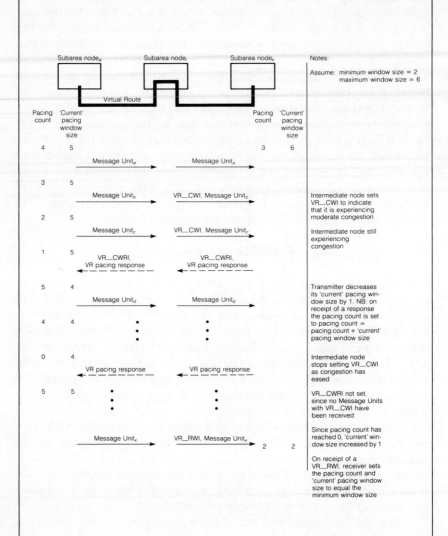

Figure 7.12: *Use of VR_CWI, VR_CWRI and VR_RWI in VR pacing to control the pacing counts and 'current' pacing window sizes*

268

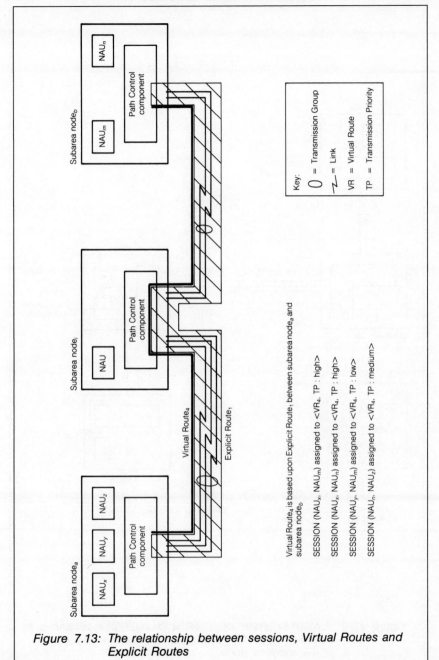

Figure 7.13: The relationship between sessions, Virtual Routes and Explicit Routes

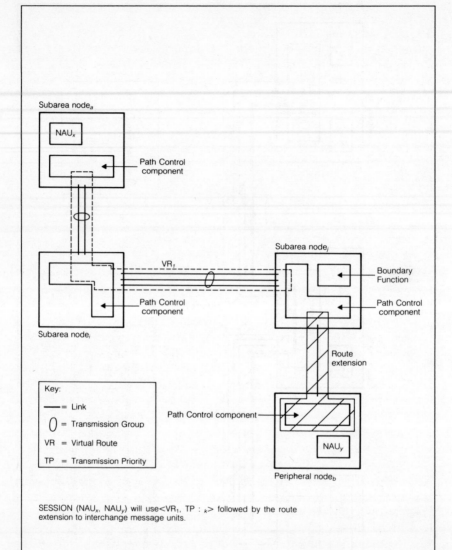

Subarea node$_a$

NAU$_x$

Path Control component

VR$_1$

Subarea node$_j$

Boundary Function

Path Control component

Path Control component

Subarea node$_i$

Route extension

Key:

—— = Link

$\bigcirc$ = Transmission Group

VR = Virtual Route

TP = Transmission Priority

Path Control component

NAU$_y$

Peripheral node$_b$

SESSION (NAU$_x$, NAU$_y$) will use$<$VR$_1$, TP : $_k>$ followed by the route extension to interchange message units.

Figure 7.14: A route extension completing the path for a session between an NAU in a subarea node and an NAU in a peripheral node

270

PU_T4 are conveyed on either SSCP-PU or SSCP-SSCP sessions. (If they are just between adjacent subarea nodes or are being conveyed on a 'hop-by-hop' basis between adjacent nodes, NC requests can be thought of as being PU-PU requests.) The NC requests are as follows:

1 ACTIVATE VIRTUAL ROUTE (NC_ACTVR) – used to activate a given VR, overlayed upon a previously activated ER.

2 DEACTIVATE VIRTUAL ROUTE (NC_DACTVR) – used to deactivate a previously activated VR.

3 EXPLICIT ROUTE ACTIVATE (NC_ERACT) – used to activate a given Explicit Route between two subarea nodes. (It is normally issued as a part of the NC_ACTVR processing to activate an ER to support the subject VR.)

4 EXPLICIT ROUTE ACTIVATE REPLY (NC_ER_ACT_REPLY) – used as the reply to an NC_ER_ACT request to denote whether the Explicit Route activation was successful or unsuccessful. (The RERN for the activated ER is specified in this reply.)

5 EXPLICIT ROUTE INOPERATIVE (NC_ER_INOP) – used when a TG forming a part of one or more ERs becomes inoperative. The subarea nodes on either side of the inoperative TG propagate NC_ER_INOP requests to notify the other subarea nodes that either use or are traversed by these ERs that the subject ER(s) are no longer operative.

6 EXPLICIT ROUTE OPERATIVE (NC_ER_OP) – used when a TG forming a part of one or more ERs becomes operative. The subarea nodes on either side of that TG exchange NC_ER_OP requests specifying which ERs can be supported across that TG.

7 EXPLICIT ROUTE TEST (NC_ERTEST) – used to determine if an ER between the issuing sub area node and a specified destination node exists.

8 EXPLICIT ROUTE TEST REPLY (NC_ER_TEST_REPLY) – used as the reply to an NC_ER_TEST to denote whether the ER is available or not.

9 IPL INITIAL (NC_IPL_INIT), IPL TEXT (NC_IPL_TEXT) and IPL FINAL (NC_IPL_FINAL) – used by subarea node PUs to load Type 2 nodes attached to that subarea.

10 IPL ABORT (NC_IPL_ABORT) – used to prematurely terminate the load of a Type 2 node which was initiated by an NC_IPL_INIT request.

11 (LOST SUBAREA (LSA) - used by pre-SNA 4 subarea node implementations to notify an adjacent subarea node that a link to another subarea node has become inoperative. It is superseded in SNA 4 by NC_ER_OP.)

Figure 7.15 depicts the activation of ERs and VRs.

Network Services: Configuration Services requests

In addition to NC requests a set of function management data services (FMDS) – network services: configuration services (NS(C)) requests – are also used by Path Control Network components to activate, deactivate and control Path Control Network resources. These FMDS NS(C) requests are exchanged either between SSCP and subarea node PUs via SSCP-PU sessions or directly between adjacent subarea node PUs outside any SNA sessions. The FMDS NS(C) requests used by Path Control Network components (in alphabetical order of their mnemonics) are as follows:

1 ABANDON CONNECTION (ABCONN) – used to request a PU to deactivate a specific link.

2 ABANDON CONNECT OUT (ABCONNOUT) – used to request a PU to terminate 'dialled-out' switched link connection.

3 ACTIVATE CONNECT IN (ACTCONNIN) – used to request a PU to enable a specific link station to start accepting in-coming – ie 'dialled-in' – calls, for switched link connections.

4 ACTIVATE LINK (ACTLINK) – used to request a PU to initiate a procedure at a specified link station in its node to activate the interface between that link station and the link connection attached to that station.

5 ADD LINK (ADDLINK), ADD LINK STATION (ADDLINKSTA) – used for dynamic assignment of network addresses. These two requests are used by an SSCP to request

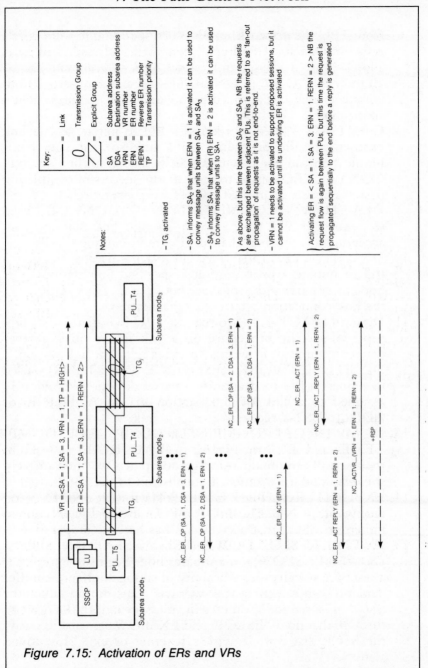

Figure 7.15: Activation of ERs and VRs

273

from a PU the network address corresponding to a link's or a link station's local address. (Network addresses and local addresses are discussed in Chapter 8, *SNA addressing*.)

6 CONNECT OUT (CONOUT) – used to request a PU to initiate a 'dial-out' procedure to establish a switched link connection.

7 CONTACT – used to request a PU to initiate a data link protocol-specific procedure on a link so that data communication can begin with a specified adjacent link station.

8 CONTACTED – used to indicate the successful completion of a previously requested CONTACT operation.

9 DEACTIVATE CONNECT IN (DACTCONNIN) – used to request a PU to disable a specific link station from accepting any further 'dialled-in' – ie in-coming – calls.

10 DEACTIVATE LINK (DACTLINK) – used to request a PU to initiate a procedure at a specified link station in its node to deactivate the interface between that link station and the link connection attached to that station.

11 DISCONTACT – used to request a PU to initiate a data link protocol-specific procedure on a link to terminate further data communication with a specified adjacent link station.

12 DELETE NETWORK RESOURCE (DELETENR) – used to request a PU to deallocate a network address previously assigned to a link or link station via an ADDLINK or ADDLINKSTA request.

13 DUMP INITIAL (DUMPINIT), DUMP TEXT (DUMP-TEXT) and DUMP FINAL (DUMPFINAL) – used to request a PU to obtain a storage dump of a specified adjacent subarea node for eventual transmission to the SSCP.

14 EXPLICIT ROUTE INOPERATIVE (ER_INOP) – on receipt of an NC_ER_INOP a PU can use ER_IN_OP to inform its SSCP that a given ER has become inoperative.

15 ENTERING SLOWDOWN (ESLOW), EXITING SLOW-DOWN (EXSLOW) – if a subarea node begins to experience a resource scarcity – eg a scarcity of storage buffers, ie buffer depletion – it can enter a 'slowdown' state, during which the SSCP must reduce or quiesce the message unit traffic flowing through that node. ESLOW and EXSLOW are used to notify the SSCP that a node wishes to enter or exit 'slowdown' state.

16 INITIATE PROCEDURE (INITPROC) – issued by an SSCP to instruct a subarea node PU to initiate a load operation to a Type 2 node attached to the subarea node it is responsible for.

17 INOPERATIVE (INOP) – used by a PU to inform its SSCP that a link connection or a contact process has failed, affecting one or more of its adjacent nodes.

18 IPL INITIAL (IPLINIT), IPL TEXT (IPLTEXT) and IPL FINAL (IPLFINAL) – used by an SSCP to request a Type 5 or Type 4 node to load a specified adjacent Type 4 node.

19 LOST CONTROL POINT (LCP) – used by a PU to inform an SSCP that an SSCP-PU session it had with another SSCP has failed.

20 LOAD REQUIRED (LDREQD) – used by a PUT2 to request its SSCP to load it with a specific software module.

21 NETWORK SERVICES IPL INITIAL (NS_IPL_INIT), NETWORK SERVICES IPL TEXT (NS_IPL_TEXT), NETWORK SERVICES IPL FINAL (NS_IPL_FINAL) and NETWORK SERVICE IPL ABORT (NS_IPL_ABORT) – these requests are used by an SSCP to load a Type 2 node (cf the NC counterparts, which are used by a subarea node PU as opposed to an SSCP to load a Type 2 node.)

22 (NETWORK SERVICES LOST SUBAREA (NS_LSA) – used by pre-SNA 4 subarea node PUs to inform their SSCPs on the loss of a subarea, following the receipt of an LSA.)

23 PROCEDURE STATUS (PROCSTAT) – used by a subarea node PU to report to its SSCP either the success or the failure of a Type 2 node load operation it had been previously instructed to perform.

24 REQUEST CONTACT (REQCONT) – used by a subarea node PU to notify its SSCP that it has activated a connection with an adjacent secondary link station in a peripheral node, either via a connect-out, ie 'dial-out', or a connect-in, ie 'call-answer', procedure.

25 REQUEST DISCONTACT (REQDISCONT) – used by a peripheral node PU to request its SSCP to initiate a procedure that will ultimately 'discontact' the secondary link station in the peripheral node.

26 REQUEST POWER OFF (RPO) – issued by an SSCP to a subarea node PU requesting it to initiate a data link control-

specific procedure to power-off a specified adjacent Type 4 node.

27 VIRTUAL ROUTE INOPERATIVE (VR_INOP) – used by a PU to inform its SSCP that a VR has become inoperative because the ER it was based on has become inoperative.

In addition to the above Path Control Network-oriented requests there are six more FMDS NS(C) requests:

1 ASSIGN NETWORK ADDRESS (ANA).
2 FREE NETWORK ADDRESS (FNA).
3 REQUEST ACTIVATE LOGICAL UNIT (REQACTLU) – used by a subarea node PU to request that its SSCP issue an ACTLU to a specific LU resident within the same subarea node as the PU issuing the request.
4 REQUEST FREE NETWORK ADDRESS (REQFNA) – used by a PU to request its SSCP to issue an FNA request to it, in order for it to release all network addresses assigned to a particular LU.
5 REQUEST NETWORK ADDRESS ASSIGNMENT (RNAA).
6 SET CONTROL VECTOR (SETCV) – used by a SSCP to convey certain status information to a given subarea node PU.

ANA, FNA and RNAA are described in Chapter 8.

Network Services: Maintenance Services requests

FMDS, Network Services: Maintenance Services (NS(MA)) requests are exchanged either between SSCPs and PUs via SSCP-PU sessions, or between SSCPs and LUs via SSCP-LU sessions, to activate or deactivate diagnostic procedures, convey data obtained from diagnostic procedures or to record statistics on various resources. The FMDS NS(MA) requests are as follows:

1 ACTIVATE TRACE (ACTTRACE) and DEACTIVATE TRACE (DACTTRACE) – used by an SSCP to instruct a subarea node PU to either activate or deactivate a data transmission trace on a specified link or a TG.

2 DISPLAY STORAGE (DISPSTOR) – used by an SSCP to instruct a subarea node PU to transmit a specified number of bytes of its node's storage, starting at a specified address, to the SSCP.

3 REQUEST ECHO TEST (REQECHO) and ECHOTEST – an LU issues a REQECHO request to its SSCP to ask the SSCP to transmit back to it a given number of times the test data included in the REQECHO request. The SSCP uses the ECHOTEST request to transmit the test data back to the subject LU.

4 ROUTE_TEST and EXPLICIT ROUTE TESTED (ER_TESTED) – an SSCP issues ROUTE_TEST to request a subarea node PU to supply it with the status of one or more ERs or VRs supported by the subarea node. The statuses of the ERs or VRs requested are returned to the SSCP in a ROUTE_TEST RESPONSE and an ER_TESTED request.

5 EXECUTE TEST (EXECTEST) – issued by an SSCP to a subarea node PU to request it to perform a specified test on either itself, an LU within the subarea node or a link station within the subarea node.

6 RECORD FORMATTED MAINTENANCE STATISTICS (RECFMS) – used by a PU to convey to its SSCP maintenance-related data pertaining to resources within its node.

7 RECORD MAINTENANCE STATISTICS (RECMS) – used by a subarea node PU to convey maintenance-related data pertaining to itself, its node, links supported by its node or adjacent stations of links supported by its node, to its SSCP.

8 RECORD STORAGE (RECSTOR)–used by subarea node PUs to transmit the data requested via a DISPSTOR request.

9 RECORD TEST DATA (RECTD) – used by subarea node PUs to convey the results of a test performed on receipt of an EXECTEST request.

10 TEST MODE (TESTMODE) and RECORD TEST RESULTS (RECTR) – an SSCP uses TESTMODE to request a subarea node PU to perform an implementation-dependent test procedure. The results of this test are returned via a RECTR request.

11 RECORD TRACE DATA (RECTRD) – used to return the data collected during a trace operation.
12 REQUEST MAINTENANCE STATISTICS (REQMS) – used by an SSCP to request a PU to supply it with maintenance statistics on a particular resource, via an RECFMS request.
13 REQUEST TEST PROCEDURE (REQTEST) – used by a subarea node PU or a LU to request its SSCP to instruct a particular LU to perform a specific test on a specified LU or link station.
14 SET CONTROL VECTOR (SETCV) – issued by an SSCP to set a diagnostic related parameter maintained in subarea node PUs, known as the Intensive Mode Control Vector.

Network Services: Management Services requests

FMDS Network Services: Management Services (NS(MN)) requests are exchanged between SSCPs and LUs via SSCP-LU sessions. Only two NS(MN) requests are defined; they are:

1 DELIVER – used by an SSCP to transmit an embedded FMDS NS(MA) request to a LU. The FMDS NS(MA) requests that may be embedded in a DELIVER request are RECFMS, RECMS, RECSTOR and RECTR. (Note that these FMDS NS (MA) requests, when not embedded in a DELIVER request, are restricted to SSCP-PU sessions.)
2 FORWARD – used by an LU to request its SSCP to relay the FMDS NS(MN) request embedded in the FORWARD request to a specified PU or LU via the appropriate SSCP-PU or SSCP-LU session. The FMDS NS(MN) requests that can be embedded in a FORWARD request are SETCV, DISPSTOR, TESTMODE and REQMS.

Implementational notes

Links

ACF/VTAM supports IBM System/370 channels as link connections to locally (ie channel) attached terminal control units or communication control units executing ACF/NCP, and switched or non-switched telecommunication links as link connections to stand-alone terminals, terminal control units, processors or remote communication control units executing ACF/NCP, via ACF/NCP(s) running in one or more locally-attached communication control units.

Channel link connections for locally-attached SNA terminal control units – *viz* 3274-1As, 3791s, 3730s, or a loop adaptor on 4331 processors – are implicitly specified when the control units are defined as minor nodes within a local SNA major node (qv implementational notes in Chapter 4). The channel address of a locally-attached SNA control unit is specified either in the CUADDR= operands of the PU macro that defines the minor node, or in the VARY command used to activate that control unit. This channel address is the 'link-level' address used by the channel programs within ACF/VTAM to interact with the secondary link station within the control unit. The PU and the LUs within the control unit are addressed by means of their network or local addresses (qv Chapter 8, *SNA addressing*) and not in terms of this channel address. The local addresses of the LUs within these control units – which also indicate which LU services which terminal – are specified via the LOCADDR= operand of the LU macros that follow the PU macro, for each local SNA control unit.

ACF/VTAM also allows locally-attached non-SNA 3270 control units – *viz* 3272s, 3274-1Bs or 3274-1Ds – to participate within an SNA environment. Non-SNA 3270 local control units are defined to ACF/VTAM by means of a Local Non-SNA Major Node. The ACF/VTAM LBUILD macro is used to specify these major nodes. Each 3270 terminal attached to the local non-SNA control unit is then defined as a minor node, within a local non-SNA major node, via a LOCAL macro. The CUADDR= operand of the LOCAL macro specifies the channel addresses assigned to the terminal, while the TERM= operand indicates whether the terminal is a display or a printer. (Note that a non-SNA control unit will not contain a PU or LU and each terminal needs to be directly addressed via its subchannel address.) Channel link connections to local non-SNA 3270 control units are implicitly specified when one or more terminals attached to such control units are defined as local non-SNA minor nodes.

Figure 7.16 outlines how channel-attached terminal control units are defined to ACF/VTAM.

ACF/NCPs – irrespective of whether they are to execute in local or remote communication control units – are defined to ACF/VTAM as individual NCP Major Nodes. If an ACF/NCP is to execute in a locally-attached communications control unit, the mandatory ACT/VTAM PCCU macro prefixing the ACF/NCP definition statements will contain a CUADDR= operand specifying the channel address of the appropriate local communication control unit. (If CUADDR= is not specified for an ACF/NCP, that NCP can still be executed in a locally-attached communications control unit, by specifying a channel address of a local communications control unit, when activating that NCP major node via a VARY command.) ACF/VTAM will automatically provide a channel link connection to a locally-attached communications control unit when asked to activate an ACF/NCP for that communications control unit.

All telecommunication link connections in an ACF/VTAM-based SNA environment are provided and supported by ACF/NCPs executing in local or remote communication control units. ACF/VTAM per se only supports channel link connections. With the exception of link connections to 3270 control units that use Binary Synchronous Communication (BSC) as their link control protocol and certain asynchronous (ie start-stop) terminals supported via the Network Terminal Option (NTO) program product, all other telecommunication link connections in an ACF/VTAM, ACF/NCP SNA environment use Synchronous Data Link Control (SDLC) as their link control protocol. (NTO is described in Chapter 12, *SNA implementation.*)

SDLC link connections are defined in ACF/NCP by means of a hierarchically structured set of macros: GROUP, LINE, SERVICE, PU and LU. This hierarchical structure enables parameters that are common to multiple links or to multiple devices attached to the links to be specified once at a higher level, rather than having to duplicate the parameters on each link or device specification.

The GROUP macro precedes a set of LINE macros that define a group of links and devices having common characteristics. (Each LINE macro must be associated with a GROUP macro: even a LINE macro specifying a unique link or device

```
LOCALSNA   VBUILD   TYPE = LOCAL                          - Defines a local SNA major node
LOC32741   PU       CUADDR = 080,                       + - 3274–1A, minor node with
                                                            channel address = X'080'
                    MODETAB = ISTINCLM.                 + - log-on mode table name
                    DLOGMOD = D4A32783,                 + - default log-on mode entry name
                    USSTAB = ISTINCDT.                  + - USS table name
                    SSCPFM = USSSCS,                    + - LUs in this control unit only
                                                            support character-coded messages
                    PUTYPE = 2,                         + - PU type
                    VPACING = 4                         + - PLU-to-SLU pacing count
L32741T1   LU       LOCADDR = 2                           - LU serving terminal on port 0
L32741T2   LU ...   LOCADDR = 3                           - LU serving terminal on port 1
LOC32742   PU ...   CUADDR =                              - 2nd local SNA minor node
L32742T1   LU ...                                         - Filed as a member in SYS1.VTAMLST

LCNONSNA   LBUILD                                         - Defines a local, non-SNA. 3270 major node
L32771T1   LOCAL    CUADDR = 040. TERM = 3277.          + - 3277 display minor node
                    MODETAB = ISTINCLM.                 +
                    DLOGMODE = D4B32782.                + - 1920 character display
                    FEATUR2 = MODEL2,                     - automatic log-in to application program 'TSO1'
                    LOGAPPL = TSO1,                       - Filed as a member in SYS1.VTAMLST
...
```

Notes:

Figure 7.16: Outline of the definition of channel-attached terminal control units to ACF/VTAM executing under OS/VS

must still be preceded by a GROUP macro.) The GROUP macro defines whether the link connections specified by the LINE macros following it are switched or non-switched, SDLC or non-SDLC etc. Each LINE macro defines a single SDLC link. If an SDLC link consists of more than one secondary link station – ie a multipoint link – a SERVICE macro is required for that link to specify the sequence – ie order – in which the primary link station should service the secondary link stations. The PU macro is used to represent a device attached to the link, while the LU macro defines the individual LUs within a given device.

Switched – dial-in or dial-out – SDLC links, in addition to being specified in an ACF/NCP, are also directly defined to ACF/VTAM by means of minor nodes within a Switched Major Node. A Switched Major Node has the following structure:

SWTCHND0	**VBUILD**	**TYPE = SWNET,** **MAXERP = 1,** **MAXNO = 2**	Defines switched major node
CU3276A1	**PU**	**ADDR = 01,**	Start of a 3276 minor node. SDLC address=X'01'
		PUTYPE = 2, **IDBLK = 018,**	Specifies the device as being a 3276
		IDNUM = 15678 . . .	Terminal ID
	PATH	**DIALNO =** **0582764564,**	Defines a dial-out link
		GRPNM = **SWTCGRP0**	Reference to appropriate GROUP macro in the ACF/NCP definition
T3276A10	**LU**	**LOCADDR = 2, . .**	LU definitions for the devices attached to the 3276 control unit

T3276A11   **LU**   **LOCADDR = 3, . .**
.
.
.
TE3767A1   **PU**   **ADDR = C0, . . .**   Start of next
.   minor node
.
.

BSC links to 3270 control units – *viz* 3271s, 3274-1Cs, 3274-51Cs, 3274-61Cs, 3276-1/2/3/4s – are defined in a similar manner to SDLC links, but CLUSTER and TERMINAL macros are used in place of PU and LU macros. Figure 7.17 outlines how SDLC and BSC links are defined in ACF/NCP.

Transmission Groups

TGs are only supported by ACF/VTAM Release 3 and ACF/NCP Release 3. Prior versions of VTAM and NCP only permitted one active link between subarea nodes.

A TG can consist of a single channel link between an IBM System/370 host containing ACF/VTAM Release 3 and a locally-attached communications control unit executing ACF/NCP3, or one or more SDLC links between local or remote communication control units executing ACF/NCP 3.

A TG consisting of a channel link is always assigned, implicitly, a TGN of 1, even if a host has multiple communications control units – each requiring a separate TG – attached to it. Since each communications control unit will have a unique subarea address, multiple TGs, all with a TGN of 1, emanating from a host can be differentiated by their 'end' subarea node address.

SDLC links between communications control units are grouped into TGs by means of the TGN= operand of the PU macro that defines a communications control unit on an SDLC link. The link defined by the LINE macro associated with the PU macro specifying TGN= is assigned to the TG corresponding to the TGN indicated. (The TGN specified for a given link between two communications control units must be the same at both ends.

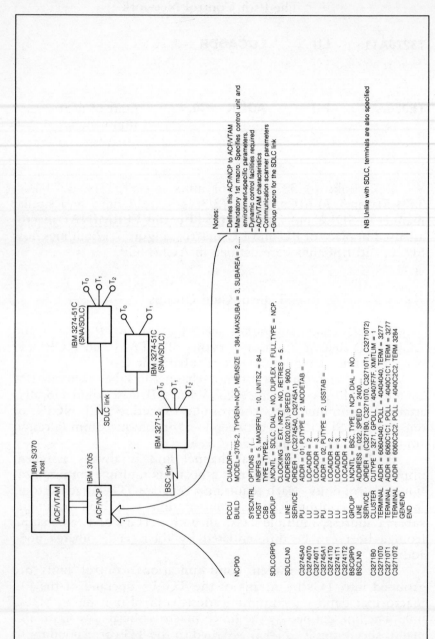

Figure 7.17: Skeleton of an ACF/NCP that defines an SDLC link and a BSC link

284

To simplify this correlation, TGN=ANY may be coded at one end. If so, the TGN specified at the other end is used to assign the link, on activation, to a TG.)

Figure 7.18 illustrates how TGs are defined in an ACF/VTAM Release 3, ACF/NCP 3 environment.

Explicit Routes and Virtual Routes

Since ERs and VRs are based on TGs, only ACF/VTAM Release 3 and ACF/NCP Release 3 support them.

ACF/VTAM Release 3 (and ACF/NCP 3) permit up to eight ERs between any two subareas. VRs are then overlayed onto these ERs. In an ACF/VTAM environment at least one end of each VR defined must be in a 'host' subarea. As such, VRs are only defined to ACF/VTAMs.

VRs are defined to ACF/VTAM, in conjunction with the relevant ERs onto which they are overlayed, by means of PATH statements filed in the ACF/VTAM definition library. A PATH statement has the following structure:

label **PATH DESTSA**=n (n_1, n_2, n_3,...)
   [,ER0=(*adjsub*,**TGN)]**
   [,ER1=(*adjsub*,**TGN)]**
    .
    .
    .
   [,ER7=(*adjsub*,**TGN)]**
   [,VR0=*er#*]
   [,VR1=*er#*]
    .
    .
    .
   [,VR7=*er#*]

where the DESTSA= operand specifies one or more destination subarea addresses (or numbers) – n_i – for the ERs and VRs being defined; the ERx= operand, where x is the ER number, specifies the adjacent subarea to which message units assigned to this ER should be forwarded, and the TGN parameter specifies the TG

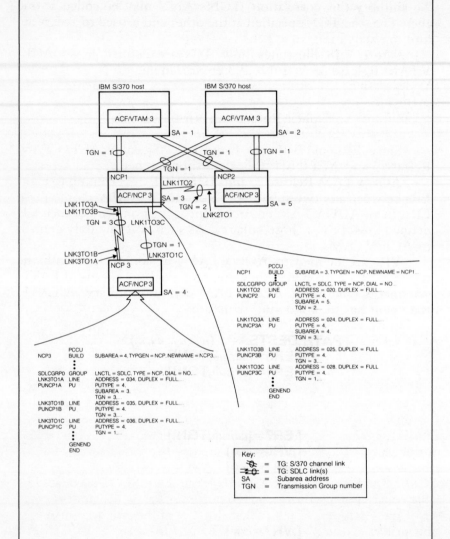

Figure 7.18: Defining Transmission Groups between subarea nodes in an ACF/VTAM Release 3, ACF/NCP 3 environment

that will be used to transmit the message units from the 'host' subarea to the subject adjacent subarea (since TGs consisting of a channel link are always assigned a TGN of 1, this parameter may be omitted); the VRx= operand, where x is the VR number, specifies the ER number into which this VR should be overlayed. (At least one ER and VR must be defined in each PATH statement.)

Within ACF/NCPs, only ERs are defined. These are defined by means of PATH macros, which have the following structure:

label   **PATH DESTSA**=$n|(n_1, n_2, n_3, ...)$
             [,ER0=(*adjsub***,TGN)]**
             [,ER1=(*adjsub***,TGN)]**
             .
             .
             .
             [,ER7=(*adjsub***,TGN)]**

where the operands and the parameters have the same meanings as their counterparts in the ACF/VTAM PATH statement.

Figure 7.19 illustrates how ERs and VRs are defined in an ACF/VTAM Release 3, ACF/NCP 3 environment.

Class of Service

The VR to be used for conveying the traffic of a given LU-LU session is specified via a Class of Service (COS) reference in the log mode table entry associated with that session. A COS table is constructed within ACF/VTAM Release 3 by means of the ACF/VTAM macros COSTAB, COS and COSEND. The COS table consists of a series of named entries, each of which defines a set of one or more VRs by means of VR numbers and transmission priorities – ie by means of <VRN,TP> pairs. The COS= operand of the MODEENT macro (which defines log mode table entries) refers to the COS table entry that will specify the possible VRs for the LU-LU sessions that quote that log mode table entry at session activation. (One unnamed entry can be included in the COS table to cater for all LU-LU sessions that refer to a log mode table entry that does not contain a COS= operand.)

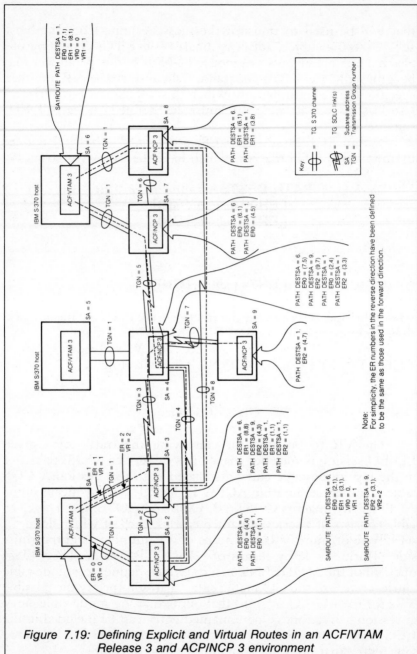

Figure 7.19: Defining Explicit and Virtual Routes in an ACF/VTAM Release 3 and ACP/NCP 3 environment

288

The COS table – which must be named ISTSDCOS – is defined by means of the COSTAB macro, which precedes all the COS macros which define each of the COS table entries.

The COS macro has the following structure:

name   **COS VR=(*vr#*,*tp*)|((*vr#*,*tp*),(*vr#*,*tp*),(*vr#*,*tp*),...)**

where *vr#* specifies a VR number and *tp* specifies a transmission priority using the codes 0 = low, 1 = medium, 2 = high.

Each COS entry may specify up to 24 possible VRs. When an LU-LU session is activated, the VR to be used by that session is selected from the relevant COS table entry in the order in which the <*vr#*,*tp*> pairs are specified. The selection process picks the first physically available route listed in the COS entry.

(NB ACF/VTAM Release 3 does not cater for alternate routing, so if a VR becomes inoperative, all sessions using that VR are terminated. ACF/VTAM does not attempt to reinitiate these disrupted sessions over another VR, even if multiple possible VRs were specified in the COS entries corresponding to these sessions. A failed session will only be reinitiated – providing another VR is available – if one of the session partners explicitly requests ACF/VTAM to initiate that session again.)

The COS table is terminated by a COSEND macro.

Figure 7.20 depicts the structure of the COS table, while Figure 7.21 illustrates the process used to identify the route to be used by a given LU-LU session.

VR pacing window size specification

ACF/VTAM Release 3 'automatically' calculates the minimum and maximum window sizes for VRs, using an internal 'subroutine', without any explicit instructions or data from the system implementor. If the implementor wishes to override these window sizes, the 'subroutine' itself has to be modified or replaced.

SLOWDOWN

The criteria for an ACF/NCP to enter SLOWDOWN are specified in the SLOWDOWN= operand of the ACF/NCP

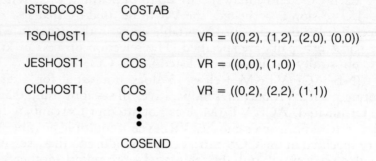

ISTSDCOS   COSTAB

TSOHOST1   COS   VR = ((0,2), (1,2), (2,0), (0,0))

JESHOST1   COS   VR = ((0,0), (1,0))

CICHOST1   COS   VR = ((0,2), (2,2), (1,1))

$\vdots$

COSEND

Figure 7.20: Structure of the Class of Service Table

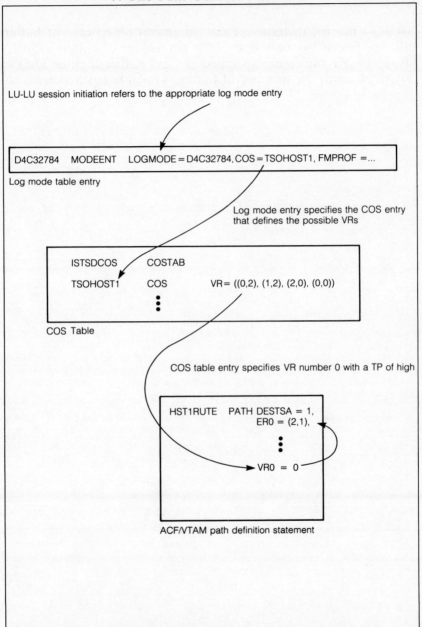

Figure 7.21: The process of identifying the route to be used by an LU-LU session

BUILD macro, in terms of the minimum percentage of buffers that are free at any one time. If the percentage of buffers available drops below the figure specified, ACF/NCP will enter SLOW-DOWN, until the number of buffers available again exceeds the threshold figure.

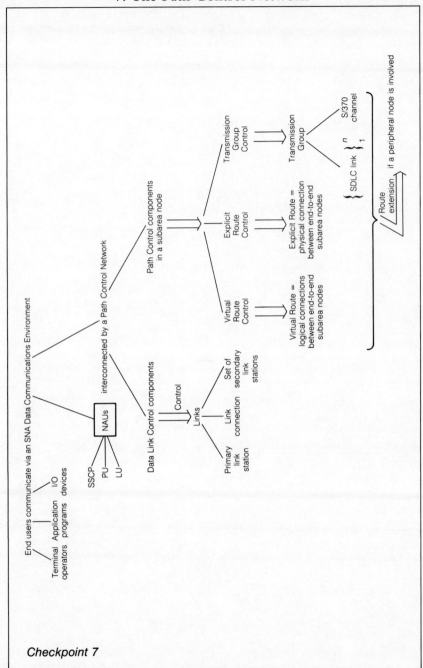

Checkpoint 7

Chapter 8:
SNA addressing

☐ Network Address ☐ Parallel Sessions ☐ Subarea Address ☐ Element Address ☐ Network Names ☐ Uninterpreted/ Alternative Names ☐ Local Addresses ☐ LSID ☐ RNAA/FNA

Chapter 8:
SNA addressing

Addressing rules

Each NAU and link station in an SNA environment has at least one unique address assigned to it. These addresses are referred to as *network addresses*. SNA specifies the following rules on the allocation of network addresses:

- Each SSCP is assigned a single network address
- Each PU is assigned a single network address
- Each LU, resident in a peripheral node, is assigned a single network address
- Each LU, resident in a subarea node, is assigned one or more network addresses
- Each primary link station, resident in a subarea node, is assigned a single network address
- Each secondary link station, on a link emanating from a subarea node, is assigned a single network address
- (The network address assigned to a secondary link station, on a switched link, will be numerically one greater than the network address assigned to the primary link station of that link, ie network address: secondary link station on a switched link = network address: primary link station for link + 1.)

Since a session can be uniquely identified by the ordered pair <primary NAU network address, secondary NAU network address>, it is only LUs intending to establish parallel sessions that need multiple network addresses. (An LU that wishes to establish multiple, but non-parallel, sessions does not need multiple network addresses, as each session will have a different primary NAU or secondary NAU network address.) When parallel sessions exist between two LUs each uses a different network address for each parallel session for which it is the primary LU. But a single secondary network address – which has not been used in sessions for which it is the primary – is used for all sessions, irrespective of whether they are parallel or non-parallel sessions. This secondary address is also used for the SSCP-LU session. As such, only an LU in a subarea node can act as the primary LU in parallel sessions. LUs in peripheral nodes can only participate in parallel sessions as the secondary. (Note that parallel sessions are only possible between LUs. SSCPs support multiple, but non-parallel, sessions. PUs can only support one session – an SSCP-PU session – at any one time.)

Network addresses

A network address is 16 bits long and is made up of two parts:

1 A subarea address component.
2 An element address component.

Each subarea, ie a subarea node and all the peripheral nodes attached to it, in an SNA environment is assigned a unique address. This address is known as the subarea address, subarea number or subarea ID.

The network addresses of all NAUs and link stations, within nodes that are part of the same subarea, have the same subarea address component, which consists of the subarea address assigned to the subarea.

Each NAU and link station, within nodes that are part of the same subarea, is assigned a distinct element address relative to the subarea. An element address is only unique within a given subarea. The same element addresses can be used in different subareas. This element address is used as the element address component of the network address. SNA specifies that the PU_T5 or PU_T4 in the subarea node, of each subarea, is assigned an element address of 0.

SNA does not specify how the 16 bits of the network address should be split between the subarea address component and the element address component. The subarea address component, which occupies the most significant bits of the network address, can vary in length from one to eight bits, while the element address component can vary from eight to 15 bits. (The total length of the subarea address component and the element address component cannot exceed, or be shorter than, 16 bits.) Figure 8.1 depicts the format of an SNA network address.

The number of bits to be used for the subarea address and element address components of the network address is defined at system installation. The component lengths chosen must be used in all network addresses used within the environment, ie all network addresses in a given environment use the same number of bits to specify the subarea and element address components. (Once defined at system installation, the component lengths can only be modified by regenerating the system definitions.)

(This 16-bit addressing scheme, capable of addressing up to 65 536 elements, and the variable-length subarea and element address component comprise the original addressing scheme introduced with SNA 0. SNA 4 defined a new transmission header – known as FID4 – for message units passing between subarea nodes. Though the addressing scheme was not changed by SNA 4, FID4 – which is described in Chapter 10 – specifies 32 bits for the subarea address component of a network address and 16 bits for the element address component of a network address. At present the subarea and element address components of the 16-bit network addresses, when used with FID4, need to be separated and then inserted into the respective 32-bit and 16-bit fields in the FID4. All SNA requests that specify network addresses, eg CINIT or CDINIT, still use the 16-bit addressing scheme.)

Network names

Each LU, PU and primary link station in an SNA environment is given an EBCDIC character-encoded name. This name is referred to as the *network name* of that resource. Network names, unlike network addresses which are unique across the environ-

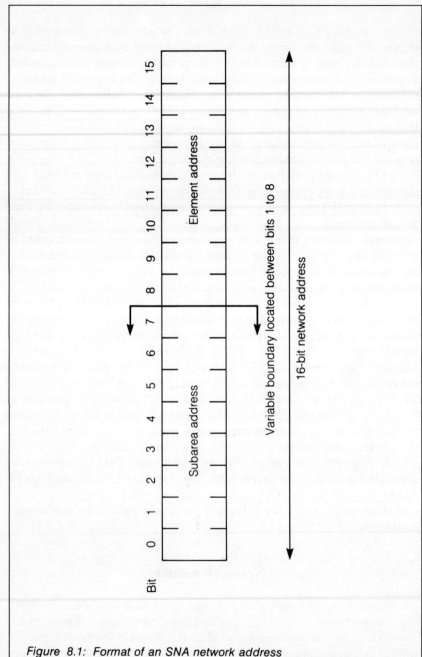

Figure 8.1: Format of an SNA network address

ment, need only be unique within the domains in which the resources they identify are used. That is, network names within a domain must be unique, but it is only the names of resources that are to be used for cross-domain applications that need to be unique across the domains intending to use them. Therefore, the same network name may occur in more than one domain, provided that the name does not refer to a resource that may be used in cross-domain applications with a domain containing another resource with the same name. Figure 8.2 illustrates how the same network name can be used in multiple domains provided that they do not cause cross-domain use conflicts.

The network name of a PU, a primary link station or a peripheral node LU, corresponds to a unique network address, while the network name of a subarea node LU may correspond to a single network address or a set of network addresses, depending on the number of network addresses assigned to the LU. An SSCP maintains translate tables pertaining to the resources within its domain so that it can convert the network names of resources in its domain to the corresponding network address(es) or *vice versa*. (Note that in cross-domain session initiations it is always the SSCP that controls the relevant LU that converts the network name to the corresponding network address, as the other SSCPs do not have the necessary translate tables.)

Uninterpreted names

In addition to its network name an LU may have one or more alternate names associated with it. These alternate names are referred to as the *uninterpreted names* of that LU.

Uninterpreted names are only used during LU-LU session initiation or termination. An end user instructing the LU via which it accesses the environment to establish or terminate an LU-LU session can identify the other LU by means of its associated uninterpreted name (rather than by its network name) ie the DLU in INIT-SELF or TERM-SELF requests, or both DLU and OLU in INIT-OTHER or TERM-OTHER requests, can be specified by means of uninterpreted names.

An LU's uninterpreted name is always translated to the network name of that LU by the SSCP that receives the INIT-

Domain (Subarea 1)	Domain (Subarea 4)	Domain (Subarea 9)
LUs defined within domain	LUs defined within domain	LUs defined within domain
LU1 LU2 LU4	LU2 LU3 LU4 LUA LUX	LU2 LU4 LUA LUX LUY
Other domain LU usage	Other domain LU usage	Other domain LU usage
LU3 in domain (subarea 4) LUX in domain (subarea 9)	LU1 in domain (subarea 1) LUY in domain (subarea 9)	LU1 in domain (subarea 1)

Note:

Domain(subarea *n*) = domain of the SSCP which is assigned subarea address '*n*'

Figure 8.2: Use of the same network name in different domains

SELF, INIT-OTHER, TERM-SELF or TERM-OTHER request containing the uninterpreted name(s). (LUs are specified by network name, rather than by uninterpreted name, in all other session initiation or termination requests, such as INIT-OTHER-CD, CDINIT, TERM-OTHER-CD, CDTERM.) As such, uninterpreted names need only be unique within each domain. An LU that will be involved in cross-domain sessions can be referred to by the same uninterpreted name in all the relevant domains or by a different uninterpreted name in each domain. For example, in Figure 8.2, LU3 in domain (subarea 4), could be known in domain (subarea 1) by the uninterpreted name APL1. When the SSCP (domain (subarea 1)) receives an initiation or termination request from one of its LUs specifying APL1, it will first translate that to LU3 before proceeding with the initiation or termination request. The network name LU3 will be used during the rest of the initiation or termination process.

Local addressing

All message units transmitted from one NAU to another contain the network address of the NAU to which the message unit is being sent and the network address of the NAU that sent the message. The network address of the NAU to which the message unit is being sent is known as the *destination address*, while the network address of the NAU that sent the message is known as the *origin address*. The destination address and origin address, for a given message unit, are contained in the *transmission header* of the message unit. (Message units and transmission headers are dealt with in Chapter 10, *Message units.*)

NAUs and Path Control Network components in subarea nodes have little difficulty coping with the 16-bit destination and origin network addresses of message units – with their variable length subarea and element address components – since the functions that need to be performed by these nodes dictate that they are implemented in machines or devices that are programmable and have significant processing powers. However, the same is not true for NAUs and Path Control Network components in peripheral nodes. Peripheral devices are usually implemented in devices which have limited processing capabilities. These devices also tend to be either non-programmable devices, or devices with restricted programming or reprogramming facilities. As such, assigning 16-bit network addresses to resources in peripheral nodes, especially in view of the variable length subarea and element address components, and expecting them to decipher the destination and origin network address in message units, is impractical. Thus, in deference to implementational considerations, for peripheral node resources SNA specifies a simpler addressing scheme to network addressing. This simpler addressing scheme is known as *local addressing*. (It is a good example of the pragmatism that is inherent in the SNA specification!)

Local addressing is intended to provide the following:

- A simple identification scheme to denote the destination and origin of message units to or from peripheral nodes
- A means of being able to either pre-assign, or very easily assign, addresses to peripheral node resources.

Local addresses are assigned to each PU, LU and secondary link station in each peripheral node, in addition to the network addresses that are associated with them. But peripheral node resources are not aware of their network addresses, or the network addresses of any of the other resources in the environment. Peripheral node NAUs always refer to other NAUs, eg in an INIT-SELF request, by their uninterpreted or network name. The local addresses assigned to the resources of a particular peripheral node are not known, and therefore not used, by NAUs in subarea nodes or in other peripheral nodes. These NAUs will identify the resources in the peripheral node either by uninterpreted name, network name or network address, but never by local address.

Only the boundary function in the subarea node to which a peripheral node is attached is aware of, and therefore able to use, the local addresses assigned to the resources of that peripheral node. As such, local addresses can only be used to identify the destination and source of message units when they are in transit between a peripheral node and the boundary function, in the subarea node to which the peripheral node is attached. These message units must, if destined for a peripheral node NAU, arrive at the boundary function with, or if originated from a peripheral node NAU, leave the boundary function with network addresses denoting the destination and origin NAUs. So the boundary function, in a subarea node, is responsible for transforming network addresses specifying destination and origin NAUs of message units to local addresses, and vice versa. (Note that local addresses can only be used as a substitute for network addresses in identifying the destination and origin of message units. They cannot be used in an SNA request to specify a resource.)

Local addresses assigned to peripheral node NAUs need only be unique within each peripheral node, ie the same local address can be assigned to NAUs in different peripheral nodes, even if these peripheral nodes are all attached to the same subarea node. The local addresses assigned to secondary link stations in peripheral nodes tend to be the data link control dictated address for the device containing the peripheral node. Hence, the local address for a secondary link station is unique relative to the link it is on, ie local addresses for secondary link stations can only be the same if they are on different links. Within this addressing structure, a peripheral node NAU can be uniquely identified: it qualifies its local address with the link that the peripheral node containing the NAU is on, and with the local address of the secondary link station serving the peripheral node. The link that a peripheral node is on can be identified by the network address of the link's primary link station. So, the boundary function, in a subarea node, uses the following transformations to convert network addresses of peripheral node resources to distinct local addresses, and *vice versa*:

> network address (secondary link station)⟺network address
> (primary link station for link),
> local address (secondary link station)
> network address (NAU) ⟺ network address (primary link
> station),
> local address (secondary link station),
> local address (NAU)

Note that these transformations cannot be used to convert network addresses of other NAUs to appropriate local addresses. That depends on the local addressing scheme used.

There are two different local addressing schemes, one for Type 1 nodes and the other for Type 2 nodes.

(The subarea node to which a peripheral node is attached is known as the peripheral node's *adjacent subarea node*. This term will be used during the rest of this chapter instead of 'the subarea node to which the peripheral node is attached'.)

Local addressing: Type 1 nodes

The local addressing scheme for Type 1 nodes reflects the limited processing capabilities (and requirements) of these nodes, and the limits that this imposes upon the LU-LU session characteristics of LUs within these nodes. The local addressing scheme for Type 1 nodes is based upon the following attributes of Type 1 nodes and of the LU they contain:

1 A Type 1 node will not contain more than 64 LUs.
2 LUs in Type 1 nodes will always be the secondary LUs in all the LU-LU sessions that they participate in.
3 LUs in Type 1 nodes will only support one LU-LU session at any given time (ie they cannot support multiple LU-LU sessions).

These characteristics indicate that:

1 Six bits will suffice to uniquely identify the maximum number of LUs that can occur in a Type 1 node.
2 An LU in a Type 1 node will only have, at most, two sessions at any one time: an SSCP-LU session and an LU-LU session.
3 Since an LU in a Type 1 node can only have one LU-LU session at a time, the address of the other LU (ie the PLU) is not required to indicate the source of message units that an LU in a Type 1 node receives on its LU-LU session (via its adjacent subarea node boundary function); nor is it required to indicate the destination of a message unit an LU in a Type 1 node transmits on its LU-LU session (via its adjacent subarea node boundary function). The adjacent subarea node boundary function, by monitoring BIND and UNBIND requests to the LUs in a Type 1 node, can obtain the network address of the LU that a given LU in a Type 1 node is in session with.

Thus, the local addressing scheme for Type 1 node NAUs consists only of eight bits. The structure of this eight-bit addressing scheme – which is referred to as a *Local Session Identification* (LSID) – is shown in Figure 8.3.

With LSID, six bits, (bits 2 to 7) are used to address the LUs within the Type 1 node. Thus, an LU within a Type 1 node could have a local address in the range X'00' to X'3F'. (Which address within the range 0 to 63 is given to which LU is an implementational option.) The other two bits (0 and 1) are used to denote the type of session to which the message unit associated with the LSID belongs. If a message unit belongs to an LU-LU session, both these bits will be on. If it belongs to an SSCP-LU session, bit 0 will be off, while bit 1 will be on. For both these session types, bits 2 to 6 will specify the local address of the LU in the Type 1 node which is either to receive, or has transmitted, the associated message unit. If, however, the message unit belongs to the SSCP-PU session, all the eight bits of the LSID will be off. Figure 8.4 summarises the bit configurations used in the LSID scheme. (Note that bit 0 being on and bit 1 being off, which would indicate an LU-PU interaction, is not a permitted bit setting.)

The data link control protocol address (ie SDLC) serves as the local address for secondary link stations in Type 1 nodes.

Figure 8.5 illustrates the conversion of network addresses specifying the destination and origin of message units to LSIDs.

(Note that the LSID addressing scheme will not permit a Type 1 node to have more than 64 LUs or these LUs to support more than one LU-LU session at a time.)

Local addressing: Type 2 nodes

Type 2 nodes are expected to have more processing capabilities than Type 1 nodes, and so they should be able to support more LUs than Type 1 nodes. These LUs should also be capable of participating in multiple LU-LU sessions. Hence, a more comprehensive local addressing scheme than that provided by LSID is required for Type 2 nodes. LUs in Type 2 nodes, being capable of participating in multiple LU-LU sessions, dictate that each message unit to or from them specifies the LU-LU session it relates to. So the local addressing scheme for Type 2 nodes is based on

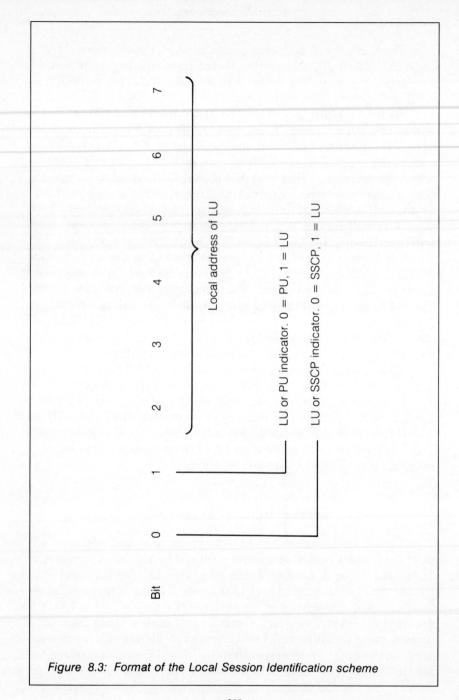

Figure 8.3: Format of the Local Session Identification scheme

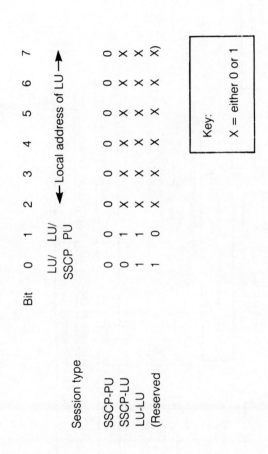

Session type	Bit 0 LU/ SSCP	1 LU/ PU	2	3	4	5	6	7
			←— Local address of LU —→					
SSCP-PU	0	0	0	0	0	0	0	0
SSCP-LU	0	1	X	X	X	X	X	X
LU-LU	1	1	X	X	X	X	X	X
(Reserved)	1	0	X	X	X	X	X	X)

Key:
X = either 0 or 1

Figure 8.4: *Bit settings used in Local Session Identification*

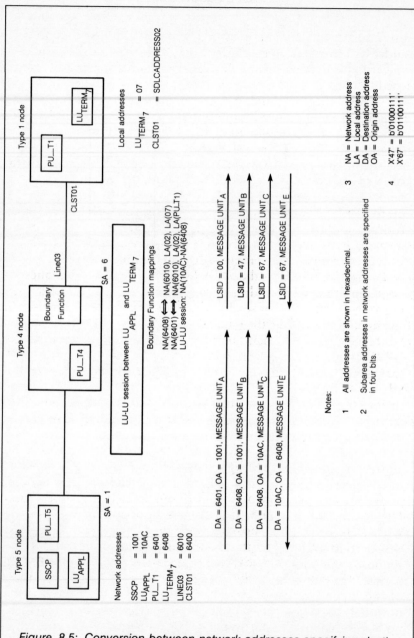

Figure 8.5: Conversion between network addresses specifying destination and origin of message units and LSIDs

310

prefixing each message with a destination address and an origin address. However, instead of using 16-bit network addresses to specify the destination and origin, eight-bit local addresses are used.

Thus, the local addressing scheme for Type 2 node NAUs consists of an eight-bit destination address and an eight-bit origin address. (As with Type 1 nodes, the Data Link Control protocol (channel or SDLC)-specified address is used as the local address for secondary link stations in Type 2 nodes.) The eight-bit local addresses allow a Type 2 node to contain up to 256 NAUs. Since one of these addresses – usually X'00' – is required for the PU_T2, up to 255 LUs can be implemented within a Type 2 node. (Which address within this range is assigned to which LU is left as an implementational option.)

In addition to the local addresses assigned to them, another set of eight-bit 'local addresses' is required for each LU in a Type 2 node, to indicate which LU-LU session a particular message unit belongs to. These 'local addresses' are assigned, by the adjacent subarea node Boundary Function, when an LU-LU session is established. The Boundary Function does this by monitoring the BIND requests to the LUs in Type 2 nodes, and assigning the LU that is not resident in the Type 2 node, a notional eight-bit local address that will be used to uniquely identify it for the duration of that session. The Boundary Function will then transmit the BIND request to the Type 2 node-resident LU, with the eight-bit destination address specifying the local address of the Type 2 node LU and the eight-bit origin address specifying the notional local address assigned to the other LU. (Though not precluded by the SNA specification or the local addressing scheme, LUs in Type 2 nodes are not envisaged as being the PLUs in LU-LU sessions. Hence, an LU in a Type 2 node will only have LU-LU sessions with LUs resident in subarea nodes.) All further message units that pertain to the LU-LU session that was proposed by the BIND request – including the positive or negative response to it – will be identified by the notional local address and the actual local address of the Type 2 node-resident LU. SNA does not specify how the notional local addresses will be assigned to the non-Type 2 node-resident LUs. (In practice, for each LU in a Type 2 node, X'00' is used to denote messages on its SSCP-LU session and the remaining addresses – X'01' to X'FF' – are allocated sequentially to identify each LU-LU session that is established. That is, the other LU, in the first LU-LU session that is established, is assigned a notional local address of X'01'; the other LU in the second LU-LU session that is established is assigned a notional local address of X'02' etc.) Figure 8.6 illustrates the conversion of network addresses to notional and actual local addresses.

Note that this addressing scheme limits to 255 the number of concurrent LU-LU sessions that an LU in a Type 2 node can participate in.

Advantages of using local addresses

The advantages of using local addresses for peripheral node resources are as follows:

1 Peripheral node resources do not have to work with 16-bit network addresses with variable length subarea and element address fields. (While the 16-bit addresses *per se* could be catered for, the variable length fields would present a problem, especially with non-programmable devices, not only in decoding and encoding of addresses, but also in terms of the procedure for notifying the device of these lengths.)
2 Since the local addresses for NAUs are only unique relative to each peripheral node, these local addresses can be pre-assigned when the node is being manufactured.
3 The local address of a peripheral node secondary link station can be assigned via a set of switches or by means of a simple customisation process.
4 Reconfiguration of SNA environments is greatly simplified. A regeneration could result in all the resources in the environment, including peripheral node resources, being assigned new network addresses. But since this does not in any way impact the local addresses assigned to the resources within peripheral nodes, LSIDs, or the notional local addresses allocated by a Boundary Function, reconfigurations are totally transparent to peripheral nodes and no modifications have to be performed to them to reflect the changes caused by the reconfiguration.

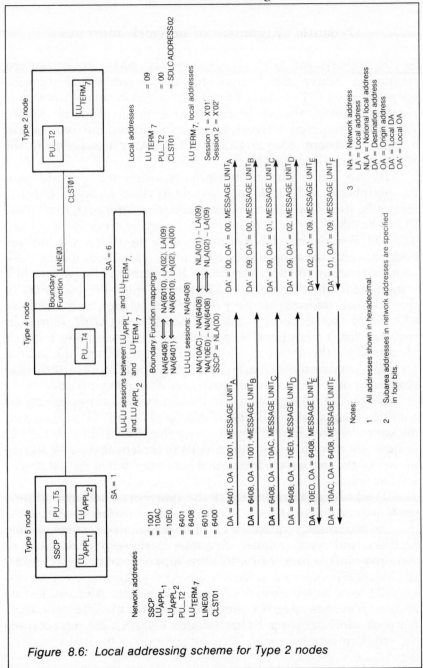

Figure 8.6: Local addressing scheme for Type 2 nodes

313

Dynamic assignment of network addresses

If a peripheral node is dynamically added to or moved within an 'active' SNA environment, or additional network addresses need to be assigned to an LU so that it can accommodate parallel sessions, the SSCP can request the appropriate PU to allocate the required network addresses. This is done by means of a *Request Network Address Assignment* (RNAA) message from the SSCP to the relevant PU.

RNAA can be used to dynamically assign network addresses for peripheral node LUs and secondary link stations. (RNAA cannot be used to request a network address for a peripheral node PU. The SSCP must allocate the network address for the PU.) The SSCP issues the RNAA message to the PU in the subarea node to which the subject peripheral node is attached. If a network address is required for a secondary link station, the subject link station is identified to the adjacent subarea node PU by means of the network address of the primary link station and the local address of the secondary link station. If a network address is required for a peripheral node-resident LU, the subject LU is identified by the network address of the secondary link station serving the node the LU is in, and by the local address of the LU (six bits if in a Type 1 node, eight bits if in a Type 2 node).

When RNAA is used to allocate network addresses so that parallel sessions can be established between two LUs, it is issued during the session initiation process by the SSCP (PLU) to the PU of the node that the PLU is in. The PLU is identified to the PU by means of the network address that was used when its SSCP-LU session was set up.

The PU returns to the SSCP the appropriate network addresses requested by an RNAA via the response to the RNAA.

An SSCP can request a PU (in a subarea node) to release the network addresses assigned to either peripheral node LUs or secondary link stations, or a PLU to support parallel sessions, by sending a *Free Network Addresses* (FNA) message.

(RNAA supersedes the Assign Network Address (ASA) request that was used in previous versions of SNA to assign network addresses for peripheral node LUs. ASA did not cater for the requirements for secondary link stations or parallel sessions.)

SSCP ID

Each SSCP in an SNA environment is assigned a unique 48-bit numerical identifier called the SSCP ID.

The SSCP ID is contained in all SSCP-SSCP interactions and in all ACTPU requests. It serves as another means of uniquely identifying an SSCP, in addition to its network address, so that cross-checks can be made on the validity of requests emanating from SSCPs.

SSCP IDs are also used to resolve the contention that could arise if the SSCPs send ACTCDRM requests, to establish an SSCP-SSCP session, to each other simultaneously. SNA specifies that the SSCP with the numerically greater SSCP ID should be given priority and be the primary for the proposed SSCP-SSCP session.

Implementational notes

Network names

The name (up to eight characters) assigned to the ACF/VTAM or ACF/NCP macro that defines a resource, or, in the case of application program LUs, optionally specified within the definition macro, serves as that resource's network name. (The implementational notes in Chapter 4 deal with the definition of resources to ACF/VTAM and ACF/NCP.)

For application program LUs the name assigned to the ACF/VTAM APPL macro serves as the network name for that LU that is valid through the environment (and, as such, must be unique across the environment). A network name that is only valid for use within the domain that is controlled by the ACF/VTAM that processes the particular APPL macro definition can be specified in the ACBNAME= operand of the APPL macro.

The network names for the other LUs are the names assigned to the ACF/VTAM or ACF/NCP LU macros that define that LU. Network names for PUs are the names assigned to the ACF/VTAM or ACF/NCP PU macros that define that PU. Primary link stations are given network names corresponding to the name as signed to the ACF/NCP LINE macro that defines that line. Note that the names assigned to the various macros within an

ACF/VTAM major node definition must be unique. In addition, the same name can only be assigned to macros in different major nodes if the major nodes will not be active concurrently.

Uninterpreted names

Only application program LUs can be known by uninterpreted names. These uninterpreted names, which can be up to 255 characters in length, are specified to ACF/VTAM by means of *interpret tables*. The ACF/VTAM INTAB macro is used to define an interpret table. (The interpret table is known by the name assigned to the INTAB macro that defines it.) Within each interpret table, the uninterpreted name by which an application program LU is known, and its network name, are defined by means of LOGCHAR macros.

If multiple interpret tables are present, the table to be searched to determine the network name of an application program LU, given its uninterpreted name, can be specified by means of the LOGTAB= operand of ACF/VTAM and ACF/NCP, PU and LU macros. (If LOGTAB= is coded in the PU macro it will apply to all the LUs in that device, unless specially overidden in the LU macros.)

Subarea addresses

The subarea address for a Type 5 node centred subarea, ie a host with ACF/VTAM and the Type 2 devices channel attached to it, is specified by means of the ACF/VTAM HOSTSA= start option.

The subarea address for a Type 4 node centred subarea, ie a communication controller with ACF/NCP and all the peripheral nodes attached to it by telecommunication links, is specified by means of the SUBAREA= operand of the ACF/NCP BUILD macro.

Network addresses

The network addresses for each domain are allocated by the ACF/VTAM that controls that domain. (The unique subarea address of each subarea ensures that the network addresses generated for each domain will be unique across the environment.) However, before network addresses can be generated, the number of bits to be used to specify the subarea address component and the element address component need to be defined. This is done by means of the ACF/VTAM MAXSUBA= start option. MAXSUBA= does not directly specify the number of bits required for the subarea address component, but the highest subarea address to be used in the environment (ie, it does not specify the number of bits for the subarea nor the element address components). (Since subarea addresses need not be contiguous, the value specified for MAXSUBA= may not reflect the actual, or planned, number of subareas in the environment.)

ACF/VTAM determines from the value specified in MAXSUBA= the number of bits that it needs to use to specify subarea addresses within network addresses. (In a multidomain environment, MAXSUBA= value specified for all the domains must be the same.)

The composition of the network addresses is specified to ACF/NCPs by means of the ACF/NCP BUILD macro, MAXSUBA= operand. The value quoted for ACF/NCP cannot deviate from that quoted for ACF/VTAM.

Once the composition of the network address has been determined, the network addresses are assigned by subarea when the environment is activated. For each subarea, the element addresses for LUs, PUs and link stations are allocated sequentially in the order that they are defined within the relevant major nodes.

ACF/VTAM only permits parallel sessions between application program LUs. Whether an application program LU will participate in parallel sessions or not is specified by means of the PARSESS= operand of the ACF/VTAM APPL macro. PARSESS= only indicates yes or no, and not the number of parallel sessions that the application program LU intends to support. Since network addresses for parallel sessions can be assigned dynamically, ACF/VTAM only needs to allocate one network address to application program LUs when it activates the environment.

SSCP ID

A unique decimal number in the range 0 to 65 535 can be specified for each ACF/VTAM in the environment by means of the SSCPID= start option. ACF/VTAM converts the decimal number to a 16-bit binary value and prefixes this value by X'05000000' to obtain the 48-bit SSCP ID. (The X'05' at the start of the SSCP ID indicates that the node containing the SSCP, identified by the SSCP ID, is a PU_T5.)

Local addresses of LUs

The local address assigned to a peripheral node LU is specified by means of the LOCADDR= operand of the ACF/VTAM or ACF/NCP LU macro. For LUs in Type 1 nodes a decimal value in the range 0 to 63 can be specified, while for LUs in Type 2 nodes a decimal in the range 0 to 255 can be used.

Local addresses of secondary link stations

The local addresses for secondary link stations in peripheral nodes are specified either in the ADDR= operand of the ACF/NCP PU macro for non-switched SDLC links, in the CUADDR= operand of the ACF/VTAM PU macro for channel links, or in the ADDR= operand of the ACF/VTAM PU macro for switched SDLC links.

8: SNA addressing

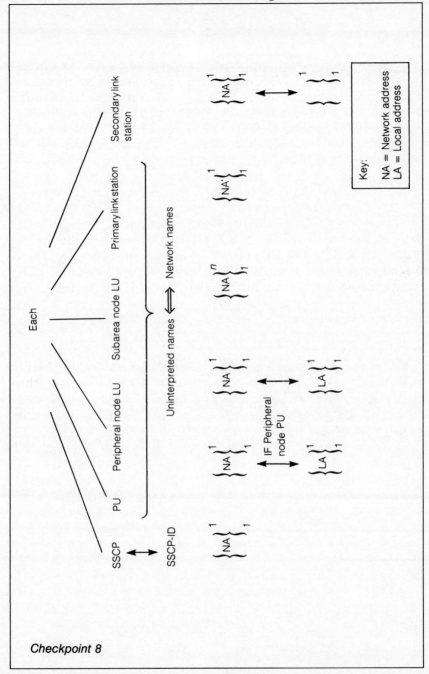

Key:

NA = Network address
LA = Local address

Checkpoint 8

319

Chapter 9:
SNA 'commands'

☐ Request Categories ☐ Request Codes ☐ Network Services Headers ☐ ACTPU ☐ ACTLU ☐ SDT ☐ Control Vectors

Chapter 9:
SNA 'commands'

SNA requests

The 125 requests (or 'commands') defined by SNA are assigned to one of four functional categories:

- Data Flow Control (DFC) requests
- Session Control (SC) requests
- Network Control (NC) requests
- Function Management Data Services (FMDS) requests.

End-user data requests are also classified as FMDS requests, since these requests enter LU–LU half-sessions via the FMDS component of these half-sessions (qv Chapter 5, *Half-sessions*).

The functional category of each request is denoted by two bits, the RU category bits, in the request header prefixing the request. SNA-specified FMDS requests are further sub-divided into four subcategories corresponding to their network services functions:

- Configuration services requests
- Maintenance services requests
- Management services requests
- Session services requests.

(Measurement services and network operator services sub-categories of FMDS network services are not included since there are no SNA requests defined for them as yet.)

Each SNA-defined request is identified by a one-byte request code. Request codes are unique within each of the request categories, or in the case of FMDS requests within each of the network services subcategories, ie a given request code could represent different SNA requests within different request categories. (Note that the request category is indicated by the RH RU category bits, rather than by the request code.)

With DFC, NC and SC requests, the request code for that request is always the first – or, in some cases, the only – byte of the request. However, the SNA-defined FMDS requests begin with a three-byte header, referred to as a *network services header*. An NS header has the format shown in Figure 9.1.

For example, the NS header for a CDINIT request is X'818641', indicating:

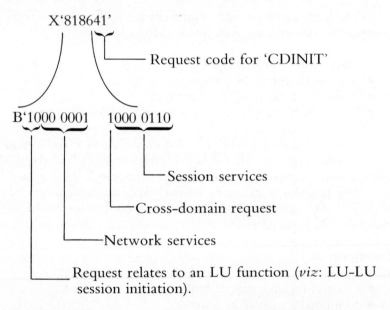

X'818641'

Request code for 'CDINIT'

B'1000 0001   1000 0110

Session services

Cross-domain request

Network services

Request relates to an LU function (*viz*: LU-LU session initiation).

The SNA-defined FMDS requests are referred to as being 'field-formatted' since their formats are specified by SNA in terms of discrete and predefined parameter fields. However, certain requests transmitted from an LU to its controlling SSCP, via their SSCP-LU session, to perform specific FMDS NS functions may have implementation-dependent formats; eg a Character-Coded

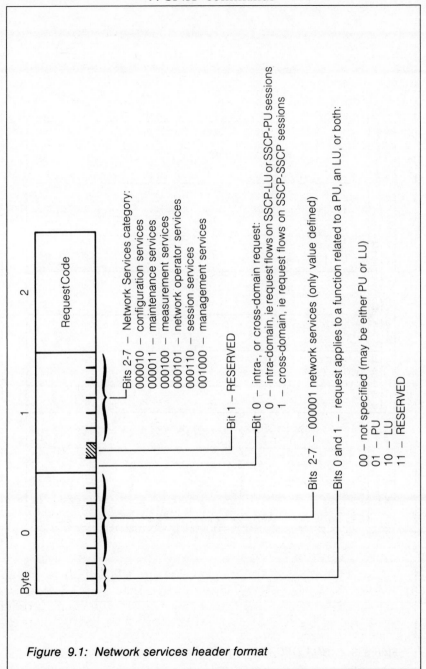

Figure 9.1: Network services header format

Figure 9.2: SNA DFC, SC and NC requests

Request mnemonic	Request code	LU-LU	SSCP-LU	SSCP-PU	SSCP-SSCP	(PU-PU)	Expedited (E) or normal (N) flow	Positive response may contain data
Data Flow Control (DFC) requests								
BID	X'C8'	>					N	
BIS	X'70'	>					N	
CANCEL	X'83'	>					N	
CHASE	X'84'	>					N	
LUSTAT	X'04'	>	>				N	
QC	X'81'	>					N	
QEC	X'80'	>					E	
RELQ	X'82'	>					E	
RSHUTD	X'C2'	>					E	
RTR	X'05'	>					N	
SBI	X'71'	>					E	
SHUTC	X'C1'	>					E	
SHUTD	X'C0'	>					E	
SIG	X'C9'	>					E	
Session Control (SC) requests								
ACTCDRM	X'14'				>		E	>
ACTLU	X'0D'		>				E	>
ACTPU	X'11'			>			E	>
BIND	X'31'	>					E	>
CLEAR	X'A1'	>					E	
CRV	X'C0'	>					E	
DACTCDRM	X'15'				>		E	
DACTLU	X'0E'		>				E	
DACTPU	X'12'			>			E	
RQR	X'A3'	>					E	
SDT	X'A2'	>					E	>
STSN	X'A0'	>					E	
UNBIND	X'32'	>					E	
Network Control (NC) requests								
(LSA)*	X'05'					>	E	
NC_ACTVR	X'0D'					>	E	
NC_DACTVR	X'0E'					>	E	
NC_ER_ACT	X'0B'					>	E	
NC_ER_ACT_REPLY	X'0C'					>	E	
NC_ER_INOP	X'06'					>	E	
NC_ER_OP	X'0F'					>	E	
NC_ER_TEST	X'09'					>	E	
NC_ER_TEST_REPLY	X'0A'					>	E	
NC_IPL_ABORT	X'46'					>	E	
NC_IPL_FINAL	X'02'					>	E	
NC_IPL_INIT	X'03'					>	E	
NC_IPL_TEXT	X'04'					>	E	

* Pre-SNA 4 request, not used in SNA 4

326

Logon sent by a terminal or control unit that is unable to construct a *bona fide* INIT-SELF request, (qv *Implementational notes* in Chapter 4, *Sessions*). Such implementation-dependent requests that originate from an LU are referred to as character-coded FMDS NS requests, and do not begin with, or contain, NS headers. Character-coded requests are translated by the SSCP to the corresponding field-formatted FMDS NS request before it is processed. (All FMDS requests from an SSCP to an LU, and all requests flowing on SSCP-PU or SSCP-SSCP sessions are field-formatted.)

SNA does not specify a request code or an NS header to signify end-user data requests. Since there are no SNA-defined FMDS requests that flow on LU-LU sessions, any request flowing on an LU-LU session whose RH specifies that it is an FMDS request is deemed to be an end-user data request.

Figure 9.2 tabulates the SNA DFC, SC AND NC requests – in alphabetical order within each category – and denotes their request code, the type of session they are transmitted on, whether they are transmitted on the normal or expedited flow and whether a positive response to them may contain data. Figure 9.3 tabulates the FMDS NS requests in the same manner but specifies the NS header corresponding to each request rather than just the request code.

Figure 9.4 summarises the type of flow – *viz* expedited or normal – on which the various request types are transmitted.

SNA responses

With the exception of the 17 SNA-defined requests – indicated in Figures 9.2 and 9.3 – whose positive responses may contain data, all other positive responses generated may only contain the request code (in the case of responses to DFC, SC or NC requests) or the NS header (in the case of responses to FMDS NS requests) specified in the request the response refers to. Since end-user data requests or character-coded FMDS NS requests do not contain request codes or NS headers, responses of these requests consist of just a response header. Figure 9.5 summarises the contents and length of the positive response units corresponding to the various request categories. A request code or an NS

FMDS Network Services: Configuration (NS(C)) requests

Request mnemonic	NS header	Session type SSCP-LU	Session type SSCP-PU	Session type SSCP-SSCP	Session type (PU-PU)	Expedited (E) or normal (N) flow	Positive response may contain data
ABCONN	X'01020F'		>			N	
ABCONNOUT	X'010218'		>		>	N	
ACTCONNIN	X'010216'		>		>	N	
ACTLINK	X'01020A'		>		>	N	>
ADDLINK	X'41021E'		>			N	>
ADDLINKSTA	X'410221'		>			N	
(ANA)*	X'010219'		>			N	
CONNOUT	X'01020E'		>		>	N	
CONTACT	X'010201'		>		>	N	
CONTACTED	X'010280'		>		>	N	
DACTCONNIN	X'010217'		>		>	N	
DACTLINK	X'01020B'		>		>	N	
DISCONTACT	X'010202'		>		>	N	
DELETENR	X'41021C'		>			N	
DUMPFINAL	X'010208'		>			N	
DUMPINIT	X'010206'		>			N	
DUMPTEXT	X'010207'		>			N	
ER_INOP	X'41021D'		>		>	N	
ESLOW	X'010214'		>			N	
EXSLOW	X'010215'		>			N	
FNA	X'01021A'		>		>	N	
INITPROC	X'410235'		>			N	
INOP	X'010281'		>		>	N	
IPLFINAL	X'010205'		>			N	
IPLINIT	X'010203'		>			N	
IPLTEXT	X'010204'		>			N	
LCP	X'410287'		>			N	
LDREQD	X'410237'		>			N	
NS_IPL_ABORT	X'410246'		>			N	
NS_IPL_FINAL	X'410245'		>			N	
NS_IPL_INIT	X'410243'		>		>	N	>
NS_IPL_TEXT	X'410244'		>			N	
(NS_LSA)*	X'010285'		>			N	
PROCSTAT	X'410236'		>			N	
REQACTLU	X'410240'		>			N	
REQCONT	X'010284'		>			N	
REQDISCONT	X'01021B'		>			N	
REQFNA	X'410286'		>			N	
RNAA	X'410210'		>			N	
RPO	X'010209'		>			N	
SETCV	X'…'		>			N	

Figure 9.3: SNA FMDS Network Services requests

Command	Code
ACTTRACE	X'010302'
DACTTRACE	X'010303'
DISPSTOR	X'010331'
ECHOTEST	X'810389'
ER_TESTED	X'410386'
EXECTEST	X'010301'
RECFMS	X'410384'
RECMS	X'010381'
RECSTOR	X'010334'
RECTD	X'010382'
RECTR	X'410385'
RECTRD	X'010383'
REQECHO	X'810387'
REQMS	X'410304'
REQTEST	X'010380'
ROUTE_TEST	X'410306'
SETCV	X'010311'
TESTMODE	X'410305'

FMDS Network Services: Management Services (NS(MN)) requests

Command	Code
DELIVER	X'810812'
FORWARD	X'810810'

FMDS Network Services: Session Services (NS(S)) requests

Command	Code
BINDF	X'810685'
CDCINIT	X'81864B'
CDINIT	X'818641'
CDSESSEND	X'818648'
CDSESSSF	X'818645'
CDSESSST	X'818646'
CDSESSTF	X'818647'
CDTAKED	X'818649'
CDTAKEDC	X'81864A'
CDTERM	X'818643'
CINIT	X'810601'
CLEANUP	X'810629'
CTERM	X'810602'
DSRLST	X'818627'
INIT_OTHER	X'810680'
INIT_OTHER_CD	X'818640'
INIT_SELF	X'010681'
NOTIFY	X'810620'/X'818620'
NSPE	X'010604'
SESSEND	X'810688'
SESSST	X'810686'
TERM_OTHER	X'810682'
TERM_OTHER_CD	X'818642'
TERM_SELF	X'010683'
UNBINDF	X'810687'

*Pre-SNA 4 requests not used in SNA 4

Request type	Normal flow	Expedited flow
Data Flow Control	√	√
Session Control		√
Network Control		√
FMDS: Network Services	√	
FMDS: end-user data	√	

Figure 9.4: The flow on which the various request types are transmitted

Type of request the response is for	Contents of Response Unit	Length of Response Unit
DFC	Request code	1
SC	Request code	1
NC	Request code	1
SNA-defined FMDS NS (ie field-formatted)	NS header	3
FMDS NS (character-coded)	—	0
FMDS: end-user data	—	0

Figure 9.5: Contents and lengths of the positive Response Units – that do not convey data – corresponding to the various request categories

header returned in a response only serves as an auxiliary means of relating that response with the request it applies to. Since a response echoes the sequence number or identifier assigned to the request it refers to, response to request correlation is based on sequence number or identifier matching.

All negative responses contain four bytes of sense data indicating why the subject request could not be processed or the type of error that was encountered while processing the request. A negative response unit always begins with the four bytes of sense data. The sense data is followed by up to three further bytes specifying either the request code in the case of responses to DFC, SC or NC requests, the NS header in the case of responses to SNA-defined FMDS NS requests, or the first three bytes of the subject request irrespective of the request type.

ACTPU request

The ACTPU request has two formats: format 0 and format 3. Format 3 is only issued to subarea nodes that support Virtual and Explicit Routes, while format 0 is used for all other types of node. (See Figure 9.6.) The two possible *control vectors* indicated in Figure 9.6 have formats as shown in Figures 9.7 and 9.8.

ACTLU request

The format of the ACTLU request is shown in Figure 9.9.

Start Data Traffic (SDT) request

The SDT request format is as follows:

Byte	0
	Request code X'A0'

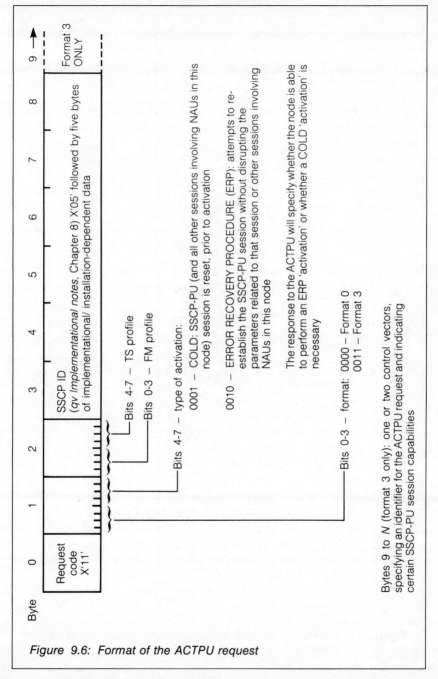

Figure 9.6: Format of the ACTPU request

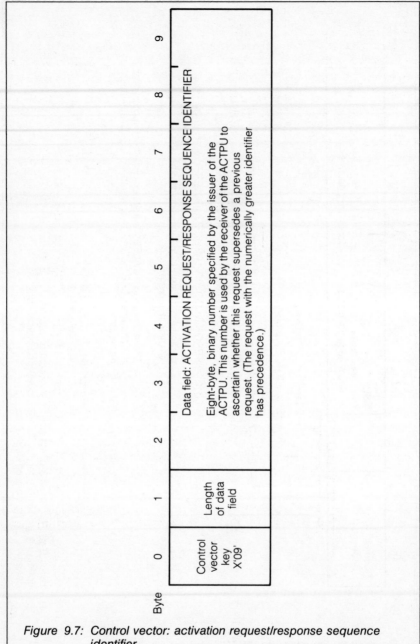

| Byte | 0 | 1 | 2 | 3 | 4 | 5 | 6 | 7 | 8 | 9 |

Byte 0: Control vector key X'09'

Byte 1: Length of data field

Bytes 2–9: Data field: ACTIVATION REQUEST/RESPONSE SEQUENCE IDENTIFIER

Eight-byte, binary number specified by the issuer of the ACTPU. This number is used by the receiver of the ACTPU to ascertain whether this request supersedes a previous request. (The request with the numerically greater identifier has precedence.)

Figure 9.7: Control vector: activation request/response sequence identifier

334

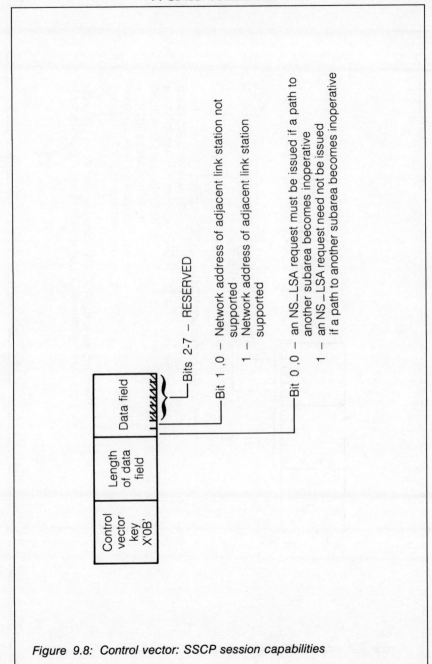

Figure 9.8: Control vector: SSCP session capabilities

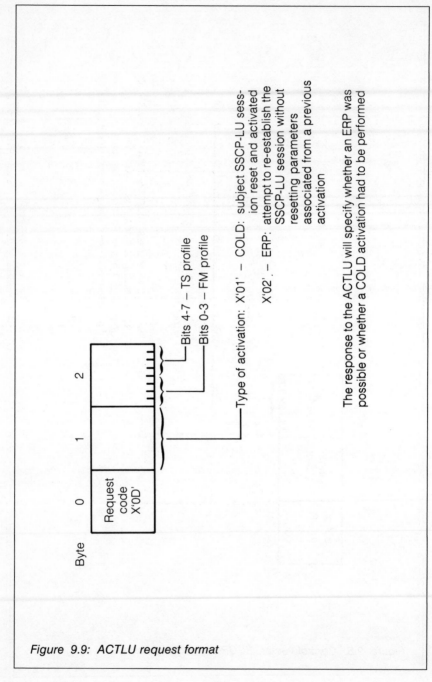

Figure 9.9: ACTLU request format

Request category	Request mnemonic
SC	ACTPU DACTPU ACTLU DACTLU BIND UNBIND SDT CLEAR
DFC	CANCEL CHASE LUSTAT SHUTD SHUTC RTR BID SIGNAL
FMDS NS(MA)	REQMS RECFMS
FMDS NS(S)	NOTIFY

Figure 9.10: SNA requests supported by the IBM 3274 SNA/SDLC control unit

Implementational notes

Requests/responses

The implementational notes in Chapter 5, *Half-sessions*, describe how requests and responses are generated by ACF/VTAM application programs.

The exact repertoire of the possible SNA requests that are supported by a given node will be node type- and implementation-dependent. For example, the NC requests will only be supported by subarea node implementations: *viz* ACT/VTAM and ACF/NCP.

Figure 9.10 tabulates the SNA requests supported by the IBM 3274 SNA/SDLC control unit, which, due to its ubiquity, is treated as the *de facto* standard for node Type 2 implementations. Note that it does not support any of the FMDS NS session services requests associated with session initiation or termination, since all IBM 3270 devices use character-coded requests for session initiation and termination.

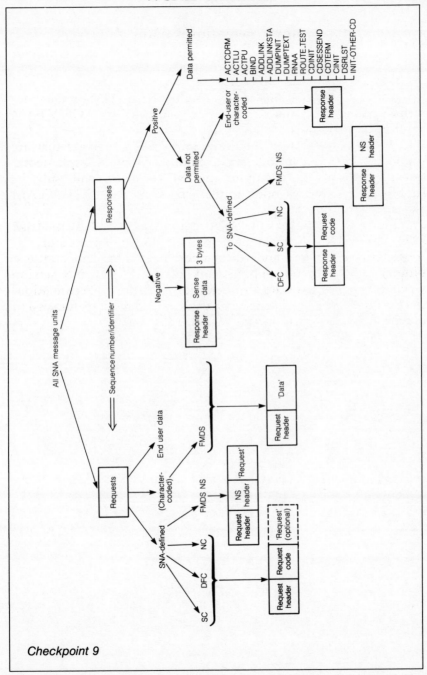

Checkpoint 9

Chapter 10:
SNA message units

☐ BIU ☐ Segmenting ☐ BIU Segment ☐ PIU ☐ BTU
☐ Blocking ☐ BLU ☐ Request Headers ☐ Response Headers
☐ Transmission Headers ☐ FID 0/1/2/3/4 and F ☐ Boundary
Function

Chapter 10:
SNA message units

Message units

A typical SNA message unit consists of three discrete components:

1 A Request or Response Unit (RU).
2 A Request or Response Header (RH).
3 A Transmission Header (TH).

The exceptions to this are: responses to end-user data and character-coded FMDS NS requests or isolated pacing responses which consist of only an RH and a TH, and VR pacing responses and Transmission Group sequence number field wrap acknowledgements which consist only of a TH.

All RUs must be prefixed by an RH. The sub-message unit consisting of an RH followed by an RU, or a message unit consisting of an RH on its own, is referred to as a *Basic Information Unit* (BIU). A BIU is the fundamental unit of information exchanged between half-sessions via the Path Control Network. SNA permits the Path Control Network to split, or segment, a BIU into two or more *BIU segments* if the transmission of smaller message units improves the overall transmission efficiency, reduces the need for retransmission due to transmission errors or suits the availability of processing or storage resources. Figure 10.1 illustrates the structure of a BIU and shows how a BIU may be split into two or more BIU segments. Note that when a BIU is segmented the RH appears in the first BIU segment and is not repeated in subsequent ones. The Path Control Network will not segment BIUs which are less than 11 bytes in length, BIUs destined for a half-session in an NAU supported by a boundary function, BIUs containing session activation or deactivation requests or responses or BIUs containing NC requests or responses.

Half-sessions only support unsegmented BIUs: therefore the Path Control Network must reassemble a segmented BIU to its entirety prior to conveying it to its destination NAU. Since sequence numbers to RUs are assigned by the transmitting half-session, rather than by the Path Control Network, all the segments of a segmented BIU contain the sequence number assigned to the original BIU.

The Path Control Network prefixes each BIU or BIU segment with a Path Control Network-specific header – the transmission header. The TH specifies information needed by the Path Control Network components to allow a message unit to be conveyed through the Path Control Network: for instance, the address of the NAU to which the message unit is bound. THs are described in detail later in this chapter.

A BIU, a BIU segment prefixed by a TH, or a TH by itself (eg VR pacing response) is referred to as a *Path Information Unit* (PIU). Figure 10.2 depicts the various PIU structures.

The Transmission Group Control subcomponent of a subarea node Path Control component is permitted to combine, or block together, two or more PIUs to form an extended message unit (referred to as a *Basic Transmission Unit* (BTU)) when it is passing message units to its DLC component for transmission to an adjacent subarea node via a single link transmission group. (Multiple-PIU BTUs are not used over multi-link Transmission Groups.) This process of combining multiple PIUs to form a BTU is known as blocking and the converse operation, performed by a receiving Transmission Group Control subcomponent, of disassembling a BTU into the separate PIUs, is known as deblocking. A BTU is defined as consisting of one or more PIUs, and is the fundamental unit of data exchanged between the Path Control and Data Link Control components of the Path Control Network. Figure 10.3 illustrates the composition of a BTU.

The fundamental unit of data transmitted across an SNA link is referred to as a *Basic Link Unit* (BLU). A BLU consists of a BTU prefixed by a DLC header and postfixed by a DLC trailer

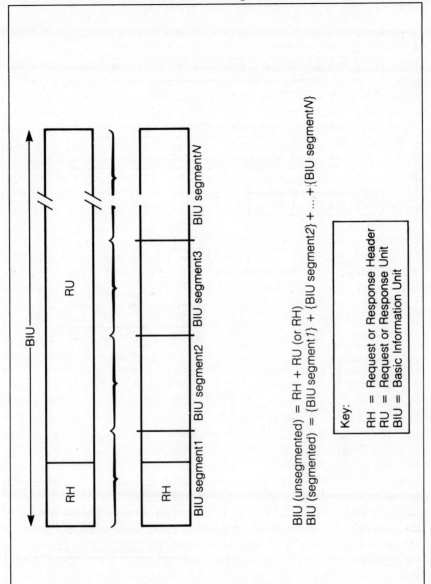

Figure 10.1: Structure of a Basic Information Unit and the way it may be split into multiple BIU segments

345

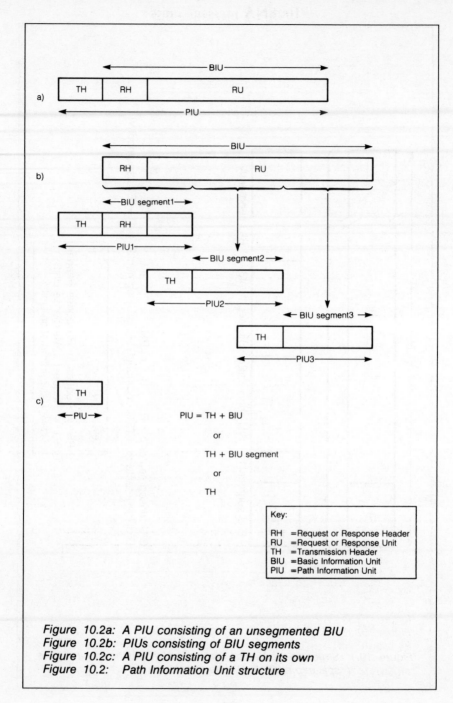

Figure 10.2a: A PIU consisting of an unsegmented BIU
Figure 10.2b: PIUs consisting of BIU segments
Figure 10.2c: A PIU consisting of a TH on its own
Figure 10.2: Path Information Unit structure

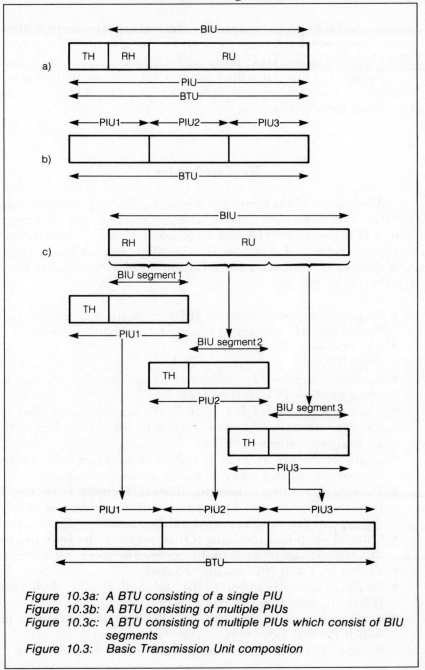

Figure 10.3a: A BTU consisting of a single PIU
Figure 10.3b: A BTU consisting of multiple PIUs
Figure 10.3c: A BTU consisting of multiple PIUs which consist of BIU segments
Figure 10.3:   Basic Transmission Unit composition

containing DLC protocol-specific information. Figure 10.4 illustrates the general structure of a BLU and also the structure if SDLC is used as the DLC protocol for a link.

Figure 10.5 illustrates the various SNA message units that are utilised to convey an end-user data request along a route traversing three nodes.

Request header

All Request Units conveyed within an SNA environment are prefixed by a three-byte request header. Only one type of request header is defined by SNA and all Request Units, irrespective of category, origin or destination, use this single request header type. The indicators contained in a request header, and what they specify, are as follows:

- Request/Response Indicator (RRI): that the RU attached to the subject RH contains a request rather than a response
- RU category: the category of the request, ie SC, NC, DFC or FMDS
- Format Indicator (FI): which one of two possible formats is being used by FMDS requests
- Sense Data Included Indicator (SDI): whether sense data is present within the RU, ie the request has been transformed to an Exception Request (EXR)
- Begin Chain Indicator (BCI) and End Chain Indicator (ECI): the position of this request, within a chain of requests
- Definite Response 1 Indicator (DR1I), Definite Response 2 Indicator (DR2I) and Exception Response Indicator (ERI): the type of response expected by the request
- Queued Response Indicator (QRI): whether the response to this request can be queued during transmission
- Pacing Indicator (PI): pacing requests
- Begin Bracket Indicator (BBI) and End Bracket Indicator (EBI): the beginning or end of a bracket
- Change Direction Indicator (CDI): that the direction in which normal flow requests are being transmitted is to be reversed if a half-duplex send/receive mode is being used

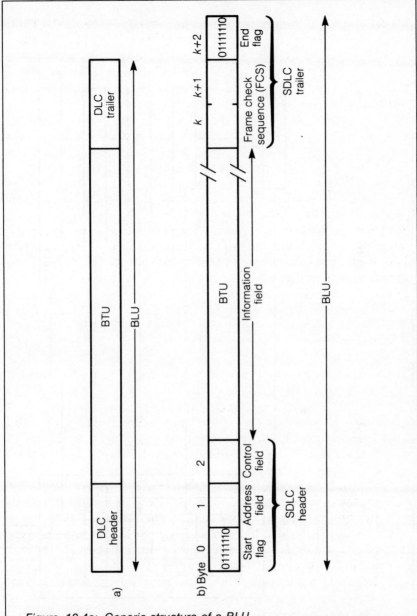

Figure 10.4a: Generic structure of a BLU
Figure 10.4b: The BLU format if SDLC is the DLC protocol being used
Figure 10.4: BLU structures

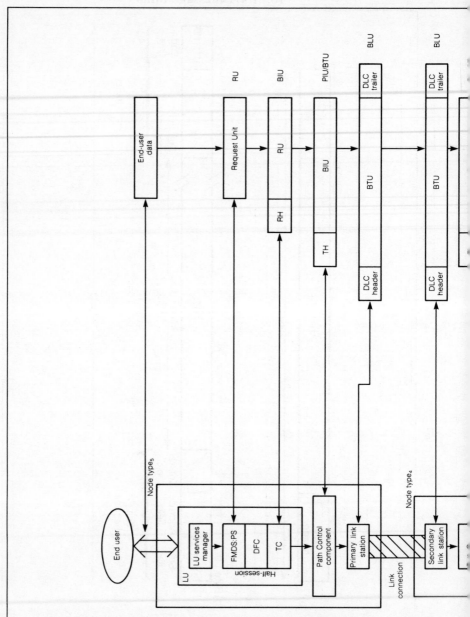

Figure 10.5: The SNA Message Units that are utilised to carry an end-user data request along a route traversing three nodes

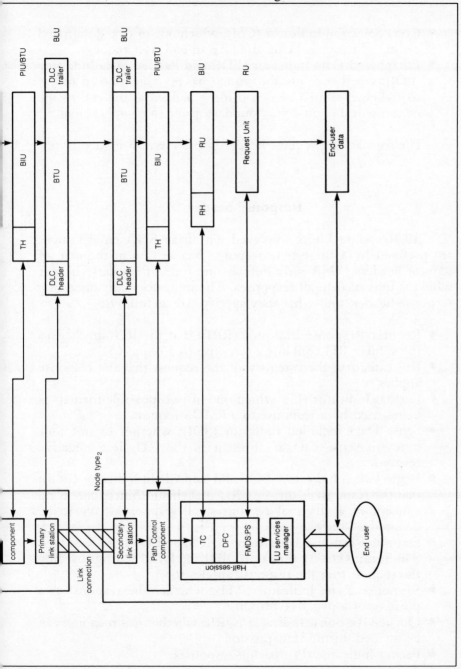

- Code Selection Indicator (CSI): which one of two designated coding schemes is being used by an end-user request
- Enciphered Data Indicator (EDI) and Padded Data Indicator (PDI): whether or not the request has been enciphered and, if so, whether the RU has had to be padded at the end to the next integral eight-byte boundary prior to encipherment.

The format of a request header is as shown in Figure 10.6.

Response header

All Response Units conveyed within an SNA environment are prefixed by a three-byte response header. As in the case of request headers, SNA only defines one type of response header which is universal to all responses. The indicators contained in a response header, and what they specify, are as follows:

- Request/Response Indicator (RRI): that the RU attached to the subject RH contains a response to a request
- RU category: the category of the request that the response applies to
- Format Indicator (FI): which one of two possible formats is being used by a response to a FMDS request
- Sense Data Included Indicator (SDI): whether or not four bytes of sense data are present in the RU, ie a negative response
- Begin Chain Indicator (BCI) and End Chain Indicator (ECI): that the response is the only RU of a chain. (Since there is no concept of a chain of responses, all responses have to be denoted as 'only in chain'.)
- Definite Response 1 Indicator (DR1I) and Definite Response 2 Indicator (DR2I): the same DR1I and DR2I settings used by the request that the response applies to
- Response Type Indicator (RTI): whether the response is a positive or a negative response
- Queued Response Indicator (QRI): whether this response can be queued during transmission
- Pacing Indicator (PI): pacing responses.

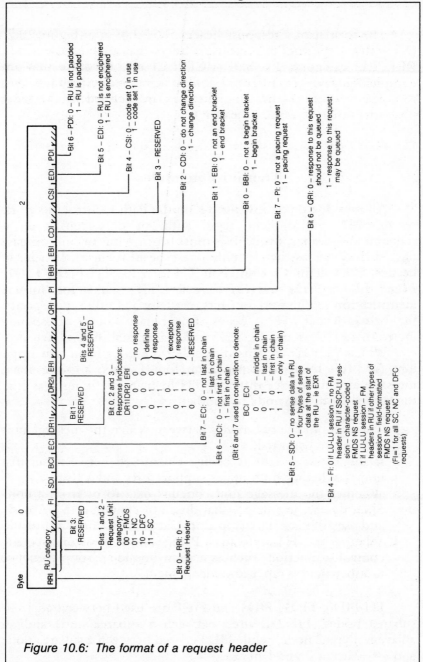

Figure 10.6: The format of a request header

The format of a response header is as shown in Figure 10.7. (Note that indicators in response headers that are equivalent, *viz* RRI, RU category, FI, SDI, BCI, ECI etc, or those that are complementary, *viz* ERI and RTI, pacing request and pacing response, to request header indicators are defined in the same positions as in the request header.)

Transmission header

All message units flowing within the Path Control Network of an SNA environment begin with, or only consist of, a transmission header, ie all PIUs must begin with, or only consist of, a TH. Whereas there is only one type of request or response header, SNA defines six different TH formats: TH *FID0*, *FID1*, *FID2*, *FID3*, *FID4* and *FIDF*, where FID stands for 'format identification'. (The first four bits of all six TH FID types specify the format of that TH by means of the binary values corresponding to 0, 1, 2, 3, 4 and 15, ie 15 = hexadecimal 'F'.)

Which TH format is used to either prefix or form a message unit (ie PIU) by itself depends on four factors; and the same message unit may have different TH formats prefixing it as it is forwarded from one node to another:

1 The types of the two nodes between which the message unit is being transmitted.
2 If the message unit is being transmitted between subarea nodes, whether both nodes support ERs and VRs.
3 Whether the message unit contains data to or from a non-SNA device, ie a device that does not contain an SNA node and uses BSC or start/stop as its Data Link Control protocol.
4 Whether the TH performs a Path Control Network-specific control – function, such as a Transmission Group sequence number field wrap acknowledgement.

TH FID0, FID1, FID4 and FIDF are used between adjacent subarea nodes, FID2 is used between a subarea node and an adjacent Type 2 node, while FID3 is used between a subarea node and an adjacent Type 1 node.

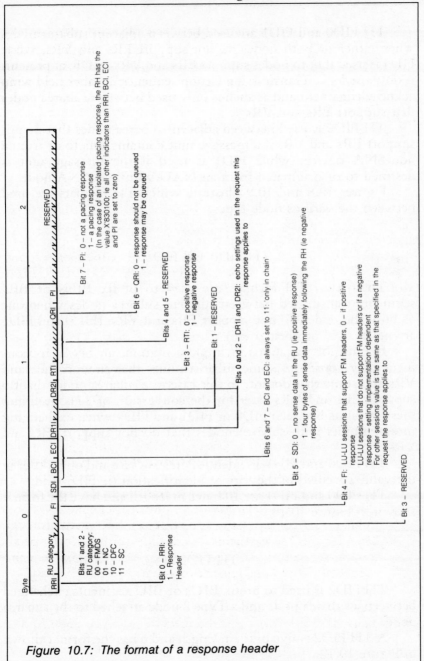

Figure 10.7: The format of a response header

TH FID0 and FID1 are used between adjacent subarea nodes when either or both nodes do not support ERs and VRs, while FID4 is used if both nodes support ERs and VRs. FIDF, at present, is only used as a Transmission Group sequence number field wrap acknowledgement and as such is only used between subarea nodes that support ERs and VRs.

TH FID0 is used between adjacent subarea nodes that do not support ERs and VRs if a message unit contains data to or from a non-SNA device, while FID1 is used if the message unit is destined to or originated from an NAU within an SNA node.

Figures 10.8 and 10.9 illustrate which TH formats are used between the various node types.

TH FID0 and FID1

These two TH formats are used to prefix BIUs or BIU segments transmitted between adjacent subarea nodes when one or both the nodes do not support ERs and VRs. (FID0 and FID1 are never used on their own.)

Because of variations in implementation, an SNA environment may consist of some subarea nodes that support ERs and VRs and some that do not. In this case, the subarea nodes that do support ERs and VRs cater for the conversion of THs prefixing message units between FID0 or FID1 and FID4 when exchanging message units with subarea nodes that do not support ERs and VRs.

TH FID0 and FID1 are identical in structure and only differ in the value specified in the format identification (ie FID) field.

TH FID0 and FID1 are 10 bytes in length and have the format shown in Figure 10.10.

TH FID2

TH FID2 is used to prefix BIUs or BIU segments exchanged between a subarea node and a Type 2 node attached to the subarea node.

A TH FID2 is five bytes in length and 6 has the format shown in Figure 10.12.

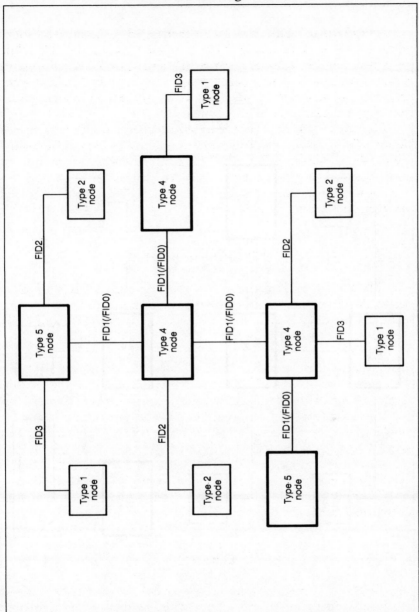

Figure 10.8: The transmission header formats used between the
various SNA node types in an environment where the
subarea nodes do not support ERs or VRs

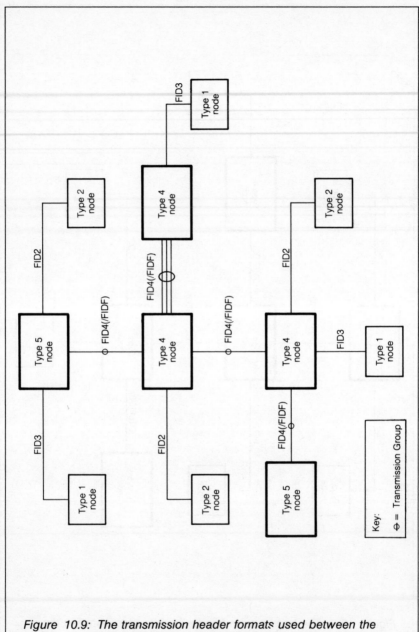

Figure 10.9: The transmission header formats used between the various SNA node types in an environment where the subarea nodes support ERs and VRs

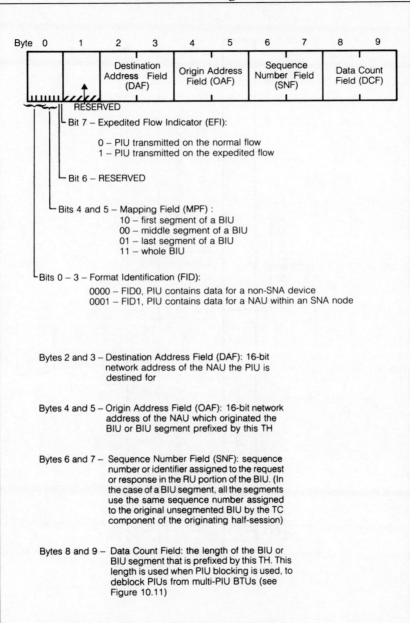

Figure 10.10: The format of a TH FID0 and FID1

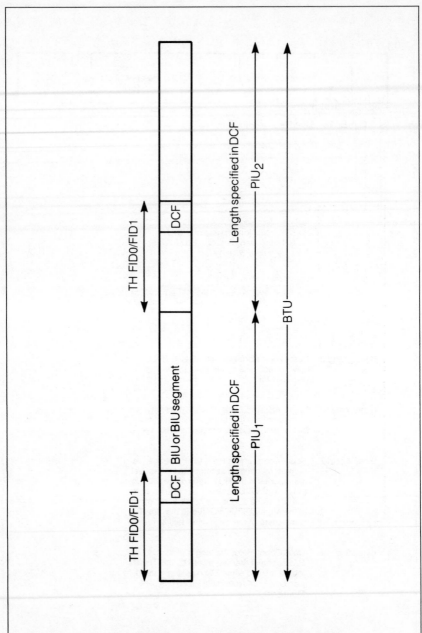

Figure 10.11: Use of the Data Count Field to deblock PIUs from a BTU consisting of multiple PIUs

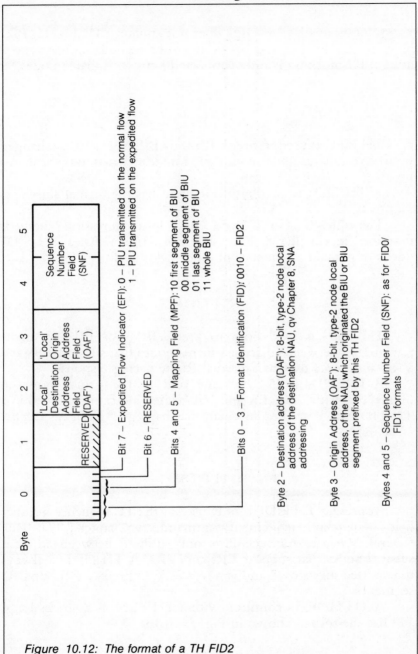

Figure 10.12: The format of a TH FID2

(Note that since an FID2 does not contain a DCF field, PIU blocking cannot be used between a subarea node and a Type 2 node. PIU blocking is only supported between subarea nodes.)

TH FID3

TH FID3 is used to prefix BIUs or BIU segments exchanged between a subarea node and a Type 1 node attached to that subarea node.

A TH FID3 is two bytes long and has the format shown in Figure 10.13.

The eight–bit, LSID, Type 1 node local addressing scheme is described in Chapter 8, *SNA addressing*. (Note that a TH FID3 does not contain a sequence number field (SNF).)

TH FID4

TH FID4 is used both to prefix BIUs or BIU segments transmitted between adjacent subarea nodes that support ERs and VRs, and on its own as a Virtual Route pacing response.

A TH :FID4 is 26 bytes long, and has the format shown in Figure 10.14 (the TG, ER and VR–related indicators defined in a TH FID4 are described in detail in Chapter 7, *The Path Control Network*).

TH FIDF

At present TH FIDF is only used as the TG sequence number field wrap acknowledgement command, qv Chapter 7, *The Path Control Network*. As such it is only utilised between adjacent subarea nodes that support ERs and VRs. A TH FIDF is always transmitted on its own and is never used to prefix a BIU or BIU segment.

A TH FIDF, in common with a TH FID4, is 26 bytes long, and has the format shown in Figure 10.15.

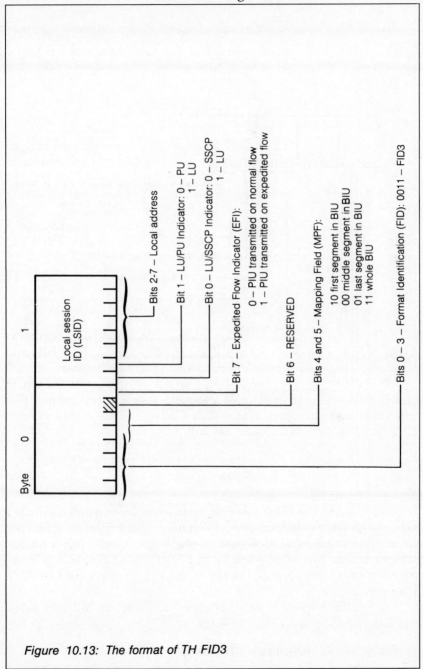

Figure 10.13: The format of TH FID3

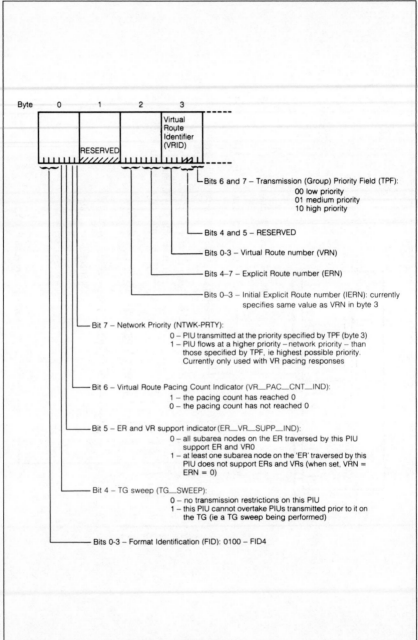

Figure 10.14: The format of TH FID4

364

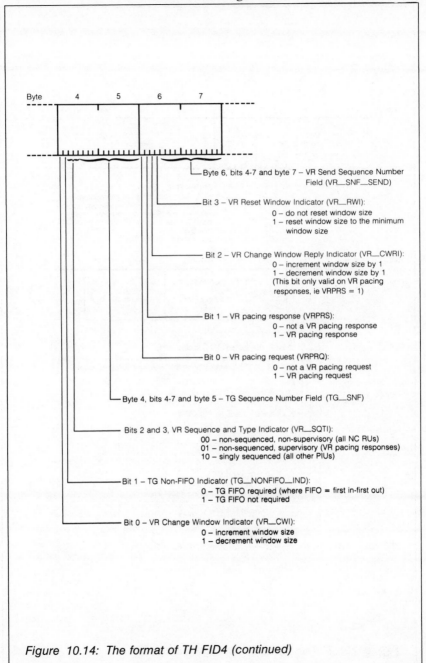

Figure 10.14: The format of TH FID4 (continued)

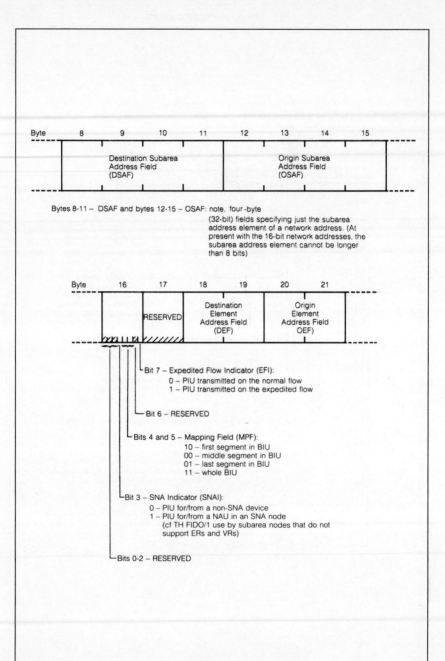

Figure 10.14: The format of TH FID4 (continued)

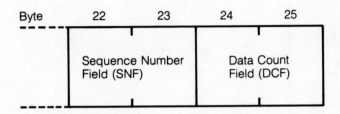

Bytes 22 and 23 – Sequence Number Field (SNF): sequence number or identifier assigned to the request or response in the RU portion of the BIU

Bytes 24 and 25 – Data Count Field (DCF): the length of the BIU or BIU segment that is prefixed by this TH. This length is used to deblock PIUs when PIU blocking is used

Figure 10.14: The format of TH FID4 (continued)

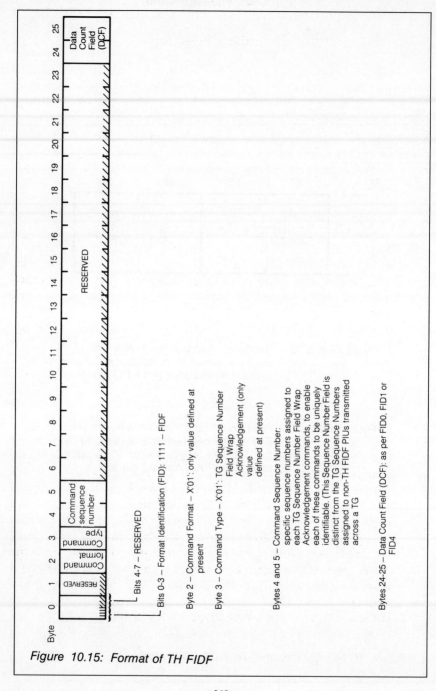

Figure 10.15: Format of TH FIDF

368

Boundary Function

Subarea nodes that have peripheral nodes attached to them support message unit interchange with these peripheral nodes through a Boundary Function component. Figure 10.16 illustrates the location of the Boundary Function component within a subarea node and the control and data interchange paths between it and the other components within that subarea node.

A Boundary Function component is responsible for the following:

1 It transforms the THs used to prefix BIUs transmitted between subarea nodes – *viz* TH FID0, FID1 or FID4 – to the TH formats used between subarea nodes and peripheral nodes – *viz* TH FID2 or FID3 – and *vice versa*. (Note that BIU segments are not sent to a Boundary Function component.) This also entails the conversion of the 16-bit network address used in TH FID0, FID1 and FID4 to specify the destination and origin NAUs, of the message unit, to the local addressing scheme relevant to the peripheral node for which the message unit is bound – ie eight-bit local addressing for NAUs in Type 2 nodes or LSID local addressing for NAUs in Type 1 nodes – and *vice versa* for message units received from a peripheral node. (Non-SNA devices do not support SNA commands, response procedures, SNA message unit structures or the SNA headers. These devices are only capable of handling their particular data stream commands and data structures – ie their Device Control protocol – in conjunction with an appropriate Data Link Control protocol – *viz* BSC or S/S. Since non-SNA devices are located as pseudo-peripheral nodes, the boundary function component of a subarea node that has non-SNA devices attached to it must perform the transformations between the SNA procedures and conventions to the procedures and conventions supported by the non-SNA device, and *vice versa*.)
2 It forwards message units destined to peripheral node NAUs to the primary link station controlling the link to the subject peripheral node.

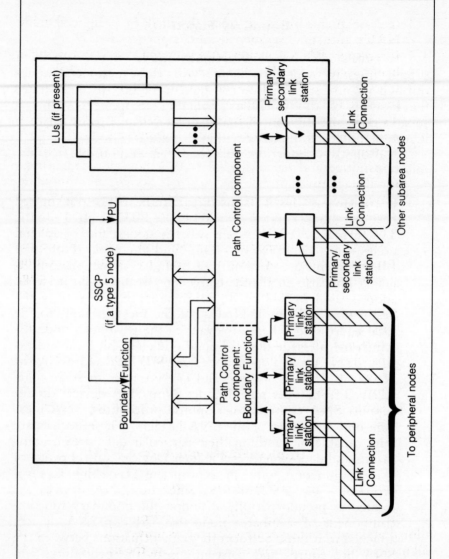

Figure 10.16: Location of the Boundary Function component within a subarea node and the control and data paths between the boundary function component and the other components within that subarea node

3 It re-segments message units destined to peripheral node NAUs into small segments, when appropriate.

4 It is responsible for session-level pacing if two-stage pacing is being used by an LU-LU session.

5 It assigns and checks the sequence numbers (or identifiers) of message units to or from NAUs in Type 1 nodes, since the TH FID3 used to prefix BIUs to and from NAUs in Type 1 nodes does not include a sequence number field (SNF). Since sequence number (or identifier) correlation between requests transmitted and responses received is the fundamental basis for Data Flow Control-level error recovery, the following conventions are used by sessions that involve an NAU in a Type 1 node:

• Secondary NAU (ie NAU in Type 1 node) to primary NAU: either immediate request mode with definite response chains (or exception-response chain indicating 'change direction') is used, or the primary NAU is designated as being responsible for error recovery

• Primary NAU to secondary NAU: either immediate request mode with definite response chains (or exception response chain indicating 'change direction') is used, or a pacing count of 1 is used for transmissions between the boundary function and the peripheral node NAU with a further caveat that precludes the secondary NAU from issuing an isolated pacing response prior to any responses – positive or negative – that may need to be returned.

Implementational notes

Message unit sizes

In an ACF/VTAM, ACF/NCP environment, there is no global maximum message unit size that is universally applicable to all message unit transfer operations. Instead, the maximum size of a message unit that can be exchanged between any two machines or devices in the environment will vary depending on the following:

1 The type of link across which the message unit is to be transmitted.

2 The node types contained in the machines or devices between which the message unit is to be transmitted.
3 The direction in which the message unit is to be transmitted.

The maximum PIU length that can be transmitted by an ACF/VTAM to a local ACF/NCP – ie an ACF/NCP resident in a communications controller channel attached to the host containing the subject ACF/VTAM – is specified in bytes in the MAXDATA= operand of the PCCU macro defining that ACF/NCP as an NCP major node (qv Chapter 4's *Implementational notes*). The maximum length that can be specified – which is also the default if the operand is not included in a PCCU macro – is 65 535 bytes. (If an environment contains multiple local ACF/NCPs, intra- or cross-domain, with links between them, the same MAXDATA= value must be specified for all of them.) While the MAXDATA= is only explicitly specified for local ACF/NCPs, it also applies to all remote ACF/NCPs associated with a local ACF/NCP and, as such, storage capacities of remote ACF/NCPs associated with it must also be considered when specifying the MAXDATA= value for a local ACF/NCP. BIUs that are longer than the value specified in MAXDATA= are segmented such that each PIU does not exceed the maximum PIU length.

The maximum PIU length that a local ACF/NCP can transmit to an ACF/VTAM located in its local host is specified by means of two operands – UNITSZ= and MAXBFRU= – in the ACF/NCP HOST macro relating to that ACF/VTAM. UNITSZ= indicates the length, in bytes, of the data buffers being used by the ACF/VTAM to receive message units from the ACF/NCP, while MAXBFRU= indicates the number of buffers the ACF/VTAM will have allocated at any one time to receive data from the ACF/NCP. Thus, the maximum number of bytes that the ACF/VTAM can accept from the ACF/NCP in one data transfer operation, is its buffer length – ie UNITSZ= value – multiplied by the number of receive buffers allocated – ie MAXBFRU= count. This maximum number of bytes that can be transferred to the ACF/VTAM imposes the upper limit on the maximum length of a PIU that may be transmitted from the ACF/NCP to ACF/VTAM. However, ACF/NCP may block one or more PIUs to form a BTU when transmitting message units to ACF/VTAM. In this case, the length of a BTU cannot exceed the maximum transfer count – ie 'UNITSZ=' × 'MAXBFRU'. (The value specified in the MAXDATA= operand of the PCCU for a local ACF/NCP – ie maximum PIU length from ACF/VTAM to that ACF/NCP – should not be greater than the product of 'UNITSZ' × 'MAXBFRU' – ie the maximum number of bytes the ACF/NCP can transmit to the ACF/VTAM.)

The actual size of the data buffers used by an ACF/NCP is specified by the BFRS= operand of the ACF/NCP BUILD macro. The value specified in BFRS= does not have to reflect the maximum permitted PIU length. A PIU may span multiple ACF/NCP buffers.

The maximum PIU length that can be sent to a device containing a peripheral node is specified by the MAXDATA= operand of the ACF/VTAM PU macro for locally attached devices and for devices on switched links, and by the equivalent operand of the ACF/NCP PU macro for devices on non-switched links. The maximum amount of data bytes that an ACF/NCP must be ready to accept from a device on one of its links is specified by the TRANSFR= operand of the LINE macro corresponding to the link. The TRANSFR= operand specifies the maximum number of ACF/NCP data buffers – of length as specified by the BFRS= operand of the BUILD macro – that should be allocated for receiving data during a single data transfer operation.

SDLC or IBM channel protocols *per se* do not impose any upper limits on the amount of data that may be transferred in a single data transfer operation. However, certain devices may impose implementation-specific limits on the maximum amount of data they may receive or transmit. For example 3270 SNA/SDLC control units restrict the maximum number of data bytes, excluding the TH and RH, that may be transferred by one SDLC frame to 256, ie the information field in an information transfer SDLC frame may only contain a TH, a RH and up to 256 bytes of a Request Unit.

The maximum Request Unit sizes established, for each direction, when an LU-LU session is activated are independent of the above maximum message unit length limitations. ACF/VTAM, ACF/NCP will segment Request Units in LU-LU sessions to suit the appropriate maximum message unit lengths.

Non-SNA device support

The only non-SNA devices directly supported by ACF/VTAM and ACF/NCP are non-SNA 3270 devices, that is, channel-attached 3272s or 3274-1B/1Ds or BSC 3271s, 3274-1C/51Cs, 3275s or 3276s. However, certain link-attached, start/stop (asynchronous) devices, such as 2740s, 2741s, Model 33/35 teletypes, 3101s, can be supported via the Network Terminal Option (NTO) program product which executes in communication controllers along side ACF/NCP. (NTO is described in Chapter 12, *SNA implementations*.)

Boundary Function

Boundary Function support does not have to be explicitly requested in an ACF/VTAM, ACF/NCP environment. Boundary Function support will be automatically included in ACF/VTAM (provided these are channel-attached SNA (or local 3270) devices other than communications controllers executing ACF/NCPs) and in ACF/NCPs that have link-attached SNA (or 3270 BSC) devices.

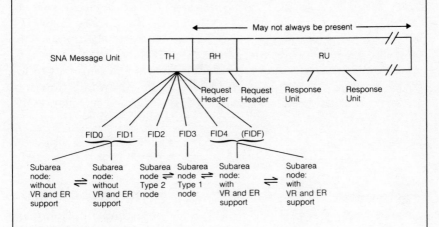

BIU (unsegmented) = RH + RU

BIU (segmented) = $\{ \text{BIU segment} \}_1^1$ + $\{ \text{BIU segment} \}_1^n$

RH + [RU segment$_1$] [RU segments]

PIU = TH + BIU
      or
    TH + BIU segment

BTU = $\{ \text{PIU} \}_1^n$

BLU = DLC header + BTU + DLC trailer

Checkpoint 10

Chapter 11:
Functional Layers

☐ Functional Layers ☐ Hierarchically Layered Architectures ☐ Reference Model for Open Systems Interconnection ☐ Physical Layer ☐ Data Link Layer ☐ Network Layer ☐ Transport Layer ☐ Session Layer ☐ Presentation Layer ☐ Application Layer

Chapter 11:
Functional Layers

Overview

SNA is a classic example of a hierarchically layered architecture. The repertoire of functions defined in SNA is clearly and cleanly divided into discrete, mutually independent, non-redundant and non-overlapping sets. The execution of a particular set of functions within a given SNA entity, eg a NAU or a node, is always performed by a specific component in the subject entity. In addition, a given set of functions is always performed by the same component, for a given entity type, and the components are always structured in the same hierarchical order within each entity: hence the concept of 'Functional Layers'. All interactions in an SNA environment – whether end-user data transfer- or environmental control-related - are conducted and managed by means of a series of dialogues between peer components in either end-to-end or adjacent peer entities, via protocols specific to the functions performed by those components. For example:

- Session-level pacing, to regulate the rate of data flow in a given direction within a session, is performed by the Transmission Control components in the two half-sessions forming the session, using a protocol based on pacing requests, pacing responses and a pacing window size. Figure 11.1 illustrates the concept of a session-level pacing protocol between end-to-end Transmission Control components to realise session-level pacing.
- Message unit transmission between adjacent subarea nodes,

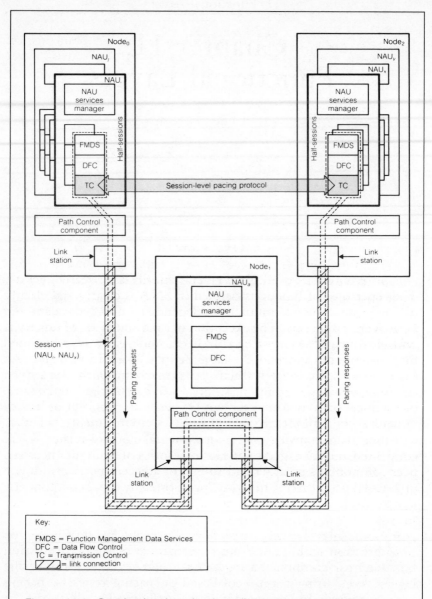

Figure 11.1: Session-level pacing is performed by the Transmission Control components in the two (end-to-end) half-sessions forming the session, using a Transmission Control component-specific protocol based on pacing requests, pacing responses and a pacing window size

across a transmission group, is handled by the Transmission Group Control subcomponents of the two Path Control components in the two nodes, using a protocol based on Transmission Group sequence numbers, 'multi-level' retransmissions, Transmission Group sweeps and Transmission Group sequence number field wrap acknowledgement requests (see Figure 11.2).

- Quiescing, the process whereby a half-session can temporarily stop its session partner from transmitting requests on the normal flow of a session, is performed by the Data Flow Control components in the two half-sessions forming the session, using a protocol based on QEC, QC and RELQ requests.

The functional layering of SNA is taken for granted in most current discussions on SNA *per se*. The term 'functional layering' itself only tends to crop up now when SNA is being compared to other contemporary communication architectures (such as the International Standards Organisation's (ISO) seven-layer Reference Model of Open Systems Interconnection (OSI)) rather than when SNA is being discussed in isolation. The various components, eg Path Control, Data Flow Control, Transmission Control etc, are described in terms of the functions they are responsible for; the peer-component-to-peer-component interaction aspect is often just alluded to rather than explicitly stated.

The need for functional layering – not only for facilitating the specification and validation but mainly for permitting modular and thus easily maintainable and modifiable implementations – in an architecture as abundant in functions as SNA is now effectively assumed. However, this was not always the case. When announced in 1974, SNA pioneered the concept of functional layering for communication architectures. Early descriptions of SNA – *viz* SNA0, SNA1 and SNA2 – stressed its functional layering aspect, but these early versions were based on three functionally 'thick' layers: the Application (or End-User) Layer, the Function Management Layer and the Transmission Subsystem Layer. This layering structure was refined, in two stages, with SNA3 and SNA4 when more functions were added. Rather than attempting to integrate these additional functions into the previously defined three layers, and thus risking defeating the fundamental objective

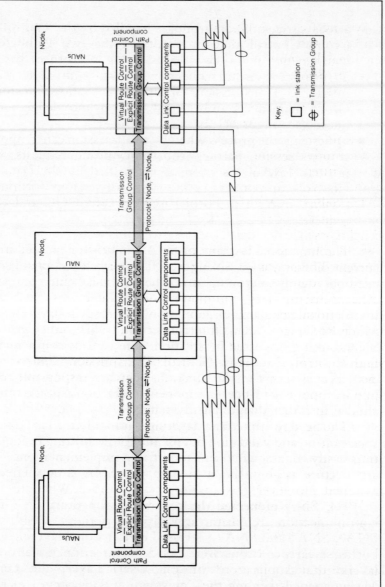

Figure 11.2: Message unit transfer between adjacent subarea nodes, across Transmission Groups, is handled by the Transmission Group Control subcomponents of the Path Control components in these nodes, using a Transmission Group Control-specific protocol

of layering (ie, an easily isolatable set of functions) by bloating each layer, the layering scheme was 'revamped' to provide more functional layers. (The de-emphasis of the functional layering aspect of SNA coincided with this realignment of layers!)

SNA: the Functional Layers

To study the functional layering of SNA one must consider both the structures of NAUs and nodes since the Path Control Network components that are needed to provide interconnection between the NAUs only occur within nodes. Since all the functions that the constituent components of NAUs and nodes are responsible for have been discussed in detail in Chapters 4 to 7, this section only attempts to highlight the peer-to-peer span of these functions. This is best achieved schematically and Figure 11.3 illustrates all the discrete functional components defined in SNA and summarises the functions that each Functional Layer is responsible for. (The fact that Path Control components comprising Virtual Route Control, Explicit Route Control and Transmission Group Control subcomponents only occur within subarea nodes need not distract from their being considered in a generalised node representation. If their functions are not applicable to a given node these Functional Layers could be thought of as still being present but being transparent in terms of functions performed; ie the Path Control component will convey messages between NAUs and the Data Link Control component without altering in any way the message units or the environment.)

The Reference Model for Open Systems Interconnection

The Reference Model for Open Systems Interconnection is a data communications architecture, postulating a data communication environment for supporting distributed data processing, similar in capability and functionality to that specified by SNA. In 1982 it was put forward by the International Standards Organisation in the form of a Draft International Standard (ISO/DIS 7498) for potential adoption as a reference standard for such architectures, following a

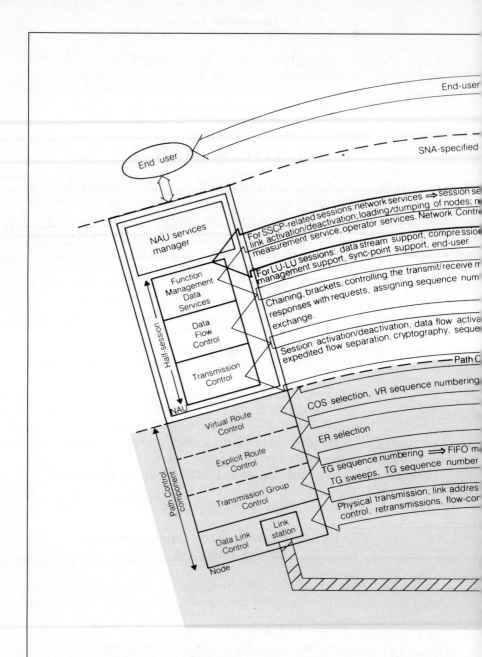

Figure 11.3: The functional layering of SNA, with a summary of the
functions that each layer is responsible for

384

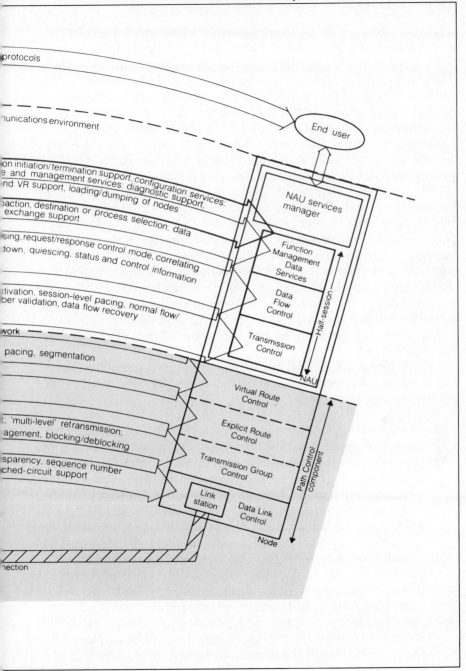

protocols

munications environment

End user

on initiation/termination support, configuration services:
and management services: diagnostic support,
nd VR support, loading/dumping of nodes

action, destination or process selection, data
exchange support

sing, request/response control mode, correlating
own, quiescing, status and control information

tivation, session-level pacing, normal flow/
er validation, data flow recovery

work

pacing, segmentation

, 'multi-level' retransmission,
agement, blocking/deblocking

sparency, sequence number
ched-circuit support

nection

NAU services
manager

Function
Management
Data
Services

Data
Flow
Control

Transmission
Control

Half-session

NAU

Virtual Route
Control

Explicit Route
Control

Transmission Group
Control

Path Control
component

Link
station

Data Link
Control

Node

five-year gestation. Its total independence from, and impartiality to, any commercial organisation is becoming increasingly appealing to a significant sector of the computer and communications industries. They are vociferously advocating that it should be treated as the universal standard for communication architectures in preference to SNA, which by sheer dint of the number of active implementations, the volume of documentation available and the general awareness of it within the computer fraternity, is gaining momentum as the *de facto* standard for communication architectures even though SNA is IBM proprietary and all developments on it are dictated entirely by IBM. A full, or even adequate, description of the Reference Model is beyond the scope of this book. (Suitable references are cited in the bibliography.) However, a cursory comparison of the Reference Model and SNA is of interest in order to appreciate how they both provide a similar repertoire of functions and to observe the similarities in the functional layering schemes in both architectures. To this end, a very brief description of the Reference Model follows, concentrating only on its salient features to enable a meaningful and relatable comparison to be made with SNA. (This description should not be treated as a comprehensive list of the features offered by the Reference Model.)

The Reference Model for Open Systems Interconnection is based on seven Functional Layers, hierarchically structured in the following ascending order:

1: *the Physical Layer*. This is the lowest layer of the architecture and is responsible for establishing, maintaining and disconnecting point-to-point or multipoint, full- or half-duplex mode, serial or parallel, switched or non-switched physical connections with adjacent 'system entities' (where a 'system entity' can be either an individual distributed data (processing product – a là SNA node – or a distributed data processing system consisting of multiple interconnected products) over which any data stream can be transmitted. This layer specifies the mechanical aspects: the physical dimensions of the circuit terminating plugs and sockets to be used, the number of pins required in these plugs and sockets and how these pins will be assigned to the various control and data signals that will be used; the electrical property: the voltage levels that will be employed by the various signals; the functional aspect: the significance of a signal being at a certain voltage level; and the procedural aspects: the exact sequences in which the various signals need to be activated or deactivated, and characteristics of the interface to the physical connection so that it can be activated, deactivated and used for the physical transmission and reception of bit streams. (Note that SNA does not explicitly address this aspect of an SNA link. A link connection is only referred to as being either an IBM System/370 channel or a switched or non-switched telecommunications link, along with the appropriate DCEs. The details of activating, deactivating, using and interfacing with these link connections are not dealt with in the specification.)

2: *the Data Link Layer.* This layer is responsible for the error–free, transparent, sequence-controlled and full-duplex transmission and reception of data over a physical connection provided by layer 1. To this end layer 2 specifies the following: how data units will be delimited (or framed), the physical connection-specific addressing scheme for identifying the destination or source of a data unit and the procedures, ie the sequences of defined control commands, that will be used for transmission and reception of data between adjacent 'system entities'. (ISO's High-level Data Link Control (HDLC), which is a Data Link Control protocol similar to SDLC, is an example of a protocol recommended as suitable for the implementation of this layer.)

3: *the Network Control Layer.* The main concern of this layer is to provide a 'logical route' through the environment (which may involve several intermediate 'system entities') for two–way data communication between two interacting 'end users'. This layer specifies the following: the overall network addressing scheme (cf SNA's Network Addresses), the control commands required, the formats of message units – whether for control commands or for data units – to be used over a route, the sequences of control commands needed for requesting, establishing and disestablishing a route and for maintaining an error-free flow of message units over the route, the mechanism for providing an expedited flow over the route for control and status message units, the segmentation and blocking techniques available to restructure message units and the message unit sequence control and assurance procedures needed to provide this 'logical routing' capability. However, this layer does not provide or maintain 'logical routes' on an end–to–end basis: the routing is provided on a 'hop-by-hop' basis between each 'system entity' forming the route. Figure 11.4 illustrates this 'hop-by-hop' routing provided by layer 3 and the span of the functions offered by the two lower layers.

4: *the Transport Layer.* The first three layers of the Reference Model do not provide any end–to–end control functions between two interacting end users: their span of control is only between adjacent 'system entities' (qv Figure 11.4). Layer 4 is responsible for providing end–to–end flow control, sequence control, blocking and segmentation, 'pacing', error recovery and delivery assurance for data units being exchanged between two interacting end users. The Transport Layers at each end 'system entity' rely on their underlying Network Layers to provide them with the appropriate 'logical route' through the environment, and offer their higher layers a guaranteed end–to–end 'quality of service' based on a specified Class of Service, where each Class of Service designates the characteristics of the communications resources needed for a particular type of interaction, eg batch or interactive (cf SNA's VR COS). Two interacting end users may have multiple concurrent dialogues with each other (cf SNA's parallel sessions). In such instances, the Transport Layer may multiplex the data units belonging to several dialogues onto one 'route' provided by its underlying layers. In addition, it may split the data units belonging to one dialogue (irrespective of whether there are multiple active dialogues or not) for transmission over multiple 'routes'.

5: *the Session Layer.* This layer is responsible for establishing, maintaining and disestablishing a 'session' between two end users (a 'session' in this context being equivalent to an SNA session – *viz* all end-user dialogues are conducted relative to a session). In addition, this layer also deals with the following tasks: coordinating the end-user-to-end-user transmit and receive mode – *viz* two-way-simultaneous (ie full-duplex), two-way-alternate (ie half-duplex) and one-way (ie simplex); providing an SNA 'synch-point'-type feature coupled with a request and response control mode mechanism; supporting the 'quarantining' of data units – ie a means whereby a group of data units (designated as a single entity) are queued (ie 'quarantined')

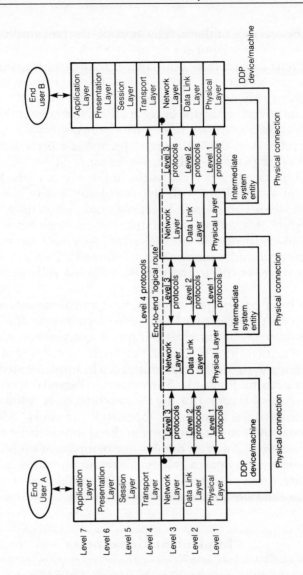

Figure 11.4: The span of the functions offered by the first three layers of the ISO Reference Model, and how the network layers provide an end-to-end logical route for two interacting end users via a 'hop-by-hop' technique between the intermediate system entities that occur between the system entities serving the end users

by the receiver of the data units until the transmitter explicitly releases them or purges them (cf SNA chaining).

6: *the Presentation Layer.* This layer provides the transformations required to convert and reformat the data being exchanged between two interacting end users, so that the data transmitted by one is received by the other in a form that is acceptable to it: ie in the correct character set with the necessary device control characters and the appropriate format if a presentation – *viz* display or printer – medium is being used.

7: *the Application Layer.* This is the highest layer of the Reference Model and it deals with the actual support of the end-user processes involved in the data communication operations, the transfer of control and status information between these end-to-end processes and the system operator functions needed to control and monitor the communications environment. (This layer is still in the process of being fully defined.)

This brief description of the salient functions offered by the seven layers of the Reference Model demonstrates that the Reference Model proposes a communications function repertoire very similar to that specified in SNA and, as such, data communication environments with similar capabilities can be implemented based on either architecture. Figure 11.5 attempts to illustrate the similarities in the functional layering of the two architectures. However, this two-dimensional schematic comparison can only address the fundamental and crucial functions in the layering structures of the two architectures. An exact one-to-one mapping of the layers of the two architectures is not feasible since certain functions, available in both architectures, are catered for in completely different hierarchical levels in the two architectures.

Implementational notes

Figure 11.6 illustrates where the various SNA Functional Layers occur within a typical SNA implementation.

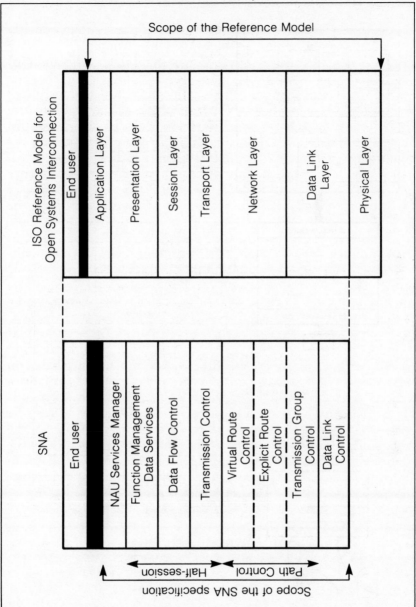

Figure 11.5: Comparison of the SNA layering and the Reference Model functional layering

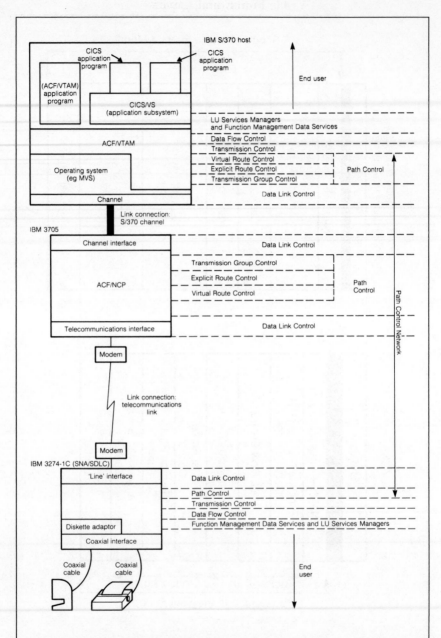

Figure 11.6: The 'implementation' of the SNA Functional Layers in a typical SNA-based environment

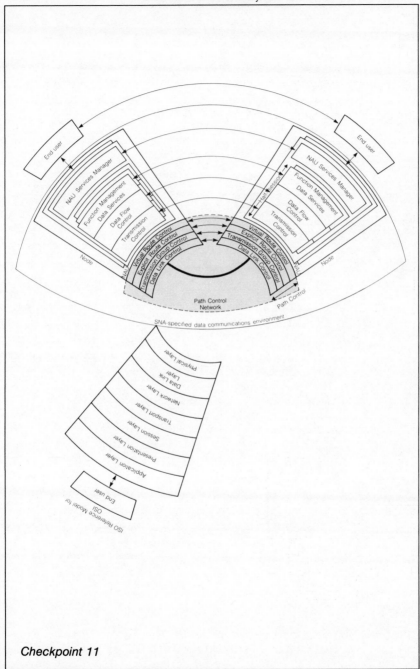

Checkpoint 11

393

Chapter 12:
Products for realising an SNA environment

☐ ACF/VTAM ☐ TOLTEP ☐ CNM ☐ ACF/TCAM ☐ ACF/
VTAME ☐ MSNF ☐ ACF/NCP ☐ EP ☐ NTO ☐ ACF2/3
☐ Resource   Takeover   ☐ NCCF   ☐ NPDA   ☐ CPDA
☐ VM/VCNA ☐ X.25 Support

Chapter 12:
Products for realising an SNA environment

Overview

The *Implementational notes* at the end of each of the preceding chapters described how the various features and functions of SNA were provided by ACF/VTAM and ACF/NCP and how they were selected, specified or invoked. This chapter briefly examines the main – IBM proprietary – software products currently available to realise an SNA-based communications environment. A list of the more common terminals and devices that can be found in such an environment was tabulated in Figure 2.7. The functional and characteristic scope, diversity and complexity of these terminal and device families are so great that a functional description of each component, or even a generic description of a complete family, is beyond the scope of this book. However, a synopsis of their salient capabilities can be found in the *Glossary*.

Figure 12.1 depicts the main software products germane to realising an SNA-based communications environment and illustrates where they occur within the environment. (The 'VTAM', 'TCAM' and 'NCP' releases that correspond to the various SNA versions, ie SNA-2, SNA-3, SNA-4 etc, were tabulated in Figure 2.8.)

ACF/VTAM

ACF/VTAM (Advanced Communications Function for the Virtual Telecommunications Access Method) is the core of most current SNA implementations. (ACF/TCAM can be used as an

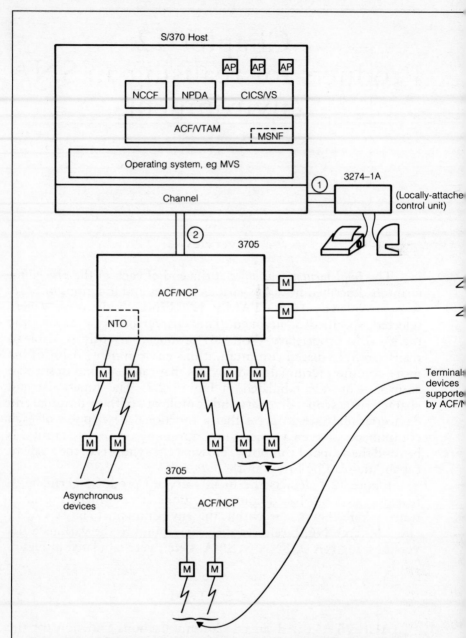

Figure 12.1: *IBM proprietary software products germaine to realising
an SNA-based communications environment*

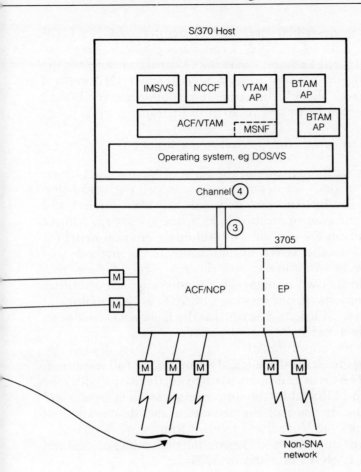

Key:

M = Modem

AP = Application program

EP = Emulation program

NTO = Network Terminal Option

Notes:

(1) Only one 'device address', ie subchannel address, is used, irrespective of the number of terminals or printers attached to the control unit. SNA addressing is used over this channel interface to identify the NAUs

(2) Only one 'subchannel address' is used between ACF/VTAM and ACF/NCP irrespective of the number of lines supported by the 'NCP'

(3) Each line supported by the EP will require a unique subchannel address, as the EP and BTAM APs represent a pre-SNA terminal

(4) Locally-attached devices – 3274-1As, 3705s, 3725s etc – supported by 'VTAM' are normally attached to a Block Multiplexor Channel

alternative and is described later in this chapter.) ACF/VTAM implements the bulk of an SNA Type 5 node functionality: the SSCP, the PU_T5, the Path and Data Link Control components, the boundary function (for supporting locally-attached SNA control units) and some of the LU functions for supporting ('VTAM') application program end users resident in the same host as it (qv Figure 3.8).

ACF/VTAM carries out the following functions:

1 It provides a mechanism – in the form of 'system' definition 'VTAM' macros – for defining the resources, *viz* application programs, locally- and remotely-attached SNA devices and terminals, and communication links, that constitute its control domain and, in the case of a multidomain environment, for specifying the other telecommunications access methods that control the other domains and the resources in them that resources in its own domain wish to interact with or utilise. These definitions are one by means of ACF/VTAM major and minor nodes, which are described in the *Implementational notes* in Chapters 4 and 7.

2 It controls the allocation of the resources in its domain by supervising the establishment and termination of all sessions in which the NAUs in its domain participate. (It also provides the logmode and USS tables for supporting session initiation and termination). It controls the activation and deactivation of physical links and Virtual and Explicit Routes (qv *Implementational notes* in Chapters 4 and 7) including the loading of local and remote ACF/NCPs in 3705s or 3725s.

3 It handles the transmission and reception of message units between NAUs located in its host and between them and NAUs located in other parts of the environment. To do this it utilises locally-attached ACF/NCPs in the case of NAUs located in remote devices, terminals or machines.

4 It supplies S/370 Assembler macros to enable application program end users to do the following:
  • To create an LU (*viz* the Access-method Control Block (ACB) and Node Initialisation Block (NIB) macros)
  • To establish and terminate LU-LU sessions (*viz* OPNDST, CLSDST, SIMLOGON, OPNSEC, TERMSESS – qv *Implementational notes* in Chapter 4)

- To transmit and receive end-user data or SNA–defined control commands (*viz* SEND, RECEIVE, SESSIONC – qv *Implementational notes* in Chapter 5)
- To set, exchange and modify parameters to be used by the other macros (*viz* RPL, MODCB – qv *Implementational notes* in Chapter 5)
- To define Exit Routines to handle session initiation and termination requests or certain exception conditions (*viz* Exit List (EXLST) macro)
- To build control blocks that will be accessed by other macros (*viz* Generate Control Block (GENCB) macro)
- To extract parameters from control blocks (*viz* SHOWCB macro)
- To test the values in certain fields of a control block (*viz* TESTCB).

(An Exit Routine is an application program routine that is invoked by ACF/VTAM when it encounters a condition such as one of the following:

- An LU–LU session establishment or termination request
- Failure of an LU–LU session
- A specific system operator command
- Certain errors or certain SNA–defined requests or responses received from a session partner, for which a 'VTAM' application program has designated an Exit Routine by means of an EXLST macro, which specifies the subject condition and the storage address of the routine to be invoked.)

5 It offers an extensive array of problem–determination aids:
- Hardware and software error logging and notification
- Traces for I/O activity, buffer use (including recording of the contents), storage use and certain processing conditions
- Obtaining storage dumps of local or remote ACF/NCPs
- The performance of on-line test procedures on lines and certain devices in its domain (via a component known as Teleprocessing On-line Test Executive Program (TOLTEP)).

6 It provides a System Operator Interface via a set of 'VTAM' operator commands that can be entered at the host system console to enable the host system operator to:

- Activate and deactivate individual or all resources in the domain by means of the major and minor node definitions
- Monitor the status of the resources
- Initiate or terminate sessions
- Modify the physical configuration of its domain (ie dynamic reconfiguration)
- Activate or deactivate certain ACF/VTAM facilities such as traces, statistics recording, dumps from NCPs, link tests etc. (ACF/VTAM also allows certain 'authorised' application programs to issue – and receive the results of – system operator commands by means of two Assembler macros: SENDCMD and RCVCMD. Another environment control-related feature offered by ACF/VTAM is Communication Network Management (CNM) application programs. These 'authorised' application programs can request and receive status and error statistics from PUs in their domain for processing. The NCCF – described later in this Chapter – is an example of a CNM Application Program.)

The SSCP, PU_T5 and the system operator interface responsibilities of ACF/VTAM dictate that it must be active within the host to control and sustain its domain. So, unlike BTAM – its best known predecessor – which was just a library of Assembler macros that expanded at application program assembly time to calls to the operating system (ie SVCs), ACF/VTAM is a program in its own right, which executes as such in the host machine, under the operating system, and provides real-time, interactive support and services to the resources in its domain, to the other SNA teleprocessing access methods – if present – that control resources that can interact with resources in its domain and to the system operator. If ACF/VTAM fails, all LU-LU sessions involving 'VTAM' application programs executing in its host would also fail, since the LUs for these programs are provided through ACF/VTAM. The LUs in its domain, not serving application programs, ie those in local or remote devices or terminals, will be unable to establish any LU-LU sessions with application programs in other domains since the session establishment has to be conducted via the LU's controlling SSCP. However if an LU in a remote device or terminal already had a LU-LU session established with an application program in another domain, before ACF/VTAM failed, this session would not be affected by the failure of the LU's controlling ACF/VTAM (since the failed ACF/VTAM would not have been involved in the transmission of the data on the LU-LU session. (This would not be the case with LUs in locally-attached devices, since transmissions to or from them would be through the ACF/VTAM's boundary function.) Figure 12.2 illustrates the sessions that are affected when an ACF/VTAM fails.

ACF/VTAM supports the following:

1 Channel-attached SNA devices, *viz* 3274-1A, the 3790 Communication System and the 3730 Distributed Office Communication System.
2 Channel-attached non-SNA 3270s, *viz* 3272, 3274-1B/1D and the IBM 4331 Display/Printer Adaptor.
3 If executing in an IBM 4331 host, SNA or non-SNA devices attached to the 4331 loop adaptor.
4 Devices accessing it via a local ACF/NCP (ie any device supported by ACF/NCP).

Note that ACF/VTAM only directly communicates with channel-attached devices. Remote devices are only supported via ACF/NCP. As such, ACF/VTAM, only contains Data Link Control components that support S/370 channels. It does not deal with teleprocessing protocols, *viz* SDLC, BSC or Start/Stop. ACF/NCPs provide all the teleprocessing protocol support, ie BLUs exchanged between ACF/VTAM and a local ACF/NCP are in S/370 channel format and the BTUs in them do not contain any teleprocessing protocol-related information. The BIUs or BIU segments in the BTU will only contain end-user data or SNA commands.

Cryptography support, when required, is provided through the Encrypt/Decrypt feature of ACF/VTAM. This feature is currently only available with OS/VS Operating Systems.

ACF/TCAM

ACF/TCAM (Advanced Communication Function for the Telecommunications Access Method) is the other IBM teleprocessing access method that can be used to implement an SNA-based data

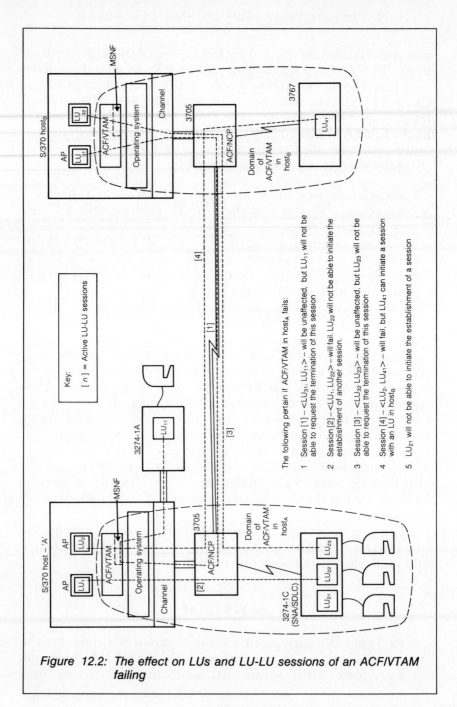

Figure 12.2: The effect on LUs and LU-LU sessions of an ACF/VTAM failing

Key:
[n] = Active LU-LU sessions

The following pertain if ACF/VTAM in host$_A$ fails:

1 Session [1] – <LU$_{31}$, LU$_{11}$> – will be unaffected, but LU$_{11}$ will not be able to request the termination of this session

2 Session [2] – <LU$_1$, LU$_{22}$> – will fail. LU$_{22}$ will not be able to initiate the establishment of another session.

3 Session [3] – <LU$_{32}$ LU$_{23}$> – will be unaffected, but LU$_{23}$ will not be able to request the termination of this session

4 Session [4] – <LU$_2$, LU$_{41}$> – will fail, but LU$_{41}$ can initiate a session with an LU in host$_B$

5 LU$_{21}$ will not be able to initiate the establishment of a session

404

communications environment. It provides the same type of facilities as ACF/VTAM, but in addition provides the following features: a Message Control Program (MCP) feature that facilitates time stamping, control character addition or deletion, message editing, message reconstruction etc, support for a wider range of non-SNA devices and queuing of messages (even for ACF/TCAM application programs that might not be active). However, ACF/VTAM usually gains preference over ACF/TCAM, at least in Europe, as the teleprocessing access method used for realising SNA-based environments. This is partly due to the considerably lower rental price of ACF/VTAM and the fact that most environments do not require the MCP and queuing features offered by ACF/TCAM.

ACF/VTAME

ACF/VTAME (Advanced Communication Function for VTAM Entry) is a version of ACF/VTAM that operates only under DOS/VSE on an IBM 4331 host. It directly supports telecommunication links – to SNA devices, non-SNA 3270s or to ACF/NCPs supported by SNA teleprocessing access methods in other hosts – attached to the 4331 Communications Adaptor. (This Adaptor can support up to eight links.) In addition, it supports locally-attached SNA or non-SNA 3270 devices and caters for cross-domain LU–LU sessions.

MSNF

MSNF (Multisystem Networking Facility) is an optional feature of ACF/VTAM and ACF/TCAM that is required if inter-(cross-) domain LU–LU sessions are needed in a multidomain environment.

ACF/NCP

ACF/NCP (Advanced Communications Function for Network Control Program) – in recent years formally referred to as ACF/NCP/VS, where the VS signifies virtual storage – is a control program that executes in either a local or remote communications controller and provides functions of an SNA Type 4 node: PU_T4, Path Control, Data Link Control and Boundary Function. (qv Figure 3.8.) An ACF/NCP is required if a data communications environment is to contain any remote devices or, in the case of a multidomain environment, if inter- (cross-) domain communication is required. (SNA teleprocessing access methods, unless they are in the same host, can only communicate with each other via an ACF/NCP.)

ACF/NCP is responsible for providing all the teleprocessing protocol support required to establish and disestablish communication with and control and maintain communications with devices, terminals and other ACF/NCPs attached to the telecommunications links connected – permanently or on a switched basis – to the communications controller it executes in. It is also responsible for routing message units to or from these devices, terminals or ACF/NCPs. ACF/NCPs in locally-attached communication controllers liaise with the teleprocessing access method (ie ACF/VTAM and ACF/TCAM) in the host computer(s) across an S/370 channel. However, unlike pre-SNA environments, only one 'device address' (subchannel address) is used irrespective of the number of links supported by the ACF/NCP. ACF/NCP supports any remote SNA terminals and devices and non-SNA 3270s.

EP

EP (Emulation Program) is a feature available on local ACF/NCPs that enables application programs written for pre-SNA systems to interact with telecommunications links attached to a local 3704/3705 or 3725 communications controller. (qv Figure 12.1.) EP emulates the operation of a specified pre-SNA transmission control unit (TCU), ie a 2701, 2702 or 2703. This feature enables a pre-SNA network to be implemented using a modern communication controller, ie 3705, as opposed to a now obsolete 270X TCU, or for a pre-SNA network to coexist alongside – but not to interact with – an SNA network. Since EP emulates a pre-SNA environment, each line supported by EP must have a unique 'device' (subchannel) address and the pre-SNA network supported by EP will still retain all the drawbacks inherent in pre-SNA systems. (qv *Why SNA?* in Chapter 1.)

(A 'combined' ACF/NCP and EP control program executing in a local communications controller, ie a local communication controller supporting an SNA and a pre-SNA network, is referred to as a Partitioned Emulation Program (PEP).)

NTO

NTO (Network Terminal Option) is a control program (supplied as an IBM Program Product) that executes alongside ACF/NCP in a communications controller and enables certain non-SNA devices – IBM 2740 Model 1, IBM 2741, Teletype (TTY) Models 33 or 35 (switched support only), World Trade teletypewriter terminal (WTTY) (non-switched support only), IBM 3101, IBM 1750/3750 and 3780 BSC (not fully supported) – to participate in an SNA environment as if they were *bona fide* SNA devices: that is as if these devices had SNA PUs and LUs. NTO acts as a 'protocol converter' between the SNA teleprocessing access method (and the application programs associated with the access method) and the non-SNA devices it supports, and presents the non-SNA devices to the access method and the application programs as single LU IBM 3767 terminals. Figure 12.3 illustrates the operation of NTO.

ACF/VTAM and ACF/NCP environments

Figures 12.4 and 12.5 illustrate some of the possible SNA-based data communications environment configurations that could be realised with ACF/VTAM Release 2 and ACF/NCP Release 2/2.1 (sometimes collectively referred to as 'ACF 2'). These environments correspond to SNA version 4.1. (qv Chapter 2.)

Figure 12.6 illustrates the type of multidomain environment that can be realised with ACF/VTAM Release 3 and ACF/NCP Release 3 (collectively referred to as 'ACF 3').

Note that with an 'ACF 3' environment only eight different routes are permitted between any given pair of subarea nodes even though SNA 4 caters for up to 48 virtual routes. These environments do not offer 'alternate routing'. When a route between subarea nodes becomes inoperative, all the sessions associated with that route are disrupted. If the affected LUs wish to resume communications via

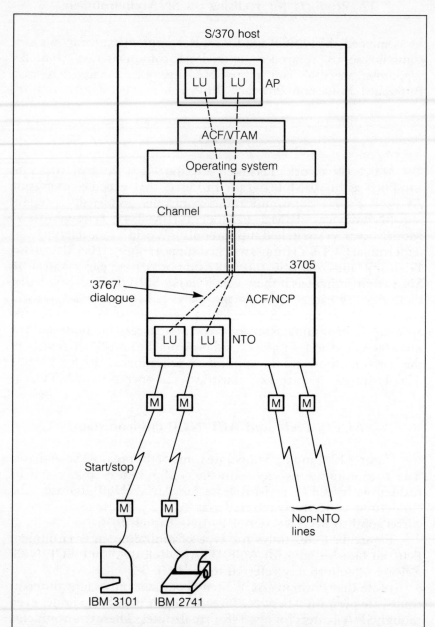

Figure 12.3: Network Terminal Option (NTO): presents designated non-SNA terminals to SNA-based application programs as if the terminals were 3767 SNA terminals

408

another route they need to explicitly initiate a new session specifying the relevant COS. (qv Chapter 7.)

A 'resource takeover' capability is provided in 'ACF' environments. The ownership of resources, ie lines, PUs and LUs, specified in an ACF/NCP may be transferred from one SNA teleprocessing access method to another, ie the resources can be moved from one domain to another. This feature enables shared resources to be 'reactivated' if they lose 'contact' with their original SSCP, ie teleprocessing access method, due to either failure of the access method or the disruption of the route(s) between their adjacent ACF/NCP and the access method. 'Resource takeover' can be catered for by one of two means:

1 Having multiple SNA teleprocessing access methods – in the same host or in different hosts – share an ACF/NCP and the resources specified by it. (Up to eight access methods can concurrently share a local or remote ACF/NCP in an 'ACF 3' environment, while up to four access methods may share an ACF/NCP in an 'ACF 2' environment.) If an access method fails, another one of the access methods can reactivate the shared resources.
2 Having one SNA teleprocessing access method own an ACF/NCP and the resources specified by it and then, using the OWNER= and BACKUP= operands of the ACF/VTAM PCCU macro, define another access method that will acquire the resources if the access method owning the resources fails.

NCCF

NCCF (Network Communications Control Facility) is an IBM-supplied program product that executes as an ACF/VTAM- (or ACF/TCAM-) authorised CNM application program. It allows system operators using either locally- or remotely-attached 3270 terminals to control a single- or multidomain environment using ACF/VTAM-defined operator commands or 'operator-defined' command lists (CLISTS) consisting of ACF/VTAM and NCCF-defined commands. It also allows the operators to communicate with each other and provides for the collection, storage and retrieval of network error data for processing by NPDA.

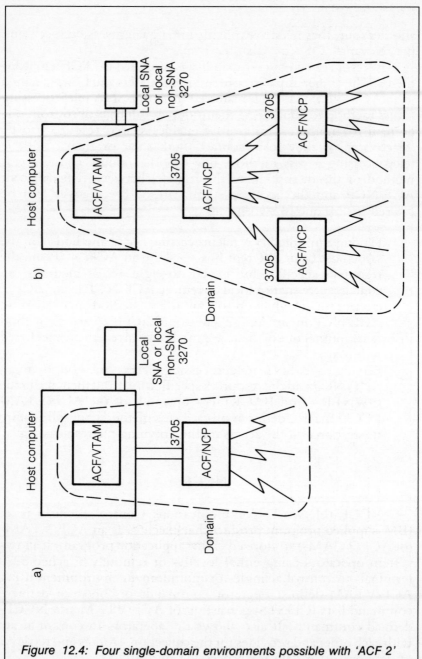

Figure 12.4: Four single-domain environments possible with 'ACF 2'

410

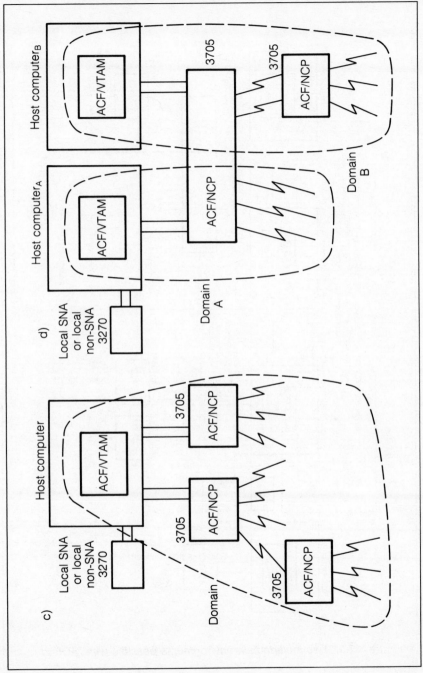

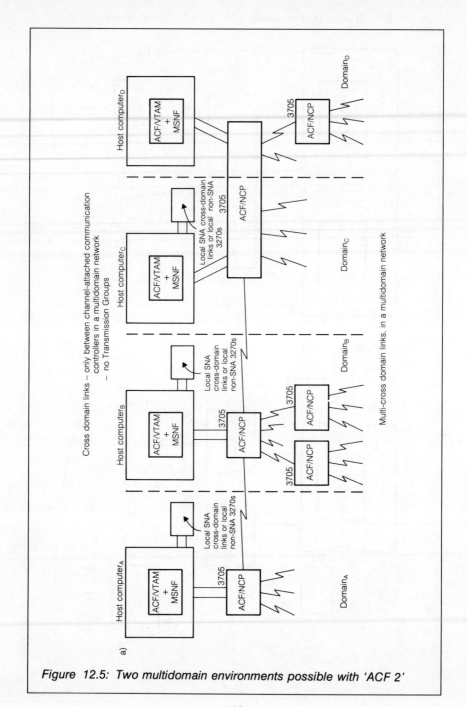

Cross domain links – only between channel-attached communication controllers in a multidomain network
– no Transmission Groups

Multi-cross domain links, in a multidomain network

Local SNA cross-domain links or local non-SNA 3270s

Figure 12.5: Two multidomain environments possible with 'ACF 2'

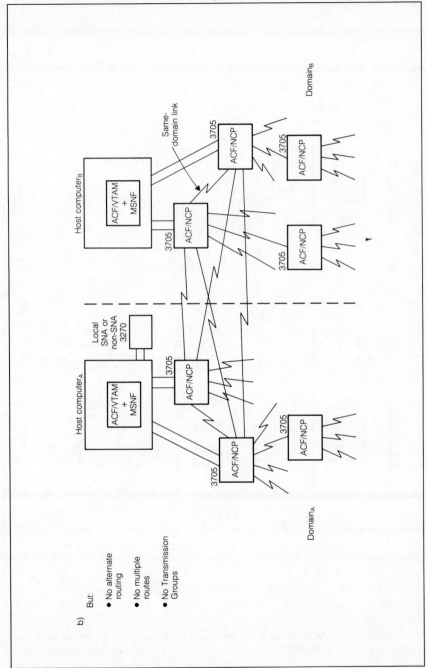

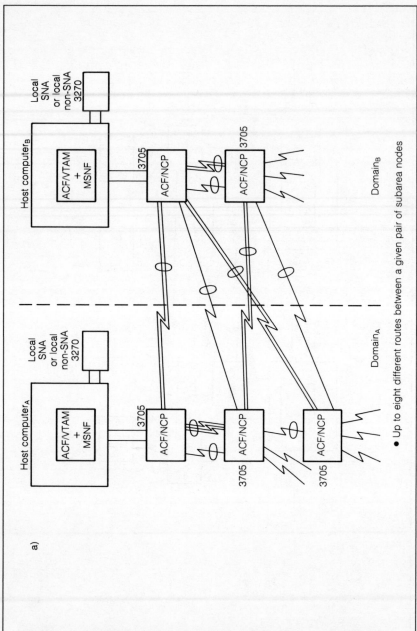

Figure 12.6: Multidomain environment configurations possible with 'ACF 3'

414

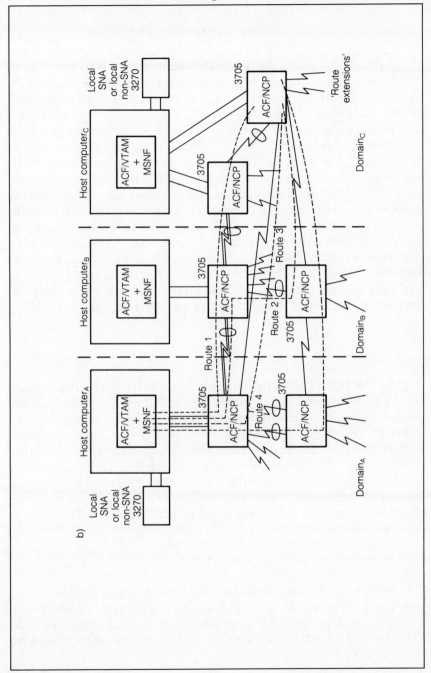

NPDA

NPDA (Network Problem Determination Application) is an IBM-supplied program product that executes as an authorised CNM application 'process' under NCCF that acts as a central problem determination function – using error data collected for it by NCCF – and assists users in locating resources in the environment that have failed or are liable to fail. Via 3270 terminals, NPDA provides its users with the following: a hierarchical perspective of error counts for communication controllers; SDLC, BSC and S/S lines attached to communication controllers; local or remote control units and the devices attached to these or stand-alone, remote devices or terminals; an analysis of the probable cause of a failure or problem; and a list of recommended actions to resolve a failure or problem. (In OS/VS-based systems, NPDA can be extended to also display error data on selected tapes, disks and printers attached to the host.) NPDA also provides an alert feature, which will dynamically display prespecified error conditions which warrant operator action.

LPDA

LPDA (Link Problem Determination Aid) is a feature provided by ACF/NCP Release 2.1 and ACF/NCP Release 3 to exploit the on-line test and problem determination features available on the microprocessor-based IBM modems, *viz* 3863, 3864 and 3865. LPDA generates diagnostic test commands to these modems, either dynamically upon detection of a permanent link or link station error condition, dynamically upon an error count being exceeded or upon receipt of or request from NPDA. The results obtained from the diagnostic tests are then forwarded to NPDA for processing.

VM/VCNA

VM/VCNA (Virtual Machine/VTAM Communications Network Application) is an IBM-supplied program product that executes under the VM operating system and provides VM Conversational Monitor System (CMS) users with access to resources in an SNA environment by acting as an SNA teleprocessing access method.

Support of X.25

There are currently two products – one hardware and one software – available from IBM to interface SNA-based products with packet-switched networks, via X.25. They are the 'X.25 NCP Packet-Switching Interface', which is a program product that executes in a communication controller in conjunction with ACF/NCP, and the Network Interface Adaptor (NIA), which is a stand-alone hardware 'protocol converter' unit that enables remote SNA terminals or devices to access a packet-switched network, using X.25, as packet-mode terminals or devices. Figures 12.7 and 12.8 depict the operation of these two products. In effect, they both present X.25 virtual calls or permanent virtual circuits as leased SDLC links to the appropriate SNA product.

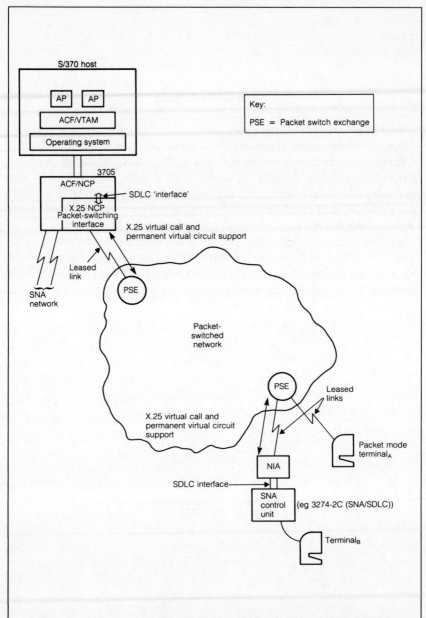

Figure 12.7: X.25 NCP packet switching interface enables terminals A and B to interact with ACF/VTAM via a packet-switched network that they access using X.25

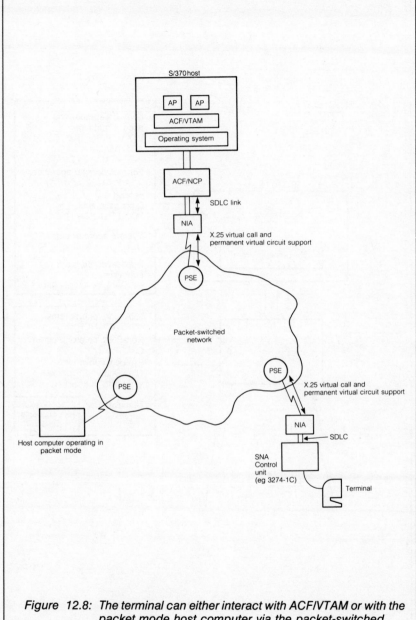

Figure 12.8: The terminal can either interact with ACF/VTAM or with the packet mode host computer via the packet-switched network

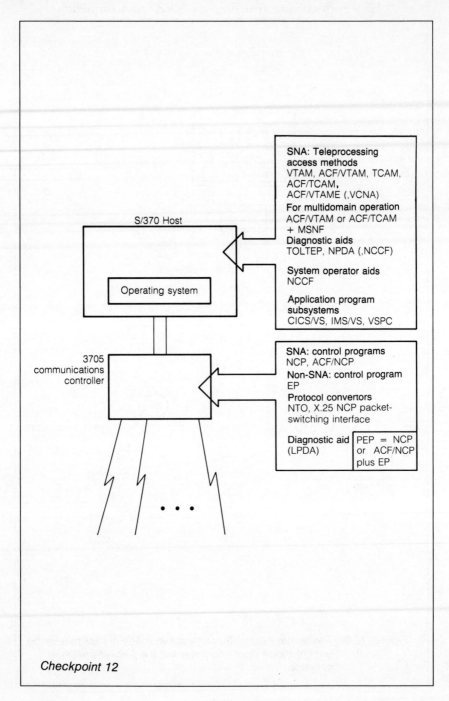

SNA: Teleprocessing
access methods
VTAM, ACF/VTAM, TCAM,
ACF/TCAM,
ACF/VTAME (,VCNA)
For multidomain operation
ACF/VTAM or ACF/TCAM
+ MSNF
Diagnostic aids
TOLTEP, NPDA (,NCCF)

System operator aids
NCCF

Application program
subsystems
CICS/VS, IMS/VS, VSPC

S/370 Host

Operating system

3705
communications
controller

SNA: control programs
NCP, ACF/NCP
Non-SNA: control program
EP
Protocol convertors
NTO, X.25 NCP packet-
switching interface

Diagnostic aid (LPDA)	PEP = NCP or ACF/NCP plus EP

• • •

Checkpoint 12

Appendix A:
TS and FM profiles

Transmission services (TS) profiles

TC-related 'characteristics'	TS profile 1	TS profile 2	TS profile 3	TS profile 4	TS profile 5	TS profile 7	TS profile 17
Pacing: in both directions	No pacing	Yes	Yes	Yes	No pacing	Yes	Yes
Normal flow requests/responses identified by	IDENTIFIERS	SEQ. NUMBERS	SEQ. NUMBERS	SEQ. NUMBERS	SEQ. NUMBERS	SEQ. NUMBERS	IDENTIFIERS
SDT command supported	No	No	Yes	Yes	Yes	No	Yes
CLEAR command supported	No	Yes	Yes	Yes	No	No	N/A⊕
RQR command supported	No	No	No	Yes	No	No	N/A⊕
STSN command supported	No	No	No	Yes	No	No	No
CRV command supported	No	No	Yes, if session-level cryptography selected via BIND	Yes, if session-level cryptography selected via BIND	No	Yes, if session-level cryptography selected via BIND	No
Maximum RU size, for normal flow requests, in either direction	256 bytes*	+	+	+	No maximum size	+	No maximum size
TS USAGE FIELD SPECIFIES:							
Pacing counts	N/A	✓	✓	✓	N/A	✓	✓
Maximum RU sizes	N/A	✓	✓	✓	N/A	✓	N/A

* Unless a different value is specified in the positive response to the ACTLU, when this profile is used on SSCP – LU sessions

+ Maximum RU sizes specified in the TS usage field

⊕ These commands not used on SSCP – SSCP sessions, for which TS Profile 17 is intended.

Key:

N/A = not applicable

TC = Transmission Control

Function Management (FM) profiles

DFC-related 'characteristics'	FM profile 0	FM profile 2	FM profile 3	FM profile 4	FM profile 5	FM profile 6	FM profile 7	FM profile 17	FM profile 18
Primary's request control mode	Imm.	*	*	*	Delayed	Delayed	Imm.	Delayed	*
Primary's response control mode	Imm.	*	Imm.	Imm.	-	Delayed	*	Delayed	Imm.
Secondary's request control mode	Imm.	Delayed	*	*	Delayed	Delayed	Imm.	Delayed	*
Secondary's response control mode	Imm.	Imm.	Imm.	Imm.	Delayed	Delayed	*	Delayed	Imm.
Chaining	Single-RU	Single-RU	*	*	Single RU	Single-RU	*	Single-RU	*
Response type expected by primary	Definite	*	*	*	Definite	Any	*	Definite	*
Response type expected by secondary	Definite	No-resp.	*	*	No - or def.	Any	*	Definite	*
Compression	No	No	Yes	Yes	No	No	No	No	Yes
BID command supported	No	No	No	No	No	No	No	No	Yes
BIS command supported	No	No	Yes	Yes	No	No	Yes	No	Yes
CANCEL	No	No	Yes	Yes	No	No	Yes	No	Yes
CHASE	No	No	Yes	Yes	No	No	No	No	Yes
LUSTAT	(1)	No	Yes	Yes	No	No	Yes	No	No
QC	No	No	No	Yes	No	No	No	No	No
QEC	No	No	No	Yes	No	No	No	No	No
RELQ	No	No	No	Yes	No	No	No	No	No
RSHUTD	No	No	Yes	Yes	No	No	Yes	No	Yes
RTR	No	No	No	No	No	No	No	No	Yes
SBI	No	No	No	Yes	No	No	No	No	No
SHUTC	No	No	Yes	Yes	No	No	No	No	No
SHUTD	No	No	Yes	Yes	No	No	No	No	No
SIG	No	No	Yes	Yes	No	No	Yes	No	Yes
FM HEADERS	No	No	*	*	No	No	*	No	*
BRACKETS	No	*	*	*	No	No	*	No	*
Usage of alternate code set	No	No	*	*	No	No	*	No	*
Send/receive mode	HDX-cont	FDX	*	*	FDX	FDX	*	FDX	*
Contention winner	Sec.	N/A	*	*	N/A	N/A	*	N/A	*
Recovery responsibility	Primary	Primary	*	*	N/A	N/A	*	N/A	*
FM usage field specifies:									
Bracket reset states	N/A	>	>	>	N/A	N/A	>	N/A	>
Bracket termination rule	N/A	(2)	>	>	N/A	N/A	>	N/A	>
Issuance of END BRACKET	N/A	Primary	>	>	N/A	N/A	>	N/A	>
HDX-FF reset states	N/A	N/A	>	>	N/A	N/A	>	N/A	>

(1) – Secondary may issue LUSTAT
(2) – If brackets used, termination Rule 2 will apply
＊ – Specified in the FM usage field

Key:

N/A = not applicable   Resp. = response
Imm. = immediate   Sec. = secondary
Def. = definite

Appendix B:
3270 Data Stream and SCS

Appendix B:
3270 Data Stream and SCS

3270 Data Stream

Introduction

'3270 Data Stream' is the term used to describe the device control protocol used between an IBM host computer and an IBM 3270 control unit – *viz* 3271, 3272, 3274, 3275 or 3276 – to exchange user or control data, to or from displays or printers attached to the control unit, and application programs executing in the host. 3270 Data Stream consists of user data, *commands* to initiate data transfer operations, *orders* to 'control' and modify the representation of the data, a *buffer addressing scheme* to denote the location of user and control data within the display or printer presentation space and *control fields* to convey control or status information.

3270 Data Stream is data-link protocol independent, ie the same data stream is used by local (channel-attached) and remote (SDLC or BSC, link-attached) control units, and it supports both EBCDIC and ASCII character coding schemes. 3270 Data Stream does not deal with link-level control unit addressing or the addressing of displays and printers relative to a control unit. This addressing is performed by a combination of SNA addressing and data-link control protocol-defined addressing schemes:

- Local, non-SNA: each display and printer is addressed via its designated subchannel address
- Local, SNA: the control unit is identified by a subchannel

address and displays and printers addressed via their SNA local addresses

- Remote, SDLC: the control unit is identified by a control unit address specified in the SDLC frame's address field and the displays and printers addressed via their SNA local addresses
- Remote, BSC: control unit and the displays and printers addressed via predefined poll/select addresses.

3270 Data Stream can be divided into four categories:

- *Outbound Data Stream*: data stream sent from a host to a control unit
- *Inbound Data Stream*: data stream sent to a host by a control unit
- *Standard Data Stream*: the basic data stream, as announced with the first 3270 control unit in 1972, and supported by all 3270 control units
- *Extended Data Stream*: enhancements to the stan dard data stream required to support the seven-colour, the extended highlighting and the programmed symbol features announced in 1979 and only supported by control units that contain an optional feature referred to as the 'structured field and attribute processing function'.

(Standard Data Stream is sometimes referred to as *Base Data Stream*, while Extended Data Stream is sometimes referred to as *Structured-field Data Stream*.) Figure B.1 depicts the direction of flow of inbound and outbound data streams. (ASCII character codes are not supported by the Extended Data Stream.)

Fields

3270 Data Stream is based on the concept of *fields*. A display or printer presentation space may be defined by an application program to consist of one or more discrete and uniquely identifiable fields, each of which is assigned a set of presentation-related characteristics, eg whether a field may be used by a display

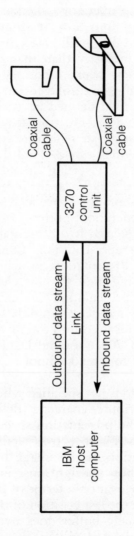

Figure B.1: Direction of flow of inbound and outbound data streams. (Note that the terms are relative to the host computer as opposed to the control unit)

operator for entering input data, whether the application program-supplied contents of a field should be protected from being overwritten by a display operator, whether, for security reasons, the data being entered into a field should not be displayed, whether a field should be highlighted by having its contents displayed in a higher intensity than that normally used and, if Extended Data Stream is being used, the colour in which the contents of a field should be displayed etc. A presentation space which has at least one field defined in it is known as a *formatted presentation space*, while a presentation space which has no fields defined in it is known as an *unformatted presentation space*. An application program defines a field – and the presentation-related characteristics of it – by inserting an *attribute character* in the display's or printer's *image buffer*, at the location corresponding to the position in the presentation space at which the field is to beg in. (The image, or regeneration, buffer is the storage in which the graphic character – converted to an internal code from EBCDIC or ASCII if necessary – representation of the 'text' to be displayed or printed is stored. Presentation is achieved by accessing a character generator, using these graphic characters as indices and obtaining the image representation (ie shapes) corresponding to these characters.) Note that fields can only be defined, ie attribute characters can only be inserted into the image buffer, by application programs, using 3270 Outbound Data Stream. Fields or the characteristics assigned to a field cannot be defined by a terminal operator.

The length of a field is not specified when it is defined. A field extends from the attribute character defining it to the next attribute character in the presentation space when traversing the presentation space row by row from left to right and top to bottom. The last position of the image buffer, ie the position corresponding to the bottom rightmost location of a displayed image, has no special relevance in terms of field definition. A field does not have to end at the last position of the image buffer. If the last position of the image buffer does not contain an attribute character, the last field defined will wraparound, ie continue to the first, ie top leftmost, position of the buffer. Figure B.2 illustrates the relationship between the image buffer and the presentation space, while Figure B.3 depicts examples of formatted presentation spaces.

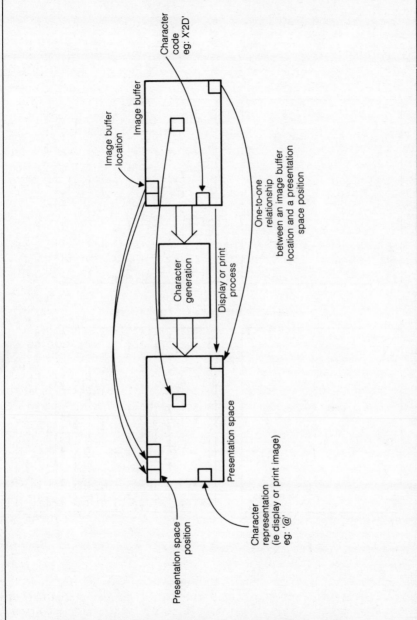

Figure B.2: Relationship between the image buffer and the presentation space of a 3270 display or printer

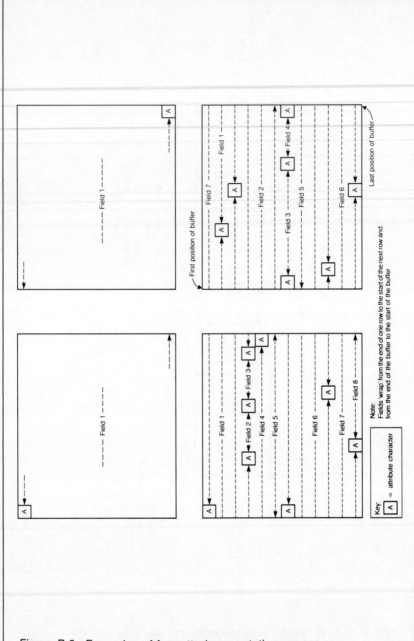

Figure B.3: Examples of formatted presentation spaces

432

The characteristics, which are in the main display, as opposed to printer oriented, that can be assigned (ie attributed) to a field, with Standard Data Stream, by the attribute character (or byte) defining the start of that field are as follows:

1 Protected or unprotected:
   - Protected: the display operator cannot enter data into this field or modify the contents displayed in the field by the application program
   - Unprotected: the display operator can either enter data into the field or modify the contents displayed in the field by the application program, ie an 'input' field.
2 Display, non-display and high-intensity display:
   - Display: the contents of the field – whether application program or display operator originated – are displayed in normal intensity
   - Non-display: the contents of the field are not displayed (or printed). This feature caters for the entry of security passwords
   - High-intensity display: the contents of the field are displayed in a higher intensity to that normally used.
3 Alphanumeric or numeric:
   - Alphanumeric: alphabetic or numeric data may be entered into the field
   - Numeric: has no effect if data is being entered into the field from a typewriter type keyboard. If, however, a data-entry type keyboard is being employed, the keyboard will be automatically 'shifted' to upper (ie numeric) shift whilst entering data into the field, but this may be overridden to enter any type of data. If the Optional Numeric Lock feature is fitted to a data entry keyboard this feature will ensure that only numeric (ie 0 to 9), minus (ie '-'), decimal point (ie '.') and DUPLICATE (DUP) characters can be entered into the field.
4 Selector light pen detectable or non-detectable: A display operator can use a selector light pen to 'select' a field that is defined as being detectable. When a read operation is performed the application program is notified of the fields that have been 'selected' via a selector light pen.

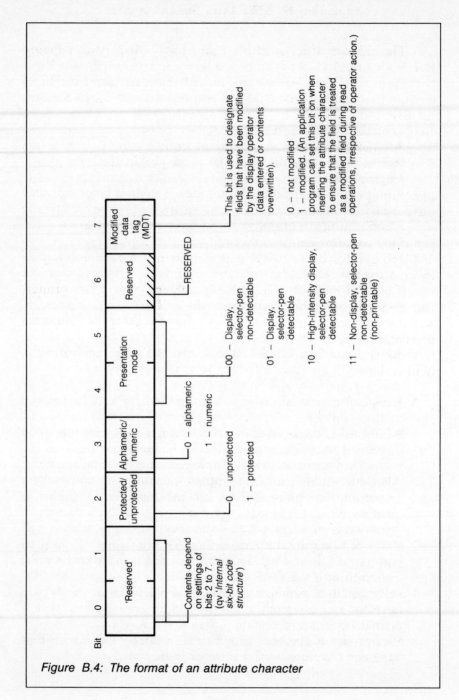

Figure B.4: The format of an attribute character

434

The format of an attribute character is as shown in Figure B.4.

Figure B.5 tabulates the permissible combination (of characteristics that can be defined for a field using Standard Data Stream, the EBCDIC and ASCII hexadecimal values corresponding to the attribute character bit settings needed to specify these characteristic combinations and the graphic characters that can be used in the data stream to denote the relevant hexadecimal values.

Attribute characters, though they occupy a character position in the image buffer, are not displayed or printed. The positions in the presentation space corresponding to attribute characters in the image buffer appear as 'spaces'. However, attribute characters are protected against being 'overwritten' by the display operator, ie a display operator cannot enter a character into the space occupied by an attribute character.

If a 3270 control unit, and the subject display, or printer, contain the appropriate features to support Extended Data Stream and the colour and programmed symbol features, the following presentation characteristics can be assigned to a field, in addition to those that can be specified via Standard Data Stream when the field is defined:

1 Extended colour: the contents of the field are displayed in one of seven colours: red, green, blue, pink, yellow, turquoise or white. (More than one colour – all seven if required – can be displayed within a single character position by utilising the triple plane capability of the programmed symbol feature). Alternatively they may be printed in one of four colours: red, green, blue or black. (The high-intensity display option is ignored when extended colour is specified, ie two levels of display intensity are not supported on colour displays.)

2 Extended highlighting: the contents of the field can be emphasised by being displayed in one of three extended highlighting modes: reverse-video, blink or underscore. (Reverse-video and underscore can be applied to space or NULL (ie X'00') characters.) Only the underscore option is supported by printers.

3 Programmed symbols: this feature permits users to define characters, symbols or arbitrary shapes of their choice, for display or print presentation, to augment the standard char-

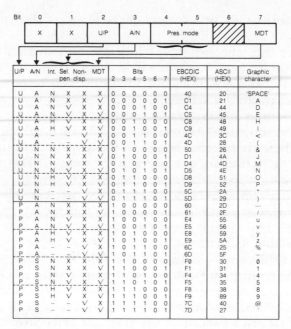

U/P	A/N	Int.	Sel. pen	Non-disp.	MDT	2	3	4	5	6	7	EBCDIC (HEX)	ASCII (HEX)	Graphic character
U	A	N	X	X	X	0	0	0	0	0	0	40	20	'SPACE'
U	A	N	X	X	√	0	0	0	0	0	1	C1	21	A
U	A	N	√	X	X	0	0	0	1	0	0	C4	44	D
U	A	N	√	X	√	0	0	0	1	0	1	C5	45	E
U	A	H	X	X	X	0	0	1	0	0	0	C8	48	H
U	A	H	√	X	√	0	0	1	0	0	1	C9	49	I
U	A	–	–	√	X	0	0	1	1	0	0	4C	3C	<
U	A	–	–	√	√	0	0	1	1	0	1	4D	28	(
U	N	N	X	X	X	0	1	0	0	0	0	50	26	&
U	N	N	X	X	√	0	1	0	0	0	1	D1	4A	J
U	N	N	√	X	X	0	1	0	1	0	0	D4	4D	M
U	N	N	√	X	√	0	1	0	1	0	1	D5	4E	N
U	N	H	X	X	X	0	1	1	0	0	0	D8	51	O
U	N	H	√	X	√	0	1	1	0	0	1	D9	52	P
U	N	–	–	√	X	0	1	1	1	0	0	5C	2A	*
U	N	–	–	√	√	0	1	1	1	0	1	5D	29	)
P	A	N	X	X	X	1	0	0	0	0	0	60	2D	–
P	A	N	X	X	√	1	0	0	0	0	1	61	2F	/
P	A	N	√	X	X	1	0	0	1	0	0	E4	55	u
P	A	N	√	X	√	1	0	0	1	0	1	E5	56	v
P	A	H	X	X	X	1	0	1	0	0	0	E8	59	y
P	A	H	√	X	√	1	0	1	0	0	1	E9	5A	z
P	A	–	–	√	X	1	0	1	1	0	0	6C	25	%
P	A	–	–	√	√	1	0	1	1	0	1	6D	5F	–
P	S	N	X	X	X	1	1	0	0	0	0	F0	30	0
P	S	N	X	X	√	1	1	0	0	0	1	F1	31	1
P	S	N	√	X	X	1	1	0	1	0	0	F4	34	4
P	S	N	√	X	√	1	1	0	1	0	1	F5	35	5
P	S	H	X	X	X	1	1	1	0	0	0	F8	38	8
P	S	H	√	X	√	1	1	1	0	0	1	F9	39	9
P	S	–	–	√	X	1	1	1	1	0	0	7C	40	@
P	S	–	–	√	√	1	1	1	1	0	1	7D	27	'

Key:

U = unprotected
P = protected
A = alphameric
N = numeric

Int = intensity — H – high / N – normal

Sel. pen = selector pen — √ – detectable / X – non-detectable

Non disp = non-display — X – display / √ – non-display

MDT = modified data tag — √ – set / X – not-set

S = Auto – Skip: The cursor will not enter or be positioned within this field. (NB – a cursor will enter or be moved into a protected field)

Figure B.5: The permissible combination of characteristics that can be specified for a field using standard data stream, the EBCDIC and ASCII hexadecimal codes corresponding to the relevant attribute character bits settings and the graphic characters that can be used in the data stream to denote these hexadecimal values

acter set and the optional APL/TEXT character set. This feature is provided by means of up to six, 190-character, application program-loadable character generators. (Note that these character generators can only be loaded from an application program using outbound Extended Data Stream. They cannot be loaded from the control unit or from a keyboard.) When the programmed symbol feature is used the character generator – including the standard or APL/TEXT – to be used to display or print the contents of a field is specified, explicitly or implicitly, for each field. (Note that in the case of a display, the character generator specified for a field also applies to data entered into the field by the operator.)

Note that if the display or printer has the appropriate features to support them, all three Extended Data Stream functions can be specified for a given field, in addition to Standard Data Stream field characteristics, such as protection, alphanumeric or numeric, or light pen detectability.

(IBM 3279 colour displays operating in base colour mode, as opposed to extended colour, use the bit settings of bits 2, 4 and 5 of the attribute character, ie protected/unprotected bit and the presentation mode bits, to display the contents of the field in one of four colours as follows:

Attri-bute 2	Byte 4	Bits 5	Characteristics denoted by bit setting	Colour contents of field displayed in
0	0	0/1	Unprotected, normal intensity	Green
0	1	0	Unprotected, high intensity	Red
1	0	0/1	Protected, normal intensity	Blue
1	1	0	Protected, high intensity	White

If neither base nor extended colour is being used with a 3279 colour display, the contents of high intensity display fields are displayed in white and the contents of normal intensity display fields are displayed in green.)

A display or printer that supports Extended Data Stream requires an extended attribute buffer in addition to the standard image buffer. The extended attribute buffer has a location corresponding to each location of the image buffer (and thus to each position of the presentation space) and the same buffer addressing scheme, ie the same addresses, is used to place data in both buffers. Figure B.6 illustrates the relationship between the extended attribute buffer and the image buffer. However, whereas each location of the image buffer only needs, at most, eight bits to represent the graphic character codes denoting the characters to be presented or control characters such as attribute characters, each extended attribute buffer location needs to contain at least nine bits to represent the characteristics provided for by Extended Data Stream. Extended Data Stream presentation characteristics for a field are specified by inserting an extended attribute into the extended attribute buffer at the location corresponding to the location in the image buffer containing the attribute character which defines the start of that field and its Standard Data Stream-specifiable characteristics.

Extended Data Stream characteristics are specified via a scheme referred to as *type/value pairs*. A type/value pair is a two-byte ordered pair, where the first byte indicates the Extended Data Stream feature, ie extended colour, extended highlighting or programmed symbols, being specified, while the second byte specifies a particular characteristic relative to this feature. The type codes denoting extended colour, extended highlighting and programmed symbols are X'42', X'41' and X'43', respectively.

With extended colour, ie type code X'42', the following value codes are used to specify the supported colours: X'F1' – blue, X'F2' – red, X'F3' – pink, X'F4' – green, X'F5' – turquoise, X'F6' – yellow and X'F7' – white or neutral. (Neutral enables the triple plane colour specification capability of programmed symbols to be used to display a character position in more than one colour.) The following three value codes are used to specify the three highlighting modes available with extended highlighting, ie type code X'41': X'F1' – blink, X'F2' – reverse-video and X'F3' – underscore. Although the six user-definable character generators provided by the programmed symbol feature are numbered X'02'

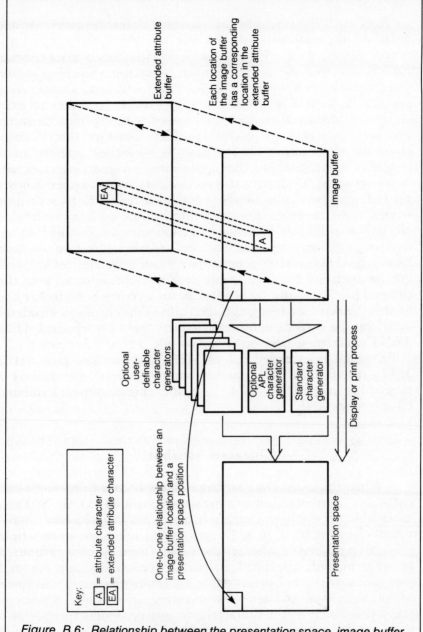

Figure B.6: Relationship between the presentation space, image buffer and the extended attribute buffer

to X'07' – X'00' refers to the standard character generator and X'01' to the optional APL/TEXT character generator – these numbers are only used when a user-defined character set is being loaded into one of these character generators. The application program assigns a 'loaded' character set a one byte identification code in the range X'40' to X'EF'. The character set is then referred to by this identification code as opposed to the specific character generator it has been loaded into. This ensures that a given character set does not always have to be loaded into the same character generator, as the application program accesses the character set by its identification code, ie its 'name', rather than via the character generator number containing the character set. (This is vital since the programmed symbol feature does not insist that all six user-definable character generators are installed in all devices. Options are available for ordering just two or four user-definable character generators.) When programmed symbols IW are specified by a type code of X'43', the value code of the ordered pair will indicate the identification code – X'40' to X'FE' – of the character set being specified. (In addition, a value code of X'01' can be used to indicate characters from the optional APL/ TEXT character generator.) For example, a type/value pair X'42', X'F2' specifies extended colour – red, a type/value pair X'41', X'F2' specifies extended highlighting – reverse video, and a type/value pair X'43', X'4F' specifies programmed symbols, character set X'4F'.

Character attributes

When Extended Data Stream is being used the presence of an extended attribute buffer enables Extended Data Stream-specifiable presentation characteristics to be assigned on an individual character basis, in addition to being able to do so on a field basis, irrespective of whether the presentation space is formatted or unformatted. Extended colour, extended highlighting and programmed symbol presentation characteristics can be assigned to an individual character by inserting an *extended attribute* – specifying the relevant characteristics via type/value pairs – into the extended attribute buffer corresponding to the location in the image buffer, containing the character. This feature can thus be used to selectively override, on a character-by-character basis, the Extended Data Stream characteristics that have been specified for a field. Each character of a field may be assigned a different set of Extended Data Stream-specifiable characteristics. However, note that Standard Data Stream-related characteristics, such as protected, unprotected, alphanumeric, numeric, normal or high intensity, cannot be specified on a character basis. These can only be specified on a field basis by an attribute character in the image buffer.

There is rarely a need to override the characteristics of just one isolated character within a field. Normally, it would be a contiguous block of characters whose characteristics will be overridden. To facilitate this, when an extended attribute is inserted into the extended attribute buffer, at a location corresponding to a data character location in the image buffer (as opposed to an attribute character), this extended attribute specification is automatically propagated through the extended attribute buffer, irrespective of field boundaries, until another extended attribute character applying to a data character is encountered. This enables the same character attributes to be specified for multiple, contiguous characters in one operation rather than on a character-by-character basis (equivalent to the concept of specifying characteristics on a field basis). However, when one, two or all three characteristics are to revert to those specified for the field, this can be achieved by inserting another extended attribute, at the extended attribute buffer location corresponding to the appropriate character location, specifying that the relevant characteristics should revert to being inherited from those characteristics specified for the field. This is indicated by the use of a value code of X'00' – designating 'default' characteristic – with the type code for the subject characteristic, eg an extended data character attribute specified with a type/value pair X'42', X'00' would denote that the extended colour characteristic should revert – starting at that data character – to that specified for the field.

With the aid of a special 87-key typewriter keyboard, referred to as an Attribute Select Keyboard, and with the explicit consent of the application program, a display operator may override the Extended Data Stream-specifiable characteristics on a character-by-character basis, ie extended data character attributes may be directly entered into the extended attribute buffer from this keyboard, provided the application program has authorised this mode of operation. The application program can determine which character attributes have been entered or modified by using a special read mode.

Internal six-bit code structure

The original remote 3270 control units, *viz* 3271 models 1 and 2 and 3275 models 1 and 2, only supported one data link control protocol: non-transparent mode BSC. As such, Standard Data Stream control codes, eg attribute characters and buffer addresses, had to be greater than X'40' if EBCDIC was being used or greater than X'20' if ASCII was being used. This ensured that there would be no conflict with the reserved BSC control codes. To this end, all Standard Data Stream control codes other than the orders are based on a six-bit code structure. Only bits 2 to 7 of the control codes are used. Settings of bits 0 and 1 for all Standard Data Stream control codes are determined for transmission via a 'conversion' formula, which ensures that each control code can be represented by a displayable graphic character. Figure B.7 depicts the conversions of six-bit control codes into EBCDIC or ASCII graphic characters.

Control units that support Extended Data Stream utilise BSC transparent mode if operating on a BSC link. As such, Extended Data Stream control characters can use all bit configurations with no conversion being required.

Buffer addressing

3270 Data Stream currently caters for six different display buffer sizes: 480 characters (12 rows, each of 40 characters; denoted as 12 × 40), 960 characters (12 × 80), 1920 characters (24 × 80), 2560 characters (32 × 80), 3440 characters (43 × 80) and 3564 characters (27 × 132).

Two buffer addressing schemes are available, both of which use two characters to specify a given buffer location. A universally applicable scheme, referred to, as 12-bit buffer addressing, is used with outbound and inbound Standard Data Stream, inbound Extended Data Stream and outbound Extended Data Stream if necessary. The second scheme, referred to as 14-bit buffer addressing, can only be used with outbound Data Stream to control units which support Extended Data Stream. (Provided the control unit supports Extended Data Stream, 14-bit buffer addressing can be used outbound, with Standard or Extended Data Stream and 12- and 14-bit buffer addressing can be used interchangeably within the same outbound Data Stream.)

12-bit buffer addressing

Obtaining the two character buffer address, corresponding to a given presentation space position – identified by a row and column reference:

1 (Row Number-1) × Presentation Space Width + (Column Number-1) ⇒ absolute buffer position.
2 Absolute Position ÷ 64⇒ quotient = bits 2-7 of first address character
remainder = bits 2-7 of second address character
3 Convert two address characters to the appropriate graphic characters used for transmission, using the Standard Data Stream control code conversion formula (qv Figure B.7).

(Presentation Space Width = number of columns per row, in the presentation space.)

Examples:
12-bit buffer address, corresponding to the Row 2, column 20 position of a 1920 character (24 × 80) display:

1 (2 − 1) × 80 + (20 − 1)
1 × 80 + 19 ⇒ 99 − absolute buffer position.
2 99 ÷ 64⇒ quotient = 1
remainder = 35
as six-bit binary values: quotient   00 0001 } bits 2-7.
remainder 10 0011

Bits 2-7	EBCDIC	ASCII	Graphic character
00 0000	40	20	'SPACE'
00 0001	C1	41	A
00 0010	C2	42	B
00 0011	C3	43	C
00 0100	C4	44	D
00 0101	C5	45	E
00 0110	C6	46	F
00 0111	C7	47	G
00 1000	C8	48	H
00 1001	C9	49	I
00 1010	4A	5B	¢ or [
00 1011	4B	2E	•
00 1100	4C	3C	<
00 1101	4D	28	(
00 1110	4E	2B	+
00 1111	4F	21	1 or !
01 0000	50	26	&
01 0001	D1	4A	J
01 0010	D2	4B	K
01 0011	D3	4C	L
01 0100	D4	4D	M
01 0101	D5	4E	N
01 0110	D6	4F	O
01 0111	D7	50	P
01 1000	D8	51	Q
01 1001	D9	52	R
01 1010	5A	5D	! or]
01 1011	5B	24	$
01 1100	5C	2A	*
01 1101	5D	29	)
01 1110	5E	3B	;
01 1111	5F	5E	⌐ or n
10 0000	60	2D	-
10 0001	61	2F	/
10 0010	E2	53	S
10 0011	E3	54	T
10 0100	E4	55	U
10 0101	E5	56	V
10 0110	E6	57	W
10 0111	E7	58	X
10 1000	E8	59	Y
10 1001	E9	5A	Z
10 1010	6A	7C	¦ or	
10 1011	6B	2C	,
10 1100	6C	25	%
10 1101	6D	5F	_
10 1110	6E	3E	>
10 1111	6F	3F	?
11 0000	F0	30	0
11 0001	F1	31	1
11 0010	F2	32	2
11 0011	F3	33	3
11 0100	F4	34	4
11 0101	F5	35	5
11 0110	F6	36	6
11 0111	F7	37	7
11 1000	F8	38	8
11 1001	F9	39	9
11 1010	7A	3A	:
11 1011	7B	23	#
11 1100	7C	40	@
11 1101	7D	27	'
11 1110	7E	3D	=
11 1111	7F	22	"

Figure B:7: Conversion table to transform six-bit Standard Data Stream control codes to EBCDIC or ASCII graphic characters that are used to exchange the control characters across the data link between the host and the 3270 control unit

3 Use conversion specified in Figure B.7

00 0001 $\Rightarrow$ EBCDIC – X'C1' or ASCII – X'41'

10 0011 $\Rightarrow$ EBCDIC – X'E3' or ASCII – X'54'

if EBCDIC, buffer address = X'C1E3'

if ASCII, buffer address = X'4154'.

12-bit buffer address, corresponding to the Row 25, Column 131 position of a 3564 character (27 × 132) display:

1 (25-1) × 132 + (131-1)

24 × 132 + 130 $\Rightarrow$ 3298 – absolute buffer position

2 3298 ÷ 64 $\Rightarrow$ quotient = 51

remainder = 34

as six-bit binary values: quotient   11 0011 $\left.\right\}$ bits 2-7.

remainder   10 0010

3 Use conversion specified in Figure B.7

11 0011 $\Rightarrow$ EBCDIC – X'F3' or ASCII – X'33'

10 0010 $\Rightarrow$ EBCDIC – X'E2' or ASCII – X'53'

if EBCDIC, buffer address = X'F3E2'

if ASCII, buffer address = X'3353'

Determining the presentation space position – in terms of a row and columns reference – corresponding to a two character buffer address:

1 Discard the top two bits – *viz* bits 0 and 1 – of both characters.

2 Multiply bits 2-7 of the first character by 64.

3 Add bits 2-7 of the second character to results of step 2

$\Rightarrow$ absolute buffer position.

4 Absolute buffer position ÷ Presentation Space Width

$\Rightarrow$ quotient + 1 = Row Number

remainder + 1 = Column Number.

Example:

Row and Column Number reference of the position in a 1920 character (24 × 80) display, corresponding to 12-bit buffer address EBCDIC X'C1E3' or ASCII X'4154':

EBCDIC   ASCII

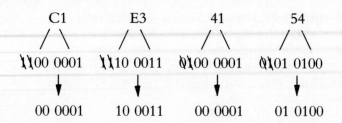

	C1	E3	41	54

1100 0001	1110 0011	0100 0001	0101 0100

00 0001	10 0011	00 0001	01 0100

Once bits 0 and 1 are discarded, bits 2-7 are the same for both EBCDIC or ASCII.

2 b'00 0001' × 64 ⟹ b'100 0000'.

3 b'100 0000' + X'10 0011' ⟹ b'110 0011' ⟹ 99.

4 99 ÷ 80 ⟹ quotient 1
$\qquad\qquad$ remainder 19
$\quad$ Row = 1 + 1 = 2
$\quad$ Column = 19 + 1 = 20.

3270 reference manuals (Component Description or the Reference Summary) tabulate the 12-bit buffer addresses in EBCDIC and ASCII corresponding to all the possible presentation space positions for all the possible presentation space sizes. This table can be used to obtain the two-character buffer address given a row and column reference, relative to a presentation space width, or to obtain the row and column reference, again relative to a particular presentation space width, given a two-character buffer address.

14-bit buffer addressing

Obtaining the two-character buffer address corresponding to a given presentation space position – identified by a row and column reference:

1 (Row Number-1) × Presentation Space Width + (Column Number-1) ⟹ absolute buffer address.

2 Represent absolute buffer address as a 14-bit binary number.

3 Prefix this 14-bit binary number with two zero bits to obtain the two-character, 16-bit buffer address. (Note that Extended Data Stream support, which is a prerequisite of 14-bit

addressing, only operates with EBCDIC, ie eight-bit characters.)

12- and 14-bit buffer addressing schemes are differentiated in outbound data streams by the value of the first two bits of the first character. If they are both zero, 14-bit buffer addressing is being used; any other value indicates 12-bit buffer addressing. (The conversion to graphic characters that is used with 12-bit buffer addressing ensures that the first two bits of both characters are either b'11' or b'10' and never b'00'.)

Example:
14-bit buffer address corresponding to the Row 27, Column 123 position of a 3564 character (27 × 132) display:

1 (27-1) × 132 + (123-1)
        26 × 132 + 122 ⇒ 3554 – absolute buffer address.
2 3554 = X'DE2' ⇒ b'00110111100010'.
3 b'00': b'00110111100010' =
        b'0000110111100010' ⇒ X'0DE2'
        Buffer address = X'0DE2'

Determining the presentation space position – in terms of row and column reference – corresponding to a two-character buffer address:

1 16-bit buffer address (ie both characters) presentation space width:
        ⇒ quotient + 1 = Row Number
        remainder + 1 = Column Number.

Orders

Nine general-purpose and five printer-specific orders are defined in 3270 Data Stream. Figure B.8 summarises the data streams in which the various orders may appear, and the control code assigned to each order. The orders are as follows:

1 *Set Buffer Address.* In outbound data streams it indicates that a two-character buffer address follows, specifying the buffer

ORDER	Control code		Applies to:	May appear in:			
	EBCDIC	ASCII		Standard Data Stream		Extended Data Stream	
				Outbound	Inbound	Outbound	Inbound
Set Buffer Address (SBA)	X'1D'	X'1D'	Either	√	√	√	√
Start Field (SF)	X'11'	X'11'	Either	√	√	√	√
Insert Cursor (IC)	X'13'	X'13'	Either	√	x	√	x
Program Tab (PT)	X'05'	X'09'	Either	√	x	√	x
Repeat to Address (RA)	X'3C'	X'14'	Either	√	x	√	x
Erase Unprotected to Address (EUA)	X'12'	X'12'	Either	√	x	√	x
Start Field Extended (SFE)	X'29'	–	Either	x	x	√	√
Modify Field (MF)	X'2C'	–	Either	x	x	√	x
Set Attribute (SA)	X'28'	–	Either	x	x	√	√
New Line (NL)	X'15'	X'0A'	Printers	√	–	√	–
End of Message (EM)	X'19'	X'19'	Printers	√	–	√	–
Forms Feed (FF)	X'0C'	X'0C'	Printers	√	–	√	–
Carriage Return (CR)	X'0D'	X'0D'	Printers	√	–	√	–

Figure B.8: 3270 orders – their control codes and the data stream in which they may appear

address at which subsequent 'write' operations are to start at or to continue, ie resets the 'current' buffer address. In inbound data streams it indicates that a two-character buffer address follows, specifying the buffer address at which a field being read in begins.

2 *Start Field.* In outbound data streams it indicates that the next character in the data stream is an attribute character, defining the start – and the Standard Data Stream-specifiable presentation characteristics – of a field, and that it should be stored in the image buffer at the 'current' buffer address. The current buffer address is then incremented by 1. In inbound data streams it indicates that an attribute character follows.

3 *Insert Cursor.* It repositions the cursor to the position specified by the 'current' buffer address. (This order itself does not alter the 'current' buffer address.)

4 *Program Tab.* This is used when performing a 'write' operation to a previously formatted presentation space. This order causes the 'current' buffer address to be set to the address of the start of the next unprotected field in the image buffer, plus 1, ie to the address of the first position following the attribute character defining the unprotected field.

5 *Repeat to Address.* This order consists of a four-character sequence. The order is followed by a two-character buffer address and a one-byte character, which is to be repeated. The order causes the character which is to be repeated – third character following the order – to be propagated through the image buffer, starting at the 'current' buffer address and finishing at – but not including – the address specified by the two buffer address characters following the order. The 'finish' address becomes the 'current' buffer address on completion of the order.

6 *Erase Unprotected to Address.* This is used when performing a 'write' operation to a previously formatted presentation space. This order is followed by a two-character buffer address. The order causes nulls, ie X'00', to be stored in the data locations of all unprotected fields, starting at the 'current' buffer address and finishing at – but not including – the address specified by the two buffer address characters following the order. On completion of the order, the 'finish' address specified becomes the 'current' buffer address.

7 *Start Field Extended.* In outbound data streams this is used to define the start of a field and to assign Extended and Standard Data Stream-specifiable characteristics to this field. (SF, though supported, is not required with Extended Data Stream. The 'standard' attribute character required to define the start of the field and its Standard Data Stream characteristic is specified by means of a type/value pair: type code X'C0' indicating 'standard field attribute' and the appropriate attribute character specified as the value code.) The characteristics to be assigned to the new field are specified as a sequence of type/value pairs following the order. This order inserts an extended attribute character into the extended attribute buffer at the 'current' buffer address, and a 'standard' attribute character into the image buffer at the 'current' buffer address. In inbound data streams SFE indicates that one or more type/value pairs specifying the Extended or Standard Data Stream-specifiable characteristics for a field follows.

8 *Modify Field.* This is used to modify selectively one or more Standard or Extended Data Stream characteristics previously assigned to a field, via an SFE order, without having to respecify all the characteristics.

9 *Set Attribute.* In outbound data streams it is used to assign character attributes. In inbound data streams it is used to indicate the type/value chains indicating that the Extended Data Stream characteristic that has been entered or modified from an attribute select keyboard follows.

10 *New Line.* A new line function is performed: print position advanced to left margin of the next print line.

11 *End of Message.* This causes the print operation to be terminated.

12 *Forms Feed.* This advances the print position to the left margin of a predetermined print line on the next form (or page).

13 *Carriage Return.* This moves the print position to the left margin of the current print line.

The printer-specific orders have no effect if they are included in data streams bound for displays.

Commands

Three 'write' commands are defined in 3270 data streams: Write, Erase/Write and Erase/Write Alternate. They all use a common outbound data stream format:

Byte 0	1	2 // n
Write command code	Write Control Character (WCC)	Orders and data

The one-byte Write Control Character (WCC) is mandatory, and has the format shown in Figure B.9.

Write

The Write command can be used to fully or partially load the image buffer and, if Extended Data Stream is supported, the extended attribute buffer. This command allows attributes or data to be inserted into specified positions in these buffers without affecting the contents in other parts of the buffers.

Erase/Write

This is a two-phase command: an Erase-operation command followed by a Write command. The Write command performed is identical to the Write command described above, but before this command is executed the contents of the image buffer and, if Extended Data Stream is supported, the contents of the extended attribute buffer, are cleared (erased); ie null – X'00' – characters are placed in all the locations.

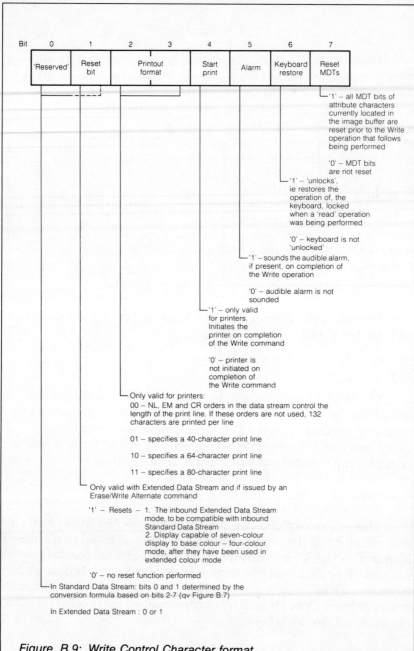

Figure B.9: Write Control Character format

Erase/Write Alternate

This command is used with devices that can operate in one of two presentation space sizes: a default size and an alternate size. This command is identical to an Erase/Write command, except that it invokes and uses the alternate presentation space size, while the Erase/Write command always selects and uses the default presentation size.

Figure B.10 depicts a typical 3270 formatted display and shows the outbound data stream required to format it.

A Write Structured Field command is provided by Extended Data Stream to issue Extended Data Stream-specific control information to devices that support Extended Data Stream features. The Write Structured Field command is used to issue one or more Outbound Structured Fields to 3270 devices supporting Extended Data Stream. Three outbound structured fields are defined:

1 Load Programmed Symbols – used to load the user-definable character generators, provided by the Programmed Symbol feature, with the character shapes of the character sets required by the user.
2 Set Reply Mode – used to specify one of three modes dictating the content and format of inbound Extended Data Streams: Field mode, Extended Field mode and Character mode. It is also used to selectively authorise the entry or modification of character attributes from an attribute select keyboard.
3 Read Partition:Query – used to solicit the following characteristics from a device: colour availability, extended highlighting availability, user-defined character sets – ie programmed symbols – that are resident in the user-definable character generators, the inbound Extended Data Stream mode currently in effect and the usable presentation space details of the device. These characteristics are conveyed to the application program that issued the Read Partition:Query via five Inbound Structure Fields: Query Reply:Colour; Query Reply:Extended Highlighting; Query Reply:Programmed Symbols; Query Reply:Reply Mode; Query Reply:Usable Area.

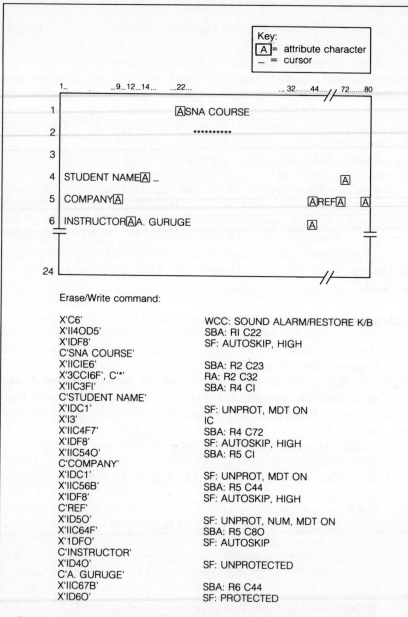

Key:
Ⓐ = attribute character
_ = cursor

```
1..        ...9..12..14...   ...22...                    ...32......44.... // 72.......80
 1                        ⒶSNA COURSE
 2                              **********
 3
 4   STUDENT NAMEⒶ _                                         Ⓐ
 5   COMPANYⒶ                                          ⒶREFⒶ    Ⓐ
 6   INSTRUCTORⒶA. GURUGE                          Ⓐ

24
```

Erase/Write command:

X'C6'	WCC: SOUND ALARM/RESTORE K/B
X'II4OD5'	SBA: RI C22
X'IDF8'	SF: AUTOSKIP, HIGH
C'SNA COURSE'	
X'IICIE6'	SBA: R2 C23
X'3CCI6F', C'*'	RA: R2 C32
X'IIC3FI'	SBA: R4 CI
C'STUDENT NAME'	
X'IDC1'	SF: UNPROT, MDT ON
X'I3'	IC
X'IIC4F7'	SBA: R4 C72
X'IDF8'	SF: AUTOSKIP, HIGH
X'IIC54O'	SBA: R5 CI
C'COMPANY'	
X'IDC1'	SF: UNPROT, MDT ON
X'IIC56B'	SBA: R5 C44
X'IDF8'	SF: AUTOSKIP, HIGH
C'REF'	
X'ID5O'	SF: UNPROT, NUM, MDT ON
X'IIC64F'	SBA: R5 C8O
X'1DFO'	SF: AUTOSKIP
C'INSTRUCTOR'	
X'ID4O'	SF: UNPROTECTED
C'A. GURUGE'	
X'IIC67B'	SBA: R6 C44
X'ID6O'	SF: PROTECTED

Figure B.10: A typical 3270 formatted display for data entry type applications, and the 3270 data stream used to format the display

454

Three Read commands are defined in 3270 Data Stream: Read Buffer, Read Modified and Read Modified All. In the main, read operations are performed following a specific action from the display operator indicating application program intervention: pressing the ENTER; CLEAR; a Program Function (PF); a Program Access (PA); TEST REQ or SYS REQ key, selecting a light-pen-detectable field that specifies that attention will be generated; with a light-pen or the CURSR SEL key or the reading of a magnetic strip card via the optional magnetic card reader or slot reader. Each of these actions causes a unique Attention Code to be generated to identify the subject action. These codes are referred to as Attention Identification (AID) codes. Figure B.11 tabulates the AID codes that can be generated.

Read Buffer

The contents of the image buffer of the specified device, starting at location 0 (ie the first location), if the command is not chained to a previous command, or, if the command is chained, from the 'current' buffer address, through to the last location of the buffer are transferred to the application program. The 3270 control units prefix all attribute characters with SF orders to indicate the start of each field. (If the display was unformatted, no SF orders will be present in the inbound data stream.) The inbound (standard) data stream would have the following format:

Byte 0	1 2	3 // n
AID code	Address at which the cursor is located	Data (and in the case of a formatted display, SF orders, prefixing attribute characters)

If Extended Data Stream is supported the contents of the inbound Extended Data Stream would depend on the reply mode

Action	AID code		Type of Read Modified performed
	EBCDIC	ASCII	
ENTER OR LIGHT PEN: '&' ATTN.	7D	27	Read Modified
PF 1	F1	31	
PF 2	F2	32	
PF 3	F3	33	
PF 4	F4	34	
PF 5	F5	35	
PF 6	F6	36	
PF 7	F7	37	
PF 8	F8	38	
PF 9	F9	39	
PF 10	7A	3A	
PF 11	7B	23	
PF 12	7C	40	Read Modified
PF 13	C1	41	
PF 14	C2	42	
PF 15	C3	43	
PF 16	C4	44	
PF 17	C5	45	
PF 18	C6	46	
PF 19	C7	47	
PF 20	C8	48	
PF 21	C9	49	
PF 22	4A	5B	
PF 23	4B	2E	
PF 24	4C	3C	
CLEAR	6D	5F	Short Read (AID only)
PA1	6C	25	
PA2	6E	3E	Short Read (AID only)
PA3	6B	2C	
TEST/SYS REQ	F0	30	Test Req Read
BADGE READER	E6	57	Read Modified
SLOT READER	E7	58	Read Modified
LIGHT PEN: SPACE/NULL ATTN.	7E	3D	Read Modified
NO AID: DISPLAY	60	2D	Read Modified
NO AID: PRINTER	E8	59	

Figure B.11: Attention identification (AID) codes corresponding to the various operator actions soliciting intervention from the application program. (NO AID, EBCDIC − X'60' and X'E8' are generated when an unsolicited Read is received when the operator has not requested intervention from the application program in effect. If Field mode was in effect the data stream would be identical to that used with Standard Data Stream and there would be no indication of Extended Data Stream characteristics. However, if Extended Field mode was in effect, SFE orders – as opposed to SF orders – will be inserted to indicate the start of each field and type/value pairs will follow the SFE, specifying the 'standard' field attribute-specifiable and Extended Data Stream-specifiable characteristics of the field. If character mode was in effect, SA orders will be used in addition to SFE orders to indicate character attributes that have been modified.

Read Modified

The contents of all the fields, excluding null characters, that have been modified by the display operator, ie entered into or overwritten, beginning with the first modified field encountered, when traversing the image buffer starting at location 0, if the command is unchained, or at the 'current' buffer address if it was chained through to the last modified field in the buffer (including the cases where the last field 'wraps' from the last location to the first), are transferred to the application program. The data from each modified field is preceded by an SBA order, followed by a two-character buffer address specifying the address of the first data character of that field, ie address of the attribute character defining the field plus 1. (If the display was unformatted, all the data from the image buffer – excluding nulls – are transferred irrespective of whether the data had been modified or not. Since there are no attribute characters, MDT bits are not available to indicate whether or not data has been modified.) The typical (inbound) data stream from a formatted display in response to a Read Modified would have the following format:

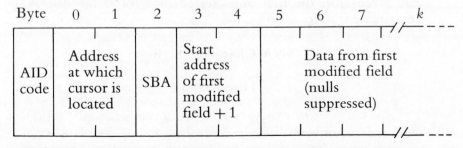

Byte	0	1	2	3	4	5	6	7	k
AID code	Address at which cursor is located		SBA	Start address of first modified field + 1			Data from first modified field (nulls suppressed)		

k+1	k+2							n
SBA	Start address of second modified field + 1	Data from the second modified field (nulls suppressed)					SBA	

If the operator action prior to the Read Modified being issued was the pressing of either the CLEAR or a PA key, a 'short read' operation is performed. This operation transfers only the AID code to the application program.

If extended attributes are supported, the contents of the inbound data stream would only be affected if Character mode was the reply mode in effect. In this case, SA orders will be included in the data stream to indicate that character attributes have been modified by the display operator.

Figure B.12 illustrates the inbound Read Modified data stream generated, for data entered into the formatted display shown in Figure B.10.

Read Modified All

This command, which is only supported by SNA-based control units, operates like a Read Modified command except that it generates a Read Modified data stream irrespective of the operator action, ie there is no 'short read' operation.

The final relevant 3270 Data Stream command is Erase All Unprotected . This command clears (erases) the contents of all unprotected fields to nulls, resets the MDT bits on all unprotected fields, unlocks the keyboard and repositions the cursor to the first data location in the first unprotected field (or if the display is unformatted, to location 0).

SNA Character String

Introduction

SNA Character String (SCS) is a device- and product-independent universal device control protocol, ie a data stream,

Appendix B: 3270 Data Stream and SCS

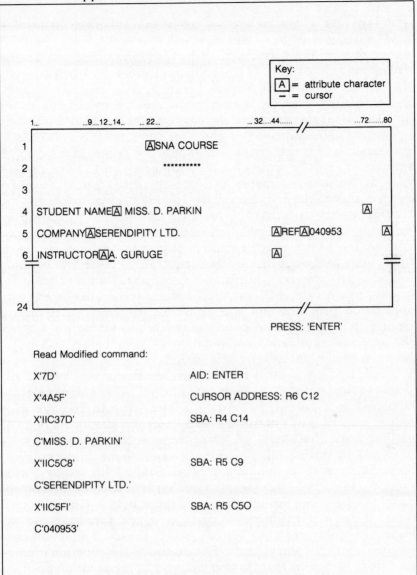

Key:
$\boxed{A}$ = attribute character
$-$ = cursor

```
1...      ...9...12..14...  ...22...        ...32....44......  //        ...72......80
1  |                    ⒶSNA COURSE
2  |                          **********
3  |
4  | STUDENT NAMEⒶ MISS. D. PARKIN                              Ⓐ
5  | COMPANYⒶSERENDIPITY LTD.              ⒶREFⒶ040953          Ⓐ
6  |_INSTRUCTORⒶA. GURUGE                  Ⓐ
24 |                                       //
                                           PRESS: 'ENTER'
```

Read Modified command:

X'7D'	AID: ENTER
X'4A5F'	CURSOR ADDRESS: R6 C12
X'llC37D'	SBA: R4 C14
C'MISS. D. PARKIN'	
X'llC5C8'	SBA: R5 C9
C'SERENDIPITY LTD.'	
X'llC5FI'	SBA: R5 C5O
C'040953'	

Figure B.12: The inbound data stream that would be generated if a Read Modified command was issued as Read Data entered into the formatted display. (Refer to Figure B.10 for definitions of the various fields.)

that provides a comprehensive set of control mechanisms for: manipulating data on a visual presentation space – eg a display screen or a printout, controlling the operating mode of a device, exchanging control information to and from a device, modifying the manner in which a designated sequence of data characters will be interpreted, and conveying 'status' information between an application program and a device operator or between device operators independently of the data presented on the visual presentation space. Devices that support SCS – eg 3287 or 3289 printers interacting with an application program LU via a type 1 LU-LU session – 'map' the SCS-specified 'virtual' control mechanisms to the relevant device-specific control sequences and control modes to realise the presentation-oriented functions defined via SCS, on receipt of an outbound SCS data stream, and convert the device-specific control sequences and control mode indications to the appropriate SCS equivalents when transmitting inbound data streams. (While SCS is essentially a data stream for visual presentation space-oriented devices, to be used between an application program and such a device, or between two such devices, it is general and powerful enough to be used to control the representation and manipulation of data being exchanged between two application programs.)

All the SCS control mechanisms are based on 47 EBCDIC control codes, referred to as the *SCS control codes*. These codes are tabulated in Figure B.13. An SCS Data Stream consists of a sequential string of intermixed SCS control codes and EBCDIC graphic data characters. (A transparent mode of operation is provided to enable all bit configurations to be interchanged.) Some SCS control codes must be immediately followed by one or more parameters qualifying the function specified by the control code. (These codes are identified in Figure B.13.) There are two types of parameter: functional parameters and value parameters. Functional parameters define, or qualify, the exact function corresponding to a control code. For example, the functional parameter of a SCS code that changes the current presentation position would specify whether the move is in the vertical or horizontal direction. Value parameters are used to specify a binary coded numeric value to govern the execution of the function designated by the SCS control code. For example, the value parameter of an SCS code that moves the current presentation position would

SCS control codes (hex)	Abbreviation	Control function	
16	BS	BACKSPACE	*
2F	BEL(STP)	BELL (STOP)	*
0D	CR	CARRIAGE RETURN	*
2B	CSP	CONTROL SEQUENCE PREFIX	+
11	DC1		
12	DC2	DEVICE SPECIFIC CONTROL	
13	DC3		
3C	DC4		
14	ENP	ENABLE PRESENTATION	*
36	EBS(NBS)	EXPANDED BACKSPACE (NUMERIC BACKSPACE)	
E1	ESP(NSP)	EXPANDED SPACE (NUMERIC SPACE)	
0C	FF(PE)	FORM FEED (PAGE END)	*
08	GE	GRAPHIC ESCAPE	+
05	HT	HORIZONTAL TAB	*
39	IT	INDENT TAB	
33	IR	INDEX RETURN	
24	INP	INHIBIT PRESENTATION	*
1C	IFS	INTERCHANGE FILE SEPARATOR	
1D	IGS	INTERCHANGE GROUP SEPARATOR	
1E	IRS	INTERCHANGE RECORD SEPARATOR	*
1F	IUS	INTERCHANGE UNIT SEPARATOR	
2S	LF(INX)	LINE FEED (INDEX)	*
1S	NL(CRE)	NEW LINE (CARRIER RETURN)	*
00	NUL	NULL	
34	PP	PRESENTATION POSITION	+
17	POC	PROGRAM OPERATOR COMMUNICATION	+
0A	RPT	REPEAT	
3A	RFF(RPE)	REQUIRED FORM FEED (REQUIRED PAGE END)	
06	RNL(RCR)	REQUIRED NEW LINE (REQUIRED CARRIER RETURN)	
41	RSP	REQUIRED SPACE	
0450	SSR	SECURE STRING ID READER	+
04	SEL	SELECT	
2BD1	SCI	SET CHAIN IMAGE	+
2BC8	SGEA	SET GRAPHIC ERROR ACTION	+
2BC1	SHF	SET HORIZONTAL FORMAT	*+
2BC6	SLD	SET LINE DENSITY	*+
2BC2	SVF	SET VERTICAL FORMAT	*+
38	SBS	SUBSCRIPT	
3F	SUB	SUBSTITUTE	
09	SPS	SUPERSCRIPT	
2A	SW	SWITCH	
CA	SHY	SYLLABLE HYPHEN	
35	TRN	TRANSPARENT	*+
1A	UBS	UNIT BACKSPACE	
04XX	VCS	VERTICAL CHANNEL SELECT	*+
0B	VT	VERTICAL TAB	*
23	WUS	WORD UNDERSCORE	

Key:

* = SCS control codes supported by 3274/3276 control units that have printers interacting with application programs via Type 1 LU–LU sessions

\+ = SCS control codes which require parameters (or consist of a sequence of multiple control codes)

Figure B.13. The SCS control codes

specify the exact number of positions – vertical or horizontal, as specified by the functional parameter – to be moved.

Three of the SCS control codes – ie Expanded Space (X'E1'), Required Space (X'41') and Syllable Hyphen (X'CA') – are essentially graphic data characters. But in certain applications, ie when used with a device that can support that function, these three codes denote specific presentation space 'format'-related functions. These functions are described when these control codes are discussed in the section *Control function descriptions* later in this appendix.

Virtual presentation space

The SCS control codes or control sequences for manipulating data on a visual presentation space are based on virtual presentation space which consists of a two-dimensional array of character positions. Devices that support SCS must map this virtual presentation space onto their device-specific visual presentation space. The format of this virtual presentation space and the positional parameters used by SCS to define the physical, ie absolute, and logical, ie application-dependent, boundaries of this presentation space are shown in Figure B.14. A given presentation position within this virtual presentation space is specified via its coordinates: row number, column number.

Control function descriptions

1 *Backspace*: moves the presentation position horizontally one position to the left. If the presentation position is at the leftmost position, ie column 1, of a line, this control code has no effect, ie it is treated as a 'no-op'.
2 *Bell*: an implementation-dependent code that can be used to communicate with the device operator, eg sound an audible alarm. This control code may be implemented to include a STOP function: the device stops processing the data stream until the device operator performs a specific operation that is signalled by the BELL code.
3 *Carriage return*: moves the presentation position horizontally

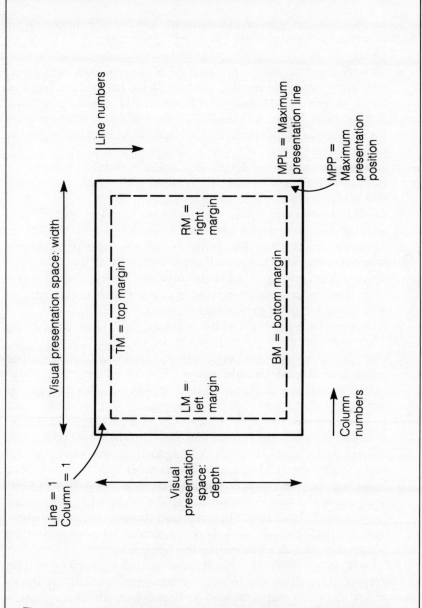

Figure B.14:   The SCS virtual presentation space and the positional
              parameters used by SCS to define its physical and logical
              boundaries

to the left margin of the current line. If the presentation position is already at the left margin, this control code has no effect.

4 *Control sequence prefix*: prefixes SCS control code sequences that are of variable length, viz Set Chain Image, Set Graphic Error Action, Set Horizontal Format, Set Line Density and Set Vertical Format. The X'2B' control code that precedes these control sequences is, in fact, this control sequence prefix.

5 *Device-specific control*: DC1, DC2, DC3 and DC4: used for implementing device-specific control functions. These control codes have no SCS-assigned functions.

6 *Enable presentation*: resets the device to begin visually representing the data, in the data stream or entered by the device operator, following this control code, on the presentation space. It is used when visual representation of data has been temporarily inhibited – via the Inhibit Presentation Control code – so that a security-related operation such as the entry of a password can be performed.

7 *Expanded backspace*: provides a large, fixed–size backspace. This permits tables or columns to be structured without the risk of distortion on proportional spacing devices. The normal backspace would not suffice as its size, on proportional spacing devices, is dictated by the 'shape' of the preceding character.

8 *Expanded space*: provides a large, fixed–size space. This permits the justification of text and the structuring of tables and columns without the risk of distortion on proportional spacing devices (cf Expanded Backspace).

9 *Form feed*: moves the presentation position to the top and left margins of the next presentation space. If the MPL parameter (qv Figure B.14) has not been set and there is no implementation-defined default this code positions the presentation position to the left margin of the next line.

10 *Graphic escape*: used to extend the standard character set. The graphic data character following the graphic escape is interpreted using an implementation-dependent, alternate character set definition. This enables two character sets to be implemented on a device, eg a standard and an APL character set.

11 *Horizontal tab*: moves the presentation position horizontally to the right, to the next tab stop position defined in the current line. (Tab stops are defined using the Set Horizontal Tab control code.) If no horizontal tab stops are defined to the right of the current presentation position on the same line, this control code is treated as 'space' function, ie the presentation position moves to the next column.

12 *Indent tab*: enables 'paragraph' indentation mode on the device, ie one or more horizontal tab operations are automatically performed after each new line function – encountered in the data stream or entered at the device. The number of horizontal tabs performed is determined by the number of indent tab control characters used to enable the indentation mode. Each indent tab control character results in one horizontal tab function being performed. Indentation mode is cancelled, ie reset, when an Index Return control code or a Required New Line control code is encountered.

13 *Index return*: mandatorily moves the presentation position to the left margin of the next line and resets (cancels) indentation mode. (Index Return may also be used to delimit the end of a field within a record or the end of a line that is stored on a magnetic disk.)

14 *Inhibit presentation*: on encountering this control code, the device inhibits the visual representation of data that is entered at the device. However, this data is stored and will be included in the next outbound data stream transmitted. This feature enables secure data, such as passwords, to be entered. This control code only inhibits the visual representation of data entered at the device; data received by the device, via outbound data streams, is not affected.

15 *Interchange separators: interchange unit separator, interchange record separator, interchange group separator* and *interchange file separator*: implementation–dependent control codes that can be used to separate (ie delimit) 'logical' units of data. These control codes can be used in a hierarchical manner, ie different codes delimiting progressively larger 'logical' units. If used in this manner, these codes are structured in the following ascending order: IUS, IRS, IGS and IFS, ie IUS is used to delimit the smallest 'logical' unit of data, while IFS delimits the largest 'logical' unit.

16 *Line feed*: moves the presentation position vertically down to the next line 5 while remaining in the same column position.

17 *New line*: moves the presentation position horizontally to the left margin and then vertically down to the next line. (In effect, a CR followed by LF.)

18 *Null*: can be used with devices that suport it as a 'space' character.

19 *Presentation position*: a three-byte control sequence – control code, function parameter, value parameter – used to move the presentation position to the location specified by the two parameters. The function parameter specifies the following: whether the move is vertical or horizontal, whether it is absolute, ie a specific line or column number is specified, or relative, ie move specified in terms of an increment to the current line or colum number; whether an erase function, ie insertion of an implementation-dependent graphic character such as 'space' or NULL, is to be performed on presentation positions traversed when performing the move; whether an erase function should be performed to the specified position but then return the presentation position to the original position it occupied prior to the move. The value parameter specifies either an absolute line or column number or an incremental value that is dependent on the function parameter. The permitted function parameters are shown in Figure B.15.

20 Program operator communication: a three-byte control sequence – control code, function parameter, value parameter – which can be used for inter-end-user communications, providing that at least one of the end users is a terminal operator, ie application program to terminal operator, terminal operator to application program or between two terminal operators. Application program to terminal operator, or terminal operator to terminal communication is operator defined in terms of a series of illuminable indicators, while terminal operator to application program is defined in terms of a series of function keys that can be activated by the terminal operator. The meanings attributed to an indicator being on or off, or a function key being activated is implementation dependent. The permitted parameters are shown in Figure B.16.

Function parameter code	Function code specifies				Value parameter			
	Absolute (A) or relative (R) move	Horizontal (H) or vertical (V) move	Erase while moving	Erase to position specified, but then return to original	Line Absolute	Line Relative	Column Relative	Column Absolute
X'C0'	A	H	×					✓
X'C1'	A	H	✓					✓
X'C2'	A	H		✓				✓
X'C4'	A	V	×		✓			
X'C5'	A	V	✓		✓			
X'C6'	A	V		✓	✓			
X'C8'	R	H	×				✓	
X'C9'	R	H	✓				✓	
X'4A'	R	H		✓			✓	
X'4C'	R	V	×			✓		
X'4D'	R	V	✓			✓		
X'4E'	R	V		✓		✓		

Figure B.15: Presentation position function parameters

Function parameter code	Application program to terminal operator or terminal operator to terminal operator: DEFINES INDICATOR 'FUNCTION'	Terminal operator to application program: DEFINES A FUNCTION KEY ACTIVATION	Value parameter specifies (Range 1 to 255)
X'C0'	No-op	No-op	Nothing, but a value must be included
X'C1'	Illuminate specified indicator	Specified function key activated	Indicator or function key number
X'C2'	Extinguish specified indicator	—	Indicator number
X'C3'	Illuminate specified indicators	—	An eight-bit mask. Each bit corresponds to an indicator
X'C4'	Extinguish all indicators	—	Nothing, but a value must be specified

Figure B.16: Program operator communication parameters

468

21 *Repeat*: used with devices that contain a print buffer. This code, when encountered in the print buffer during a print operation, causes the contents of the print buffer to be printed again. (This control code, in conjunction with the Switch control code, enables 'mail-list merging', ie the preparation of 'mail-shots', to be achieved.)

22 *Required form feed*: mandatorily moves the presentation position to the top and left margins of the next presentation space. (It differs from form feed, which may be ignored by devices that perform automatic text-alignment.)

23 *Required new line*: mandatorily moves the presentation position to the left margin of the next line. (It differs from new line, which may be ignored by devices that perform automatic text-alignment.)

24 *Required space*: alternate space character, which is treated as a *bona-fide* graphic character and, as such, is not treated as a normal space by devices that perform automatic text-alignment.

25 *Secure string ID reader*: used to prefix an operator identification number read by a device, off an operator identification card via a magnetic stripe reader. (The identification number is post-fixed with an IRS code.)

26 *Select*: a two-byte control code sequence – control code, function parameter. The function parameter identifies one of two functions within the device. X'50' – Secure String ID Reader, X'7A' to X'7C' or X'81' to X'89' – Vertical Channel Select. (Vertical Channel Select is described later in this section.)

27 *Set chain image*: a variable-length control code sequence used to load a character set image (or chain image), ie slug position on a chain corresponding to a given graphic code, into a chain printer. The format of the control code sequence is shown in Figure B.17.

28 *Set graphic error action*: currently a five-byte control code sequence (with a capability of being extended to a variable-length sequence). It specifies the action to be performed if an undisplayable, unprintable, graphic character – other than an SCS code – is received by a device. The control code sequence specifies whether an error message should be issued, or whether a substitute graphic character should be

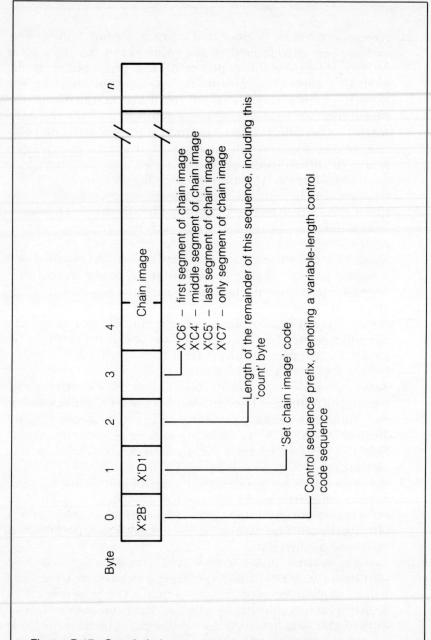

Byte

0	1	2	3	4		n
X'2B'	X'D1'			Chain image		

X'C6' – first segment of chain image
X'C4' – middle segment of chain image
X'C5' – last segment of chain image
X'C7' – only segment of chain image

Length of the remainder of this sequence, including this 'count' byte

'Set chain image' code

Control sequence prefix, denoting a variable-length control code sequence

Figure B.17: Set chain image control code sequence

used. The format of the control code sequence is shown in Figure B.18.

29 *Set horizontal format*: a variable-length control code sequence used to set the horizontal presentation space parameters: Maximum Presentation Position (MPP), left and right margins (LM and RM) and the horizontal tab stops (qv Figure B.14). The format of the control code sequence is shown in Figure B.19.

30 *Set line density*: specifies the vertical distance to be moved by the presentation position when executing a single-line vertical move, eg LF or NL. The control sequence (two bytes: control sequence prefix, X'2B', set line density, X'C6') is followed by a count field – specifying X'02' – and a value parameter, which specifies the vertical distance to be moved in terms of standard typographical points, ie one point = 1/72 inch.

31 *Set vertical format*: the control code sequence complementary to Set Horizontal Format which is used to set the vertical presentation space parameters Maximum Print Line (MPL), top and bottom margins (TM and BM) and vertical tab stop positions. The format is equivalent to that used by SHF.

32 *Subscript*: moves the presentation position downwards by a fraction of a line feed so that subscripts can be represented. (A superscript control code must be used to return the presentation position to the original line.)

33 *Substitute*: an error control code, used to replace a character that is deemed to be invalid or in error.

34 *Superscript*: moves the presentation position upwards by a fraction of a line, so that superscripts can be represented.

35 *Switch*: used with devices that contain two print buffers. This control code causes the print operation to switch from printing the contents in one buffer to printing the contents of the other (qv 'repeat').

36 *Syllable hyphen*: provides a graphic code that prints as a normal hyphen character (ie '-'). It is used when splitting a word between two lines to indicate the continuation of the word. Devices capable of automatic text alignment can discard this 'hyphen' if the word is moved so that it is no longer split between two lines.

37 *Transparent*: used to define the start of a block of 'transparent-

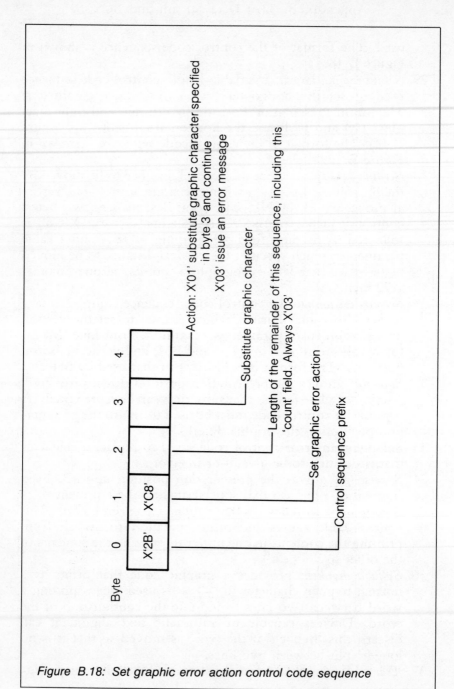

Figure B.18: Set graphic error action control code sequence

472

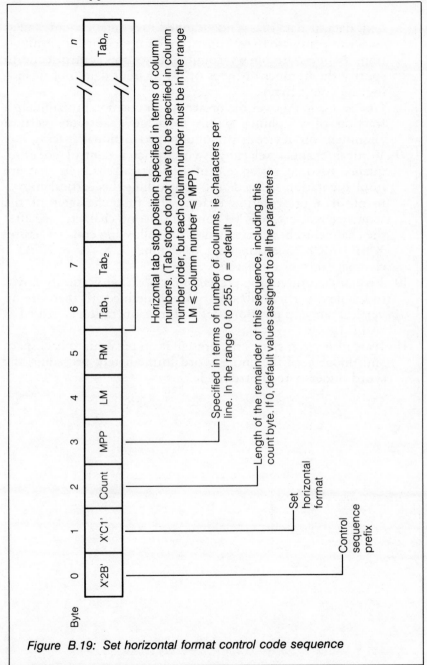

Figure B.19: Set horizontal format control code sequence

473

text' data, ie data that is not scanned for control codes, and as such can comprise bytes consisting of any eight-bit permutation. A one-byte binary count follows the control code to specify the number of bytes of transparent data (not including the count byte).

38 *Unit backspace*: moves the presentation position horizontally a fraction of a column width to achieve absolute vertical alignment on devices that support proportional spacing.

39 Vertical channel select: a two-character control code sequence used to select one of 12 vertical channels that are implementation defined, for controlling the vertical movement of a presentation space. The first character of the sequence is select, ie X'04', and the second character specifies the channel to be selected using the following code structure: X'81' to X'89' – channel one to channel 9, X'7A' to X'7C' – channel 10 to channel 12.

40 *Vertical tab*: moves the presentation position vertically down to the next vertical tab stop position defined. (If there are no vertical tab stop positions defined, this operation is treated as an LF.)

41 *Word underscore*: causes the presentation position to backspace and underscore the entire word immediately preceding the word underscore control code.

Glossary

Glossary

This glossary defines the SNA and SNA-implementation related terms used in this book. Terms more commonly referred to by an acronym or abbreviation, rather than by their full title, eg SSCP, NAU, ACF/VTAM, MVS etc, are listed under the acronym or abbreviation; these are shown in capital letters. Their explanations are given in the *'Table of acronyms and abbreviations'*.

A

Access method –
> A set of system control macros and associated routines – provided either as an intrinsic feature of the operating system or as a program product – for facilitating I/O operations between application programs and locally- or remotely-attached I/O devices.

ACF –
> The prefix used to identify IBM proprietary program products that can be used to realise environments based on SNA 3 or higher.

ACF/NCP –
> A network control program that executes in a communications controller and provides the teleprocessing protocol support for all the telecommunication links that are attached to that communications controller and are a part of the SNA-based environment, and, in the case of local communications controllers, liaises with the host-resident SNA-oriented access method.

ACF/TCAM –

A host-resident teleprocessing access method that can be used to realise an SNA environment in a manner similar to that of ACF/VTAM.

ACF/VTAM –

A host-resident SNA-oriented teleprocessing access method that provides the host-based control functions needed to implement an SNA environment and some of the LU functions for host application programs.

ACF/VTAME –

An entry-level ACF/VTAM that only operates under DOS/VSE on an IBM 4331 host and directly supports telecommunication links attached to the 4331 communication adaptor.

ACP –

A real-time high-performance operating system for airline operation-related transaction processing systems such as airline reservation systems.

APL –

A high-level, symbolic operator-based, general-purpose programming language that is ideally suited for mathematical applications. (The number of symbols used by the language necessitates a special character set, with more symbols than those offered by EBCDIC.)

Application program –

A user-oriented program, either written for or by the user, for achieving a particular user-related task or solving a user-related problem.

B

Bidder –

In an LU-LU session, the bidder is the half-session which is defined at session activation as having to request and receive permission from the other half-session (ie first speaker) before it may begin a bracket.

BIND –

The SNA command used to activate an LU-LU session.

BIU –

The fundamental unit of information exchanged between half-sessions via the Path Control Network: it consists of an RH followed by an RU.

BIU segment –

A portion of a BIU, ie a BIU may be split into two or more BIU segments. A BIU segment consists of either a part of an RU or an RH followed by a part of an RU.

Blocking –

The process of combining multiple PIUs to form a single BTU.

BLU –

The fundamental unit of data transmitted across an SNA link. A BLU consists of a BTU prefixed by a DLC header and postfixed by a DLC trailer containing DLC protocol-specific information.

Boundary Function –

A component of subarea nodes that provides message unit interchange support for the peripheral nodes attached to that node. Examples: transforming THs used between subarea nodes to those used by peripheral nodes and *vice versa*, converting network addresses to local addresses and *vice versa*; performing intermediatory, ie two-stage, session-level pacing; assigning and checking sequence numbers (identifiers) for message units to, or from, Type 1 nodes.

Bracket –

A series of requests (one or more chains) and their responses, in either or both directions, that form a designated unit of work.

Bracket protocol –

The DFC protocol used for supporting brackets, between LUs, in LU-LU sessions.

BSC –

A synchronous, teleprocessing, data link control protocol. Though not ideally suited as a remote data link control protocol for SNA, current ACF/NCPs support BSC 3270 devices as components in an SNA environment.

BTAM –

A non-SNA, host-resident, teleprocessing access method.

BTU –

The fundamental unit of data exchanged between the Path Control and data link control components of the Path Control Network. A BTU consists of one or more PIUs.

C

Cascade level –

A term, based on the analogy to a series of waterfalls, used to graphically describe the number of 'drops' – or levels – of remote communications controllers that can be supported by a local communications controller. A cascade level of 1 indicates that a remote communications controller can only be one drop away from – ie directly attached to – a local communications controller: a cascade level of 2 indicates that a local communications controller can support remote communications controllers that are not directly attached to *it*, but are attached to other remote communications controllers that are.

Chain –

A series of related requests that are transmitted consecutively, on a given flow, and are treated as one entity forming a complete message.

Channel –

The I/O processors on S/360- and S/370-architectured machines that perform all control and data transfer operations between I/O devices and main storage.

Channel-attached –

Attachment of a device, directly to a channel on an S/360- or S/370-architectured machine, via a set of multiwire cables. This is also referred to as 'locally attached'. Contrast with 'remotely attached', which refers to devices that are not directly attached to a channel, but are attached via one or more telecommunications links to a channel-attached device.

Character-coded –

SNA commands, on SSCP-LU sessions, that are entered by an end user and forwarded by its supporting LU in unformatted, character form – as opposed to the SNA-specified, bit-encoded, format for the command – and which need to be transformed to the standard format, by the SSCP, before they can be processed.

CICS –

A general-purpose data communications monitor that facilitates the development of terminal-oriented transaction-processing application programs by providing a high-level programming interface between these programs, teleprocessing access methods and database managers.

CICS/VS –

The generic term used to refer to the two currently supported versions of CICS – CIS/OS/VS and CICS/DOS/VS. CICS/OS/VS operates under OS/VS1 or MVS operating systems, while CICS/DOS/VS operates under DOS/VS or DOS/VSE operating systems.

Class of service –

A virtual route number and transmission priority pair, identifying a virtual route between two subarea nodes. The virtual route to be used to convey the traffic of a given LU-LU session is specified via a class of service reference. The class of service reference consists of a class of service name, identifying an entry in a predefined class of service table. Each entry in the table defines a set of one or more virtual routes. The class of service name, referring to the set of possible virtual routes to be used by an LU-LU session, is specified in the mode table entry used when initiating that session.

Cluster controller –

A device that controls the I/O operations of multiple terminals or devices that are attached to it.

CMS –

An interactive timesharing system that operates under VM.

CNM application programs –

Special application programs that are authorised to request and receive for processing, status and error statistics from a PU in its domain.

Communications control unit –

Another term for a communications controller.

Communications controller –

A control unit that supports the attachment of, and controls data transmission and reception over, telecommunication links.

Compaction –

Compaction is a feature wherein up to 16 predesignated characters are assigned a four-bit code, so that if two such characters are contiguous in a message they can be packed into a single byte to reduce the length of the message unit.

Compression –

Compression occurs when a repetitive sequence of up to 63 consecutive occurrences of a character is replaced by a one- or two-byte code to reduce the length of the message unit.

Configuration services –

The set of network services requests used by SSCPs and PUs to activate and deactivate Path Control Network components, convey status changes in Path Control Network components, load Type 4 or Type 2 nodes, dump Type 4 nodes and to dynamically assign network addresses.

Connection point manager –

A subcomponent of the Transmission Control component of a half-session, responsible for sequence number checking, session-level pacing, cryptography, ensuring that request units do not exceed the maximum RU length stipulated for the session, constructing and checking RHs and segregating normal and expedited flow data traffic.

Cross-domain –

Another term for 'interdomain' operations, ie operations between two domains.

Cross-domain link –

A telecommunication link between two communication controllers in separate domains, providing a communication path between the two domains.

Cross-domain resource manager –

The SSCP 'component' that controls cross-domain operations.

Cross-domain sessions –

Sessions between NAUs in different domains.

Cryptographic algorithm –

The cryptographic process used to encode and decode data whose meaning is to be concealed during transmission.

Cryptographic key –
>A code used as an input to a cryptographic algorithm, to dictate the encoding, or decoding, of data.

Cryptography –
>The encoding of data during transmission to conceal the true meaning of the data.

D

Data count field –
>A field in a TH specifying the length of the BIU or BIU segment that is prefixed by the TH.

Data flow control –
>The component of a half-session responsible for the following: grouping RUs into chains, supporting bracket protocol, controlling the transmit and receive mode, imposing the designated request and response control modes, assigning sequence numbers, correlating responses to requests and providing the means to interrupt the flow of normal-flow requests.

Data link control –
>The Path Control Network components responsible for transferring SNA message units between nodes via SNA links.

Data link control protocol –
>A protocol used by Data Link Control components to control the exchange of data between two components.

Data stream –
>A generic term used to refer to the end-user-specific protocols and data structures used to exchange data between end users.

DCA –
>A complementary architecture to SNA, put forward by IBM in 1983, that specifies the correct interpretation of the form and meaning of the content of a document that is interchanged between machines via an SNA environment.

DCE –
>The unit responsible for establishing, maintaining and disconnecting a connection, and for providing the necessary signal conversion between a machine, device or terminal and

a telecommunications link. (For analogue telecommunication links, the DCE will be a modem.)

Definite response –

One of the three possible types of response expected, that can be specified for a request. Definite response specifies that a response – whether positive or negative – must be issued by the receiver of the request.

Delayed request mode –

One of the two control modes defined for regulating the issuing of requests. This mode permits multiple requests to be issued without any restriction – irrespective of the type of response requested and expected by previous requests.

Delayed response mode –

One of the two control modes defined for regulating the order in which responses to requests may be issued. This mode permits responses to be issued in any order, irrespective of the order in which the requests were received.

DIA –

Another complementary architecture to SNA, put forward by IBM in 1984, that specifies the end-user-oriented protocols and data streams necessary to interchange documents between end users, via an SNA environment, in a compatible, consistent and predictable manner.

Domain –

An SSCP and all the PUs, LUs and Path Control Network components that the SSCP can activate via SNA-defined 'activation' requests.

DOS/VS –

A virtual storage operating system for S/370-architectured machines, similar in concept to OS/VS1 but better suited for the smaller System 370 machines as it requires less storage and processing resources.

E

Element address –

The portion of a network address that uniquely identifies NAUs and link stations within a given subarea.

Emulation program –

A function of NCPs, executing in 370X communication controllers that enable telecommunication links to operate as if they were attached to pre-SNA era, 270X transmission control units.

End user –

The possible sources or destinations of information exchanged via an SNA-specified data communications environment: application programs, terminal users or I/O devices.

Exception request –

A request in which an error has been detected by an intermediate component, and which has been modified by that component to convey this error to the request's eventual destination NAU.

Exception response –

One of the three possible types of response expected that can be specified for a request. An exception response specifies that a response should be issued only if the request cannot be processed or if an error was encountered during the processing of the request.

Exit routine –

A user-written routine within an ACF/VTAM application program which is invoked by ACF/VTAM when it encounters a condition such as an LU-LU session establishment or termination request, failure of an LU-LU session, a specific system operator command, certain errors or certain SNA-defined requests or responses received from a session partner.

EXLST –

The ACF/VTAM macro used to define the exit routine to be invoked when a specific condition is encountered by ACF/VTAM, qv exit routine.

Expedited flow –

One of two possible bidirectional, logical, data transmission 'channels' within a session, for conveying requests and responses. Requests and responses transmitted on the expedited flow can overtake requests or responses flowing on the other data 'channel' – ie normal flow – at queuing points. As such, this flow is used for session control, network control and data flow control commands, and their responses, which can affect the data transfer on the normal flow.

Explicit Route –

A physical path between two end-to-end subarea nodes, consisting of a fixed set of transmission groups and a set of subarea node path control components.

Explicit Route control –

A subcomponent of the subarea node path control component, responsible for providing and controlling Explicit Routes.

EXTM –

A CICS/DOS/VS-only telecommunications access method that interfaces with ACF/NCP and supports both SNA and non-SNA terminals that wish to interact with CICS/DOS/VS application programs.

F

FID –

The first four bits of all THs, which specify the type of TH.

Field formatted –

SNA commands, when represented in their SNA-specified bit-encoded format. Contrast with 'character coded'.

First speaker –

The half-session that is designated at session establishment as having priority in a begin-bracket contention condition, and which can begin a bracket without seeking permission from the other half-session.

FM Headers –

Headers inserted into requests containing end-user data by an FMDS: Session Presentation Services component to convey control information to its counterpart, either to instruct it on how certain data requests bound for the end user being served by it should be restructured and presented, or to update operational parameters relevant to the data stream or the operational procedures being used by the end users.

FM profiles –

Predefined sets, each identified by a number of various permutations of DFC functions that can be used by two half-sessions forming a session, and which can be referred to by their identification numbers during session-activation to specify the DFC functions that will be used during the session.

FMDS –

The highest-level component of a half-session. The functions performed by the RFMDS component depend on the type of session the half-session is involved in. For sessions involving an SSCP – *viz* SSCP-PU, SSCP-LU or SSCP-SSCP sessions – this component is further qualified as being Session Network Services, and is responsible for controlling and monitoring the resources associated with the subject NAUs. For LU-LU sessions, this component – referred to as Session Presentation Services – is responsible for manipulating data accepted from, or to be delivered to, an end user.

Full duplex –

The send/receive control mode, wherein both half-sessions can transmit and receive normal-flow requests simultaneously.

H

Half duplex –

The send/receive mode, wherein a half-session may either transmit or receive normal-flow requests, at any one time. Simultaneous transmission and reception is not permitted.

Half-session –

A session consists of two half-sessions; one in the primary and one in the secondary NAU, interconnected by the Path Control Network. A half-session is the set of FMDS, DFC and TC functions used by a NAU to provide the protocols needed to support the communications within a particular session.

Host computer –

A computer controlling a total, or a part of a, data communications environment.

Host LU –

An application program LU, resident within a Type 5 node.

Host node –

An informal name for a Type 5 node.

Immediate-request mode –
> One of the two control modes defined for regulating the issuing of requests. With this mode no further requests may be issued until a response is received for a previously transmitted request that specified that it expects a definite response.

Immediate-response mode –
> One of the two control modes defined for regulating the order in which responses are issued. With this mode responses must be issued in the same order as the requests to which they apply were received.

IMS –
> A comprehensive database management system – with a feature offering data communication facilities – for OS/VS1 or MVS systems. (The DOS equivalent is known as DL/1.)

Intermediate node –
> A subarea node whose Path Control Network components are used to route message units to other subarea nodes. The intermediate node does not contain either the NAUs originating the message units, the NAUs that are the destination of the message units nor the Boundary Function supporting any of the destination NAUs.

Interpret table –
> An optional, user-definable translate table in ACF/VTAM that enables the APPLID portion – specifying the application program that will act as the PLU of a session – of field- or character-formatted logon requests to be either converted to specify the name of another application program or to invoke a 'logon-interpret' routine (sometimes referred to as 'APPLID routines') which will further validate the logon request prior to determining the name of the application program to receive the logon request. This facility enables installations to use application programs with different names, especially during the testing of an application program, without having to use different logon sequences, ie the changes will be transparent to the terminal end users. When interpret tables are to be used, the name of the table to be used to process a logon request from a terminal LU is specified by means of

the LOGTAB= operand of ACF/VTAM and ACF/NCP LU and PU macros. Interpret tables are defined by means of the ACF/VTAM macros INTAB, LOGCHAR and ENDINTAB.

Isolated pacing response –

A response to a session-level pacing request, indicating that a further batch of requests may be transmitted, issued as a pacing-specific response, rather than combining the pacing response with the response to a data or command request. (Isolated pacing responses may be transmitted either in the normal or expedited flow, even though session level only applies to the normal flow.)

J

JES –

The generic term for the job entry subsystem facility of MVS systems that is responsible for spooling, job queuing, I/O management and, in conjunction with NJE (a feature of JES), for controlling the exchange of I/O data with other computer systems.

L

Line group –

An ACF/NCP-related term referring to a set of one or more telecommunication lines that have been defined by ACF/NCP as having the same transmission characteristics.

Link –

The SNA-defined mechanism used by the data link control components of the Path Control Network for transferring message units between nodes. A link consists of a single primary link station, a set of one or more secondary link stations and a link connection which physically interconnects the primary link station with each of the secondary link stations.

Link attached –

A device or machine containing an SNA node that is

physically attached by a telecommunication link to another device or machine also containing an SNA node.

Link connection –
>A physical transmission medium which is either an S/370 channel or a switched or non-switched telecommunication link and the appropriate data circuit-terminating equipment.

Link station –
>The hardware and software required to attach a link connection to the device or machine containing an SNA node, and to support the data link control protocol used to establish, coordinate and sustain error-free data transfer over the link connection.

Local –
>A device that is channel-attached to an S/360- or S/370-architectured machine.

Local address –
>A simplified addressing scheme used between a subarea node boundary function and the peripheral nodes that it supports, to identify the resources within the peripheral nodes and the NAUs that the peripheral node NAUs are interacting with, in place of the mandatory network addresses of these resources.

Logical Unit –
>One of the three types of NAU defined in SNA. LUs are the communication ports through which end users can access and use the resources of an SNA data communication environment to interact with other end users. An LU is a set of end-user-specifiable functions used to perform the necessary data transformation and data-flow management needed to support end-user-to-end-user communications.

Logoff –
>A generic term for a request to terminate an LU-LU session existing between an application program LU and a terminal or I/O device LU.

Logon –
>A generic term for a request to initiate an LU-LU session between an application program LU and a terminal or I/O device LU.

Logon mode table (log mode table) –
>The ACF/VTAM table containing sets of named, predefined

session characteristics and protocols. During LU-LU session initiation, the characteristics and protocols for the proposed session are specified by naming the appropriate set within a logon mode table.

LPDA –
A feature provided by ACF/NCP Release 2.1 and ACF/NCP Release 3, to exploit the on-line test and problem determination features available on the microprocessor-based IBM modems, viz 3863, 3864 and 3865.

LSID –
The local addressing scheme used by Type 1 node NAUs.

LU-LU session –
One of the four types of session defined by SNA. LU-LU sessions are used for end-user-to-end-user interactions.

LU-LU session type –
SNA defines six types of LU-LU session – type 0, 1, 2, 3, 4 and 6 – essentially based on the type of end-user pair served by the session. LU-LU session type refers to which one of these six session types applies to a given LU-LU session.

LU Services Manager –
The NAU Services Manager component of an LU.

LU type –
An informal, and now obsolete and inappropriate, term used in the past to mean 'LU-LU session type'.

M

Maintenance Services –
A class of FMDS Network Services requests exchanged either between SSCPs and PUs via SSCP-PU sessions or between SSCPs and LUs via SSCP-LU sessions, to activate or deactivate diagnostic procedures, convey data obtained from diagnostic procedures or to record statistics on various resources.

Major node –
The basic resource definition mechanism used by ACF/VTAM. A major node is a data file containing the definitions for a set of resources of a given type (viz application program LUs, PUs and LUs in locally-attached devices, PUs and LUs

in remotely-attached devices and teleprocessing links specified in NCPs, PUs and LUs in devices accessing NCPs via switched SDLC links, locally-attached non-SNA 3270 control units) that have been grouped together and can be activated and deactivated as a group. (ACF/VTAM major nodes are not related to SNA nodes and should not be confused with them.)

Management Services –
A class of FMDS Network Services requests exchanged between SSCPs and LUs via SSCP-LU sessions, to dispatch and receive diagnostic-related requests and data.

Message unit –
The generic term for all units of data exchanged between components in an SNA environment.

Minor node –
A resource definition entry within an ACF/VTAM major node. (ACF/VTAM minor nodes are not related to SNA nodes and should not be confused with them.)

Modem –
A term derived from combining the first letters of 'modulator-demodulator', which refers to the units used to convert digital signals to analogue signals, for transmission on digital data or analogue transmission systems, and *vice versa*.

MSNF –
An optional feature of ACF/VTAM and ACF/TCAM that is required if inter- (cross-) domain LU-LU sessions are needed in a multidomain environment.

Multidomain environment –
An environment containing multiple SSCPs.

Multidrop link –
Another term for a multipoint link.

Multipoint link –
A shared communication link between a device designated as a control (master or primary) station and two or more devices designated as tributary (slave or secondary) stations.

MVS –
A virtual storage operating system for S/370-architectured machines, where each task is assigned its own 16 Mbyte virtual addressing space.

N

NAU –

A Logical Unit, a Physical Unit or an SSCP: the fundamental functional entities in an SNA environment, which are the source or destination of all information flowing within an SNA environment.

NAU Services –

The functions provided by a NAU Services Manager.

NAU Services Manager –

The component, present in all NAUs, that controls and monitors the configuration and operation of its NAU and, where appropriate, of other NAUs, by exchanging Network Services requests and responses with other NAU Services Managers via the relevant SSCP oriented sessions.

NCCF –

An IBM-supplied program product executing as an ACF/ VTAM (or ACF/TCAM)–authorised CNM application program, that allows communication between system operators using either locally- or remotely-attached 3270 terminals to control a single- or multidomain environment using ACF/VTAM-defined operator commands or 'operator-defined' command lists consisting of ACF/VTAM- and NCCF-defined commands. It also provides for the collection, storage and retrieval of network error data for processing by NPDA.

NCP –

A control program that executes in either a local or remote communications controller and provides the functions of an SNA Type 4 node – *viz* PU—T4, Path Control, data link control and Boundary Function – to remotely-attached devices containing peripheral nodes or for 3270 BSC control units.

Negative response –

A response indicating that the request that it applies to could not be processed or that an error was encountered during the processing of the request.

Negotiable BIND –

One of the two possible types of BIND request. With a negotiable BIND, the SLU may propose an alternative set of session characteristics for establishing the LU-LU session proposed by the PLU.

Network –

In informal terms, any set of interconnected nodes, and, as such, invariably used in an SNA context to refer to all private data communications environments.

Network address –

An unique address assigned to each NAU and link station in an SNA environment.

Network control –

A set of SNA defined requests and responses used for controlling explicit and virtual routes.

Network name –

An EBCDIC character-encoded name given to each LU, PU and primary link station in an SNA environment.

Network Services –

A set of SNA-defined requests and responses, used by NAU Services Managers, to control and monitor the configuration and operation of SNA environments.

Network Services Header –

A three-byte header that prefixes all SNA-defined FMDS requests and the responses to these requests.

NIB –

An ACF/VTAM control block, used during the initiation and establishment of LU-LU sessions, involving an ACF/VTAM application program and, for SSCP-LU sessions, involving CNM application programs, to identify and define parameters for these sessions.

No response –

One of the three possible types of response expected, that can be specified for a request. No response specifies that a response is not required and so should not be issued, irrespective of whether the processing of the request was successful or unsuccessful.

Node –

A collection of one or more NAUs and a set of Path Control Network components.

Node type –

The designation of a node according to the presence and absence of certain NAU types and the functional capabilities of the NAUs and Path Control Network components present.

Non-negotiable BIND –

One of the two possible types of BIND request. With a non-negotiable BIND, the SLU cannot request any changes to the session characteristics when accepting the establishment of an LU-LU session proposed by the PLU.

Non-SNA device –

A device that does not contain an SNA node.

Non-switched link –

A leased (ie dedicated) telecommunication link.

Normal flow –

One of two possible bidirectional, logical, data transmission 'channels' within a session for conveying requests and responses. The normal flow is used for end-user data, FMDS and certain DFC requests and responses.

NOSP –

An IBM-supplied ACF/VTAM application program to enhance the system operator capabilities in a single- or multi-domain environment.

NPA –

A program product consisting of a host application program and a modified NCP, which collects message traffic, error and resource usage statistics for devices attached to SDLC links and for 3270 BSC control units and enables this information to be analysed in graphic form.

NPDA –

An IBM-supplied program product executing as an authorised CNM application 'program' under NCCF, that acts as a central problem determination function – using error data collected for it by NCCF – and assists users in locating resources in the environment that have failed or are liable to fail.

NTO –

A control program that executes alongside ACF/NCP in a communications controller and enables certain non-SNA devices to participate in an SNA environment as if they were *bona fide* SNA devices.

O

OS/VS –
> The generic term for OS/VS1 and OS/VS2 operating systems.

OS/VS1 –
> A virtual storage operating system for S/370-architectured machines, where the 16 Mbyte virtual storage is divided into a fixed number of partitions, each of which can execute a task that does not exceed the storage size of the partition.

OS/VS2 –
> The collective term for OS/VS2 Release 1 and OS/VS2 Release 2 operating systems.

OS/VS2 Release 1 –
> A virtual storage operating system for S/370 architectured machines, where the 16 Mbyte virtual storage can be dynamically shared by a variable number of tasks.

OS/VS2 Release 2 –
> The original formal name for MVS. This term is no longer used to refer to current versions of MVS which are now officially referred to as MVS followed by a Release number, eg MVS Release 3.8.

P

Pacing –
> The technique used in SNA whereby the receiving component of a data flow can regulate the rate at which data is transmitted to it, to ensure that it does not get inundated with data.

Pacing request –
> The mechanism employed by the transmitter of a data flow, when pacing is in use, to notify the receiver that it will cease transmission until it receives a pacing response, after it has transmitted the next group of requests (the number of requests in the group being equal to the pacing window size), the first request of which will contain the 'pacing request' as an indicator in the RH.

Pacing response –
> The mechanism employed by the receiver of a data flow, when pacing is in use, to indicate to the transmitter that it is capable of receiving another group of requests – the number of requests that can be in the group being equal to the pacing window size.

Pacing window size –
> The maximum number of requests that can be accepted at any one time by a receiving component of a data transfer operation that uses pacing.

Parallel links –
> Multiple links between adjacent subarea nodes.

Parallel sessions –
> Multiple concurrent sessions between the same two NAUs.

Path –
> The overall route through an SNA environment traversed by a message unit transmitted from one NAU to another.

Path control –
> The components of the Path Control Network responsible for routing message units between nodes using the appropriate data link control components.

Path Control Network –
> The set of path control and data link control components responsible for transmitting message units between the NAUs in an SNA environment.

PEP –
> A 'combined' ACF/NCP and EP control program executing in a local communications controller.

Peripheral node –
> A collective term for a Type 1 or Type 2 node.

PIU –
> A BIU or a BIU segment prefixed by a TH, or a TH by itself.

PLU –
> The LU that attempts to establish an LU-LU session by issuing a session activation – ie BIND – request.

Point-to-point link –
> A non-shared data link between two devices.

Positive response –
> A response indicating that the request to which it applies can be, is being, or has been successfully processed.

Primary link station –
The link station of a link, responsible for controlling all data transfer operations that occur over that link, using the command and procedure repertoire of the data link control protocol specified for that link.

Prime compression character –
A character that is nominated, when compression is being used, for replacement by a one-byte string control byte – as opposed to a two-byte string control byte – sequence, when repetitive sequences of it are encountered in a data stream.

Primary NAU –
The NAU which requests a session to be established by issuing the appropriate session activation request for that session.

Primary half-session –
The half-session resident within the primary NAU of a given session.

Profiles –
Predefined sets of related functions, identified by a number, that can be offered by two half-session subcomponent – ie DFC, TC and FMDS – partners of a session, that can be selected and specified at session activation by means of its identification number relative to the subject half-session subcomponent functions.

Protocol –
The set of conventions used for achieving error-free, orderly and efficient data interchange between two components.

POWER –
The spooling subsystem on DOS/VS systems.

PS profiles –
The set of profiles that specify the various possible functions that can be provided by the FMDS Session Presentation Services components in conjunction with the LU Services Managers for an LU-LU session.

PU –
A NAU present in every node, which controls the configuration and operation of the physical entities – eg data communication links – that the node is responsible for.

PUCP –
A set of functions, provided by PUs in non-Type 5 nodes, that are a subset of the functions performed by an SSCP, and are used for activating and deactivating resources local to that node.

PU-PU flow –
Though sessions between PUs are not defined in SNA, PUs in adjacent nodes may sometimes exchange NC requests and responses for controlling and monitoring certain Path Control Network components.

PU type –
The designation of the functional capability of a PU according to the type of node in which it resides.

Q

Quiescing –
A protocol supported by the DFC components of LU-LU sessions, which enables either half-session to temporarily stop its partner from transmitting requests on the normal flow.

R

Request –
In SNA, a message unit that conveys data or initiates a data transfer or control operation.

Request Unit –
A message unit that contains a request.

Response –
In SNA, a message unit that indicates that a request reached its destination and whether the receiver of that request can process it or not. (A response, contrary to the expected connotation, is not the reply to a request: a reply to a request will be in the form of another request.)

Response Unit –
A message unit that contains a response.

RH –
A three-byte prefix that precedes all RUs.
Route extension –
The portion of a path, consisting of Path Control Network components, between a Boundary Function in a subarea node and a NAU in an adjacent peripheral node, completing the data transfer route to be used by a session between the NAU in the peripheral node and a NAU in a subarea node.
RPL –
An ACF/VTAM control block used to supply or receive operands from ACF/VTAM macros.
RU –
A generic term for a message unit that contains either a request or a response.

S

SCS –
A device- and product-independent, universal and compre-hensive device control protocol – ie a data stream – based on 47, EBCDIC control code.
SDLC –
A synchronous, bit-oriented, inherently transparent data link control protocol – with acknowledgement window size of seven – that supports full- or half-duplex serial transmission on point-to-point or multipoint telecommunication links or on data communication loops. The main teleprocessing data link control protocol employed by SNA.
Secondary half-session –
The half-session resident within the secondary NAU of a given session.
Secondary NAU –
The NAU which accepts a session establishment request issued by a potential primary NAU of a session.
Segmenting –
An optional function of the Path Control Network, which will split a BIU into two or more BIU segments if the transmission of smaller message units is deemed to improve the overall transmission efficiency, reduce the need for

retransmission due to transmission error or suits the availability of processing or storage resources.

Sequence numbers –

Numeric identifiers assigned to a stream of contiguous requests, in a given direction, by the DFC components of the transmitting half-session, in serially ascending order.

Series/1 –

A powerful and versatile general-purpose minicomputer – with many features pioneered on DEC PDP-11s – introduced by IBM in 1976.

Session –

A formal, bilateral and temporary relationship which must be established between two NAUs before they can participate in any form of dialogue. Sessions are a fundamental and intrinsic concept of SNA: all end-user-to-end-user data communications and the conveyance of most of the SNA-specified commands and their responses are based on sessions.

Session activation request –

A request used to establish a session between two NAUs, eg ACTLU, ACTPU, BIND, ACTCDRM.

Session control –

One of the two subcomponents of a transmission control component of a half-session, responsible for: activating and deactivating the session in which its half session is to be, or already is, a partner; activating and deactivating the data flow within a session; and receiving the data flow following an error.

Session control requests –

The set of SNA-specified requests used by session control subcomponents to: activate and deactivate sessions; activate and deactivate the data flow within a session; recover a data flow following an error.

Session deactivation request –

A request used to bring about the termination of a session between two NAUs.

Session-level pacing –

Pacing that is used in both directions to regulate the rate of transmission of requests on the normal flow within SSCP-SSCP and LU-LU sessions.

Session limit –

    The maximum number of concurrently-active sessions a given NAU – usually a LU – can support.

Session Services –

    A category of FMDS Network Services requests and responses, used on SSCP-LU and SSCP-SSCP sessions to support the initiation and termination of LU-LU sessions.

Shared control –

    Refers to PUs and Path Control Network components that belong to more than one domain.

Single-domain –

    An SNA environment with only one SSCP.

SLU –

    The LU that accepts an LU-LU session establishment request – ie BIND – issued by the potential PLU of an LU-LU session.

SNA –

    A design specification, proffered by IBM in 1974 and since updated four times, that comprehensively specifies the various data communication-oriented facilities and functions that need to be provided and performed by products intended for either operating within, or supporting, a distributed data processing system, so that the total set of facilities and functions within the system result in an efficient, reliable, cost-effective and resource-sharable data communication environment that not only enables the relevant products to be fully interconnected but also enables data transfer operations to be performed between these products in a homogeneous manner irrespective of the nature of the products.

SSCP –

    The NAU, or NAUs, in an SNA environment that controls and manages the physical configuration of all the resources, the addition or removal of resources, the activation and deactivation of resources, the establishment of sessions between NAUs, the testing of resources, the recovery of resources and the interactions with the system operator.

SSCP-ID –

    A unique, 48-bit, numerical identifier assigned to each SSCP in an SNA environment.

Subarea –
A subarea node and all the peripheral nodes attached to it.

Subarea address –
The unique address assigned to each subarea in an SNA environment.

Subarea node –
A collective term for Type 4 and Type 5 nodes.

SVS –
The informal name for the OS/VS1 operating system.

Switched link –
A point-to-point telecommunications link established between a communications controller and a device or terminal, via a telephone dial operation.

Sync points –
An optional feature on LU-LU sessions for checkpointing the processing of specific units of work, such as the updating or deleting of a database entry.

S/32 –
A single-workstation minicomputer system.

S/34 –
A minicomputer announced by IBM in 1977.

S/38 –
A sophisticated minicomputer announced by IBM in 1978.

S/360 –
A powerful, comprehensive, compatible and immensely popular range of host computers introduced by IBM in 1964 and now considered as a *de facto* standard for mainframe computers.

S/370 –
Announced in 1971 as the replacement of the S/360 family. The S/370 range retained the basic S/360 architecture but enhanced it with the support of virtual addressing (in the basis of virtual storage). While IBM no longer market any machines bearing the S/370 designation *per se*, 4300, 303X and 308X systems are all based on, and fully compatible with, the S/370 architecture.

TCU –

Another term for communication controllers, but usually used to indicate non-programmable, low-functionality (pre-SNA) communication controllers as opposed to the more modern programmable communication controllers.

Terminal –

A device with a system user interface that can be operated by a *bona-fide* user, such as a visual display unit, as opposed to a device that is normally operated by a system operator, such as a disk or tape unit.

TH –

A header that prefixes all message units – or forms a complete message unit – flowing within the Path Control Network, containing Path Control Network-specific data related to routing, sequencing, blocking and virtual route pacing.

Transmission control –

The half-session component responsible for: activating and deactivating the session it is to be, or already is, a partner in; activating and deactivating data flow within a session; receiving a data flow following an error; session-level pacing; checking the sequence numbers of requests on the normal flow; cryptography; ensuring that requests do not exceed the maximum length designated for the session; segregating the normal and expedited flow; constructing RHs for message units transmitted by its half-session; checking the RHs of message units received by its half-session.

Transmission Group –

A bidirectional logical connection between two adjacent subarea nodes, consisting of one or more links between them.

Transmission Group control –

A subcomponent of a subarea node path control component, responsible for providing and controlling one or more transmission groups between adjacent subarea nodes.

Transmission priority –

A three-level ranking mechanism used by Transmission Group control to determine the order in which it transmits message units forwarded to it for transmission to an adjacent subarea node via a Transmission Group.

TSO –
> A timesharing system available on MVS systems for interactive computing from a terminal.

TS profile –
> Predefined sets, each identified by a number, of various permutations of TC functions that can be used by two half-sessions forming a session, and which can be referred to by its identification number during session activation to specify the TC functions that will be used during the session.

U

Unformatted –
> Another term for 'character coded'.

Unformatted system services –
> A set of functions within an SSCP used for translating character-coded requests to their field-formatted equivalent, prior to subsequent processing by other components within the SSCP.

Uninterpreted name –
> One or more alternative names associated with an LU, in addition to its network name, that can be used during LU-LU session initiation or termination to identify that LU.

USS tables –
> ACF/VTAM definition tables used to convert character-coded logon requests from non-standard formats to the standard format prior to their being translated into a field-formatted logon request.

V

VCNA –
> An IBM-supplied program product that executes under the VM operating system and provides VM Conversational Monitor System users with access to resources in an SNA environment by acting as an SNA teleprocessing access method.

Virtual Route –
> A bidirectional logical connection between two end-to-end subarea nodes, which is mapped onto an underlying ER, that

supports one or more sessions either between NAUs resident within the two end-to-end subarea nodes, NAUs in one of the subarea nodes and NAUs within a peripheral node supported by the other subarea node, or between NAUs in two peripheral nodes, each supported by one of the end-to-end subarea nodes. (In the case of intra-subarea node NAU-NAU sessions, the VR is contained within the Path Control Network components of that subarea node.)

Virtual Route pacing –
An end-to-end dynamic pacing mechanism used to regulate the rate, in both directions, at which the combined data flow of all the sessions associated with a particular Virtual Route are transmitted.

VM –
A virtual storage operating system for S/370-architectured machines, which provides multiple virtual machines whereby each virtual machine appears as a dedicated S/370-architectured machine and can execute any S/370-compatible operating system. VM was originally referred to as VM/370, but current versions are known as VM/SP, where SP denotes 'System Product'.

VSPC –
An interactive subsystem, available as a program product for OS/VS1 and MVS Systems, aimed at users who wish to develop programs interactively using programming languages such as APL, BASIC, FORTRAN or PL/I.

VTAM –
A host-resident, SNA-oriented teleprocessing access method that only supported single-domain environments. Now superseded by ACF/VTAM.

W

Window size –
When pacing is being used this is the number of requests that can be transmitted before a pacing response is received indicating that the receiver can accept a further batch of requests.

X

X.25 –

A recommendation put forward by the CCITT in 1976 for the interface between data terminal equipment and data circuit-terminating equipment, for terminals operating in packet mode on public data networks.

2260 –

A local or remote display system based on 2260 Display Stations and 2848 Control Units. Now made obsolete by 3270s.

270X –

A family – *viz* 2701, 2702 and 2703 – of hard-wired, ie non-programmable, pre-SNA TCUs.

2740 –

An IBM SELECTRIC typewriter modified so that it can either be used as a *bona fide* typewriter or as a communications terminal.

2741 –

An IBM SELECTRIC typewriter-based terminal similar to the 2740.

2780 –

A remote job entry terminal, comprising a card reader, line printer and an optional card punch.

3101 –

A table-top remote VDU that operates in start-stop mode.

3270 –

A comprehensive, versatile, local or remote, clustered or stand-alone display system consisting of monochrome and colour VDUs and printers and a range of control units.

3271 –

A remote – BSC or SDLC – control unit in the 3270 family.

3272 –

A non-SNA local control unit in the 3270 family.

3274 –

A range of local and remote control units in the 3270 family.

3276 –

A range of remote control units in the 3270 family, each built into a VDU and capable of supporting up to seven more VDUs or printers.

3274-1A –

An SNA local control unit in the 3270 family.

3274-1B –

A non-SNA local control unit in the 3270 family.

3274-1D –

A non-SNA local control unit in the 3270 family.

3600 –

A finance communication system consisting of a programmable control unit and a selection of terminals, some of which are specially designed for financial application – eg passbook printers.

3624 –

An unattended self-service banking terminal – ie cash dispenser.

3630 –

A range of programmable plant communication controllers that act as control units for ruggedised 3640 reporting terminals used in industrial work zones that are not conducive to the operation of standard terminals.

3650 –

A retail store system consisting of a control unit and a selection of terminals, some of which are specially designed for point-of-sale transactions.

3660 –

Supermarket key-entry system consisting of a control unit and a selection of terminals, some of which are specially designed for point-of-sale transactions at supermarkets.

3680 –

A programmable store system for point-of-sale applications.

3704 –

A programmable communications controller capable of executing EP, NCP or PEP.

3705 –

A programmable communications controller capable of executing EP, ACF/NCP or PEP.

3725 –

A programmable communications controller capable of executing ACF/NCP.

3730 –

The Distributed Office Communication System, based on a 3790 control unit, for document preparation.

3767 –

A compact, desk-top, remote SNA terminal consisting of a keyboard and a printer, with an optional feature for emulating 2740 or 2741 terminals.

3770 –

A family of BSC or SDLC remote terminals offering a variety of keyboard and printer configurations.

3780 –

A remote job entry terminal, comprising a card reader, line printer and an optional card punch, which superseded the 2780.

3790 –

A user-programmable minicomputer that can be locally or remotely attached to an S/370 system, and can act as an intelligent host to a variety of terminals and devices.

4300 –

A family of S/370-architectured machines addressing the needs of the users requiring small-to-medium-scale S/370 systems.

4331 DPA –

A built-in control unit, capable of supporting up to 15 3270 displays or printers on 4331 host computers in the 4300 family.

6670 –

An intelligent copying machine. A document copier-based information distributor which is a multifunction terminal acting as a text formatter, text printer and communication terminal as well as a copier.

8100 –

A user-programmable, multipurpose minicomputer which is aimed at distributed data processing applications and which can act as an intelligent host to a variety of terminals and devices and offers extensive communications capabilities.

8775 –

A stand-alone 3270 data stream-compatible VDU offering screen partitioning and field validation features.

Table of Acronyms and Abbreviations

Table of acronyms and abbreviations

A

ABCONN	Abandon Connection
ABCONNOUT	Abandon Connect Out
ACB	Access Method Control Block
ACF	Advanced Communications Functions
ACF/NCP	Advanced Communications Function for Network Control Program
ACF/TCAM	Advanced Communications Function for the Telecommunications Access Method
ACF/VTAM	Advanced Communications Function for the Virtual Telecommunications Access Method
ACF/VTAME	Advanced Communications Function for the Virtual Telecommunications Access Method Entry
ACP	Airline Control Program
ACTCDRM	Activate Cross-Domain Resource Manager
ACTCONNIN	Activate Connect In
ACTLINK	Activate Link
ACTLU	Activate Logical Unit
ACTPU	Activate Physical Unit
ACTTRACE	Activate Trace
ADDLINKSTA	Add Link Station
ADJSUB	Adjacent Subarea

AID	Attention Identification
ANA	Assign Network Address
APL	A Programming Language
ASCII	American Standard Code for Information Interchange

B

BB	Begin Bracket
BBI	Begin Bracket Indicator
BC	Begin Chain
BCC	Block Check Characters
BCI	Begin Chain Indicator
BEL	Bell
BF	Boundary Function
BINDF	BIND Failure
BIS	Bracket Initiation Stopped
BIU	Basic Information Unit
BLU	Basic Link Unit
BS	Back Space
BSC	Binary-Synchronous Communications
BTAM	Basic Telecommunications Access Method
BTU	Basic Transmission Unit

C

CCITT	The International Telegraph and Telephone Consultative Committee
CD	Change Direction
CDCINIT	Cross-Domain Control Initiate
CDI	Change Direction Indicator
CDINIT	Cross-Domain Initiate
CDRM	Cross-Domain Resource Manager
CDRSC	Cross-Domain Resource
CDSESSEND	Cross-Domain Session Ended
CDSESSSF	Cross-Domain Session Setup Failure
CDSESSST	Cross-Domain Session Started

CDSESSTF	Cross-Domain Session Take Down Failure
CDTAKED	Cross-Domain Take Down
CDTAKEDC	Cross-Domain Take Down Complete
CDTERM	Cross-Domain Terminate
CICS	Customer Information Control System
CICS/VS	Customer Information Control System/Virtual Storage
CINIT	Control Initiate
CLISTS	Command Lists
CLSDST	Close Destination
CMS	Conversational Monitor System
CNM	Communication Network Management
COBOL	Common Business Oriented Language
CONNOUT	Connect Out
COS	Class of Service
CP	Connection Point
CPMGR	Connection Point Manager
CR	Carriage Return
CRE	Carrier Return
CRV	Cryptographic Verification
CS	Configuration Services
CSI	Code Selection Indicator
CSP	Control Sequence Prefix
CTERM	Control Terminate

D

DACTCDRM	Deactivate Cross-Domain Resource Manager
DACTCONNIN	Deactivate Connect In
DACTLINK	Deactivate Link
DACTLU	Deactivate Logical Unit
DACTPU	Deactivate Physical Unit
DAF	Destination Address Field
DC	Device Control
DCA	Document Content Architecture
DCE	Data Circuit-Terminating Equipment

DCF	Data Count Field
DDP	Distributed Data Processing
DEC	Digital Equipment Corporation
DEF	Destination Element (Address) Field
DELETENR	Delete Network Resource
DES	Data Encryption Standard
DFC	Data Flow Control
DIA	Document Interchange Architecture
DISPSTOR	Display Storage
DLC	Data Link Control
DLU	Destination Logical Unit
DOS	Disk Operating System
DOS/VS	Disk Operating System/Virtual Storage
DPCX	Distributed Processing Control Executive
DPPX	Distributed Processing Programming Executive
DR	Definite Response
DR1	Definite Response 1
DR2	Definition Response 2
DR1I	Definite Response 1 Indicator
DR2I	Definite Response 2 Indicator
DSAF	Destination Subarea Address Field
DSRLST	Direct Search List
DTE	Data Terminal Equipment
DUMPINIT	Dump Initial
DUP	Duplicate

E

EA	Element Address
EB	End of Bracket
EBCDIC	Extended Binary Coded Decimal Interchange Code
EBI	End of Bracket Indicator
EBS	Expanded Backspace
EC	End of Chain
ECI	End of Chain Indicator

ECMA	European Computer Manufacturers Association
EDI	Enciphered Data Indicator
EFI	Expedited Flow Indicator
EM	End of Message
ENP	Enable Presentation
EP	Emulation Program
ER	Explicit Route *or* Exception Response
ERC	Explicit Route Control
ERI	Exception Response Indicator
ER__INOP	Explicit Route Inoperative
ERN	Explicit Route Number
ERP	Error Recovery Procedure
ESLOW	Entering Slowdown
ESP	Expanded Space
ETB	End of Text Block
ETX	End of Text
EUA	Erase Unprotected to Address
EXECTEST	Execute Test
EXLST	Exit List
EXR	Exception Request
EXSLW	Exiting Slowdown
EXTM	Extended Telecommunications Modules

F

FCS	Frame Check Sequence
FDX	Full Duplex
FF	Flip-Flop (*in SNA*) or Form Feed (*in SCS*)
FI	Format Indicator
FID	Format Identification
FIFO	First-in, First-out
FM	Function Management
FMD	Function Management Data
FMDS	Function Management Data Services
FMH	Function Management Header
FNA	Free Network Address

G

GE	Graphic Escape
GENCB	Generate Control Block

H

HDLC	High-Level Data Link Control
HDX	Half-Duplex
HDX-CONT	Half-Duplex Contention
HDX-FF	Half-Duplex Flip-flop
HSID	Half-Session Identification
HT	Horizontal Tab

I

IBM	International Business Machines Corporation
IC	Insert Cursor
IFS	Interchange File Separator
IGS	Interchange Group Separator
ILU	Initiating Logical Unit
IMS	Information Management System
IMS/VS	Information Management System Virtual Storage
INIT-OTHER	Initiate-Other
INIT-OTHER-CD	Initiate-Other Cross-Domain
INIT-PROC	Initiate Procedure
INIT-SELF	Initiate Self
INOP	Inoperative
INP	Inhibit Presentation
INX	Index
IPL	Initial Program Load
IPLINIT	IPL Initial
IPR	Isolated Pacing Response
IR	Index Return
IRS	Interchange Record Separator

ISO	International Standards Organisation
IT	Indent Tab
IUS	Interchange Unit Separator

J

JES	Job Entry Subsystem

L

LCP	Loss Control Point
LDREQDNS	Load Required
LF	Line Feed
LPDA	Link Problem Determination Application
LS	Link Station
LSA	Lost Subarea
LU	Logical Unit
LUSTAT	Logical Unit Status

M

MDT	Modify Data Tag
MF	Modify Field
MOC	Middle of Chain
MODCB	Modify Control Block
MPF	Mapping Field
MSNF	Multisystem Networking Facility
MVS	Multiple Virtual Storage

N

NAU	Network Addressable Unit
NBS	Numeric Backspace
NC	Network Control

NCCF	Network Communication Control Facility
NCP	Network Control Program
NIA	Network Interface Adaptor
NIB	Node Initialisation Block
NL	New Line
NOSP	Network Operation Support Program
NPA	Network Performance Analyser
NPDA	Network Problem Determination Application
NS	Network Services
NS(C)	Network Services, Configuration Services
NSH	Network Services Header
NSLSA	Network Services Lost Subarea
NS(MA)	Network Services, Maintenance Services
NS(ME)	Network Services, Measurement Services
NS(MN)	Network Services, Management Services
NSP	Numeric Space
NSPE	Network Services Procedure Error
NS(S)	Network Services, Session Services
NTO	Network Terminal Option
NUL	Null

O

OAF	Origin Address Field
OC	Only in Chain
OLU	Originating Logical Unit
OPNDST	Open Destination
OPNSEC	Open Secondary
OSAF	Originating Subarea (Address) Field
OSI	Open Systems Interconnection
OS/VS	Operating System/Virtual Storage

P

PA	Program Access
PC	Path Control
PCC	Programmed Communication Controller or Prime Compression Character
PCCU	Programmed Communication Control Unit
PDI	Padded Data Indicator
PE	Page End
PEP	Partitioned Emulation Program
PF	Program Function
PI	Pacing Indicator
PIU	Path Information Unit
PL/I	Programming Language/I
PLU	Primary Logical Unit
POC	Program Operator Communication
PP	Presentation Position
PROCSTAT	Procedure Status
PS	Presentation Services
PSE	Packet-Switch Exchange
PT	Program Tab
PTT	Post, Telephone and Telegraph (Authority)
PU	Physical Unit
PUCP	Physical Unit Control Point
POWER	Priority Output Writers, Execution (Processors and Input) Readers

Q

QC	Quiesce Complete
QEC	Quiesce at End of Chain

R

RA	Repeat to Address
RC	Request Code
RCR	Required Carrier Return

RECFMS	Record Formatted Maintenance Statistics
RECMD	Record Measurement Data
RECMS	Record Maintenance Statistics
RECSTOR	Record Storage
RECTD	Record Test Data
RECTR	Record Test Results
RECTRD	Record Trace Data
RELQ	Release Quiesce
REQACTLU	Request Activate Logical Unit
REQCONT	Request Contact
REQDISCONT	Request Discontact
REQECHO	Request Echo Test
REQFNA	Request Free Network Address
REQMS	Request Maintenance Statistics
REQTEST	Request Test
RERN	Reverse Explicit Route Number
RFF	Required Form Feed
RH	Request/Response Header
RNAA	Request Network Address Assignment
RNL	Required New Line
RPE	Required Page End
RPL	Request Parameter List
RPO	Remote Power Off
RPT	Repeat
RQR	Request Recovery
RRI	Request/Response Indicator
RSHUTD	Request Shutdown
RSP	Required Space (*in SCS*) Response (*in SNA*)
RTI	Response Type Indicator
RTR	Ready To Receive
RU	Request/Response Unit

S

SA	Set Attribute
SBA	Set Buffer Address
SBI	Stop Bracket Initiation

SBS	Subscript
SC	Session Control
SCI	Set Chain Image
SCS	SNA Character String
SDI	Sense Data Included Indicator
SDLC	Synchronous Data Link Control
SDT	Start Data Traffic
SEL	Select
SESSEND	Session Ended
SESSST	Session Started
SETCV	Set Control Vector
SF	Start Field
SFE	Start Field Extended
SGEA	Set Graphic Error Action
SHF	Set Horizontal Format
SHUTC	Shutdown Complete
SHUTD	Shutdown
SHY	Syllable Hyphen
SIG	Signal
SIMLOGON	Simulated Logon
SLD	Set Line Density
SLU	Secondary Logical Unit
SN	Sequence Number
SNA	Systems Network Architecture
SNF	Sequence Number Field
SNS	Session Network Services
SOH	Start of Header
SPS	Session Presentation Services (*in SNA*) Superscript (*in SCS*)
SRL	Systems Reference Library
SSCP	System Services Control Point
SSR	Secure String ID Reader
STARTMEAS	Start Measurement
STOPMEAS	Stop Measurement
STP	Stop
STSN	Set and Test Sequence Numbers
STX	Start of Text
SUB	Substitute
SVF	Set Vertical Format

SVS	Single Virtual Storage
SW	Switch
SYNC	Synchronisation

T

TCAM	Telecommunications Access Method
TCU	Transmission Control Unit
TERM-OTHER	Terminate-Other
TERM-OTHER-CD	Terminate-Other Cross-Domain
TERM-SELF	Terminate-Self
TG	Transmission Group
TGN	Transmission Group Number
TH	Transmission Header
TLU	Terminating Logical Unit
TOLTEP	Teleprocessing On-line Test Executive Program
TPF	Transmission Priority Field
TRN	Transparent
TS	Transmission Services
TSO	Timesharing Option
TTY	Teletype

U

UBS	Unit Backspace
UNBINDF	Unbind Failure
USS	Unformatted System Services
USSTAB	Unformatted System Services Tables

V

VCNA	VTAM Communications Network Application
VCS	Vertical Channel Select
VM	Virtual Machine

VR	Virtual Route
VR—CWI	Virtual Route Change Window Indicator
VR—CWRI	Virtual Route Change Window Reply Indicator
VR—INOP	Virtual Route Inoperative
VRN	Virtual Route Number
VRPRQ	Virtual Route Pacing Request
VRPRS	Virtual Route Pacing Response Indicator
VR—RWI	Virtual Route Reset Window Indicator
VSPC	Virtual Storage Personal Computing
VT	Vertical Tab
VTAM	Virtual Telecommunications Access Method

W

WACK	Wait Before Transmit Positive Acknowledgement
WCC	Write Control Character
WP	Word Processing
WTTY	World Trade Teletypewriter Terminal
WUS	Word Underscore

X

XID	Exchange Station Identification

Bibliography

Bibliography

SNA: specification - reference

Systems Network Architecture format and protocol reference manual: architectural logic
SRL no SC30-3112 IBM Corp (current version: Revision 2 (ie -2) dated Nov 1980)

Systems Network Architecture – Logical Unit types
SRL no GC20-1868 IBM Corp

Systems Network Architecture – introduction to sessions between Logical Units
SRL no GC20-1869 IBM Corp

SNA: specification - reference summary

Systems Network Architecture: reference summary
SRL no GA27-3136 IBM Corp

SNA: specification - background

Systems Network Architecture: technical overview
SRL no GC30-3073 IBM Corp

Systems Network Architecture: concepts and products
SRL no GC30-3072 IBM Corp

Computer network architectures
Chapter 7 'IBM's Systems Network Architecture', Meijer A and Peeters P, Pitman (ISBN 0-273-01709-8) (1982)

Communications architecture for distributed systems
Cypser R J Addison-Wesley (ISBN 0-201-14458-1) (1978)
(Note that this book is pre-SNA 4.)

Proprietary network architectures
Chapter 9 'IBM – Systems Network Architecture' Gee K C E, NCC (ISBN 0-85012-327-5) (1981)

IBM contribution to ECMA TC23 on Open Systems Interconnection architecture – Part 1
European Computer Manufacturers Association ECMA/TC23/80/27 (March 1980)

IBM Systems Journal
vol 18 no 2 SRL no G321-0057 IBM Corp (1979)

SDLC – reference

IBM Synchronous Data Link Control: general information
SRL no GA27-3093 IBM Corp

S/370 channel protocol – reference

S/370 principles of operation, input/output operations
SRL no GA22-7000 IBM Corp

IBM 3270 Data Stream – reference

IBM 3270 information display system: component description
SRL no GA27-2749 IBM Corp

SCS – reference

Systems Network Architecture – Logical Unit types
Appendix B SRL no GC20-1868 IBM Corp

ACF/VTAM Releases 2 and 3 – introductory

Advanced Communications Function for VTAM (ACF/VTAM), general information: introduction
SRL no GS27-0462 IBM Corp

ACF/VTAM Release 2 – reference

Advanced Communications Function for VTAM (ACF/VTAM), pre-installation planning
SRL no SC27-0469 IBM Corp

Advanced Communications Function for VTAM (ACF/VTAM), installation
SRL no SC27-0468 IBM Corp

Advanced Communications Function for VTAM (ACF/VTAM), programming
SRL no SC27-0449 IBM Corp

ACF/NCP Releases 2 and 3 – introductory

ACF/NCP/VS network control program, system support programs: general information
SRL no GC30-3058 IBM Corp

ACF/NCP Release 2 – reference

ACF/NCP/VS network control program, system support programs: installation
SRL no SC30-3142 IBM Corp

ACF/VTAM Release 3 – introductory

Advanced Communications Function for VTAM, general information: concepts
SRL no GC27-0463 IBM Corp

ACF/VTAM Release 3 – reference

Advanced Communications Function for VTAM, planning and installation reference
SRL no SC27-0587 IBM Corp

Advanced Communications Function for VTAM, programming
SRL no SC27-0449 IBM Corp

ACF/NCP Release 3 – reference

ACF/NCP/VS network control program, system support programs: installation
SRL no SC30-3154 IBM Corp

ACF/NCP/VS network control program, system support programs: utilities
SRL no SC30-3158 IBM Corp

NPDA – introductory

Network Problem Determination Application: general information
SRL no GC34-2010 IBM Corp

NCCF – introductory

Network Communications Control Facility: general information
SRC no GC27-0429 IBM Corp

X.25 interface – introductory

The X.25 interface for attaching IBM SNA nodes to packet-switched data networks: general information manual
SRC no GA27-3345 IBM Corp

ISO Open Systems Interconnection – reference

Information processing systems. Open Systems Interconnection – Basic Reference Model
Draft International Standard ISO/DIS/7-498 International Standards Organisation (Apr 1982)

ISO Open Systems Interconnection – introductory

Computer network architectures
Chapter 2 'The Reference Model of Open Systems Interconnection', Meijer A and Peeters P, Pitman (ISBN 0-273-01709-8) (1982)

Index

SNA Index

A

D

E

F

G

H

I

L

O

P

Q

R